Jackie Robinson

IN QUOTES

Danny Peary

AUTHOR/EDITOR OF *BASEBALL IMMORTAL*
DEREK JETER: A CAREER IN QUOTES

PAGE STREET
PUBLISHING CO.

PAGE STREET
PUBLISHING CO.

First published in 2016 by
Page Street Publishing Co.
27 Congress Street, Suite 103
Salem, MA 01970
www.pagestreetpublishing.com

Distributed by Macmillan, sales in Canada by The Canadian Manda Group.

19   18   17   16   1   2   3   4   5

ISBN-13: 978-1-62414-244-4
ISBN-10: 1-62414-244-3

Library of Congress Control Number: 2016930602

Cover and book design by Page Street Publishing Co.

Printed and bound in the United States

Page Street is proud to be a member of 1% for the Planet. Members donate
one percent of their sales to one or more of the over 1,500 environmental and
sustainability charities across the globe who participate in this program.

"I WOULD FIGHT FOR MY LIBERTY SO LONG AS MY STRENGTH LASTED, AND IF THE TIME CAME FOR ME TO GO, THE LORD WOULD LET THEM TAKE ME."

—HARRIET TUBMAN

CONTENTS

Introduction

Sixty years after Jackie Robinson concluded his ten-year career as a Brooklyn Dodger, he is still regarded by those of us who saw him as the most exciting, competitive, savvy, and inspirational player in baseball history. The great man who broke Major League Baseball's color barrier in 1947, who at first held his tongue as he turned the other cheek to the torrent of abuse he was subjected to, also would lay claim to being the most outspoken. As his own quotes make clear, he never stopped speaking, never stopped agitating, never stopped striving for equality and social justice for all Americans. As a result, no player since World War II was more discussed, praised, and attacked—verbally and in print. Moreover, during the fifteen years after his retirement from the diamond, Robinson continued to speak and write about all the changes he felt were necessary in a divided America—and his personal champions (including family members, friends, teammates, opponents, and political allies) and critics continued to voice pointed opinions about him. Many have correctly stated that Robinson's death at the age of fifty-three was due, in part, to what he went through as the pioneer black baseball player; but, as becomes clear in these pages, perhaps what wore him down the most was what he willingly went through as a political activist in the years following his career. He refused to be relegated to the sidelines, and in his quest to end discrimination wherever it existed, he never let up as long as he felt he could make a difference.

The quotes by and about Robinson confirm he was the honest man Diogenes sought, an individual of impeccable principal and integrity and a person so brave that he never swayed from his righteous path, no matter whom he alienated. He never cared if anyone liked him, as long as he felt respected, a trait that is most admirable but made life much harder for him. At great personal sacrifice, he proved the courage of his convictions until his death in 1972, and that is certainly a major reason that today he is revered and celebrated like no other player. Babe Ruth is baseball, but Jackie Robinson is even more than that.

"THERE IS NOT AN AMERICAN IN THIS COUNTRY
WHO IS FREE UNTIL EVERY ONE OF US IS FREE."

—JACKIE ROBINSON

ONE

The Formative Years

"Our family name, Robinson, no doubt was borrowed by us from a master. It is difficult to realize that one's great-grandparents were chattels without human rights, that they could be bought and sold with dollar values on their heads from birth to death."

—**J. R.,** *Baseball Has Done It,* **1964**

"My grandfather was born into slavery, and although my mother and father, Mallie and Jerry Robinson [who married in 1909], lived during an era when physical slavery had been abolished, they also lived in a newer, more sophisticated kind of slavery than the kind Mr. Lincoln struck down."

—**J. R.,** *I Never Had It Made,* **as told to Alfred Duckett, 1972**

"The Robinson family, living in the heart of the [Velvet] Corridor [between Albany, Georgia, and the Atlantic Ocean], when Jackie, the fifth and last surviving child was born on January 31, 1919, was as representative as any other. The Robinsons lived in a sharecropper's cabin—a log-cabin structure with an open 'dog-track' hallway—on the Jim Sasser Plantation."

—**David Falkner,** *Great Time Coming,* **1995**

"My father worked . . . for twelve dollars a month. . . . My mother encouraged [him] to confront his boss and ask for a better deal. Since he didn't want to lose him, [Jim Sasser reluctantly] agreed to let my father become a 'half-cropper.' That means that, instead of working for a flat sum, he would get half the profits from whatever he produced from the earth."

—**J. R.,** *I Never Had It Made,* **as told to Alfred Duckett, 1972**

"Jerry wanted to move to town, but Mallie could not be swayed. . . . He left, then returned; she forgave him. He left again, and came back again; she forgave him once more. Meanwhile, their children came—Edgar in 1910, Frank in 1911, Mack in 1914, Willa Mae in 1916; and Jack in 1919."

—**Arnold Rampersad,** *Jackie Robinson: A Biography,* **1997**

"His name was Jack Roosevelt Robinson, not Jackie. Mallie Robinson, his mother, chose the middle name in honor of the former president Theodore Roosevelt, who had died a few weeks before her son's birth."

—Jonathan Eig, *Opening Day: The Story of Jackie Robinson's First Season*, 2007

"It was a difficult birth, Mallie's first with a doctor in attendance. She hoped the addition of another child would help keep Jerry at home."

—Glenn Stout and Dick Johnson, *Jackie Robinson: Between the Baselines*, 1997

"Bless you, boy. For you to survive all this, God will have to keep an eye on you."

—Mallie Robinson, Jackie's mother, to her newborn son, quoted in *Wait Till Next Year*, Carl T. Rowan with Jackie Robinson, 1960

"Six months after Jackie was born, Jerry Robinson told Mallie he was going to visit a brother in Texas. . . . Instead he . . . went to Florida with another man's wife."

—Carl T. Rowan, about the father Jackie would claim had died, *Wait Till Next Year*, Carl T. Rowan with Jackie Robinson, 1960

"We never saw [our father] again, but after Jack became famous he did show up one time. Jack didn't have anything to do with him and that was it."

—Willa Mae Robinson Walker, Jackie's sister, to Maury Allen, *Jackie Robinson: A Life Remembered*, 1987

"I COULD ONLY THINK OF [MY FATHER] WITH BITTERNESS. HE, TOO, MAY HAVE BEEN THE VICTIM OF OPPRESSION, BUT HE HAD NO RIGHT TO DESERT MY MOTHER AND FIVE CHILDREN."

—J. R., QUOTED BY ARNOLD RAMPERSAD, *JACKIE ROBINSON: A BIOGRAPHY*, 1997

"After my father left, my mother had the choice of going home to live with her people or trying to pacify the irate plantation owner [who blamed her for driving the productive Jerry Robinson away]. . . . She decided then that she would sell what little she had and take her family out of the South."

—J. R., *I Never Had It Made*, as told to Alfred Duckett, 1972

"Our destination was Pasadena [California], where my mother's brother, Burton, worked as a gardener [and] self-taught . . . landscape artist."

—**J. R.,** *Baseball Has Done It,* **1964**

"After a long, tedious train ride across the country, we were generously received by Uncle Burton. He took us in, but my mother made arrangements to move soon after we arrived because we were too crowded. Almost immediately, she found a job washing and ironing."

—**J. R.,** *I Never Had It Made,* **as told to Alfred Duckett, 1972**

"In Pasadena, the clan from Georgia moved into a ramshackle apartment of three rooms and a kitchen. Mallie and her five children slept in one room—little Jackie in the bed with his mother; her [younger] sister [Cora] and brother-in-law [Sam Wade] and their two children were in another; her brother [Burton], a nephew and her husband's cousin slept in the third room. There was no hot water, no kitchen sink, and the dishes were washed in a tin tub that was also used for baths. . . . A meal of pinto beans and bacon skins or white navy beans with a slab of salt pork was considered first class."

—**Carl T. Rowan,** *Wait Till Next Year,* **Carl T. Rowan with Jackie Robinson, 1960**

"Their mother supported the youngsters by doing domestic work, but the children had to . . . fix their own food. Jack . . . never ate a vegetable except potatoes before he met me."

—**Rachel Robinson, Jackie's wife, who met Jackie when he was in his early twenties,** *McCall's* **magazine, January 1951**

"My mother got up before daylight to go to [work] and although she came home tired, she managed to give us the extra attention we needed. She indoctrinated us with the importance of family unity, religion, and kindness toward others. Her great dream was for all of us to go to school."

—**J. R.,** *I Never Had It Made,* **as told to Alfred Duckett, 1972**

"Late in the summer of [1920], Edgar and Frank Robinson, ten and nine years old respectively, started school at Grover Cleveland Elementary School nearby; Cora Wade . . . was in charge of Mack, Willa Mae and Jack as well as her own children while her husband and Mallie worked."

—**Arnold Rampersad,** *Jackie Robinson: A Biography,* **1997**

"When Willa Mae was five or six and Jackie about three, she became [Jack's] primary caregiver. She dressed him, fed him, bathed him, and even took him along to Grover Cleveland Elementary School with her each day. Then she left her little brother to play alone in the schoolyard sandbox . . . running out to him if he needed any help."

—**Mary Kay Linge,** *Jackie Robinson: A Biography,* **2007**

"If I quit working to stay home to take care of him, I'll have to go on relief; it'll be cheaper for the city if you just let him play in the sandbox."

—**Mallie Robinson, arguing successfully with school authorities to let Jackie play in the school sandbox every day while Willa Mae and her teacher watched him through the classroom window**

"Before entering school himself, Jackie contracted diphtheria and nearly died."

—**Glenn Stout and Dick Johnson,** *Jackie Robinson: Between the Baselines,* **1997**

"Mallie . . . got a bucket of lard into which she dipped her hand [and] sat up all night, pulling phlegm out of the boy's throat. . . . Mallie had a medical book which she studied frantically, and concluded [it was] diphtheria. The next morning she sent for the doctor, who rushed out and agreed that the diagnosis was correct. 'If you hadn't used that lard Jackie would be a dead boy by now,' he said."

—**Carl T. Rowan,** *Wait Till Next Year,* **Carl T. Rowan with Jackie Robinson, 1960**

"Mallie frequently came home with used clothing passed along by her employers, or [their] friends. . . . Even the kindergarten teacher occasionally came to school with a bag of second-hand clothing for Jackie and Willa Mae, and the Robinson family rejoiced."

—**Carl T. Rowan,** *Wait Till Next Year,* **Carl T. Rowan with Jackie Robinson, 1960**

"In kindergarten I had a teacher, Miss [Beryl] Haney, who judged me as an individual and not by the color of my skin. She inspired me to believe that my chances for equal treatment from others were as good as anyone else's, provided that I applied myself to the tasks at hand."

—**J. R., about a teacher he would praise throughout his life,**
Baseball Has Done It, **1964**

"In 1922 [when Jack was three] . . . Mallie [who had income from her job and help from the Welfare Department] and Sam [had] pooled their money and bought a house at 121 Pepper Street, on an all-white block just to the north of Glorieta. . . . Two years later, in 1924, the Wades moved into their own home a few blocks away. . . . Mallie then became the sole owner of 121 Pepper Street."

—**Arnold Rampersad, about the first of three adjacent properties Mallie would eventually purchase on Pepper Street and Navarro Avenue,** *Jackie Robinson: A Biography,* **1997**

"JACKIE ROBINSON resided on the Site with his Family from 1922 to 1946."

—**Words engraved on a small plaque outside 121 Pepper Street that was placed in the ground when the house was torn down as part of a redevelopment of the neighborhood**

"The family called it 'The Big House,' a four-bedroom place where she would raise five kids on her own. It was a white neighborhood then. [Jack's mother] was able to buy the clapboard house only because the previous owner, also black, had purchased it with the help of a light-skinned relative. So Mallie had her dream home, the porch hemmed with fieldstone and bougainvillea."

—**Chris Erskine,** *Los Angeles Times,* **August 1, 2012**

"To Jack's dismay, Mallie . . . insisted on trying to help other people. Living with her at 121 Pepper Street, in addition to her five children and Frank's wife, Maxine, and their two children, were her niece Jessie Maxwell, the young daughter of Mallie's sister Mary Lou Thomas Maxwell, who had died prematurely soon after migrating from Cairo. Other relatives and friends came and went."

—**Arnold Rampersad,** *Jackie Robinson: A Biography,* **1997**

"IN 1927, [THE ROBINSONS] MADE ROOM FOR EDNA SIMS MCGRIFF, MALLIE'S [RECENTLY WIDOWED] MOTHER. . . . EDNA TOLD STORIES ABOUT HER LIFE AS A SLAVE, THE FEAR THAT SO MANY HAD FELT WHEN FREEDOM FINALLY CAME, AND THE VALUE OF STANDING UP FOR ONE'S RIGHTS AND ONE'S DIGNITY. HER WORDS WOULD STAY WITH JACK LONG AFTER HER DEATH IN 1933."

—**MARY KAY LINGE,** *JACKIE ROBINSON: A BIOGRAPHY,* **2007**

J. R. NOTE: Jackie's home made the papers soon after he did, in 1934. The *Pasadena Star-News*: "For the second time within a week fire broke out in the home of Mrs. Mollie [*sic*] Robinson, 121 Pepper Street, this time in the two bedrooms on the first floor, and in the rear of the house on the second story. The . . . Fire Department engines . . . extinguished them without much trouble. However the causes of both Thursday and today's blazes are undetermined, necessitating an investigation. Last week's fire started in the attic and burned part of the roof before it was put out."

"When we first moved to Pepper Street we had a bad time. Nobody wanted us there since the neighborhood was all white. . . . They did everything they could to get us out of there. One night we even had a cross burning. We didn't know who did it, but there was one family [who] used to call the cops all the time on us for the silliest things, mostly for being out on the street. Jack was the one who was out the most. He just didn't enjoy playing indoors."

—**Willa Mae Robinson Walker to Maury Allen,**
Jackie Robinson: A Life Remembered, **1987**

"Our white neighbors . . . signed petitions to try to get rid of us. . . . My mother never lost her composure. She didn't allow us to go out of our way to antagonize the whites, and she still made it perfectly clear to us and to them that she was not afraid of them and that she had no intention of allowing them to mistreat us."

—**J. R.,** *I Never Had It Made,* **as told to Alfred Duckett, 1972**

"Nigger! Nigger! Nigger!"

—**Neighbor girl to Jack, 1927**

"When he was eight, Dad got into a name-calling fight with the little white girl who lived across the street. The children's verbal battle was interrupted when the girl's father came outside and started throwing rocks at my father."

—**Sharon Robinson, Jackie's daughter,** *Promises to Keep,* **2005**

"Jack picked up the rocks and threw them right back until the man's wife finally pulled him inside."

—**Rachel Robinson,** *Jackie Robinson: An Intimate Portrait,* **1996**

"People used to ask me how Jack got so good throwing a baseball and a football, and I said it was from throwing rocks at the other kids who threw rocks at him."

—Willa Mae Robinson Walker to Maury Allen,
Jackie Robinson: A Life Remembered, **1987**

"Pasadena regarded us as intruders. My brothers and I were in many a fight that started with a racial slur on the very street we lived on."

—J. R., *Baseball Has Done It,* **1964**

"Pasadena was a pretty city with lots of parks and other public recreational facilities. My dad couldn't go to most of them. [Even] the local soda fountain wouldn't serve black kids. . . . The boundaries were clearly drawn."

—Sharon Robinson, *Promises to Keep,* **2005**

"He watched movies from segregated balconies, [was permitted in the YMCA only one night a week] and was allowed to swim in Pasadena's municipal pool only on Tuesdays—called 'International Day'—when the city changed the water."

—*Pasadena Star-News,* **April 7, 1987**

"Dad went to Cleveland and Washington Elementary schools in Pasadena. The students were black. The teachers were white."

—Sharon Robinson, *Promises to Keep,* **2005**

"[He] was enrolled at Washington Elementary School, along with a large proportion of Pasadena's black children. This was a deliberate move by the city, whose leaders had taken note of the influx of black and Hispanic families and had altered the school zoning to create, in effect, a segregated education system."

—Mary Kay Linge, *Jackie Robinson: A Biography,* **2007**

"His official transcript at Washington Elementary shows grades of B and C over the years, with a decline in quality between the fourth grade and sixth grade, his last year there. The transcript also includes a simple note made by a school official about his likely future occupation: 'Gardener.'"

—Arnold Rampersad, *Jackie Robinson: A Biography,* **1997**

A BUDDING ATHLETE

"I guess he was about five, and that's when our friendship started. He was a great athlete, even during . . . pickup games as kids. He hated to lose, just hated it."

—Ray Bartlett, Jackie's close friend in elementary school and junior high and sports teammate at Pasadena JC and UCLA, to Pat Karlak, *Pasadena Star-News*, April 18, 1996

"He was good at any game he took up. I think maybe soccer and handball required these moves everybody later saw in baseball."

—Ray Bartlett, Jackie's close friend and teammate in elementary school and junior high, quoted by David Falkner, *Great Time Coming*, 1995

"We played dodgeball. One by one kids would be eliminated when they were hit by the ball. Every time we played, he was left. And the game had to stop because nobody could hit him. . . . We would . . . play marbles from eight o' clock to five o' clock. . . . Boy, that dude Jackie, he cleaned us out. . . . He could concentrate better than any of us."

—Sidney Heard, Jackie's elementary-school friend, whose family also came from Georgia, to Harvey Frommer, *Rickey and Robinson*, 1982

"When I was about eight I discovered that in one sector of life in Southern California I was free to compete with whites on equal terms—in sports. I played soccer on my fourth-grade team against sixth graders who were two or three years older than me. Soon I was competing in other sports against opponents of every size, shape . . . and color."

—J. R., *Baseball Has Done It*, 1964

"[Jack's] life [by the third or fourth grade] was driven by sports, and by the need to win, whatever the game. . . . [Some] boyhood friends would later say that Jack's intense focus on winning made him hard to like."

—Mary Kay Linge, *Jackie Robinson: A Biography*, 2007

"The more I played the better I became—in softball, hardball, football, basketball, table tennis, any kind of game with a ball."

—J. R., *Baseball Has Done It*, 1964

"NO MATTER THE SPORT, HE WAS THE BEST. NOBODY CAME CLOSE."

—SAM MARDIAN, FUTURE MAYOR OF PHOENIX, WHO MET JACKIE WHEN THEY WERE FOURTH GRADERS, TO PAT KARLAK, *PASADENA STAR-NEWS*, APRIL 18, 1996

"My cousins and I used to shag flies for the older boys, and I can remember discovering that I could run faster than most of the kids in our neighborhood."

—J. R., *Jackie Robinson: My Own Story,* as told to Wendell Smith, 1948

"When he was playing with [us] older boys, he had to learn how to make up for his lack of size and strength. I have to think the quickness did it."

—Mack Robinson, Jackie's brother, to Maury Allen,
Jackie Robinson: A Life Remembered, 1987

"I think it was 1933 when he was in junior high school that we began to notice what an athlete Jack was. He was uncanny. He just took up a sport and he was the best in the neighborhood before anybody knew it. I think the first time he played Ping-Pong he won the city championship. I think that was the first time he got his name in the papers."

—Mack Robinson to Maury Allen, *Jackie Robinson: A Life Remembered,* 1987

"You might say I turned professional at an early age. . . . [The other boys would give me] sandwiches and dimes for the movies so they could play on my team."

—J. R., *Look* magazine, January 15, 1955

"In those days he would come home from school, gulp down a glass of milk, put his books on that old dresser, and be out the door playing ball with the kids. How that boy loved playing ball."

—Willa Mae Robinson Walker to Maury Allen,
Jackie Robinson: A Life Remembered, 1987

"I PLAYED HARD, AND ALWAYS TO WIN."

—J. R., *BASEBALL HAS DONE IT,* 1964

"There were so few blacks in Pasadena at that time that we were just like family. . . . We used to go down to Brookside Park where the whites were and play teams for ice cream and cake. We'd beat them. Jack loved that. We used to get an awful lot of ice cream and cake."

—**Sidney Heard, Jackie's elementary-school friend, to Harvey Frommer,**
Rickey and Robinson, **1982**

"My experiences in sports multiplied my contacts with whites. . . . I knew that the wall of segregation was not so high that it could not be breached on gridiron, court and diamond."

—**J. R.,** *Baseball Has Done It,* **1964**

"The young Robinson followed the accomplishments of white sports stars, especially Lou Gehrig and Babe Ruth, and marveled at the way the New York Yankees kept winning. . . . Baseball's color barrier precluded any thought of playing major-league baseball, but he was sure of his talents and sure that his future lay in sports."

—**Harvey Frommer,** *Rickey and Robinson,* **1982**

"My pride in my mother was tempered with a sense of sadness that she had to bear most of our burdens. At a very early age I began to want to relieve her in any small way that I could. Along with a number of other children in the neighborhood, I had a lot of free time, and a lot of freedom. Some of it I put to good use—I had a paper route, I cut grass."

—**J. R.,** *I Never Had It Made,* **as told to Alfred Duckett, 1972**

"I contributed my bit by shining shoes, running errands, selling newspapers, and hawking hot dogs at the baseball parks and football stadiums."

—**J. R.,** *Jackie Robinson: My Own Story,* **as told to Wendell Smith, 1948**

"The rest of the time, I stole—all sorts of small things from stores, particularly food."

—**J. R.,** *I Never Had It Made,* **as told to Alfred Duckett, 1972**

"I REMEMBER 1932 VERY WELL. THAT WAS OUR WORST YEAR. THERE WERE MANY TIMES THAT YEAR WHEN THERE WAS BARELY ENOUGH TO EAT."

—J. R. TO JACK SHER, *SPORT* **MAGAZINE, OCTOBER 1948**

"God bless the child who's got his own."

—Mallie Robinson, telling Jackie and her other children the importance of being self-reliant

MALLIE ROBINSON: JACKIE'S INSPIRATION

"Mallie Robinson was on her own, and she became the dominant figure in young Jackie Robinson's life, an ongoing example to her children of what hard work and determination could accomplish."

—Glenn Stout and Dick Johnson, *Jackie Robinson: Between the Baselines***, 1997**

"The Mallie Robinson family was a poor family, but they were rich in values and strengths that helped them adapt, adjust, and overcome obstacles. Although Mallie literally moved away from her support structure in the South, she created a new base and somehow began to foster positive identity, self-esteem, and an intense feeling of entitlement, especially in Jack, her youngest."

—Rachel Robinson, *Jackie Robinson: An Intimate Portrait***, 1996**

"I believe that [Jack] derived his sense of himself—his life mission, and the courage to carry it out—from his mother, Mallie Robinson. She was an extraordinary woman—courageous, determined, extremely religious, and self-reliant. . . . She was THE major influence in Jack's life."

—Rachel Robinson, interview, *Scholastic* **magazine, February 11, 1998**

"Mallie always bragged that she instilled in her young Jack a sense of racial pride. She claimed no responsibility for her boy's rage."

—Jonathan Eig, *Opening Day: The Story of Jackie Robinson's First Season***, 2007**

"My mother taught us to respect ourselves and to demand respect from others. That's why I refused to back down in later life."

—J. R., *Baseball Has Done It***, 1964**

"Those who recall most intimately the childhood of Jackie Robinson express surprise that he did not end up in a reform school. The grinding poverty, a broken home, a mother away working most of the day, the racial conflict, provided a fertile ground for delinquency. Friends of the family say that it was Mallie's love that inculcated in Jackie and his brothers and sister a sense of dignity and pride that kept them out of severe trouble."

—Carl T. Rowan, *Wait Till Next Year*, Carl T. Rowan with Jackie Robinson, 1960

"The reason Jackie made it was the strength he got from our mother. She instilled that pride in him. She wouldn't take anything from anybody. She was a real strong woman."

—Mack Robinson to Maury Allen, *Jackie Robinson: A Life Remembered*, 1987

"Jack learned early on to fight back, because Mallie . . . refused to accept abuse. . . . She wasn't well-educated in a formal sense, but she had a vision and courage to take actions of heroic dimensions. Jack always said he thought of her as 'working magic.'"

—Rachel Robinson, *Jackie Robinson: An Intimate Portrait*, 1996

"My mother never put her philosophy into precise words. She couldn't write well, she made mistakes in grammar, but she expressed herself in a way that made me understand what she meant and how she felt. As I listened I acquired her ideas. Besides, I was aggressive by nature."

—J. R., *Baseball Has Done It*, 1964

"Mallie Robinson fit no one's stereotype. She crossed the continent for her children; she crossed the street for no one. She demanded iron discipline; she opened her home. . . . More than anything, what she transmitted was the sense that the spiritual life that she demanded from her children came first from herself. All her children, and especially Jackie, took up the challenge she posed for them in their own way."

—David Falkner, *Great Time Coming*, 1995

"JACKIE WAS A PIONEER, A CRUSADER, THE SYMBOL OF A CHANGING ORDER, IN 1946, BECAUSE HIS MOTHER HAD BEEN A CRUSADER IN HER OWN WAY, AN OPPONENT OF THE STATUS QUO."

—CARL T. ROWAN, *WAIT TILL NEXT YEAR*, CARL T. ROWAN WITH JACKIE ROBINSON, 1960

"Mallie's children each displayed unusual athletic ability. Edgar was a master on roller skates and the bicycle. . . . Frank's tall and slim stature made him a natural for track and basketball. Willa Mae excelled in basketball, track and soccer and was known as a top sprinter. But it was Mack and Jackie whose skill took them beyond the neighborhood and brought them international acclaim. Mack started by setting records in track and field in junior high, high school and junior college."

—**Sharon Robinson,** *Stealing Home,* **1996**

"He became famous long before anyone heard of me. . . . Naturally Mack was my idol. I used to watch him perform and say to myself, 'Gee, I'd like to be a great athlete some day! I'd like to be like Mack.'"

—**J. R.,** *Jackie Robinson: My Own Story,* **as told to Wendell Smith, 1948**

"Jack was only interested in sports. He wasn't a great student, but that was only because somewhere along the line he decided sports would be his life. He always talked of coaching teams in football and baseball, and I think that's what he would have done if he hadn't become a baseball player."

—**Willa Mae Robinson Walker to Maury Allen,** *Jackie Robinson: A Life Remembered,* **1987**

"When it came to work, he was lazy."

—**Mack Robinson,** *Ebony* **magazine, July 1957**

"By the age of 12 or 13, Jack would come home from Washington Junior High, dump his books on the nearest table, and run outside to play sports; next day, he would grab the unread volumes as he headed back to school."

—**Mary Kay Linge,** *Jackie Robinson: A Biography,* **2007**

THE PEPPER STREET GANG

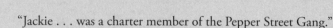

"Jackie . . . was a charter member of the Pepper Street Gang."

—*Time* magazine, September 22, 1947

"[They were] a mischievous group of youngsters expressing the general frustration of youth as well as the specific frustrations of minority-group youngsters in a community beset by many forms of discrimination and segregation."

—Carl T. Rowan, *Wait Till Next Year,* Carl T. Rowan with Jackie Robinson, 1960

"The Pepper Street Gang was mostly a sports gang. We loved to compete. We weren't out to hurt anyone. We'd go miles to get into any type of sport. . . . We played together—blacks, whites, Mexicans, Japanese. Anaheim and Long Beach were cities that were very prejudiced. Jack knew this, but he had no fear. He . . . knew we could play ball and win. Whenever we played, wherever we played, Jack was always the best."

—Sidney Heard, Jackie's elementary-school friend and Pepper Street Gang member, to Harvey Frommer, *Rickey and Robinson,* 1982

"HE PLAYED SOFTBALL ON THE CORNER LOT WITH HIS GANG, OCCASIONALLY EARNED POCKET MONEY BY SNEAKING INTO NEIGHBORING GOLF COURSES TO RETRIEVE LOST BALLS. HE COULD OUTRUN THE GANG—AND THE COPS—EVERY TIME."

—*TIME* MAGAZINE, SEPTEMBER 22, 1947

"During the Depression, things were tough for all of us. Things were especially tough for him. He didn't have a father. We kids all used to go down to chase after golf balls and make three or four dollars a day. [Jack] had tremendously good eyesight. We'd be down in the gullies, down among the boulders. Sometimes he'd find six or seven golf balls. We couldn't find them. We used to get a quarter a piece for those golf balls. Jackie'd say, 'Okay, the next one is yours, Pete. The next one is yours, Sid.' He'd share with us."

—Sidney Heard, Jackie's elementary-school friend and Pepper Street Gang member, to Harvey Frommer, *Rickey and Robinson*, 1982

"We all looked up to Jackie because he could hide in the storm drain, run out on the golf course in Brookside [Park], grab a ball and get back out of sight faster than any of the rest of us. That's how we got our Coke money. And he could get oranges, or a bunch of grapes so fast that he'd never get caught. We all did things like that during the Depression. We had to, to exist."

—**Warren Dorn, white Pepper Street Gang member and later Pasadena mayor and L.A. County supervisor, quoted by Harvey Frommer,** *Rickey and Robinson,* **1982**

"All the time we were aware of a growing resentment at being deprived of some of the advantages the white kids had. Once we were escorted at gunpoint by the sheriff because we had gone for a swim in the reservoir."

—**J. R.,** *I Never Had It Made,* **as told to Alfred Duckett, 1972**

"The roundup over, sixteen young men [including Jack Robinson] were crammed into one small room at the police station. When, after four hours, a Negro lad claimed he was 'so hot and thirsty and hungry I'm gonna faint,' the sheriff said sarcastically to a deputy, 'The coon's hungry. Go buy a watermelon.' When the deputy returned the sheriff passed out chunks of the melon and then took photographs of the [young] Negroes eating it."

—**Carl T. Rowan, about a humiliating experience Jackie never forgot,** *Wait Till Next Year,* **Carl T. Rowan with Jackie Robinson, 1960**

"[The gang] liked to break street lamps and watch the changing colors of the shattered bulbs."

—*Time* **magazine, September 22, 1947**

"Another favorite stunt of the Pepper Street gang was to perch on the curb just before going home, with the young men seeing who could hurl a clod of dirt most accurately at passing automobiles. . . . Jackie was always too fast for the policemen, but some lead-footed member of the group inevitably got caught. The policemen would show up at Jackie's house with a list of the names of the offenders, and Jackie would be hauled off to the police station for a lecture by Captain Morgan, who was in charge of youth."

—**Carl T. Rowan,** *Wait Till Next Year,* **Carl T. Rowan with Jackie Robinson, 1960**

"Jackie always seemed to get the worst of it from the cops . . . usually for defending one of his pals."

—**Warren Dorn to Shav Glick,** *Los Angeles Times,* **April 8, 1987**

"A stern talk from Ma Robinson put him out of business. She was, and is, a fervent Methodist who can be volubly graphic on the subject of hell."

—*Time* magazine, September 22, 1947

"I suppose I might have become a full-fledged juvenile delinquent if it had not been for the influence of two men who shared my mother's thinking. Carl Anderson was a mechanic who . . . said it didn't take guts to follow the crowd, that courage and intelligence lay in being willing to be different. . . . The other man . . . was the Reverend Karl Downs. He was a young minister who came to Pasadena to pastor the church [Scott United Methodist Church] where our family worshiped. . . . Reverend Downs set out to win the young members of the congregation. . . . He had the ability to communicate with us spiritually and . . . participated with us in our sports."

—J. R., *I Never Had It Made,* as told to Alfred Duckett, 1972

"It soon became apparent that athletics would be the salvation of Jackie Robinson, would help him to burn off the anger that Pasadena built up in him every day."

—Carl T. Rowan, *Wait Till Next Year,* Carl T. Rowan with Jackie Robinson, 1960

"THE DEVIL IS SENDING THE PEOPLE TO WATCH YOU PLAY AND HE'S ALSO SENDING YOU TO PLAY."

—MALLIE ROBINSON, TO HER TWELVE-YEAR-OLD SON IN 1931 FOR PLAYING BASEBALL AT BROOKSIDE PARK ON SUNDAYS BEFORE SHE DEVELOPED AN APPRECIATION FOR THE SPORT, QUOTED IN *TIME* MAGAZINE, SEPTEMBER 22, 1947

"Jack left Washington Junior High School early in 1935. As a graduation gift . . . Mallie managed to buy him a brand-new dress suit. After a lifetime of hand-me-downs, the sight of it brought the teenager to tears."

—Mary Kay Linge, *Jackie Robinson: A Biography,* 2007

"Jack enrolled at John Muir Technical High, which Willa Mae and Mack both attended, for the spring semester. Muir was known throughout southern California for its sports program."

—**Mary Kay Linge,** *Jackie Robinson: A Biography,* **2007**

"Blessed with speed and marvelous coordination, Robinson became an athletic standout at Muir Technical High School, although the scouts did not single him out immediately as a potentially great college star [because] word was quickly spread around the circuit that [for a Negro] he was 'too aggressive,' 'cocky,' 'arrogant,' and 'uppity.' Robinson's coaches were delighted with his competitive spirit, however, for it infected the entire squad. He made Muir Tech a high school terror in several sports."

—**Carl T. Rowan,** *Wait Till Next Year,* **Carl T. Rowan with Jackie Robinson, 1960**

"In his first semester at the school, Jackie made his mark, making the baseball team as a shortstop and competing alongside Mack on the track team in the broad jump and the high jump. With Jackie at short, the Terriers went all the way to the finals in the regional baseball championship, though they lost the game to Long Beach."

—**Mary Kay Linge, about the sport for which Jackie expressed only a mild interest,** *Jackie Robinson: A Biography,* **2007**

"Before the summer of 1935, he had established himself as the most versatile of the Muir Terriers. He also sang in the glee club, but sports were his mainstay."

—**Arnold Rampersad,** *Jackie Robinson: A Biography,* **1997**

"In the fall, Jack went out for football and made the team, though not as a starter. He saw some action at quarterback late in the season, showing off his running and passing skills for an undefeated Muir squad. As soon as football ended, he jumped right into basketball, excelling as a guard [and] driving the team all season. The Terriers came within a single game of capturing the league championship."

—**Mary Kay Linge,** *Jackie Robinson: A Biography,* **2007**

"The end of basketball meant the beginning of [his second season of] baseball (as a catcher . . . because the team needed one) and track."

—**Mary Kay Linge,** *Jackie Robinson: A Biography,* **2007**

"Woodrow Wilson High School put on a swell 'coming out' party yesterday as it was host to the Southern C.I.F. tracksters on Stephens Field, Long Beach, but the Bruins turned out to be very inhospitable guests. . . . John Gartner's seven spikemen totaled 27½ points. . . . Muir Tech of Pasadena trailed in second spot with 14 points. . . . Jack Robinson, brother of dusky Mack Robinson who performed for the Terriers a year ago, uncorked a tremendous leap of 23ft. ¼in. to top the broad jumpers and added a half inch to that a few minutes later."

—**Charles Curtis,** *Los Angeles Times,* **May 17, 1936**

"Jackie Robinson, all-around Muir Tech star, [took] the junior boys' singles championship . . . in the annual Pacific Coast Negro tennis tournament being staged at the Pasadena Junior College Courts yesterday. Robinson easily turned back B. Devine 6–1, 6–2, to win the crown in the 15- to 18-years class."

—*Pasadena Post,* **September 7, 1936**

"He developed his baseball skills further in a summer clinic at Brookside Park run by the baseball coach from Pasadena Junior College (PJC), John Thurman. Thurman was keeping a close eye on Jack's development, hoping he would follow his brother to PJC."

—**Mary Kay Linge,** *Jackie Robinson: A Biography,* **2007**

"[That summer] Jack and his family huddled around their kitchen-table radio to listen to 3 a.m. broadcasts from the 1936 Olympics in Berlin, where Mack represented the United States on a track team that included Jesse Owens and Ralph Metcalfe. . . . The German leader, Adolf Hitler, meant these Olympic Games to display the might of Nazi Germany and the superiority of the so-called Aryan race. Owens was the undisputed star of the group: his four gold medals were seen as a symbol of democracy's defiance against fascism. . . . Mack Robinson had his own success in the 1936 Games, earning a silver medal, behind Owens' gold, in the 200-meter dash."

—**Mary Kay Linge,** *Jackie Robinson: A Biography,* **2007**

"Mack returned to PJC as a part-time student, keeping his amateur athletic status intact. When he went out looking for paid work, though, silver medal or no, the best Mack was offered was an overnight street-sweeping job. . . . Watching Mack's triumphs and disappointments were formative experiences for his youngest brother."

—**Mary Kay Linge,** *Jackie Robinson: A Biography,* **2007**

"In 1936 when a judge ordered Pasadena pool to allow blacks, the city government responded by purging all blacks from its payrolls. Among those fired was Jackie's older brother, Mack."

—**Jules Tygiel**, *Baseball's Great Experiment,* **1983**

"MY BROTHERS, THEIR FRIENDS AND ACQUAINTANCES, ALL OLDER THAN ME, HAD STUDIED HARD AND WOUND UP AS PORTERS, ELEVATOR OPERATORS, TAXI DRIVERS, BELLHOPS. I CAME TO THE CONCLUSION THAT LONG HOURS OVER BOOKS WAS A WASTE OF TIME. CONSIDERING MY SITUATION, I WAS NOT FAR WRONG. MY KNOWLEDGE OF LIFE WAS INCREASING IN SPORTS."

—J. R., *BASEBALL HAS DONE IT,* 1964

"While the family wanted Jackie to have the mental attainments of [George Washington] Carver or a Booker T. Washington, he let them down for athletics and became a Robinson. Early at Muir Tech, he learned that a C average would keep him eligible for varsity athletics, and a C student he was."

—**Arthur Mann**, *Collier's* **magazine, March 2, 1946**

"When one subject dipped a bit, I brushed up on another subject to maintain the necessary average. To do more would have meant giving up at least one sport, and I couldn't."

—**J. R., quoted by Arthur Mann**, *Collier's* **magazine, March 2, 1946**

"He never wrote down his homework. I did. I made a copy for him and one for me and I'd just hand it to him and out the door he'd go and shove it in his pocket."

—**Elizabeth Grimley Enos, Jackie's high school classmate, to Kim Covington, KPNX-TV Channel 12 News Phoenix, April 14, 2013**

"The overriding reality of Robinson's early years was that, for black youth, the future was closed. Simple as that. It didn't take a sociologist or a Jim Crow sign to tell him that schools, jobs, opportunities, and careers were severely limited. . . . If Robinson was a precocious athlete, he was also bound by this time and place. When he left his house he was conscious that his hometown was full of invisible lines that were not to be crossed."

—**David Falkner**, *Great Time Coming,* **1995**

"There was a lot of discrimination and prejudice when we were growing up. . . . My mom used to tell Jackie and me that it'll all change one day. We didn't believe her then."

—Ray Bartlett, Jackie's lifelong friend and teammate in school and college

"His sports achievements helped give him a self-assured, almost cocky attitude. It was a front, though, a mask he wore to keep outsiders at arm's length. He did not often reach outside his comfortable circle to make friends. Within this small group of neighborhood teens, he was seen as quiet and shy, if often mischievously 'devilish.' Friends would remember him tossing firecrackers in the street, or jostling pals to make them drop their popcorn at the movies."

—Mary Kay Linge, *Jackie Robinson: A Biography*, 2007

"We never thought anything about [his being African American]. Everybody into sports loved him. [Jack was] very quiet and almost timid."

—Elizabeth Grimley Enos, Jackie's high school classmate, to Kim Covington, KPNX-TV Channel 12 News Phoenix, April 14, 2013

"Robinson's last few months at Muir Technical High School were all about football. He drove the team to victory after victory with an intense running game that had him using his . . . speed and agility in every situation. He played safety on defense, he could pass and run from tailback on offense, and his speed made him the team's best punt returner."

—Mary Kay Linge, *Jackie Robinson: A Biography*, 2007

"He was a star. . . . [If I saw him play] I thought, 'We'll win!' Always."

—Elizabeth Grimley Enos, Jackie's high school classmate, to Kim Covington, KPNX-TV Channel 12 News Phoenix, April 14, 2013

"His final football game for Muir was the conference championship of 1936, played against Glendale High in the storied Rose Bowl. As the team's mainstay, Robinson was so feared that the Glendale players decided to get him out of the game early with a deliberate hit just after the opening kickoff. Robinson, taken completely off guard, was knocked to the ground and sidelined with two broken ribs."

—Mary Kay Linge, about why Muir lost the championship game, *Jackie Robinson: A Biography*, 2007

"I SAW THEM THROWING WATER ON MY BOY AND I WANTED TO RUSH DOWN THERE AND HELP HIM. BUT HE GOT UP AND WALKED OFF THE FIELD AND I SAT DOWN. AFTER THAT I ALWAYS WORRY ABOUT MY BABY."

—MALLIE ROBINSON, QUOTED *IN TIME* MAGAZINE, SEPTEMBER 22, 1947

"[A basketball] thriller was the 43–35 loss to Muir Tech, when the Tigers led with but two minutes to go, but faulty passing upset them as Jack Robinson went on a one-man-spree."

—*Copa De Oro*, praising opponent Jack Robinson, South Pasadena High School Yearbook, 1937

"Muir Tech closed the first round of its [basketball] schedule last night on its home floor by beating Glendale Broadway, 35–25. . . . Jack Robinson, Muir Tech's stellar forward, graduated from high school yesterday, will be permitted to play in [a postponed game against Whittier] here next Wednesday. But his official 'swan song' was last night, and what a melody he played, much to Glendale's disgust. Robinson was all over the floor, and when he wasn't scoring points, he was making impossible 'saves' and interceptions and was the best player on the floor."

—*Pasadena Star-News*, January 30, 1937

"Robinson graduated from high school in [late January] 1937. At his mother's insistence, and over his own objections to adding to the family's financial burdens, he enrolled in Pasadena Junior College."

—Glenn Stout and Dick Johnson, *Jackie Robinson: Between the Baselines*, 1997

– TWO –

College Man for All Seasons

"Young Robinson had no illusions concerning the value of his education. . . . While his mother wanted him to become a doctor or lawyer, Robinson . . . was in college for one reason—to play sports."

—Glenn Stout and Dick Johnson, *Jackie Robinson: Between the Baselines,* **1997**

"Robinson chose Pasadena JC for a myriad of reasons: free tuition, a chance to display his sports skills on a bigger stage (with the hopes of attracting scholarship offers to larger universities), and a liberal campus climate that afforded black students unlimited access to all school facilities."

—*Icons of Black America,* **Volume I, edited by Matthew C. Whitaker, 2011**

"As Jack settled in at PJC, he made one friend for life, a sprinter named Jack Gordon. . . . Gordon was small in stature compared with Jack; his skin was a light brown compared with Jack's ebony; and he was as voluble and outgoing as Jack was reserved, especially with women. . . . 'I remember he used to be a spokesman for me,' [Robinson] recalled. 'He would go with me every place. Through him I met my first girlfriend. . . . I don't think I had enough courage at that time to go out on a date with a girl alone.'"

—Arnold Rampersad, about Robinson's friend Jack Gordon, who would be his best man when he married in 1946, *Jackie Robinson: A Biography,* **1997**

"That first semester, he . . . began going out with his first steady girlfriend— Elizabeth 'Bessie' Renfro—a girl from the neighborhood who had her eye on him since junior high."

—Mary Kay Linge, about the tall Pasadena beauty Robinson would date casually until he met his future wife, Rachel Isum, *Jackie Robinson: A Biography,* **2007**

"I LOST MOST OF THE SHYNESS THAT HAD ALWAYS MADE MY EARLY LIFE MISERABLE."

—J. R., ABOUT FINDING COMFORT AT PJC, EVEN AWAY FROM SPORTS, TO ED REID, *WASHINGTON POST*, AUGUST 22, 1949

"Just as he promised, Mack Robinson, second place winner in the Olympic Games 200-meters, took up his studies today at Pasadena Junior College and prepared to lead the Bulldogs to another banner season on the cinderpath. Coach Otto Anderson . . . was all smiles. He not only enticed his 1936 co-captain back to school, but also landed Mack's kid brother Jackie in the deal. The younger Robinson enrolled from Muir Tech and invades Pasadena JC with a world of promise."

—*Los Angeles Times*, **February 3, 1937**

"With the PJC track team, the younger Robinson consistently placed second to his brother, but this was one rival he did not mind losing to. . . . Mack seemed to thrive on the challenge of competing with his kid brother [and] it led to a scholarship offer from the University of Oregon . . . the next spring."

—**Mary Kay Linge,** *Jackie Robinson: A Biography*, **2007**

"That spring [Jackie] made the baseball team as a shortstop. He was an eye-catching fielder and patient hitter who quickly took the leadoff spot in the lineup. The freshman's real genius was on the basepaths: A constant threat to steal, he drove opposing pitchers to distraction. In one game Robinson stole second base, then third and home . . . for the Bulldogs. . . . When PJC went on a 14-game winning streak that April, Robinson was given much of the credit."

—**Mary Kay Linge,** *Jackie Robinson: A Biography*, **2007**

"When classes ended for the summer, Robinson played shortstop for a team in a local semi-pro Owl League, a softball-baseball hybrid that was popular in California."

—**Mary Kay Linge,** *Jackie Robinson: A Biography*, **2007**

"My first athletic achievements were as a softball player. I went in for all the other sports, too. But I liked softball best."

—**J. R., who played overhand softball with Ray Bartlett and against future National League home-run king Ralph Kiner,** *Jackie Robinson: My Own Story*, **as told to Wendell Smith, 1948**

"That isn't stealing. It's grand larceny."

—Rube Samuelson, on Robinson's ability to steal second, third, and even home with abandon in the Owl League, *Pasadena Post*, **July 10, 1937**

"As his first fall semester at Pasadena Junior College began, Robinson went out for the football team. . . . A new head coach, Tom Mallory, had arrived from Oklahoma City, Oklahoma, bringing along a contingent of players from his former whites-only school. The Oklahoma men had never competed with or against blacks. When Robinson made the team as starting quarterback, along with his friend Ray Bartlett and another black student, the transplants at first refused to take the field for an integrated practice. Coach Mallory's intervention got the white players to grudgingly accept the blacks as teammates."

—Mary Kay Linge, *Jackie Robinson: A Biography*, **2007**

"In his [second formal practice] he broke his ankle when another player rolled over it after a tackle. Jackie sat out . . . before returning for Pasadena's final six games. Without Robinson, the team . . . lost four in a row."

—Glenn Stout and Dick Johnson, *Jackie Robinson: Between the Baselines*, **1997**

"He was back in action for the fifth game, on the road against Phoenix Junior College. Segregated Phoenix, Arizona, would not house the team in one hotel, and the black players refused the rooms offered them. . . . Despite this, Robinson was itching to get into the game. He came in as a substitute and promptly scored a touchdown in the Bulldogs' first victory of the season. They would not lose again in 1937, or in 1938 either for that matter: this was the first win of what would become a 16-game winning streak, driven by the spectacular play of Jackie Robinson. . . . His tricky running style, incorporating sudden stops, nimble sidesteps, and blazing accelerations, kept opponents confused and off-balance. His team-first attitude . . . won over the Oklahomans and the other white players by the end of the season."

—Mary Kay Linge, *Jackie Robinson: A Biography*, **2007**

"I knew very well that as a quarterback I had [to make] these guys feel we were working as a unit, as a team. When we got inside the ten-yard line . . . I'd give them a chance to score. Then, if they couldn't make it, they'd come back and call my play. Well, I could walk over because they did a job [blocking for me]."

—J. R., about breaking down the barriers between him and the white players from Oklahoma, *Sport* **magazine, September 1966**

"Pasadena and Compton junior colleges spent a rather futile 60 minutes last Friday night in the Rose Bowl and ended their annual 'grudge' battle with the scoreboard sporting [a] large pair of zeros. . . . Jackie Robinson, second-string quarterback of the locals, rather stole the show as far as ground-gaining honors were concerned. . . . Robinson toted the ball for a total net of 77 yards."

—*Pasadena (JC) Chronicle*, about Robinson making the transfer from sub to star, November 5, 1937

"Jackie Robinson and Bill Busik turned in their usual four star performances [as Pasadena smashed Loyala 25–7]. . . . Robinson turned the game into a complete rout as he sprayed the field with footballs."

—Hank Shatford, *Pasadena (JC) Chronicle*, November 12, 1937

"Jackie Robinson contributed the most sparkling event to last week's [26–0 victory over Chaffey] with his brilliant 80-yard return of a punt."

—Hank Shatford, *Pasadena (JC) Chronicle*, November 19, 1937

"With Jackie Robinson doing the main share of the digging, Pasadena Junior College undermined the favored Cal Tech Engineers last Wednesday night. . . . Pasadena JC thus won the Pasadena grid championship for the first time. . . . Robinson personally accounted for the first touchdown and tossed the pass which resulted in the second tally."

—Ed van der Veen, *Pasadena (JC) Chronicle*, November 29, 1937

"His ankle fully recovered, Robinson moved onto the basketball team [after football ended in December]. He was an immediate star, leading the team in scoring and finding himself the focus of the opponent's defense. . . . Robinson's skin color made him the target of abuse."

—Glenn Stout and Dick Johnson, *Jackie Robinson: Between the Baselines*, 1997

"LONG BEACH AND PASADENA JUNIOR COLLEGES CLIMAXED THE RENEWAL OF THEIR TRADITIONAL RIVALRY LAST SATURDAY NIGHT [JANUARY 22, 1938] BY STAGING A RIOT IN THE LOCAL GYM AT THE CONCLUSION OF THEIR WESTERN DIVISION GAME, WHICH, THE GAME, NOT THE RIOT, PASADENA WON 54–47. ROBINSON, BESIDES COMING OFF WITH HIGH POINT HONORS [WITH 20 POINTS], ALSO CAME OFF TOP MAN IN HIS PERSONAL WAR WITH SAM BABICH, SUB-VIKING FORWARD. . . . THE TWO CONTINUALLY FOULED EACH OTHER ALL THROUGH THE LAST HALF AND AT THE CONCLUSION OF THE GAME HAD IT OUT. BABICH WALKED OVER TO ROBINSON, ASKED HIM IF HE WANTED TO MAKE SOMETHING OF IT AND WHEN JACKIE NATURALLY SAID, 'SURE,' LASHED OUT WITH A RIGHT HOOK THAT LANDED JUST OVER ROBINSON'S EYE. THE NEXT MOMENT BABICH WAS LYING ON THE FLOOR WITH ROBINSON ON TOP OF HIM."

—ED VAN DER VEEN, *PASADENA [JC] CHRONICLE*, JANUARY 30, 1938

"At least 50 players, coaches, and fans jumped into the subsequent melee. Incidents like this one began to give Robinson a reputation as a hothead. He was not willing to stay silent in the face of racist insults."

—**Mary Kay Linge,** *Jackie Robinson: A Biography,* **2007**

"[In January 1938,] Jackie and one of his buddies started singing a song called 'Flat-Footed Floogie' while coming home from a movie. . . . A police officer overheard the pair and (in keeping with the tradition of SoCal police) threw the two young black men in jail. A judge sentenced Robinson to 10 days but showed incredible restraint (that's sarcasm) and let him off easy with two years' probation."

—**Gavin Evans and Jack Erwin, ComplexSports.com, illustrating that Robinson continued to have problems with Pasadena law enforcement even as a college student, April 11, 2013**

"Police Judge [Kenneth C.] Newell suspended a sentence of 10 days in the city jail for a period of two years 'on condition that there be no further complaints of this kind against this defendant, Jackie Robinson.'"

—*Pasadena Star-News*, October 18, 1939

"Bill Busik and Jackie Robinson . . . combined forces once again to lead Carl Metten's Bulldog cagers to a decisive 44–36 victory over Pomona Junior College last Friday night on local courts. Busik . . . sank a bevy of shots to nose out Robinson for scoring honors with 17 points. Robinson challenged . . . with 16. . . . Robinson slipping through to drop in a short toss . . . would bring in the defense and give Busik his chance [to make long shots]."

—Ed van der Veen, *Pasadena (JC) Chronicle*, February 4, 1938

"Putting up a stiff battle against Coach Art Nunn's Fullerton Junior College's defending Southern California champions, the Pasadena JC cagers dropped a 50 to 46 thriller last Monday night in the Fullerton gym. . . . Jackie Robinson . . . took high point honors for the game. The deadly Negro forward sent 22 points through the Fullerton bucket during the game."

—*Pasadena (JC) Chronicle*, February 11, 1938

"The Bulldogs finished the season third in their conference; Robinson was one point behind the leading scorer in the division, despite his and his teammates' belief that a suspiciously large number of calls made by the all-white referees went against the integrated PJC squad."

—Mary Kay Linge, *Jackie Robinson: A Biography*, 2007

"'Honest John' Thurman is [already] looking forward to . . . the start of the new [PJC baseball] season. . . . Thurman's . . . only worry is the question of retaining [last year's] championship. . . . Shortstop will be a toss-up between Jackie Robinson and George Doleshall. Robinson led the Bulldogs in hitting last year, and is almost a unanimous choice for the all-star night league game."

—*Pasadena (JC) Chronicle*

"[In addition to playing baseball for Pasadena Junior College,] Robinson . . . played for the Pasadena Sox, a team sponsored by the Chicago White Sox as part of an integrated amateur baseball league."

—Christina Rice, Senior Librarian, *Los Angeles Public Library Blog/Huffington Post*, April 11, 2013

"IF THAT KID ROBINSON WAS WHITE, I'D SIGN HIM RIGHT NOW. NO ONE IN THE AMERICAN LEAGUE COULD MAKE PLAYS LIKE THAT."

—JIMMIE DYKES, CHICAGO WHITE SOX MANAGER, TO REPORTERS, AFTER HIS TEAM PLAYED A CHARITY GAME ON MARCH 13, 1938, AGAINST THE PASADENA SOX, WHICH WAS THE NINETEEN-YEAR-OLD ROBINSON'S INITIAL EXPERIENCE WITH MAJOR LEAGUE BASEBALL, SHAV GLICK, _LOS ANGELES TIMES_, MARCH 31, 1997

"Robinson . . . played shortstop and was the team's leadoff batter. Pasadena batters got only six hits . . . and Robinson had two of them. On his second at-bat, he singled. Immediately, he darted off first. . . . After a couple of tosses to first, the pitcher finally threw to the batter and Robinson was off. The catcher's throw to Hall of Fame shortstop Luke Appling was so late that Robinson was standing up. Later in the game, with a runner on first, Appling hit a shot toward left field, only to have Robinson make a diving catch and somehow whirl and throw to second [to turn a] hit into a double play."

—Shav Glick, _Los Angeles Times_, March 31, 1997

"In the Long Beach relays on March 5 . . . Jack Robinson leaped 23 feet 1 inch for second in the open broad jump."

—_Pasadena (JC) Chronicle_, March 18, 1938

"[Sam] Mardian [who played sports with Robinson in elementary school] remembers playing handball with Robinson and being beaten by him . . . even though Mardian was handball champion at Pasadena Junior College and Robinson had never before played the game. 'He was so spectacular that most of the teams he played on were championship teams simply because of his presence. [Jackie never shied away from] calling attention to the general attitude that existed between the races. He spoke out more often than not.'"

—Pat Karlak, _Pasadena Star-News_, April 18, 1996

"Jackie Robinson, veteran shortstop of John Thurman's varsity baseball team, and team's leading batter, was last Sunday awarded a season pass to Wrigley Field as an award for being chosen the most valuable junior college ball player in Southern California. . . . At the same time, it was announced that Robinson and Fay Starr, stellar center-fielder of the Bulldogs, were selected to the all-Southern California Junior College first team."

—_Pasadena (JC) Chronicle_, May 6, 1938

CLASSIC MOMENT: MAY 7, 1938, POMONA AND GLENDALE, CALIFORNIA

"Once again, Pasadena was forced to play second fiddle to the all-powerful Compton Tartars in the annual Southern California jaysee track meet held last Saturday [May 7] in Pomona, which Compton won with 55 points to the Bulldogs' 51. . . . Overshadowing any of the team performances, however, was the sensational 25ft. 6½in. broad jump of the phenomenal Jackie Robinson. Jackie took just three jumps, hit 24ft. 7in. on his second trial, and then sailed out to a new national junior college record a few minutes later. The old record was 25ft. 5½in. set by his brother Mack, back at the Drake relays in 1937."

—*Pasadena (JC) Chronicle*, May 13, 1938

"MY PROUDEST ACHIEVEMENT, I THINK, WAS BREAKING MACK'S BROAD JUMP RECORD. . . . TO ECLIPSE ONE'S IDOL, EVEN IN ONE EVENT, IS A GREAT THRILL FOR ANY BOY."

—J. R., *JACKIE ROBINSON: MY OWN STORY*, AS TOLD TO WENDELL SMITH, 1948

"But his schedule gave him no time to bask in the achievement; the baseball Bulldogs were at that moment taking the field in Glendale 40 miles away."

—**Mary Kay Linge,** *Jackie Robinson: A Biography,* **2007**

"Jack [Gordon, my friend and football teammate,] drove me to Glendale while I changed into my baseball uniform in the car. The ballgame was in the fourth inning. I got two hits before it was over."

—**J. R.,** *Look* **magazine, February 22, 1955**

"Robinson helped lead the [Pasadena Sox] to victory in the California State Amateur Baseball Championship, prompting the *California Eagle* newspaper to declare that this success was 'the biggest argument for the participation of the Negro in major league baseball.'"

—Christina Rice, Senior Librarian,
***Los Angeles Public Library Blog/Huffington Post*, April 11, 2013**

"Pasadena Junior College successfully defended its state title in the Fresno Relays last Saturday with 36¾ points, just nosing out Compton with 36½ points. One [Fresno] relay record was broken by Jack Robinson who made a jump of 24 feet 9¾ inches, beating his brother [Mack's] mark of 24 feet 6¼ inches."

—Manfried Geisler, *Pasadena (JC) Chronicle*, May 20, 1938

"Jackie Robinson is the greatest base runner to ever play on a junior college team. He has stolen 25 bases (in 24 games), has batted .417 for the whole season, and is one of the most sensational fielders in the business."

—Hank Shatford, *Pasadena (JC) Chronicle*, after Robinson was instrumental in PJC's 11–6 defeat of Compton to capture the championship, May 27, 1938

"The Most Outstanding All-Around Athlete of the Year—that is the title of the honor conferred upon Jackie Robinson by the Chronicle Sports Page. If the page had been naming the greatest all-around athlete ever to attend PJC, Jackie would have captured this honor. . . . About all we need to say is that he was proclaimed as one of the most outstanding participants in Southern California in each of the four major sports: football, basketball, track, and baseball. In all of them he was a champion."

—*Pasadena (JC) Chronicle*, June 4, 1938

"PJC sent Robinson to the National Amateur Athletic Association's annual track meet, held in Buffalo, New York. Mack was there, too, representing Oregon. Jack placed third in the broad jump; Mack won the 200-meter race. But it was the last competition the two would share. Mack, who had married and would soon become a father, never returned to the University of Oregon. Instead he went home to Pasadena and his street-cleaning job."

—Mary Kay Linge, *Jackie Robinson: A Biography*, 2007

HOW A JC FOOTBALL PLAYER BECAME A LOCAL SENSATION

"With the incomparable Jackie Robinson leading a perfectly balanced first string backfield, behind a tried and true line, the Bulldogs seem set for a banner [1938 football] season."

—**Johnny Beckler,** *Pasadena (JC) Chronicle*, **September 30, 1938**

"Coach Tom Mallory's eleven bumped off Santa Ana's defending co-Southern California champions in its initial game [31–19]. . . . Jack Robinson's 83-yard gallop with Larry Monroy's punt was the climax of a wild scoring game."

—*Campus*, **Pasadena Junior College Yearbook, 1939**

"Another Southern California champion fell in the second game as the Bulldogs rolled to an impressive victory over the San Bernardino Indians [39–26]. Jack Robinson of Pasadena and Hal Finney of San Bernardino were directly responsible for all ten touchdowns. Robinson scored three personally and passed to Frank Spratt, Don Winton, and Ray Bartlett for three more."

—*Campus*, **Pasadena Junior College Yearbook, 1939**

"Making its first appearance in a Western conference game in three years, Pasadena's eleven easily mangled a weak Ventura team in the third game [27–6]. . . . Al Donnell recovered a Pirate bobble on the Ventura 19, giving Jack Robinson opportunity to score. The lithe Robinson also made the last two tallies on gallops of 60 and 14 yards."

—*Campus*, **Pasadena Junior College Yearbook, 1939**

"Coach Mallory's smooth-working machine struck early and then held the battling [Los Angeles City College] Cubs behind their own 44-yard line throughout the [16–0] game. Jack Robinson took a lateral from Red Robinson and ran 83 yards for the initial score."

—*Campus*, **Pasadena Junior College Yearbook, 1939**

"Shig Kawai, 80, who played halfback with Robinson at the junior college, remembers frightening trips to places like Compton. 'It was scary. In those days Compton was all white, and, except for me, our backfield was all black,' said Kawai, a Japanese American. Compton Junior College players taunted them with racial slurs, while fans did the same from the bleachers, Kawai said."

—**Peter Y. Hong,** *Los Angeles Times*, **January 1, 1999**

"Matching the mighty power of Compton with slashing speed, Pasadena's juggernaut thrilled 40,000 fans with a second quarter thrust that netted three touchdowns and victory [20–7]. The national junior college record crowd sat stunned by the precision that marked the drives of Pasadena. . . . One man—Jack Robinson—spelled the difference between the two squads. First Bulldog tally came when Jackie went 15 yards. . . . Almost immediately, Jack pulled down a Compton aerial, then passed to Red Robinson for 14 yards and a touchdown. Third score was made on a 45-yard gallop from scrimmage by the phenomenal Jackie."

—*Campus*, **Pasadena Junior College Yearbook, 1939**

"Daytime and San Francisco failed to stop the Bulldogs as they bested the Rams in the only afternoon game of the year [33–0]. Jack Robinson was a one-man riot as he scampered 76 yards to a score on the second scrimmage play. Later Jackie went 14 yards for a touchdown and made three conversions for a total of 15 points. . . . Jackie's ball-toting averaged 14.8."

—*Campus*, **Pasadena Junior College Yearbook, 1939**

"Victory over a rough Glendale eleven [33–6] assured Pasadena a tie for the Western conference grid championship [with Santa Monica] with five wins and no losses. Playing before 32,000 Homecoming Day spectators, Jack Robinson, held in check for 59 minutes, scampered 85 yards on the last play of the game to climax the conference season."

—*Campus*, **Pasadena Junior College Yearbook, 1939**

"He just had the abilities to duck and dodge and stop quick and stop cold. It's just amazing what he could do with his body if he had a little room to do it in."

—**Ray Bartlett, Robinson's childhood friend and an end on the PJC football team, to Kevin Glew, 2006**

"JACK ROBINSON AND 16 OTHER SENIORS RANG DOWN THE CURTAIN ON THEIR PASADENA FOOTBALL CAREERS AS THEY WALLOPED CROSS-TOWN RIVAL CAL TECH [39–6] IN THE SEASON FINALE. ROBINSON'S CLOSING CHAPTER WAS A 104-YARD RUN [ON A KICKOFF RETURN] TO A TOUCHDOWN, CLIMAXING THE GREATEST INDIVIDUAL CAREER IN JAYSEE HISTORY."

—*CAMPUS*, PASADENA JUNIOR COLLEGE YEARBOOK, 1939

"Pasadena Junior College's greatest football team was sparked by its greatest individual athlete, Jack Robinson. That's what critics were saying of Coach Tom Mallory's 1938 gridiron juggernaut after the Bulldogs won 11 straight games, scoring 369 points, better than 33 per game. . . . Unanimous choice as most valuable player, Robinson's contribution was 131 points and over 1,000 yards from scrimmage."

—*Campus*, **Pasadena Junior College Yearbook, 1939**

"Coming as a surprise to almost no one, Jackie Robinson, great Negro athlete, was presented the Elks' award for the most valuable player of the season at the 12th annual Elks' banquet held Tuesday night in the club lodge. . . . One of the highlights of the affair was the presentation of a special trophy to Tom Mallory by Frank Spratt on behalf of entire grid team. The trophy pictured Jackie Robinson atop a pedestal about 18 inches high."

—*Pasadena (JC) Chronicle*, **December 9, 1938**

"Pasadena and Santa Monica dominated the 1938 all-Western Division junior college team, selected by the all-Southern California Board of Football. . . . The Bulldogs have Ray Bartlett at end, Don Winder at tackle, and the great Jackie Robinson at quarterback. . . . He was easily the outstanding player of the year."

—*Pasadena (JC) Chronicle*, **December 16, 1938**

"Newspapers in the area generally gave less coverage to Robinson than many thought was merited, and it was said that one editor at the *Pasadena Star-News* ordered a reporter not to write so much about Robinson and his black teammates, claiming readers didn't care."

—*Pasadena Star-News*, **April 7, 1987**

"Brother of Jackie Robinson Mauled by Pasadena Police."

—*California Eagle*, **headline of article in which the paper expressed outrage toward the two white policemen who beat and arrested Edgar Robinson for not producing quickly enough his valid permit for placing rented chairs along the parade route of the Tournament of Roses Parade, January 12, 1939**

"Robinson's eldest brother Edgar was beaten and robbed . . . and subsequently denied treatment at a local hospital. Edgar later explained that the policemen were angered to see a black man at the Tournament of Roses Parade and when he refused to leave they charged him with resisting arrest. After beating Edgar, they robbed him of the $60 they found in his pockets, saying, 'We don't allow Negroes in Los Angeles to make this kind of money.'"

—*Icons of Black America*, **Volume 1, edited by Matthew C. Whitaker, 2011**

"That the brother of Olympian Mack and up-and-coming star Jackie would be treated so poorly spoke to the racial animosity in Pasadena."

—**Gregory John Kaliss, providing another reason Jackie would be sensitive to the issue of police abuse of blacks in the 1950s, 1960s, and 1970s,** *Everybody's All-Americans*, **2008**

"On Colorado Boulevard, Robinson first won big-time athletic glory as a star of Pasadena Junior College's track, football, basketball and baseball teams. The boulevard is also where his brother Edgar was beaten by police in a 1939 fight over Rose Parade seats. Such experiences left Jackie Robinson . . . alienated from his hometown."

—**Peter Y. Hong,** *Los Angeles Times*, **January 1, 1999**

"Robinson and Edgar took the case to the local offices of the NAACP and convinced them to file an official complaint with the City of Pasadena. The complaint was simply ignored. The incident was one in a string of frustrating events that caused Robinson to hate Pasadena and move on [after] college."

—*Icons of Black America*, **Volume 1, edited by Matthew C. Whitaker, 2011**

"Twelve [PJC] students out of 7,000 were singled out in January, rewarded for [performing outstanding service to the school] and presented with her highest honor, the distinction of being an OMD [Order of the Mast and Dagger (Omicron Mu Delta)] member. . . . Nine new OMD [gold pins were given to] Phyllis Richmond, Becky Bradford, Phyllis Wilson, Jeannette Eastman, Shorty Grannis, Herb McDonald, Joe Landisman, Shavenau Glick, [and] Jack Robinson."

—*Campus*, **Pasadena Junior College Yearbook, 1939**

"Classes and facilities at Pasadena Junior College were open to all students, and many social activities were integrated. [Former Pepper Street Gang member] Warren Dorn, who would later become a Los Angeles County supervisor, said he remembered his college friends helping him with his run for class president without race ever becoming an issue. Speaking on his behalf at one assembly were Robinson and Billy Beedle, who changed his name to William Holden when he became a movie actor."

—**Peter Y. Hong,** *Los Angeles Times,* **January 1, 1999**

"Coach Carl Metten's cagers made it two league championships in a row for Pasadena Junior College when they took the Metropolitan League basketball crown from Compton Junior College. . . . Robinson was the only local to earn a place on the official all-league team while the sensational Jackie, who averaged 19 points a game, also made the all-state selection. . . . Graduating seniors who will be greatly missed next year are Jack Robinson, Al Sauer, Ray Bartlett, Clem Tomerlin, George Good and Neil Reese."

—*Campus,* **Pasadena Junior College Yearbook, 1939**

"I WAS A KID AT COMPTON JUNIOR COLLEGE, AND JACKIE [WOULD] WIPE US OUT IN BASKETBALL, FOOTBALL, BASEBALL. HE COULD HAVE BEEN A PRO IN ALL THREE."
—DUKE SNIDER, FUTURE BROOKLYN DODGERS OUTFIELDER AND HALL OF FAMER, QUOTED BY DICK YOUNG, *NEW YORK DAILY NEWS,* JULY 19, 1977

"As his two years in junior college drew to a close, Robinson's outstanding play made him a hot commodity for four-year colleges up and down the West Coast. . . . [When it came time to make a decision], Robinson's brother Frank took a large part in it. Frank had been Jack's most loyal fan. . . . The standout, in Frank's mind, was the University of California at Los Angeles. . . . UCLA was a new school in California's state university system and a relatively comfortable one for black students. Its football program was strong and featured black players in key roles, including receiver Woody Strode and halfback Kenny Washington."

—**Mary Kay Linge,** *Jackie Robinson: A Biography,* **2007**

"Jack was a mama's boy. Always was. When he finished Pasadena Junior College, he had scholarship offers from dozens of schools. He chose to stay home and go to UCLA. Why? Because he didn't want to leave his mama."

—**Willa Mae Robinson Walker to Maury Allen,**
Jackie Robinson: A Life Remembered, **1987**

"I chose UCLA because I planned to get a job in Los Angeles after I completed my education. I figured I'd have a better chance of getting one if I went to a local university."

—**J. R. to Jack Sher,** *Sport* **magazine, October 1948**

"Days later, Robinson . . . got word that Frank . . . had been riding his motorcycle and had collided with a car on a busy street not far from home. Jack rushed to Huntington Memorial Hospital to find that the injuries were severe. . . .Within hours, Frank was dead. Frank's loss was emotionally devastating, and it would reverberate in his brother's life for years to come."

—**Mary Kay Linge,** *Jackie Robinson: A Biography,* **2007**

"I was very shaken up by his death. It was hard to believe he was gone, hard to believe I would no longer have his support."

—**J. R.,** *I Never Had It Made,* **as told to Alfred Duckett, 1972**

"Yesterday was a red-letter day for Jackie Robinson, Pasadena Junior College's sensational Negro athlete, for he enrolled at UCLA and prepared to settle down to make up lacking units in language and mathematics to become eligible by time next football season rolls around. Robinson, ineligible for all the athletics as a member of the Bruins' various teams . . . plans to compete unattached in the cinderpath this season and has his eye on a trip to Finland next year as a member of the American Olympic Games team."

—*Pasadena Post,* **about Robinson having make up academic units and become eligible to play football in the fall, February 17, 1939**

"He couldn't bear to stay completely away from athletic competition, though. That spring he played basketball in a statewide league for black fraternity members, and in early July Robinson competed in the championship tournament of the Western Federation of Tennis Clubs, which offered African Americans a chance to play this largely segregated sport. . . . He easily won the men's singles and doubles crowns. Reporters made a point to note that Robinson, who only played tennis in the summer as a sideline, beat players who devoted themselves to the sport year-round."

—**Mary Kay Linge,** *Jackie Robinson: A Biography,* **2007**

"Jack played to win, I can tell you that. . . . Jack was a really fine tennis player. He would out-finesse you. . . . He could move from one part of the court to another so fast you wouldn't even know he was moving. He had the ability to stop suddenly and get off a shot. He had a terrific cut that would make the ball hit the ground and just stay there. Nobody taught him these things. . . . We won the Pacific Coast mixed doubles championship. But that was it. At that time, no matter how good blacks were, they were not allowed to compete in national tournaments."

—Eleanor Heard, wife of Robinson's childhood friend Sidney Heard, who was sixteen when she played mixed doubles with him, to Harvey Frommer, *Rickey and Robinson*, 1982

"On September 5 [1939], [Robinson] was in his aging Plymouth, coming home from a softball game in Brookside Park, with Ray Bartlett and other friends riding playfully on the running boards, when he pulled up at the corner of Mountain Street and Fair Oaks Avenue. . . . Bartlett remembered clearly that a car driven by a white man came alongside."

—Arnold Rampersad, *Jackie Robinson: A Biography*, 1997

"The man said something about 'niggers' to us, and I popped him with my glove, slapped him in the face. . . . I thought me and this guy were going to have a fight. But Jack got in the middle of it, as usual."

—Ray Bartlett to Arnold Rampersad, *Jackie Robinson: A Biography*, 1997

"Just then a motorcycle policeman, John C. Hall, pulled up. By this time the crowd had grown, according to a police report, to 'between 40 and 50 members of the Negro race.'. . . When Officer Hall tried to make arrests, his 'suspects' kept melting into the crowd. Suddenly he drew his gun on Robinson, who alone refused to run or hide."

—Arnold Rampersad, *Jackie Robinson: A Biography*, 1997

"I FOUND MYSELF UP AGAINST THE SIDE OF MY CAR WITH A GUN BARREL PRESSED UNSTEADILY INTO THE PIT OF MY STOMACH. I WAS SCARED TO DEATH."

—J. R.

"Charged with hindering traffic and resisting arrest, Robinson was hauled off to jail. . . . The next morning, before an acting police court judge, he pleaded not guilty to both charges."

—Arnold Rampersad, about the much-publicized incident that would add to Robinson's reputation as a troublemaker, *Jackie Robinson: A Biography*, **1997**

"Jackie Robinson, Pasadena star last year, will see his first college action Friday night, the 29th of September, when UCLA entertains Texas Christian in the Coliseum. Although [new head coach] Babe Horrell said in a recent speech that Robinson will not be used too much because his switch from jaysee to college ranks might be his downfall, Pasadena fans are confident that Jackie cannot be kept out. Ray Bartlett, another former Bulldog, will probably see action."

—*Pasadena (JC) Chronicle*, **September 22, 1939**

"We also recruited [Jackie's] friend Ray Bartlett, and they became the fourth and fifth black players on [UCLA's football] team [that fall, along with Kenny Washington, Johnny Wynn, who soon left school, and me]. The black community liked to point to us as a symbol of achievement."

—Woody Strode, UCLA end who, along with star back Washington and two others, would break the color barrier in professional football in 1946, *Goal Dust*, **1990**

"ROBINSON MADE HIS COLLEGIATE DEBUT . . . AND THE FACT THAT HE AVERAGED ALMOST 10 YARDS PER PLAY IN SIX BALL-CARRYING ATTEMPTS PLAYED A BIG PART IN UCLA'S SURPRISE 6–2 VICTORY OVER TEXAS CHRISTIAN."

—SEATTLE TIMES, OCTOBER 4, 1939

"Kenny Washington, wearing Number 13 jersey, starred along with his team-mate, Jackie Robinson of Pasadena, for the University of California, Los Angeles branch, against . . . Texas Christian University. These two sepia stars had a field day."

—*Chicago Defender*, **October 7, 1939**

"With Jackie Robinson on the right side and Kenny Washington on the left, we had the two greatest halfbacks the West Coast had ever seen."

—Woody Strode, UCLA end and future NFL player and movie actor, *Goal Dust*, **1990**

"Since I could fake pretty well, I was used as the man-in-motion on offense at UCLA. As a halfback, I [would have] a ball-carrying average of about 12 yards per try. . . . At UCLA I was more interested in football than any other sport."

—J. R., *Jackie Robinson: My Own Story*, as told to Wendell Smith, 1948

"The addition of Robinson to the UCLA backfield . . . adds effectiveness to Kenny Washington's play, giving the Bruins two of the fleetest backs in the conference. UCLA's new coach, Babe Horrell, has devised reverses, double reverses, and split backs to shake loose Robinson and Washington. The Huskies defense must be air tight to stop them."

—George Varnell, *Seattle Times*, October 4, 1939

"The spectacular Bruins from UCLA, led by Jack Robinson and Kenny Washington, Negro backfield aces, came from behind to outscore the University of Washington Huskies today, 14 to 7, before 16,000 spectators. . . . It took UCLA until the third quarter to punch across the tying touchdown, and it was a sensational 64-yard punt return by Robinson that set up the score made by [Kenny] Washington."

—*New York Times*, October 8, 1939

"Three great Negro stars, Robinson, Kenny Washington and Woodrow Wilson Strode, wrecked the Huskies in the second half. The Huskies knocked Engineer Jack down and jumped on him in highly approved fashion throughout much of the first half. But the slim Negro halfback kept getting up."

—Alex Schults, *Los Angeles Times*, October 8, 1939

"That run of Robinson's beat us. Until that occurred we had the game well in hand."

—Jimmy Phelan, Washington Huskies coach, October 7, 1939

"THERE WILL BE FRIED CHICKEN AND WATERMELON ON THE DINING CAR TABLE AND THE PULLMAN PORTERS WILL LUG IN HOT WATER BY THE BARREL TO KEEP ROBINSON'S [HURT] ANKLE WARM ON THE HOMEWARD RIDE."

—ALEX SCHULTS, TRYING TO BE FLATTERING BUT REVEALING HIS AND HIS PAPER'S CONDESCENDING VIEW OF BLACKS, *LOS ANGELES TIMES*, OCTOBER 8, 1939

"In October 1939, the [US Communist Party's *Daily*] *Worker* began to tout the young Jackie Robinson, UCLA's four-sport standout athlete, as a potential major league baseball player."

—Kelly E. Rusinack, sports historian, noting how communist and black newspapers were at the forefront of the push for the integration of Major League Baseball, from paper presented at the Jackie Robinson anniversary conference, Long Island University, Brooklyn campus, April 1997

"Jackie Robinson, Negro football player now with the UCLA team, this morning by proxy faced Judge Herbert Farrell of Alhambra, sitting in the Pasadena Police Court for Police Judge Kenneth C. Newell who was called out of town at this time, on a second charge of resisting arrest. . . . Judge Farrell accepted a technical change of plea from not guilty to guilty and allowed the defendant to forfeit bail in the sum of $25 for this second arrest. . . . The court acted on a letter from an attorney in Los Angeles who has taken a great interest in sports affairs . . . asking that the Negro football player not be disturbed during football season."

—*Pasadena Star-News*, about the court ruling on Robinson's September arrest, October 18, 1939

"[Robinson] remembered . . . that UCLA paid the fine; he also recalled that he got back his forfeit bail of twenty-five dollars, presumably from UCLA."

—Arnold Rampersad, *Jackie Robinson: A Biography*, 1997

"I got out of trouble because I was an athlete."

—J. R.

"As a result of this bad publicity, Jack recalled, his first few weeks as a full-time student at UCLA were uncomfortable; the suggestion that he was a sort of thug persisted for a long time. . . . Later Jack would call this episode 'my first personal experience with the bigotry of the meanest sort.' . . . Some press accounts treated the matter humorously, but Jack did not laugh."

—Arnold Rampersad, *Jackie Robinson: A Biography*, 1997

"This thing followed me all over and it was pretty hard to shake off."

—J. R., writing about his early life, *Brooklyn Eagle*, August 16, 1949

"Sparked by sophomore Frankie Albert's southpaw passing, Stanford was close to a 14–7 victory over UCLA in [its] third game. An Albert pass play was clicking. . . . Gambling that Albert would repeat his successful play a third time, Robinson forgot his takeout and went for the pass. Leaping high, he snared the ball on his 20-yard line, twisted in mid-air and zigzagged back to his 45 before they spilled him. As the back in motion from a single wing to the right, Jackie was the spearhead of a swift march. He carried the ball to Stanford's 19. He took a short pass from [Kenny] Washington and raced to the five. Leo Cantor ran it over for a touchdown. Robinson then kicked for the point that tied the score, 14–14."

—**Arthur Mann,** *Collier's* **magazine, March 2, 1946**

"Two spectacular plays marked UCLA's 16–6 victory over [previously unbeaten] Oregon before 40,000 in Memorial Coliseum today. . . . A 45-yard forward pass by Kenny Washington to Jackie Robinson, good for 66 yards, brought one touchdown, and Robinson broke the Oregon Spirit in the third period with an 82-yard sprint for the second Bruin tally."

—*New York Times*, **October 29, 1939**

"[ROBINSON IS] THE GREATEST BALL CARRIER ON THE GRIDIRON TODAY."
—MAXWELL STILES, *SPORTS WEEKLY*, FALL 1939

"Robinson on the run looked like a funnel cloud. . . . He was big, just under six feet tall and a bit less than two hundred pounds, solid from head to toe, yet with the agility of a much smaller man. He ran with his toes pointed slightly inward, and with his arms lashing wildly, so that even when moving in a straight line he appeared to be going this way and that."

—**Jonathan Eig,** *Opening Day: The Story of Jackie Robinson's First Season*, **2007**

"Jackie was a very intelligent and . . . had a perfect white smile and steely hard eyes that could flash angry in a heartbeat. To be honest, Jackie Robinson was not well-liked when he was at UCLA. . . . Jackie was not friendly. . . . He was very withdrawn. Even on the football field he would stand off by himself."

—**Woody Strode, UCLA end,** *Goal Dust*, **1990**

"It wasn't his size, his speed, or his agility that impressed people most. . . . That thing that struck most strongly . . . was the fire. It seemed to burn constantly, just below the surface. It fueled his competitive spirit even as it threatened at times to undermine his accomplishments."

—Jonathan Eig, about the college athlete who never stopped competing, moving seamlessly from football to basketball to baseball to track, *Opening Day: The Story of Jackie Robinson's First Season,* **2007**

"The Uclans went on to beat . . . California for the best record in school history. The Rose Bowl was a certainty . . . until Robinson injured his ankle in a scrimmage just before the Santa Clara game. Without his speed and utility, UCLA was [only] as good as Santa Clara, Oregon State, and Southern California, all of whom were tied, but the Trojans got the Bowl bid."

—Arthur Mann, *Collier's* **magazine, March 2, 1946**

"We finished with four ties and [USC] had two. They were favored against us but we came close to winning the game. . . . We wound up with fourth down at the three, with time for one more play. The ball was right in front of the goal posts, and . . . it was such an important decision the quarterback took a vote in the huddle to see whether we'd try for a touchdown or a field goal. The rest of us voted 5–5, so . . . he decided on trying for a touchdown. So we threw a pass and it missed and the game was over [a 0–0 tie]. . . . I voted for a kick, but the quarterback said the reason he couldn't go for it was that the week before we tried four extra points and missed them all. Even so I had a lot of confidence in that place-kicker. Me."

—J. R., November 1952

"It seemed impossible to earn enough [working] part-time for college expenses and still be able to provide money to relieve [my mother] of her daily grind. When I talked to Karl [Downs] about this and other problems, he helped ease some of my tensions. . . . Inspired by Karl's dedication, I volunteered to become a Sunday school teacher. On Sunday mornings, when I woke up sore and aching because of a football game the day before, I yearned to stay in bed. But no matter how terrible I felt . . . it was impossible to shirk duty when Karl Downs was involved."

—J. R., *I Never Had It Made,* **as told to Alfred Duckett, 1972**

"UCLA finally won a Pacific Coast Conference basketball game tonight, beating California, 34–32, with the invaluable aid of its Negro sharpshooter, Jackie Robinson, of Pasadena, who proved decisively he plays basketball as well as he does football. It was the Bruins' first conference victory in 31 games. . . . Early in the second period California stretched [its] lead to 29–19. At that point Robinson went to work and almost single-handedly rolled his teammates to a 32–32 tie. . . . During the remaining 10 minutes the only points scored were on one field goal sunk by Robinson. That basket gave UCLA the game. Robinson was the game's high scorer with 12 points."

—*Pasadena Post*, **February 3, 1940**

"IF JACKIE HADN'T PLAYED FOOTBALL, HE MIGHT HAVE BEEN THE GREATEST OF ALL BASKETBALL PLAYERS. HIS TIMING WAS PERFECT. HIS RHYTHM WAS UNMATCHED. HE HAD THE VALUABLE FACULTY OF BEING ABLE TO RELAX AT THE PROPER TIME. HE WAS ALWAYS IN PERFECT CONDITION—NEVER DRANK NOR SMOKED—AND HE ALWAYS PLACED THE WELFARE OF HIS TEAM ABOVE HIS CHANCE FOR GREATER STARDOM."

—WILBUR JOHNS, UCLA BASKETBALL COACH, TO ARTHUR MANN,
THE JACKIE ROBINSON STORY, 1950

"Jackie's chief rival for individual scoring honors was Ralph Vaughn, of Southern Cal. They were running neck and neck and creating all kinds of excitement in Los Angeles—all over the Pacific Coast. Then came our game with Stanford. . . . Jackie had another great night [scoring] twenty-three points. We all knew that Vaughn was going well up in Berkeley. . . . Yet, with the score close and time running out, [Jackie] deliberately held on to the ball several times, instead of shooting. . . . Schools can't teach that type of sportsmanship. . . . The whole gallery was yelling for him to shoot and pile up his record against Vaughn. But Jackie thought of the score and the team. Nothing else counted."

—**Wilbur Johns, UCLA basketball coach, to Arthur Mann,**
The Jackie Robinson Story, **1950**

"When the basketball season was over . . . Jackie was top point scorer of the Southern Division of the Pacific Coast Conference with a total of 148. He rolled up an average of 12.44 points per game. He had beaten Vaughn!"

—**Arthur Mann, about Robinson excelling at his favorite sport,**
The Jackie Robinson Story, **1950**

"Three of the greatest track athletes ever to wear the Blue and Gold brought national recognition to their alma mater in 1940 and only the cancellation of the Olympic Games limited their fame. Jack Robinson stepped from the baseball diamond to the broad-jump pit, and after two weeks practice leaped 25' to set a new record in the conference meet. He reaped national laurels [a month later at Minneapolis] when the NCAA crown was bestowed upon him [with a leap of 24' 10 ¼"]. Pat Turner . . . won the Coast Conference-Big Ten meet with a leap of 25' 6". . . . Captain Carl McBain . . . in the National AAU negotiated the 400-meter hurdles in 51.6 seconds [equaling] the American record."

—*Bruin Life,* UCLA Yearbook, 1941

"ODDLY, BASEBALL WAS ROBINSON'S WEAKEST SPORT AT UCLA. HE HAD FOUR HITS AND FOUR STOLEN BASES, INCLUDING HOME, IN HIS FIRST COLLEGIATE GAME [MARCH 10, 1940], BUT OTHERWISE BATTED .097."

—DAVID ESKENAZI AND STEVE RUDMAN, TWITTER UPDATE AT @SPORTSPRESSNW, NOVEMBER 7, 2014

"If I had known I was going to play professional baseball, I would have refrained from other sports."

—**J. R., realizing too late how much long-term wear and tear the other sports had on his body,** *New York World-Telegram and Sun,* **October 1, 1960**

MEETING RACHEL

"[Rachel Isum] was just seventeen, slender and serene, with soft brown curls stacked cloudlike atop her head. She studied nursing at UCLA and took her school work seriously. She took most things seriously. Like Jack, she neither drank nor smoked."

—**Jonathan Eig,** *Opening Day: The Story of Jackie Robinson's First Season,* **2007**

"I was born and raised in northern California. Racial discrimination was very subtle. For instance, if we went to the movies, as we entered the lobby, the usher would direct us upstairs to the balcony. We were being segregated almost without knowing it. Jackie grew up in Pasadena, California, where discrimination was even more blatant and humiliating."

—**Rachel Robinson, interview,** *Scholastic* **magazine, February 11, 1998**

"I was a freshman at UCLA and he was a senior. He was Big Man on campus, because he was the first four-letter man at UCLA—that is, he starred in all four major sports. I was introduced to him by one of his teammates on the football team."

—**Rachel Robinson, interview,** *Scholastic* **magazine, February 11, 1998**

"While studying on UCLA's campus, Mom [Rachel Isum], lived at home [with her parents, Charles and Zellee] and commuted to school each day [from west Los Angeles]. For black students, campus socializing occurred at Kerckhoff Hall, and after class, Rachel and her girlfriends . . . hung out in the corner of the hall unofficially reserved for black students. . . . It was here that my mother and father were introduced by . . . Ray Bartlett."

—**Sharon Robinson,** *Stealing Home,* **1996**

"He wanted to meet her. He was a little bashful, a little reserved. I took him by the hand and introduced them. I said, 'You're on your own now.'"

—**Ray Bartlett,** *Pasadena Star-News,* **March 31, 1997**

"There was an immediate attraction and according to Ray, my father's passion for athletics paled after meeting my mother."

—**Sharon Robinson,** *Stealing Home,* **1996**

"I DIDN'T THINK ANYTHING COULD COME INTO MY LIFE THAT WOULD BE MORE VITAL TO ME THAN MY SPORTS CAREER. I BELIEVED THAT UNTIL RAY BARTLETT, MY BEST FRIEND AT UCLA, INTRODUCED ME TO RACHEL ISUM."

—**J. R.,** *I NEVER HAD IT MADE,* **AS TOLD TO ALFRED DUCKETT, 1972**

"Later, to my dismay, I learned that when Rachel had seen me play ball at Pasadena Junior College, she felt that I was cocky, conceited and self-centered. . . . She had watched the way I had stood in the backfield with my hands on my hips, and this stance reinforced her impression that I was stuck on myself."

—J. R., *I Never Had It Made*, **as told to Alfred Duckett, 1972**

"I was extremely shy, but I was rather pleased to see that he was also shy in that encounter. However, my impression of him was that he had great self-confidence, and I was pleased to see that he was not arrogant. It's a trait I detest. He was extremely handsome, with a wonderful smile. And he was clearly comfortable and proud of being a black man. In the 1940s I was very impressed by that fact. Not all of us could carry our racial identity with such pride."

—**Rachel Robinson, interview,** *Scholastic* **magazine, February 11, 1998**

"What do you see in that big ugly ape?"

—**Charles Isum, Rachel's father, who, after being gassed by the Germans while fighting US Infantry in France during World War I, worked twenty-five years as a bookbinder for the** *Los Angeles Times*, **to Rachel, who thought him jealous of Jackie**

"The relationship flourished, although Jackie clearly lacked Rachel's sophistication. Her stoic presence was crucial to his later success. Apart from a brief breakup . . . they were together for the remainder of Jackie's life."

—**Glenn Stout and Dick Johnson,** *Jackie Robinson: Between the Baselines*, **1997**

"Despite the departure of the great Kenny Washington, giant Negro halfback [who led the nation in total offense], as well as twelve other lettermen . . . nothing but optimism illumines the UCLA campus. In fact, the rabid Westwood rooters flatly say that wing-footed Jackie Robinson will out-perform Washington. . . . Left-halfback Robinson undoubtedly is one of the swiftest backs in the nation."

—*1940 Illustrated Football Annual*

"The younger half of the 'Gold Dust Twins,' Jackie Robinson, the Pasadena flash, set out to reach new heights of football fame during his last year of varsity competition, but was injured in the Texas A&M game and didn't get back into form until he ran through Washington State."

—*Bruin Life*, **about Robinson excelling during a disappointing senior season for the Bruins, UCLA Yearbook, 1941**

"He was named football All-American, and was widely acclaimed as the best all-around athlete on the West Coast, if not the country. He was called cocky and arrogant by some, the man to stop by rival coaches and 'The Dusky Flash,' 'Midnight Express,' and 'The Dark Demon' by West Coast sportswriters."

—**Sharon Robinson,** *Stealing Home,* **1996**

J. R. NOTE: Despite UCLA finishing 1–9 in 1940 on the gridiron, Robinson received raves around the country because he led the nation in punt-return average for the second year (improving from 16½ yards to 21 yards a return), and the Bruins in rushing (383 yards), passing (444 yards), total offense (827 yards), and scoring (36 points).

"Robinson formed the nucleus of a fast-breaking attack [for the Bruins basketball team]."

—*Bruin Life,* **UCLA Yearbook, 1941**

"In one January 1941 home game, Robinson single-handedly defeated the University of San Francisco Dons. With seconds remaining in overtime and the game tied, Robinson stole the ball and got off a buzzer beater. 'It was our Jackie,' wrote the Chicago Defender, 'who [clinched] the game with a spectacular heave as the gun sounded, giving the UCLA boys a 55–53 verdict.' Robinson had sent the game into OT with a game-tying bucket with 10 seconds remaining."

—**Black Fives Foundation, January 31, 2008**

"In early 1941, after his basketball career at U.C.L.A. had ended, Robinson abandoned his senior year spring track season [for baseball]—a move that reportedly 'broke the heart' of track coach Harry Trotter, who had counted on him for the broad jump."

—Black Fives Foundation, January 31, 2008

"Up one week and down the next Coach Jim Schaeffer's varsity nine . . . was far from complete until basketball season was over, for five of the team's strongest players were tied up with basketball duties far into the baseball season. Such players as Bob Null, Ray Bartlett, Jackie Robinson, Clark George, and John Colla were highlights on the basketball floor as well as the grass field."

—*Bruin Life*, UCLA Yearbook, 1941

"When I wasn't engaged in college competition, I played shortstop on the Pasadena baseball team that won the state amateur title. I'm afraid the quality of our play was not very high, because I compiled a batting average of .400, and in one game I remember stealing seven bases! When I could find the time, I'd go out to the golf course; but the best I could shoot was in the middle eighties. I also took a crack at tennis and reached the quarter finals in the Southern California Negro tournament."

—J. R., *Jackie Robinson: My Own Story*, as told to Wendell Smith, 1948

"I guess I didn't put as much effort into baseball as I did the other sports. Like most Negro athletes, I just assumed baseball was a sport without a professional future. I played it solely for the fun of it. Football, on the other hand, held out some kind of a future. Professional teams in the Pacific Coast Leagues did not discriminate against Negro players. The same was true of basketball. There were any number of professional teams made up of both whites and Negroes."

—J. R., *Jackie Robinson: My Own Story*, as told to Wendell Smith, 1948

"Jack Robinson lived up to all the promises that preceded him from Pasadena J.C. and then some. 'Jackie' became the first Bruins athlete ever to win letters in four major sports."

—*Bruin Life*, UCLA Yearbook, 1941

"At UCLA [Jack] was working for a degree in physical education when Mack got married. The children came and his mother needed help."

—Arthur Mann, about Mallie caring for Mack's children, including one who was mentally challenged, *Collier's* magazine, March 2, 1946

"After two years at UCLA I decided to leave. I was convinced that no amount of education would help a black man get a job. I felt I was living in an academic and athletic dream world. It seemed necessary for me to relieve some of my mother's financial burdens even though I knew it had always been her dream to have me finish college. . . . Rae [Rachel's nickname], too, felt strongly about the importance of a degree. . . . To my surprise [she] reluctantly accepted my decision."

—J. R., *I Never Had It Made*, as told to Alfred Duckett, 1972

"Jackie Robinson, . . . who dropped out of UCLA yesterday for a professional athletic career, was expecting to sign up with Broadway Clowns, a basketball team, sometime today. . . . [When not playing basketball,] Robinson plans to step right into professional baseball."

—*Pasadena Star-News*, March 4, 1941

"JACKIE ROBINSON DIDN'T TURN TO PRO BASKETBALL AND BASEBALL WHEN HE QUIT SCHOOL . . . AS EVERYONE HAD SURMISED."

—PAUL ZIMMERMAN, *LOS ANGELES TIMES*, MARCH 26, 1941

"Jackie . . . took a job with the National Youth Administration [as assistant athletic director at their work camp in Atascadero, California]."

—Arthur Mann, *Collier's* magazine, March 2, 1946

"The kids—we took them up to 18 years of age—mostly came from broken homes. . . . I had been no different than many of these kids who would make good if given half a chance. The kids were of all races, creeds, and colors and the biggest kid of all, come recreation time, was yours truly, Jackie Robinson."

—J. R. to Ed Reid, *Brooklyn Eagle*, August 9, 1949

"It . . . was rewarding to be involved with the youngsters. . . . However, it was a short-lived experience because World War II [had broken] out in Europe . . . and the government closed down all the NYA projects, even though America, at the time, wasn't involved in the war."

—J. R., *I Never Had It Made*, as told to Alfred Duckett, 1972

THREE

The War Years

"Jackie Robinson . . . is on schedule to report for his physical examination for the [military] draft when he returns from Chicago after the All-Star grid game there . . . Robinson was originally scheduled to take his physical exam Monday but was given a later date when the board was notified he was in Chicago."

—*Pasadena Star-News*, about American men being required to register for the military draft after President Franklin Roosevelt signed the Selective Service and Training Act on September 10, 1940, August 1941

"Robinson was named to the College All-Star team, which [played] the world champion Chicago Bears . . . the same Bears team that had demolished the Washington Redskins, 73–0, in the NFL championship game."

—Shav Glick, *Los Angeles Times*, March 31, 1997

"The matchup was an annual competition between the strongest team in the NFL versus a squad of college all stars [on August 23, 1941]. The Bears romped the preps 37–13, but Robinson earned the respect of the Monsters of the Midway. Defensive end Dick Plasman called Robinson, 'the fastest man I've ever seen in uniform' and further, 'the only time I was worried about the game was when Robinson was in there.'"

—Gavin Evans and Jack Erwin, ComplexSports.com, April 11, 2013

"Robinson did all that was expected of him and more, too. He is the first Negro to score a touchdown [catching a spectacular pass from Boston College's Charlie O'Rourke] in the eight games played. The 98,302 paid him a tribute as he left the field."

—Frank A. Young, *Chicago Defender*, September 6, 1941

"In the general uproar about Joe Louis and his universal appeal, the colored race has lost sight of Jackie Robinson, the UCLA phenomenon whom seasoned observers consider the greatest colored athlete of all time. . . . The future holds no future riches for Robinson, who . . . intends to make his mark in coaching. So it's a shame, then . . . that Robinson isn't . . . more universally known. He has everything Joe Louis has and more as regards personality, intelligence and native talent. And though there may be another Joe Louis in boxing, the thought of another athlete such as Jackie Robinson appearing upon the scene seems utterly fantastic. He is the Jim Thorpe of his race."

—Vincent X. Flaherty, after seeing Robinson against the Bears,
Los Angeles Examiner, August 1941

"When he left school, he didn't want to be a professional football player for any length of time because he already had . . . bone chips in his ankle that could not be removed."

—Rachel Robinson, to Peter Golenbock, *Bums*, 1984

"In a one-game deal later that year, Robinson toiled in his first pro football game with the Los Angeles Bulldogs. With about 10,000 fans on hand at Gilmore Stadium for a match against the Hollywood Bears [featuring his former UCLA teammates Kenny Washington and Woody Strode], Robinson injured his ankle in the second quarter and watched the rest of the game from the sidelines. One week later, Robinson signed a contract with the Honolulu Bears of the semi-pro Hawaii Senior Football League."

—Kevin Glew, *Cooperstowners in Canada* blog, April 4, 2013

"In September 1941, the NFL wasn't ready for African American players. Robinson accepted an offer from the Honolulu Bears for $100 a game."

—Jim Mendoza, *Hawaii News Now*, April 15, 2013

"When I reported there I got a job with a construction company headquartered near Pearl Harbor. I worked for them during the week and played football on Sundays [at Schofield Barracks] with . . . the Bears. They were not major league, but they were integrated."

—J. R., whose teammates included his friend Ray Bartlett,
I Never Had It Made, as told to Alfred Duckett, 1972

"Promoters of an exhibition football contest in Hawaii distributed handbills advertising Jackie Robinson, 'the sensational All-American halfback' as the primary attraction."

—**Sharon Robinson**, *Stealing Home*, **1996**

"Robinson gave 8,000 fans a lot to talk about. All they say about the Negro Flash is true. . . . He showed off his vaunted passing ability which surpasses even his running."

—*Honolulu Star-Bulletin*, **about the Bears' 27–6 victory, in which he threw a touchdown pass and returned an interception thirty-seven yards, fall 1941**

"More than 20,000 fans showed up at his next game at Honolulu Stadium, and Robinson scored his first rushing touchdown. But, alas, his team of Mainland and local stars lost, and would only win once more that entire season. By early December, Robinson had injured his ankle, and his brief Honolulu pro football career limped to an end."

—**Bob Hogue, Honolulu** *Midweek* **magazine, April 20, 2011**

"His team was staying in Waikiki, and he was denied entrance to the hotels. So we put him up here."

—**Jean Evans, executive director of the historic Palama Settlement in Honolulu, to Jim Mendoza,** *Hawaii News Now*, **April 15, 2013**

"To our pals. Best of luck. Jack Robinson."

—**J. R., writing a note of gratitude and his signature on a photo of himself that he gave to the Palama Settlement, December 1941**

"THE FOOTBALL SEASON ENDED IN NOVEMBER AND I WANTED TO GET BACK TO CALIFORNIA. I ARRANGED FOR SHIP PASSAGE [ON THE *LURLINE*] AND LEFT HONOLULU ON DECEMBER 5, 1941. . . . [TWO DAYS LATER] WE WERE ON THE SHIP PLAYING POKER, AND WE SAW MEMBERS OF THE CREW PAINTING ALL THE SHIP WINDOWS BLACK. THE CAPTAIN SUMMONED EVERYONE ON DECK. HE TOLD US THAT PEARL HARBOR HAD BEEN BOMBED AND THAT OUR COUNTRY HAD DECLARED WAR ON JAPAN. . . . BEING DRAFTED WAS AN IMMEDIATE POSSIBILITY, AND LIKE ALL MEN IN THOSE DAYS I WAS WILLING TO DO MY PART."

—J. R., *I NEVER HAD IT MADE*, AS TOLD TO ALFRED DUCKETT, 1972

"Los Angeles Bulldogs professional football team knows there's no title at stake today when they tangle with the Hollywood Bears . . . because the Bears, undefeated in eight starts, have already sewed up . . . the Pacific Coast pro title. . . . The Bulldogs are gunning for an upset. They . . . have been strengthened by the arrival of Jackie Robinson, former Pasadena JC and UCLA star, fresh from Hawaii, where he played some pro ball. . . . The Bears will throw the great Kenny Washington, formerly a teammate of Robinson's . . . and Woody Strode, perhaps the greatest end who ever came out of UCLA."

—*Pasadena Star-News*, **December 1941**

"Robinson had always been a familiar figure at Pasadena's Brookfield Park, and the spring of 1942 was no different. He was at the park nearly every day, playing softball and an occasional baseball game—even appearing with a touring black team against major league pitcher Red Ruffing's all-stars—impressing everyone with his athletic skills."

—**Glenn Stout and Dick Johnson,** *Jackie Robinson: Between the Baselines*, **1997**

"Blacks, communists, labor unions (particularly the CIO), and white liberals escalated the campaign [to desegregate Major League Baseball] during early 1942. . . . On March 18, Herman Hill, Los Angeles correspondent for the *Pittsburgh Courier*, accompanied two California-based black players, infielder Jackie Robinson and pitcher Nate Moreland, to the Chicago White Sox training camp at Brookside Park in Pasadena, California, and requested a tryout. . . . [Chicago manager Jimmie] Dykes recognized the skills of both men, but nevertheless declined to offer a tryout, repeating the familiar excuse that it was 'strictly up to the club owners and [baseball commissioner] Judge Landis to start the ball a-rolling.'"

—**Neil Lanctot,** *Negro League Baseball,* **2004**

"It was early 1942 when Jack got his draft notice. . . . Jack fully shared the outrage that most Americans felt about the attack [on Pearl Harbor]. At the time he was a patriotic man and felt that he, as much as any American, owed it to the country to fight for freedom. . . . He decided not to seek a deferment by claiming family hardship. Despite the fact that discrimination was still widespread and the military itself was rigidly segregated, Jack, like many black men, joined the armed services with high expectations."

—**Rachel Robinson,** *Jackie Robinson: An Intimate Portrait,* **1996**

"On April 3, 1942, at a Los Angeles induction center, Robinson reported for military duty as required. He joined millions of other draftees—800,000 or more of them black—called by their Uncle Sam to serve."

—**John Vernon, archivist, historian, and teacher for the National Archives,** *Prologue* **magazine, Spring 2008**

"[In May] he went through basic training at Fort Riley, Kansas. . . . Like other African American soldiers he was assigned to a segregated unit, the Cavalry."

—**Glenn Stout and Dick Johnson,** *Jackie Robinson: Between the Baselines,* **1997**

"He was never comfortable handling a rifle, and was awkward on a horse. He wrote home giving funny descriptions of his efforts to master both."

—**Rachel Robinson, who spent a year taking classes at UCLA in the day and working at night as a riveter at Lockheed Aircraft,** *Jackie Robinson: An Intimate Portrait,* **1996**

"One of my first jobs was to hold the horses for vaccinations. . . . I held the horses' heads. . . . They lifted me off the ground once in a while and whipped me around like a feed bag, but I discovered if I twisted their ears they would listen to reason and stay quiet."

—**J. R. to Ed Reid,** *Brooklyn Eagle,* **August 19, 1949**

"He was famous enough that it was news in Kansas City that he was stationed nearby. [There was] a picture [of him running in his uniform on an obstacle course while carrying his rifle in the] Kansas City Call."

—**Aaron Stilley, talk at the Negro Leagues Baseball Museum in Kansas City, 2013**

"I APPLIED FOR OFFICERS' CANDIDATE SCHOOL. IT WAS THEN THAT I RECEIVED MY FIRST LESSON ABOUT THE FATE OF THE BLACK MAN IN A JIM CROW ARMY. . . . THE MEN IN OUR UNIT HAD PASSED ALL THE TESTS FOR OCS. BUT WE WERE NOT ALLOWED TO START SCHOOL; WE WERE KEPT SITTING AROUND WAITING FOR AT LEAST THREE MONTHS. . . . JOE LOUIS WAS TRANSFERRED TO FORT RILEY, AND WHEN WE TOLD HIM ABOUT THE DELAY, HE IMMEDIATELY CONTACTED SOME POWERFUL PEOPLE IN GOVERNMENT."

—J. R., *I NEVER HAD IT MADE,* AS TOLD TO ALFRED DUCKETT, 1972

"Cpl. Joe Louis, the former heavyweight boxing champion . . . wrote to his friend Truman Gibson, who at the time was an assistant to William H. Hastie, a civilian aide serving as a racial affairs adviser to Secretary of War Henry L. Stimson. In 1943, Robinson and several other black soldiers received their overdue commissions as second lieutenants."

—**Dwight Jon Zimmerman, Defense Media Network, October 26, 2014**

"In the early 1940s, Joe Louis . . . was our hero. [Jack and I] felt that he didn't just fight in a ring, but he was battling the world on our behalf. He was fighting for respect, opportunity, and our place in America."

—**Rachel Robinson, interview, *Scholastic* magazine, February 11, 1998**

"I became a second lieutenant in January 1943. I gave Rachel a special bracelet and ring, and we formally agreed to get married when Rachel finished school."

—**J. R., *I Never Had It Made*, as told to Alfred Duckett, 1972**

"They made [Jack] morale officer to give him an official role. This is pure speculation, but I believe they made him morale officer because the other way he would have been such a troublemaker."

—**Rachel Robinson to Peter Golenbock, *Bums*, 1984**

"Considering his past, it was not surprising that Lieutenant Robinson . . . strenuously object[ed] to many of the segregated practices at the fort. In one instance he engaged in an animated telephone shouting match with a white major over whether black soldiers deserved fuller access to the installation's post exchange (PX)."

—**John Vernon, archivist, historian, and teacher for the National Archives, *Prologue* magazine, Spring 2008**

"LIEUTENANT, LET ME PUT IT TO YOU THIS WAY. HOW WOULD YOU LIKE TO HAVE YOUR WIFE SITTING NEXT TO A NIGGER?"

—MAJOR HAFFNER, PROVOST MARSHAL AT FORT RILEY, ASSUMING THE OFFICER ON THE PHONE (ROBINSON) WAS WHITE, 1943

"I was so angry that I asked him if he knew how close his wife had ever been to a nigger. I was shouting at the top of my voice. Every typewriter in headquarters stopped. The clerks were frozen in disbelief at the way I ripped into the major. . . . Warrant Officer Chambers advised me to go to Colonel Longley immediately and tell him what happened. . . . Colonel Longley [wrote] a sizzling letter to the commanding general. . . . I have always been grateful to Colonel Longley. He proved to me that when people in authority take a stand, good can come out of it."

—J. R., *I Never Had It Made,* as told to Alfred Duckett, 1972

"The incident ended fruitfully. Additional seats became available for blacks [in the PX], and Major Haffner himself, in later encounters with Robinson, was polite and even helpful."

—Arnold Rampersad, *Jackie Robinson: A Biography,* 1997

"One day a Negro lieutenant came out for the [baseball] team. . . . An officer told him . . . , 'You have to play with the colored team.' . . . That was a joke. There was no colored team. The lieutenant didn't say anything. . . . That was the first time I saw Jackie Robinson. I can still remember him walking away."

—Pete Reiser, Dodgers center fielder stationed at Fort Riley, to Donald Honig, *Baseball When the Grass Was Real,* 1975

"Jack was barred from the baseball team, but it appears that either this year, 1943, or the next, he . . . won a table tennis competition that made him the champion player in the U.S. Army."

—Arnold Rampersad, *Jackie Robinson: A Biography,* 1997

"Gallingly, the base recruited Robinson for its football team, but he rejected the offer when told he could not play against teams from the South."

—Thomas W. Zeiler, *Jackie Robinson and Race in America,* 2014

"When his commanding officer reminded the lieutenant that he could be ordered to play [football], Robinson agreed that was so but remarked that he could not be ordered to play well."

—John Vernon, archivist, historian, and teacher for the National Archives, *Prologue* magazine, Spring 2008

"ROBINSON DEVELOPED A REPUTATION AS A HOTHEAD WILLING TO STAND UP TO JIM CROW."
—THOMAS W. ZEILER, ABOUT WHY ROBINSON'S DAYS AT FORT RILEY WERE NUMBERED, *JACKIE ROBINSON AND RACE IN AMERICA*, 2014

"In early 1944 the 25-year-old cavalry-trained officer found that he had been reassigned to Camp Hood, located about 40 miles southwest of Waco, Texas. Lieutenant Robinson soon became informally attached to a black tank unit, the 761st Tank Battalion, which later distinguished itself in the European theater's Battle of the Bulge. . . . Camp Hood had already earned a dismal reputation among black officers and enlisted men, not only because of complete segregation on the post but also because neighboring towns such as Killeen and Temple were so inhospitable."

—John Vernon, archivist, historian, and teacher for the National Archives, *Prologue* magazine, Spring 2008

"Men, I know nothing about tanks, nothing at all. I am asking you to help me out in this unusual situation."

—J. R., being honest to the men in his tank battalion, whom he was training to go overseas, 1944

"Colonel Bates, who was in charge of the battalion, was proud of the showing made by my platoon. He called me to praise me and to ask if I would go overseas with the organization as morale officer. I told the colonel two facts of life: that it had been my men who got the job done—not me—and that while I would be willing to go overseas, I would probably be unacceptable since I was on limited service because of a bad ankle."

—J. R., *I Never Had It Made*, as told to Alfred Duckett, 1972

"[Robinson's] ankle . . . contained a large bone chip, which occasionally caused the joint to lock up entirely. When aggravated . . . this condition required intermittent visits to military doctors and hospitals."

—John Vernon, archivist, historian, and teacher for the National Archives, *Prologue* magazine, Spring 2008

"The business about my ankle could be resolved [Colonel Bates] said, if I were willing to go to a nearby Army hospital and sign a waiver relieving the Army of any responsibility if anything happened to me during overseas duty because of my inability. I said I'd be willing to do that."

—J. R., *I Never Had It Made,* **as told to Alfred Duckett, 1972**

"On July 6, Jackie Robinson . . . boarded an Army bus at Fort Hood [to take him to McCloskey General Hospital in Temple, Texas]. He was with the light-skinned wife [Mrs. Virginia Jones] of a fellow black officer [who was going to her home in Belton], and the two sat down, talking amiably."

—**Jules Tygiel,** *American Heritage* **magazine, August/September 1984**

"Lt. Robinson got on and came and sat beside me. I sat in the fourth seat from the rear of the bus. . . . [Southwestern Bus Company driver Milton Reneger] . . . asked Lt. Robinson to move [to the back of the bus]. Lt. Robinson told the bus driver to go on and drive the bus. The bus driver stopped the bus, came back and balled his fist and said, 'Will you move to the back?' Lt. Robinson said, 'I'm not moving,' so the bus driver stood there and glared a minute and said, 'Well, just sit there until we get down to the bus station.'"

—**Mrs. Virginia Jones, official court statement, August 1944**

"SO BEGAN A SERIES OF EVENTS THAT LED TO HIS ARREST AND COURT-MARTIAL AND FINALLY THREATENED HIS CAREER."
—JULES TYGIEL, *AMERICAN HERITAGE* MAGAZINE, AUGUST/SEPTEMBER 1984

"On the ride from Temple to camp, Robinson obeyed Texas law requiring Jim Crow seating on the bus. But he also knew that the Army now forbade segregation on its military bases. The previous month, after the killing of a black soldier by a white bus driver in Durham, North Carolina (a civilian jury soon acquitted the driver), the Army had proclaimed its new policy. Robinson also knew about the widely publicized refusals by Joe Louis and Sugar Ray Robinson to obey Jim Crow laws at a bus depot in Alabama."

—**Arnold Rampersad,** *Jackie Robinson: A Biography,* **1997**

"Upon reaching the bus station a white lady tells me she is going to prefer charges against me. . . . I told her I didn't care . . . and she went away angry . . . and the next thing I hear is I've cursed a white lady out. I feel now that I should have but I have never cursed one out and I certainly didn't start with her."

—J. R. to Truman K. Gibson, Assistant to the Secretary of War, excerpt from a letter asking whether it was advisable to publicize the trial, July 16, 1944

"When military policemen arrived at the scene, a crowd of indignant whites, both civilian and military, had formed, adding to turmoil and confusion. The MPs on site, none of whom outranked the lieutenant, asked him to go with them to the police headquarters to straighten out the situation. He agreed to do so. However, when they arrived . . . a white MP ran up to the vehicle and excitedly inquired if they had 'the nigger lieutenant' with them. The utterance of this . . . racial epithet served to set Robinson off and he threatened 'to break in two' anyone, whatever their rank or status, who employed that word. Inside the building, further exposure to what he regarded as racially unfriendly remarks and unwarranted observations by strangers convinced the young officer that he was not going to be treated fairly."

—John Vernon, archivist, historian, and teacher for the National Archives, *Prologue* magazine, Spring 2008

"After he vehemently contradicted other persons' versions of the bus incident and failed to remain in the facility until called to give his own account [on orders of Captain Gerald M. Bear, the assistant provost marshal and commander of the military police] he was taken back to the hospital under guard and under protest. He subsequently learned that his behavior had been construed as so spectacularly incorrect that he would now be subjected to a general court-martial. The justification given was that he had committed a number of monstrously serious transgressions—including the show of disrespect toward a superior officer and failure to obey a direct command. Thirteen depositions had been taken, attesting to Robinson's gross misbehavior."

—John Vernon, archivist, historian, and teacher for the National Archives, *Prologue* magazine, Spring 2008

"At the hospital, a white doctor who knew Jack warned him that a report had come in about a drunken black lieutenant trying to start a riot; the doctor advised him to take a blood alcohol test at once [although Robinson never drank]. The test proved he had not been drinking."

—Arnold Rampersad, *Jackie Robinson: A Biography*, 1997

"[Robinson was] transferred from 761st, because Paul refused to sign court martial papers."

—**Taffy Bates, wife of Colonel Paul L. Bates, commanding officer of the 761st, to Chuck Sasser, about Robinson's transfer to the 758th Tank Battalion,** *Patton's Panthers: The African American 761st Tank Battalion in World War II,* **2005**

"Robinson determined to broadcast his account of what really happened. He and others contacted the National Association for the Advancement of Colored People (NAACP) and sought publicity from the 'Negro press.'. . . Soon afterward, headquarters at Hood started to field queries about the impending trial from other military personnel, the *Pittsburgh Courier,* Robinson's state senators, and miscellaneous others. . . . Independently, the Army was beginning to realize that it was sinking in quicksand over such matters. In a transcription of a July 17 telephone conversation between a Colonel Kimball at Hood and a Colonel Buie, XXIII Corps' chief of staff, the former referred to the Robinson predicament as 'a very serious case . . . full of dynamite.'"

—**John Vernon, archivist, historian, and teacher for the National Archives,** *Prologue* **magazine, Spring 2008**

"Jackie took a stand in hostile territory, and it terrified him that he could be railroaded. I wasn't there. He called me every night [in San Francisco] and asked me to contact different people who might help him. He knew his (legal) rights, but he was afraid he couldn't get a fair trial in Texas and he didn't want to be stranded without help."

—**Rachel Robinson, quoted by Shav Glick,** *Los Angeles Times,* **October 14, 1990**

THE COURT MARTIAL OF JACKIE ROBINSON

"At 1:45 p.m. on Aug. 2, 1944, proceedings commenced in The United States v. 2nd Lieutenant Jack R. Robinson, 0-10315861, Cavalry, Company C, 758th Tank Battalion."

—**Michael Daly,** *New York Daily News,* **April 15, 2007**

"Nine men would hear the case. One was black. . . . Six votes were needed for conviction. . . . Jack faced two charges [now that three others had been dismissed]. The first, a violation of Article of War Number 63, accused him of 'behaving with disrespect toward Capt. Gerald M. Bear, CMP, his superior officer.' . . . The second charge was a violation of Article Number 64, in this case 'willful disobedience of lawful command of Gerald M. Bear, CMP, his superior.' Dropping those charges actually hurt Jack's defense, to some extent; the defense could no longer link what happened on the bus to what had gone on with the white soldiers, although a common thread was an utter disrespect for him as an officer and a human being."

—**Arnold Rampersad,** *Jackie Robinson: A Biography,* **1997**

"Although Robinson had been counseled . . . to obtain a civilian lawyer, he failed to do so. . . . Nevertheless, his Army-appointed defense attorney, Capt. William A. Cline, a white Texan, skillfully brought out inconsistencies in prosecution witnesses' accounts, including a denial by one prosecution witness, Pfc. Ben Muckleworth, that he had used the word 'nigger' in referring to Robinson when another MP had acknowledged that Muckleworth had indeed done so. . . . Cline, by careful questioning, managed to introduce enough into evidence to strongly suggest Robinson had been consistently confronted with a racially hostile environment."

—**John Vernon, archivist, historian, and teacher for the National Archives,** *Prologue* **magazine, Spring 2008**

"Robinson took the stand near the end of the five-hour proceeding. He allowed he had indeed been outraged at being called the N-word. He offered a definition of the word given him by his maternal grandmother, Edna Sims McGriff. 'She was a slave and she said the definition of the word was a low, uncouth person, and pertains to no one in particular,' he testified. 'I don't consider that I am low and uncouth.'"

—**Michael Daly,** *New York Daily News,* **April 15, 2007**

"I DON'T MIND TROUBLE BUT I DO BELIEVE IN FAIR PLAY AND JUSTICE."
—J. R., CONCLUDING HIS TESTIMONY AT HIS TRIAL, AUGUST 2, 1944

"Robinson's lawyers presented character witnesses, and then wrapped up their defense by arguing their client had been accused not because he'd committed any real crime but because a group of white men didn't like getting lip from an 'uppity' black man. . . . He was found not guilty of all charges."

—**Jonathan Eig,** *Opening Day: The Story of Jackie Robinson's First Season,* **2007**

"It was a small victory, for I had learned that I was in two wars, one against the foreign enemy, the other against prejudice at home."

—**J. R., about his acquittal, quoted by Jules Tygiel, *American Heritage* magazine, August/September 1984**

"IT WAS A TOUGH EXPERIENCE FOR JACKIE, BUT IT PREPARED HIM FOR WHAT HE WOULD FACE IN BASEBALL. HE LEARNED EARLY THAT WHAT WAS GOING TO HAPPEN WOULDN'T BE FAIR, BUT TO NOT FILL HIMSELF WITH RAGE AND HATRED."

—RACHEL ROBINSON, QUOTED BY SHAV GLICK, *LOS ANGELES TIMES*, OCTOBER 14, 1990

"[Robinson] had a lesser-known role in helping to make history of another kind eight years later, when a driver instructed Rosa Parks to move to the back of a bus in Montgomery, Ala. Parks had worked at nearby Maxwell Air Force Base after 1944, when the Robinson incident nudged military authorities to ensure actual compliance with earlier orders integrating buses and trolleys at their facilities. Parks' arrest for refusing to budge on a civilian bus in 1955 prompted a boycott and the emergence of the Rev. Martin Luther King Jr."

—**Michael Daly, noting that Parks remembered the reason for Robinson's court martial from her time at Maxwell, *New York Daily News*, April 15, 2007**

"In the summer of 1944 . . . [his ankle] kept him from going overseas with his outfit."

—**Sergeant Bob Stone, staff writer, *Yank, The Army Weekly*, November 23, 1945**

"My CO sent me to the hospital for a physical checkup and they changed my status to permanent limited service. After that I kicked around the tank destroyers, doing a little bit of everything."

—**J. R. to Sergeant Bob Stone, *Yank, The Army Weekly*, November 23, 1945**

"I appeared before the board 21 July, 1944, and was recommended for permanent limited duty and am now with the 659th Tank Destroyer Battalion, North Camp Hood, Texas, pending orders from your office. In checking with the Special Service Branch I was told there were no openings for Colored Officers in that field. I request to be retired from the services and be placed on reserve as I feel I can be of more service to the government doing defense work rather than being on limited duty with an outfit that is already better than 100% over strength of officers."

—J. R. to Adjutant General, Washington, DC, excerpt from letter, August 25, 1944

"I wound up as a lieutenant in an infantry battalion at Camp Breckinridge [in Kentucky]. . . . I was given a 30-day leave and put on inactive duty. I'm still on inactive duty. What I'd like to know is, do I have to go back to into active duty to get separated or will they just notify me that I'm out?"

—J. R., reflecting confusion over his status, to Sergeant Bob Stone,
***Yank, The Army Weekly*, November 23, 1945**

"The Army appeared as anxious to accommodate his request as he was to make it— possibly regarding him as, if not an outright troublemaker, a chronic lightning rod for controversy—granting his release within two months. His discharge took effect in November, just as the 761st encountered severe battle conditions in Europe and eventually suffered heavy casualties."

—John Vernon, archivist, historian, and teacher for the National Archives,
***Prologue* magazine, Spring 2008**

"[The army] cut an order saying Jack Roosevelt Robinson was 'honorably relieved from active duty.' It was an honorable discharge, but barely; it did not include veterans' benefits, even as it recognized that Robinson's ankle was unfit for full deployment."

—Scott Simon, NPR host, *Jackie Robinson and the Integration of Baseball*, 2002

"Had Robinson been given a dishonorable discharge in the court-martial, there would have been no contract signing [with the Dodgers in 1947] . . . and no Hall of Fame career."

—Shav Glick, *Los Angeles Times*, October 14, 1990

"When he came back from the Army, I acted as his secretary and he wrote letters to a lot of colleges, looking for jobs. He was hired by three or four until they found out he was a Negro."

—Willa Mae Robinson Walker to Maury Allen,
***Jackie Robinson: A Life Remembered*, 1987**

"Jackie Robinson . . . has given the Los Angeles Bulldogs a new lease on life. . . . He played with the Bulldogs against the potent San Francisco Packers in San Francisco . . . and was a positive sensation. The game was in the nature of a trial, and he didn't get around to formally signing his contract until late yesterday."

—*Pasadena Star-News*, **about Robinson returning to football while he tried to find steadier work, November 8, 1944**

"A 43-yard touchdown run by Jackie Robinson and a 65-yard forward-lateral touchdown play sparked the Los Angeles Bulldogs to a 21 to 13 victory over the Hollywood Wolves in a Pacific Coast Professional Football League game today. Robinson made his jaunt in the first period and was benched in the second with an ankle injury."

—*United Press/Pasadena Post*, **November 20, 1944**

"Jackie Robinson and Kenny Washington against the undefeated Hollywood Rangers! That is the smash gridiron offering setup for next Sunday at Gilmore Stadium yesterday when Jackrabbit Robinson agreed to leave for San Francisco with Washington to join the American League All-Stars and Clippers who will meet Bill Sargent's Rangers in the Shrine charity Pro Bowl game."

—*Los Angeles Times*, **December 11, 1944**

"A job offer came from his former pastor, Karl Downs, who had moved from Pasadena to Austin, Texas, and now served as president of Sam Houston [State Teachers] College. [Robinson had visited Downs often when stationed at Fort Hood.] Downs recruited Robinson to teach physical education and coach basketball at the all-black school."

—Jonathan Eig, *Opening Day: The Story of Jackie Robinson's First Season*, 2007

"HE WAS A DISCIPLINARIAN COACH. HE BELIEVED WE SHOULD BE STUDENTS FIRST AND ATHLETES SECOND. IF YOU CUT CLASS OR ANYTHING LIKE THAT, HE WOULD PUT YOU OFF THE TEAM OR GIVE YOU SOME LAPS. HE WAS A GREAT COACH AND A GREAT TEACHER. HE WAS WAY AHEAD OF HIS TIME."
—D. C. CLEMENTS, BASKETBALL PLAYER AT SAM HOUSTON COLLEGE, QUOTED BY ERIC ENDERS, *COLLEGE BASEBALL INSIDER*, OCTOBER 21, 1999

"[In exhibition games against nearby military teams] we won them all when Jackie played. Any time the team seemed to be getting behind, Jackie would have to go in. . . . He wanted to play, but he'd have to sit on the bench when we were playing those college teams."

—Harold Adanandus, trainer for the Sam Houston College basketball team 1944–1945, quoted by Eric Enders, *College Baseball Insider*, October 21, 1999

"He liked to play around the basket, rebounding and all that. He was tough around the basket. He was just an exceptional athlete, and you could tell he still wanted to play."

—Harold Adanandus, trainer for the Sam Houston College basketball team 1944–1945, *Austin-American Statesman*, April 15, 1997

"He . . . set up the school's first complete physical training program. He transferred most of his medals and trophies to the school as an inspiration exhibit. The Negro boys got the idea immediately and defeated Bishop College, 61–59, for the city basketball title."

—Arthur Mann, *Collier's* magazine, March 2, 1946

"But the post at Sam Houston College barely paid a living wage. . . . That was why he cast his eye about for a means of livelihood."

—Arthur Mann, *The Jackie Robinson Story*, 1950

"We used to hear from him a lot after he left. He was always sending us a letter or a card, advising us and encouraging us to continue in school."

—D. C. Clements, basketball player at Sam Houston College, quoted by Eric Enders, *College Baseball Insider*, October 21, 1999

— FOUR —

A Professional Baseball Player

"The way Jackie told it in his autobiography, he happened on soldiers playing catch at a military base towards the end of his service in 1944. He noticed one was throwing some curve balls with some real snap. . . . He turned out to be a Negro leagues pitcher named Ted Alexander, most recently of the [Kansas City] Monarchs. He told Jackie that the pay and life in the Negro leagues was good and that the Monarchs were looking for players. Jackie sent a letter to Tom Baird, co-owner of the Monarchs, who invited Jackie to meet the team for spring training in [Houston,] Texas, with a promised $300 a month if he made the team. Jackie countered with a request for $400 a month and Baird agreed."

—Aaron Stilley, talk at the Negro Leagues Baseball Museum in Kansas City, 2013

"Hilton Smith was playing with the Kansas City Monarchs when Jackie Robinson asked Smith [a star pitcher] to intervene with [co-owner J. L.] Wilkinson to get Jackie a job with the Monarchs."

—Janet Bruce, stating Hilton Smith's story about how Robinson became a Monarch, *The Kansas City Monarchs,* 1985

"[Rachel and I were] engaged, but she almost broke it off. . . . She didn't want me traveling all over the country with a barnstorming team. . . . I assured her that I wouldn't stay in baseball long. 'All I want to do,' I told her, 'is to make some money. They're going to pay me a hundred dollars a week. I've got to help my mother out and I don't know where I can make that much money right away.' Rachel understood, but she didn't like it. She wanted me to get a job in Los Angeles."

—J. R., *Jackie Robinson: My Own Story,* as told to Wendell Smith, 1948

"THEY DIDN'T KNOW WHETHER OR NOT I WOULD MAKE GOOD, SO THEY DIDN'T WANT TO HAVE TROUBLE GETTING RID OF ME."

—J. R., ABOUT WHY HE WASN'T ASKED TO SIGN A FORMAL CONTRACT, *EBONY* MAGAZINE, JUNE 1948

"In private conversations before Robinson had even played a game for the Monarchs, [black newspaper] sportswriters Wendell Smith and Sam Lacy agreed that Robinson could succeed in the majors. In a preseason article in 1945 in *Negro Baseball*, Lacy named several prospective major league players, calling Robinson the 'ideal man to pace the experiment.' Lacy noted that Robinson's college experiences made him no stranger to interracial competition."

—Jules Tygiel, *Baseball's Great Experiment*, 1983

"It had been five years since his only college season, with apparently little baseball in the interim. But according to reports, he 'looked good' in his very first workout with the club on March 27. . . . Jackie reportedly had the range of a good shortstop [although] his throwing arm may not have been the strongest."

—Aaron Stilley, talk at the Negro Leagues Baseball Museum in Kansas City, 2013

"Exhibition games started on Easter Sunday, April 1, in San Antonio. His first opponent was an all-white team dubbed [Charlie] Engle's Minor League All-Stars . . . a team of minor leaguers and cadets from a nearby Air Force base. The game was called a tie after 14 innings. Jackie managed one hit in seven at-bats and turned three double plays as the shortstop."

—Aaron Stilley, talk at the Negro Leagues Baseball Museum in Kansas City, 2013

"I remember seeing Jackie for the first time. He was fat. And I thought the Monarchs had him just for a publicity stunt because he had been so great in college. We were playing an exhibition game in Houston, Texas, and Jackie hit a ball between the third baseman and the bag down the left-field line. Our left-fielder ran over and got the ball quickly and wheeled it into second base. But Jackie was . . . already there. I knew right then the guy could move. We were together for about six or seven games that spring, and during that time we couldn't get him out."

—Jimmie Crutchfield, Negro League veteran, quoted by William Brashler, *The Story of Negro League Baseball*, 1994

"No method for breaking the race barrier was evolved until 1945, when the Fair Employment Practices Commission came into being in New York State. Joe Bostic, then sports editor of the *People's Voice*, Negro weekly . . . shortly afterwards corralled Terris McDuffie, a pitcher, and Showboat Thomas, captain and fancy-dan first baseman of the New York Cubans, for a trip to Bear Mountain [where, due to war-time travel restrictions, the Brooklyn Dodgers had their training camp]. Without previous notice Bostic and the two players barged in and demanded a tryout from [Dodgers president] Branch Rickey. Mr. Rickey graciously consented to a tryout the following day . . . and they worked out under Mr. Rickey's eyes."

—J. R., *Jackie Robinson: My Own Story,* as told to Wendell Smith, 1948

"[Rickey] started talking about his concern for the black man. He actually put a show on for me. Rickey cried and talked about religion and so on. I was very cynical. I thought he was a phony. . . . He didn't sign the two players, and . . . he never spoke to me again. Of course, my move might have been ill timed from Rickey's point of view. He might have already had his eye on Robinson."

—Joe Bostic, sports editor of the *People's Voice,* to Harvey Frommer, *Rickey and Robinson,* 1982

"IT IS NO SECRET THAT FOR YEARS THERE WAS A TACIT UNDERSTANDING AMONG OWNERS IN ORGANIZED BASEBALL THAT THE NEGRO WAS TABOO. HE WAS NOT BARRED CONSTITUTIONALLY, BUT IT WAS DEFINITELY UNDERSTOOD THAT HE WAS NOT TO BE SIGNED."

—J. R., *JACKIE ROBINSON: MY OWN STORY,* AS TOLD TO WENDELL SMITH, 1948

A SHAM TRYOUT IN BOSTON

"In the middle of April, Jackie took a separate trip to Boston. . . . There was an old law still on the books in Boston prohibiting Sunday baseball, and the major league Red Sox and Braves had to secure a special permit to play on Sundays from the city council every season, which was typically just a formality. But an enterprising city councilman named Isadore Muchnick . . . who was Jewish,

(continued)

informed the two Boston clubs that he would block their Sunday permit unless they allowed an African American to try-out for them. Muchnick partnered with integration-crusading sportswriter Wendell Smith, and Smith's paper, the *Pittsburgh Courier*, bankrolled a trip to Boston for three Negro leaguers with major league potential. Smith invited Marvin Williams of the Philadelphia Stars, Sam Jethroe of the Cleveland Buckeyes, and Jackie Robinson, who had been with the Monarchs for just three weeks. Jackie's name recognition could have been part of the reason Smith invited him."

—Aaron Stilley, talk at the Negro Leagues Baseball Museum in Kansas City, 2013

"Robinson was already fatalistic about the tryout. He didn't believe the Red Sox were serious about integration. . . . When Robinson arrived in Boston, the tryout was delayed for two more days in the wake of [President] Franklin Roosevelt's death. . . . Nearly fifty-five years after Cap Anson engineered the removal of the last black major leaguers in the late nineteenth century, the tryout finally took place at Fenway Park at eleven in the morning of April 16, 1945."

—Howard Bryant, *Shut Out: The Story of Race and Baseball in Boston*, 2002

"The three Negro leaguers ran through drills for around an hour and a half at Fenway Park in front of the Red Sox GM, manager, and two coaches. Jackie wore the Monarchs uniform he brought while he stood in the Fenway batter's box and sprayed line drives over the center field wall and against the green monster. He neatly performed some fielding drills at short with Marvin Williams at second."

—Aaron Stilley, talk at the Negro Leagues Baseball Museum in Kansas City, 2013

"Hugh Duffy, the former great Red Sox outfielder, ran the tryout and took notes on index cards. . . . When it ended, [Robinson], Williams, and Jethroe received platitudes from Duffy. Joe Cashman of the *Boston Record* sat with [Joe] Cronin that day and reported that the manager was impressed with Robinson. He wrote cryptically, with virtually little comprehension that he could have been witnessing a historic moment."

—Howard Bryant, *Shut Out: The Story of Race and Baseball in Boston*, 2002

"Clif Keane [*Boston Globe* sportswriter] . . . had a general reputation as a racist . . . [but he] was also one of the few reporters to pester the Red Sox on racial issues. . . . It was Keane who sat at the Robinson tryout in 1945 and heard a belligerent voice bark out [from high in the stands], 'Get those niggers off the field.' Keane believed it to be [Red Sox owner] Tom Yawkey, a viewpoint seconded by [Boston TV sportscaster] Clark Booth."

—Howard Bryant, *Shut Out: The Story of Race and Baseball in Boston*, 2002

"Without Clif Keane, no one is ever talking about the tryout with Jackie Robinson. He put a voice to it. . . . That sentence 'get those niggers off the field' is the scarlet 'A' on the Red Sox brow. Clif brought that out."

—Clark Booth, Boston television reporter, to Howard Bryant, *Shut Out: The Story of Race and Baseball in Boston*, 2002

"Robinson himself was satisfied with his performance, although by the time he left Fenway he was smoldering about what he felt to be a humiliating charade. As the three players departed, Eddie Collins [Red Sox vice president and general manager] told them they would hear from the Red Sox in the near future. None of them ever heard from the Red Sox again."

—Howard Bryant, *Shut Out: The Story of Race and Baseball in Boston*, 2002

"In the end, the Red Sox men made excuses about their farm clubs being located in the South, and that they would need to see the players in real game action before signing them."

—Aaron Stilley, talk at the Negro Leagues Baseball Museum in Kansas City, 2013

"I was in no position to offer them a job. The general manager did the hiring and there was an unwritten rule at the time against hiring black players. I was just the manager. It was a great mistake by us. [Robinson] turned out to be a great player. . . . We all thought because of the times, it was good to have separate leagues."

—Joe Cronin, Red Sox manager, *Boston Globe*, July 22, 1979

"Jackie and Isadore Muchnick remained friends after the tryout, and Jackie later thanked Muchnick for 'all [he] meant to [Robinson's] baseball career.'"

—Aaron Stilley, talk at the Negro Leagues Baseball Museum in Kansas City, 2013

"THE RED SOX IN 1945 COULD HAVE BEEN THE FIRST TEAM TO INTEGRATE, WITH ROBINSON, BUT INSTEAD WOULD BE THE LAST [IN 1959]. THE MISSED OPPORTUNITY WOULD SHARPLY MIRROR A REVERSAL OF THE CITY'S RACIAL FORTUNES."

—HOWARD BRYANT, *SHUT OUT: THE STORY OF RACE AND BASEBALL IN BOSTON*, 2002

"Meanwhile, the three men never received the promised tryout from the [Boston] Braves, who offered the fanciful excuse that they were unable to 'look at' players already evaluated by the Red Sox."

—Neil Lanctot, *Negro League Baseball*, 2004

"Jackie returned to the Monarchs and finished out the spring training schedule. . . . [To forty-four-year-old manager Frank Duncan] Jackie had been so impressive that he was batting third in his first league game [May 6, 1945]. He stayed in the three hole for just about every game with the Monarchs. He had an RBI double in the opener, plus a stolen base and run scored. The team got off to a hot start, winning 10 of the first 14 games."

—Aaron Stilley, talk at the Negro Leagues Baseball Museum in Kansas City, 2013

"On Memorial Day at Comiskey Park, [the Monarchs' legendary star pitcher] Satchel Paige showed up and got a belated start to the season. Satchel had a good day, but Jackie had a great day. He came to the plate seven times during the double header, and reached safely all seven times with three walks, two singles, a double, and a triple."

—Aaron Stilley, talk at the Negro Leagues Baseball Museum in Kansas City, 2013

"I NEVER DREAMED OF BECOMING A FULL-TIME PROFESSIONAL BASEBALL PLAYER. ALL THE TIME I WAS PLAYING I WAS LOOKING AROUND FOR SOMETHING ELSE. I DIDN'T LIKE THE BOUNCING BUSES, THE CHEAP HOTELS, AND THE CONSTANT NIGHT GAMES. BUT I DID MEET SOME GREAT BALL PLAYERS THAT YEAR. TWO OF THEM—SATCHEL PAIGE AND JOSH GIBSON— WOULD HAVE STARRED IN ANY LEAGUE THAT EVER WAS."

—J. R., *JACKIE ROBINSON: MY OWN STORY*, AS TOLD TO WENDELL SMITH, 1948

"In mid-June . . . Jackie and the Monarchs, heading east, got plenty of media attention. Frank Duncan later claimed, 'By the time we got to [the East], those scouts were on him.'. . . If the Dodgers were watching him . . . it was probably no later than this eastern trip. They would have been impressed with what they saw."

—Aaron Stilley, talk at the Negro Leagues Baseball Museum in Kansas City, 2013

"[Jackie Robinson is] one of baseball's leading shortstops."

—*New York Times*, prior to the Monarchs' appearance at Yankee Stadium, June 1945

"[Jackie Robinson is] one of the sport's most valuable additions in years . . . and is headed for stardom."

—*New York Amsterdam*, about Robinson's first appearance at Yankee Stadium on June 17, when he singled to start the winning rally against the Philadelphia Stars, June 1945

"I had first heard the name Jackie Robinson in 1945 when he came to Newark with the Kansas City Monarchs to play against the Eagles. . . . I was more aware of Satchel Paige. . . . If you were black and a baseball fan, then you knew about Satchel Paige. He was a legend."

—Don Newcombe, Newark Eagles pitcher, to Danny Peary, *We Played the Game*, 1994

"A medically discharged Army lieutenant who formerly was one of the most versatile Negro athletes in the United States may steal the show from Satchelfoot Paige and Josh Gibson when Kansis [sic] City's Monarchs visit Griffith Stadium tomorrow for a 2 p.m. . . . Outstanding newcomer to the Monarchs is shortstop Jackie Robinson . . . who presently is being acclaimed as the 1945 Negro baseball rookie of the year."

—*Washington Post*, June 23, 1945

"Robinson actually did play in DC . . . and it was a pretty big deal. It happened June 24. The Monarchs came to town to play Washington's Homestead Grays in a double header at Griffith Stadium and over 18,000 fans—twice the size of a normal Senators crowd that season—came out to watch. . . . Though the Grays won both games easily . . . the prognostications about Robinson were spot-on. Over the two games, he equaled the National Negro League record by going 7 for 7 with a walk."

—Mark Jones, WETA.org, April 12, 2013

"If I could go back in time to watch baseball games, the doubleheader on June 24 is one I would choose. I'd get to see seven Hall of Famers take the field: Jackie, Satchel, and Hilton [Smith] for the Monarchs, and Josh Gibson, Jud Wilson, Cool Papa Bell, and Buck Leonard for the Grays. I'd also get to see Jackie reach base safely in all eight plate appearances he made in the two games (five singles, two doubles, and one walk). The Grays murderer's row was too much for the Monarchs in both games, however."

—Aaron Stilley, talk at the Negro Leagues Baseball Museum in Kansas City, 2013

"The grubby life with the Monarchs was a shock to college-bred Jackie. The Monarchs traveled around in an old bus, often for two or three days at a time (the league stretches from Kansas City to Newark) without a bath, a bed, or a hot meal, and crawled out long enough to play a game. The smart ones got aboard the bus early, rolled up their uniforms for a pillow, and slept in the aisle."

—*Time* magazine, September 22, 1947

"Sammie Haynes . . . teammate of Jackie Robinson on the 1945 team . . . stressed that Jackie sat on the floor of the [Monarchs'] bus just like the other rookies."

—Larry Lester and Sammy J. Miller, *Black Baseball in Kansas City*, 2000

"Jack . . . was impressed by the caliber of play, and the unique way that the Negro leaguers performed. He learned a great deal from them, and enjoyed the camaraderie. What he hated about playing in the Negro Leagues was . . . traveling through the South on buses, unable to stop at hotels, unable to enter restaurants, unable to use restrooms. He found it thoroughly humiliating."

—Rachel Robinson, interview, *Scholastic* magazine, February 11, 1998

"AFTER TWO MONTHS OF IT, I WAS FOR QUITTING. NO FUTURE."
—J. R., *TIME* MAGAZINE, SEPTEMBER 22, 1947

"The team started their drive to win the second half with a game against the Birmingham Black Barons in Muskogee, Oklahoma, on July 7. Jackie had a pair of home runs in the game."

—Aaron Stilley, talk at the Negro Leagues Baseball Museum in Kansas City, 2013

"We had been buying gas for years at a service station (in Muskogee, OK) that had just one restroom—and we weren't allowed to use it. We . . . gave the owner a lot of business anyway. Well, when the bus pulled into Muskogee and stopped at this station, Jackie got out and headed toward the restroom. The owner, who was filling the tank, called after him, 'Hey boy! You know . . . we don't allow no colored people in that restroom.' . . . Jackie turned to the man very calmly and said, 'Take the hose out of the tank.' The owner stopped the pump and looked at him. . . . Then he turned to his teammates and said, 'Let's go. We don't want his gas.' . . . Well, that gas station wasn't going to sell a hundred gallons of gas to one customer until the bus came back through a few weeks later. He shoved the hose back into the tank and said, 'All right, you boys can use the restroom. But don't stay long.' From then on, the Monarchs could use the restroom whenever they passed through. But more importantly, they decided never to patronize any gas station or restaurant where they couldn't use the facilities."

—Buck O'Neil, Robinson's Monarchs teammate, *I Was Right on Time,* **1996**

"We . . . pulled up in service stations in Mississippi where drinking fountains said black and white and a couple of times we had to leave without our change, he'd get so mad."

—Othello "Chico" Renfroe, Robinson's Monarchs teammate, to Jules Tygiel, *Baseball's Great Experiment,* **1983**

"We played the Kansas City Monarchs in Belleville, Illinois. . . . Jackie was a real fireball. He loved to win. We won the game . . . and afterward, when both teams were dressing in the locker room, Jackie got into it with my outfielders, Sam Jethroe and Buddy Armour. He really had a sharp tongue, and I wondered who this young cat was to be raising all that sand."

—Quincy Trouppe, Cleveland Buckeyes manager, *20 Years Too Soon,* **1977**

"[Jackie] often got hotter than a General Electric burner when he played with the Monarchs. And he had a truly copious, ever-available supply of sizzling nouns, verbs and adjectives that went awfully well with that temper."

—Othello "Chico" Renfroe, Robinson's Monarchs teammate

"Later that season, I played against him in Cleveland and he overpowered my pitcher's curve with a line drive into the left-field sands. I knew then he had the makings of a top pro."

—Quincy Trouppe, Cleveland Buckeyes manager, *20 Years Too Soon,* **1977**

"Jackie was chosen to start the East-West all-star game at Chicago's Comiskey Park July 29. Over 30,000 fans showed up to watch the annual spectacle. . . . Jackie had a rare hitless day at the plate, but put the finishing touches on the West's victory by spearing a tough grounder behind second base before nailing the runner at first for the final out."

—Aaron Stilley, talk at the Negro Leagues Baseball Museum in Kansas City, 2013

"Jackie gave the fans thrill after thrill by his brilliant fielding, base running and hitting. His drag bunt, his delayed steal of third, and his stealing home with the opposing pitcher looking right down his throat, unable to do anything about it, were his three sensational plays. Jackie proved why he is the talk of the country. He acts like a big leaguer, hits like a big leaguer, thinks like a big leaguer, throws like a big leaguer, and he fields like a big leaguer at shortstop."

—*Boston Chronicle*, after the first night game played at Braves Field in Boston, 1945

"Atomic bombs were dropped on Japan [on August 6 and 9, 1945] and World War II was starting to come to an end while the Monarchs were out East. Jackie told a reporter, 'I bet $5 it wouldn't be over before October, but that is one bet I am happy to lose.'"

—Aaron Stilley, talk at the Negro Leagues Baseball Museum in Kansas City, 2013

"We'd ride miles and miles on the bus and [Jackie's] whole talk was, 'Well, you guys better be ready because pretty soon baseball's going to sign one of us.'"

—Othello "Chico" Renfroe, Monarchs teammate, about Robinson saying the major leagues would soon be integrated, to Jules Tygiel, *Baseball's Great Experiment*, 1983

"No, I didn't. Not in my lifetime. I was afraid it might take another war before it could happen."

—J. R., when asked three years later if, in 1945, he believed that the color barrier would be torn down in the major leagues, to Jack Sher, *Sport* magazine, October 1948

"In early May, [Brooklyn Dodgers GM and controlling partner Branch Rickey had announced] he would own a team in Gus Greenlee's newly formed United States League . . . to compete with the Negro National and Negro American leagues. . . . Having created a smoke screen, Rickey sent his best scouts—George Sisler, Clyde Sukeforth, and Wid Mathews—to search for players presumably for the [Brooklyn] Brown Dodgers. . . . Wendell Smith . . . went to Brooklyn for a meeting with Rickey. . . . Rickey wanted to hear about the [Fenway Park] tryout directly from Smith. . . . Smith recommended Robinson."

—Chris Lamb, *Conspiracy of Silence*, 2012

"A Sisler report declared unequivocally that [Robinson] was a prospect and could reach the top, that he could run exceptionally fast, that he had a slightly better than average arm, though not a good one, and that he had tremendous possibilities as a hitter. Matthews' report stressed Robinson as a hitter with high potentiality, due to the fact that he protected the strike zone better than any rookie that Matthews had ever seen; a great hitter for the three-and-two pitch. . . . He also agreed, much to Branch Rickey's dismay, that the boy might not have a strong arm."

—Arthur Mann, *The Jackie Robinson Story*, 1950

"The Kansas City Monarchs are playing the Lincoln Giants in Chicago on Friday night. I want you to see that game. Tell [Jackie Robinson] who sent you. . . . If you like this fellow's arm, bring him in. And if his schedule won't permit it, if he can't come in, then make an appointment for me and I'll go out there."

—Branch Rickey, supposedly trying to find players for the Brooklyn Brown Bombers, a Negro League team he had discussed establishing, to scout Clyde Sukeforth, quoted by Sukeforth, to Donald Honig, *Baseball When the Grass Was Real*, 1975, August 1945.

"Well, I'm not the smartest guy in the world but I said to myself, 'This could be the real thing.'"

—Clyde Sukeforth, Dodgers scout, about Rickey's interest in Robinson, to Donald Honig, *Baseball When the Grass Was Real*, 1975

"Many people have the impression that I was the first man to scout Jackie Robinson, but everybody in America knew what talent he had. Nobody but Branch Rickey deserves any credit. They have given me too much credit."

—Clyde Sukeforth, whom Robinson credited as being second in importance to Rickey in making the "Great Experiment" work, to Nick Wilson, *Voices from the Pastime*, 2000

"On [August] 24th, Jackie was standing on the side of Comiskey Park's field before the game when a white man called to him from the stands. He introduced himself as Clyde Sukeforth from the Brooklyn Dodgers and said Branch Rickey was interested in [him]."

—Aaron Stilley, talk at the Negro Leagues Baseball Museum in Kansas City, 2013

"He was thunderstruck."

—Clyde Sukeforth to Hall of Fame interviewer, December 5, 1996

"I ALMOST LAUGHED IN HIS PLEASANT, CLEAN-CUT FACE. I WAS SURE THIS FELLOW STANDING BEFORE ME WAS JUST ANOTHER CRACKPOT."
—J. R., *JACKIE ROBINSON: MY OWN STORY*, AS TOLD TO WENDELL SMITH, 1948

"Sukeforth asked if Jackie could throw a few balls from shortstop so he could judge his arm strength, but Jackie explained that his shoulder was injured. . . . Sukeforth urged Jackie to come to Brooklyn to meet with Rickey. Sukeforth told Jackie that if he didn't go to Rickey, Rickey would come to him."

—Aaron Stilley, talk at the Negro Leagues Baseball Museum in Kansas City, 2013

"The significance of that last part was not lost on him. I could see that. He was no fool, this fellow. Don't ever sell Robinson cheap. No, sir! The more we talked the better I liked him. There was something about that man that just gripped you. He was tough, he was intelligent, and he was *proud*. 'Mr. Sukeforth,' he said. 'What do *you* think?' 'Jack,' I said, 'this could be the real thing.'"

—Clyde Sukeforth, Dodgers scout, to Donald Honig,
Baseball When the Grass Was Real, 1975

"[The skeptical] Robinson finally melted, and . . . they proceeded to New York, occupying the same room on the train. . . . Robinson was able to leave the Monarchs for a few days, due to his injured shoulder."

—Arthur Mann, *The Jackie Robinson Story*, 1950

"We boarded the sleeper for New York that night. I got up the next morning . . . and he's already up. 'Jack,' I said, 'let's go get some breakfast.' 'No,' he said. 'I'll eat with the boys.' He meant the porters."

—Clyde Sukeforth, Dodgers scout, to Donald Honig,
Baseball When the Grass Was Real, 1975

— FIVE —

Breaking Barriers

"The meeting took place in Rickey's office [at 215 Montague Street in Brooklyn] on August 28, 1945, and lasted about three hours."

—*EyeWitness to History*, **about the historic first meeting between Branch Rickey and Jackie Robinson, eyewitnesstohistory.com, 2005**

ROBINSON AND RICKEY: A MEETING FOR THE AGES

"You got a girl?"

—**Branch Rickey, stating his surprising first words to Robinson, August 28, 1945**

"They don't come any finer, Mr. Rickey."

—**J. R. responding cautiously to Rickey about Rachel Isum, August 28, 1945**

"Well, you marry her right away."

—**Branch Rickey, who always "encouraged" his players to marry, to Robinson,** *Jackie Robinson: My Own Story,* **as told to Wendell Smith, 1948**

"When we get through today you may want to call her up, 'cause there are times when a man needs a woman by his side."

—**Branch Rickey to Robinson, August 28, 1945**

"Oh, they were a pair, those two! I tell you, the air in that office was electric."

—Clyde Sukeforth, Dodgers scout, about how the two stared at each other,
trying to get into each other's heads, to Donald Honig,
Baseball When the Grass Was Real, 1975

"Rickey went on to ask Robinson about his church affiliations, and was elated
to learn that Robinson was a God-fearing, church-going Protestant. . . . When
Robinson told Rickey that he didn't drink, the executive's eyes lit up approvingly."

—Lee Lowenfish, *Branch Rickey: Baseball's Ferocious Gentleman,* 2007

"Branch Rickey sensed in Jackie Robinson everything that he wanted in a race
pioneer—great talent, fierce competitiveness, good personal and family values, and
a commitment to uplift his race."

—Lee Lowenfish, *Branch Rickey: Baseball's Ferocious Gentleman,* 2007

"Rickey subjected Robinson to a lengthy, agitated discourse on the hardships that
awaited him as a lonely racial pioneer."

—Charles C. Alexander, *Our Game,* 1991

"Rickey even acted out a series of probable abuses, in a kind of minipsychodrama."

—Hilma Wolitzer, novelist, *Cult Baseball Players,* edited by Danny Peary, 1990

"Mr. Rickey, do you want a ballplayer who's afraid to fight back?"

—J. R.

"I WANT A BALLPLAYER WITH GUTS ENOUGH *NOT* TO FIGHT BACK."
—BRANCH RICKEY, WHO BECAME PRESIDENT AND GENERAL MANAGER OF THE BROOKLYN DODGERS IN 1942 AFTER BEING IN THE ST. LOUIS CARDINALS ORGANIZATION SINCE 1919, TO ROBINSON, AUGUST 28, 1945

"But whosoever shall smite thee on thy right check, turn to him the other also."

—Giovanni Papini, whose words were read by Rickey to Robinson,
Life of Christ, 1923

"Robinson reading Papini on nonviolence is a story that has been told several times, always with deference and approval. . . . But every source I have found neglects a profoundly disturbing fact. Giovanni Papini, the author Rickey chose to cite at this extraordinary moment, was a bigoted fascist. . . . Robinson, in later years . . . attended university seminars on dictatorships and racism, but in 1945 he had never heard of Papini. . . . How would he have reacted if he knew Rickey was feeding him words composed by a man who believed that it was acceptable for a white European army [Mussolini's troops that annihilated roughly 275,000 blacks in Ethiopia] to bomb and shoot and gas black Africans? The Jackie Robinson I remember would have walked out. But he didn't know and he did not walk out."

—**Roger Kahn,** *Rickey & Robinson,* **2014**

"Jackie, we've got no army. There's virtually nobody on our side. No owners, no umpires, very few newspapermen. And I'm afraid that many fans will be hostile. We'll be in a tough position. We can win only if we can convince the world that I'm doing this because you're a great ballplayer, a fine gentleman."

—**Branch Rickey**

"A proud, naturally excitable and combative person, Robinson nonetheless understood what he would have to do—and also what he couldn't afford to do."

—**Charles C. Alexander,** *Our Game,* **1991**

"Robinson is reported to have said, 'I get it. What you want me to say is that I've got another cheek.'"

—**Hilma Wolitzer, novelist,** *Cult Baseball Players,* **edited by Danny Peary, 1990**

"[Before deciding if it was possible for him to not respond to abuse, Jackie] hesitated quite a bit."

—**Clyde Sukeforth, Branch Rickey's assistant,
to an interviewer from the Hall of Fame, December 5, 1996**

"Mr. Rickey . . . If you want to take this gamble, I will promise you there will be no incident."

—**J. R.**

"The concession must have been agonizing for him; he was an aggressive, hot-tempered man, one hardly inclined to be passive in the face of bigotry."

—**Hilma Wolitzer, novelist,** *Cult Baseball Players,* **edited by Danny Peary, 1990**

"I thought the old man was going to kiss him."

—Clyde Sukeforth, Dodgers scout, to Donald Honig, *Baseball When the Grass Was Real*, 1975

"I heard about racial problems that you supposedly had. I made a thorough investigation. I know that if you were white, they would never call you a troublemaker. I'm satisfied on that count. I know about your battles, Jackie, I know all about your fighting spirit. It's fine. We are going to use all those qualities."

—Branch Rickey to Robinson during their famous first meeting, August 28, 1945

"The legendary meeting ends with Robinson signing with the Dodgers—in secret; word was to be withheld until the team chose to announce it—for a signing bonus of $3,500 and an agreement for a salary of $600 a month when Robinson began play [in 1946] with the Montreal Royals, the Dodgers' number one farm team."

—David Falkner, *Great Time Coming*, 1995

"There may be trouble ahead—for you, for me, for Negroes and for baseball."

—Branch Rickey

"Rickey didn't sign Robinson solely for humanitarian reasons, though that was undeniably a consideration. He also did it for financial gain. He wanted a winning team in Brooklyn—winning teams traditionally make more money than losing ones—and he wanted to hire anyone who could help, he said, black or white. But he was also well aware of the growing pressure by government employment groups—particularly in New York State—to eliminate race prejudice in hiring practices; in this regard, he accurately foresaw a changing America."

—Ira Berkow, *Red: A Biography of Red Smith*, 1986

"It was the right thing to do and the economically profitable thing to do. We should celebrate that lovely congruence and not nit-pick at it."

—Lee Lowenfish, author of *Branch Rickey: Baseball's Ferocious Gentleman*, about Rickey's motive for signing Robinson, to Danny Peary, brinkzine.com, December 9, 2007

"IT DIDN'T HAVE TO HAPPEN. . . . BRANCH RICKEY'S DECISION TO BREAK DOWN THE COLOR BARRIER IN BASEBALL CAME FROM HIS HEART, NOT BECAUSE OF FINANCIAL INTERESTS. I ALWAYS BELIEVED THAT AND WILL GO TO MY GRAVE BELIEVING THAT. MR. RICKEY ALWAYS SAID, 'HOW CAN BASEBALL BE AMERICA'S PASTIME WHEN ALL AMERICANS AREN'T GIVEN THE OPPORTUNITY TO PARTICIPATE?'"

—DON NEWCOMBE, NEWARK EAGLES PITCHER BEFORE SIGNING WITH THE BROOKLYN DODGERS AND, ALONG WITH ROY CAMPANELLA, BREAKING THE CLASS B COLOR BARRIER WITH THE NASHUA DODGERS, TO DANNY PEARY, *WE PLAYED THE GAME*, 1994

"Critics had said, 'Don't you know that your precious Mr. Rickey didn't bring you up out of the black leagues because he loved you? Are you stupid enough not to understand that the Brooklyn club profited hugely because of what your Mr. Rickey did?' Yes, I know that. But I know what a big gamble he took. . . . There was more than just making money at stake in Mr. Rickey's decision. I learned that his family was afraid that his health was being undermined by the resulting pressures and that they pleaded with him to abandon his plan. His peers and fellow baseball moguls exerted all kinds of influence to get him to change his mind. Some of the press condemned him as a fool and a demagogue. But he didn't give in. . . . Even though he was motivated by deep principle to break the barriers in baseball, Mr. Rickey was also a keen businessman. He knew that integrated baseball would be financially rewarding."

—J. R., *I Never Had It Made,* as told to Alfred Duckett, 1972

"The August 28 meeting was kept a secret for a while. In late September, an article in the [*Kansas City*] *Call* said Jackie's absence from the team was due only to his injury."

—Aaron Stilley, talk at the Negro Leagues Baseball Museum in Kansas City, 2013

"Branch Rickey asked me how I would like to manage the Brooklyn black ballclub."

—J. R., either telling the truth or fibbing as a diversionary tactic, to Monarchs teammate Hilton Smith, quoted by Hilton Smith, University of Missouri, Kansas City Monarchs Oral History Collection

"Robinson remained with the Monarchs but left the club in early September . . . unwilling to participate in a postseason barnstorming tour."

—Neil Lanctot, *Black Baseball,* 2004

"I wouldn't have played another year in the black league. It was too difficult. The travel was brutal. Financially, there was no reward. It took everything you make to live off."

—J. R.

"I think his hatred of segregation blinded him to the positive aspects of the Negro Leagues. . . . The Monarchs and the Negro Leagues were crucial stepping stones, without which the color line is broken much later than 1947."

—Aaron Stilley, talk at the Negro Leagues Baseball Museum in Kansas City, 2013

J. R. NOTE: Although statiscal records in the Negro Leagues were sketchy at best, according to *The Baseball Encyclopedia*, Jackie played forty-seven games and went sixty-three for one hundred sixty-three for a .387 average. Along with fourteen doubles, four triples, and five homers, he stole thirteen bases.

"After the [Negro League] season was over in 1945, Blanco Chitaiqe, a Venezuelan consul official got in touch with me about playing on a team he had put together to tour Venezuela for two months. Besides Jackie Robinson and myself, the [American All-Stars] was made up of Buck Leonard, Roy Campanella, Sam Jethroe, Marvin Baker, Bill Anderson, George Jefferson, Parnel Woods, Roy Welmaker, Eugene Benson, and Verdell Mathis."

—Quincy Trouppe, Negro League star catcher, *20 Years Too Soon*, 1977

"I [had] met Jackie for the first time at the Negro League [East-West] All-Star game in 1945. . . . We talked a little that day and when we met again later that year at the Woodside Hotel in Harlem . . . we had dinner one night, and he just told me in the middle of the conversation that he would be signing soon with the Dodgers. I didn't think much of it because we all heard talk of the Brown Dodger team they were supposed to be starting. 'The Brooklyn Dodgers. The big-league club,' he said. I was shocked. . . . A day or two later the Brooklyn Dodgers contacted me. . . . I signed to play in the Brooklyn organization in 1946."

—Roy Campanella, Baltimore Elite Giants catcher before breaking the color barriers in Class B with Nashua and American Association with St. Paul, to Maury Allen, *Jackie Robinson: A Life Remembered,* 1987

"I'm glad for you, Jackie, real glad. Don't you be afraid of nothing. You're a good ballplayer, you'll make it."

—Roy Campanella to Jackie Robinson in 1945, *It's Good to Be Alive,* 1959

"While Jackie was in South America, Rachel worked in New York. . . . She found the wedding dress she wanted at Saks Fifth Avenue. . . . Rachel reminded herself that she had almost no money. She quit her relatively low-paying job [as a hostess in an expensive Park Avenue restaurant] and took a job as a nurse at the Joint Diseases Hospital."

—Carl T. Rowan, *Wait Till Next Year,* Carl T. Rowan with Jackie Robinson, 1960

"Rickey did not plan to announce the signing of just one black player. Whether the recruitment of additional blacks had always been his intention or whether he had reached his decision after meeting with Robinson in August is unclear."

—John Thorn and Jules Tygiel,
National Pastime: A Review of Baseball History journal, 1990

"There is more involved in the situation than I had contemplated. Other players are in it and it may be that I can't clear these players until after the December meetings, possibly not until after the first of the year. . . . There is a November 1 deadline on Robinson—you know that. I am undertaking to extend that date until January 1st so as to give me time to sign plenty of players and make one break on the complete story. Also quite obviously it might not be good to sign Robinson with other and possibly better players unsigned."

—Branch Rickey, about a proposed delay that fell through,
making it impossible to announce the signing of several Negro League players
at the same time as Robinson, to freelance writer and consultant Arthur Mann,
excerpt from letter, October 7, 1945

"[Branch Rickey] was such a deliberate man and this letter was so *urgent.* He must have been very nervous as he neared his goal. Maybe he was nervous that the owners would turn him down and having five people at the door instead of just [Jack] would have been more powerful."

—Rachel Robinson, quoted by John Thorn and Jules Tygiel,
National Pastime: A Review of Baseball History journal, 1990

CLASSIC MOMENT: OCTOBER 23, 1945, MONTREAL, CANADA

"Rickey originally intended to announce the contractual signing of Jackie Robinson as the first Negro in organized baseball after the 1945 football season ended [to] get the most extensive coverage in the press. Political pressures on behalf of Negro players forced Rickey to make the Robinson announcement much earlier than originally planned. . . . Rickey wired Robinson instructions to fly to Montreal, Canada. The announcement . . . was made in Montreal on October 23, 1945."

—A. S. "Doc" Young, *Ebony* magazine, December 1968

"For the first time in the long history of organized baseball a Negro player officially has been taken into its ranks. Branch Rickey, president and part owner of the Dodgers, yesterday announced that Jack Roosevelt Robinson, Georgia-born Negro, had been signed by Montreal of the International League, an organization in which Brooklyn owns a controlling interest. Robinson, 26 years old, was a four-sport star and All-America halfback for the University of California at Los Angeles. He is a shortstop and, according to Rickey, 'is the best.'"

—*New York Times*, October 24, 1945

"Jack Robinson . . . put his signature on a contract calling not only for a player's salary, but also a bonus for signing. . . . Robinson signed up in a history-making huddle with Hector Racine and Lieut. Col. Romeo Gauvreau, Royals' president and vice president respectively, and Branch Rickey Jr., who heads the Brooklyn farm system."

—*New York Times*, October 23, 1945

"Mr. Racine and my father will undoubtedly be severely criticized in some sections of the United States where racial prejudice is rampant. They are not inviting trouble, but they won't avoid it if it comes. Jack Robinson is a fine type of young man, intelligent and college bred, and I think he can take it, too. . . . It may cost the Brooklyn organization a number of ballplayers. Some of them particularly if they come from certain sections of the South, will steer away from a club with colored players on its roster. Some players now with us may even quit, but they'll be back in baseball after they work a year or two in a cotton mill."

—Branch Rickey Jr., Brooklyn Dodgers head of scouting, quoted in the *New York Times*, October 23, 1945

"OF COURSE, I CAN'T BEGIN TO TELL YOU HOW HAPPY I AM THAT I AM THE FIRST MEMBER OF MY RACE IN ORGANIZED BALL. I REALIZE HOW MUCH IT MEANS TO ME, TO MY RACE, AND TO BASEBALL. I CAN ONLY SAY I'LL DO MY VERY BEST TO COME THROUGH IN EVERY MANNER."

—J. R. TO REPORTERS IN MONTREAL, OCTOBER 23, 1945

"[Robinson signed with] the Montreal Royals in the International League, where he would be the first black [player]. Rickey's intention was to give fans and players more time to get used to the idea of integration, and to give Robinson more time to polish his skills. And if the problems arose, better to have them arise in Montreal than in Brooklyn."

—Jonathan Eig, *Opening Day: The Story of Jackie Robinson's First Season,* 2007

"Robinson is a good ball player and comes to us highly recommended by our scouts. He will join us at our training camp in Florida next spring."

—Hector Racine, Montreal Royals president, October 23, 1945

"Branch Rickey, president and general manager of the Brooklyn Dodgers, had defied the other fifteen major league owners and stunned not only the baseball world but the country in signing Jack Roosevelt Robinson to a Dodger contract. No black—or known black—had played Organized Baseball since 1884, when Cap Anson, star and manager of the Chicago White Sox, refused to take the field against Toledo, which had a black player, Fleetwood Walker."

—Ira Berkow, *Red: A Biography of Red Smith,* 1986

"During his 27-year big-league career Anson . . . batted over .300 in 22 seasons; his average was .394 in 1894, when he was forty-three years old. He was a great ball player but a heartless man."

—J. R., who thought of Cap Anson when he signed his contract with the Dodgers organization in 1945 and when he made the Hall of Fame in 1972, *Baseball Has Done It,* 1964

"This was one of the proudest moments of my life."

—J. R., *Jackie Robinson: My Own Story,* as told to Wendell Smith, 1948

THE DIVERSE RESPONSE TO ROBINSON'S SIGNING

"Mr. Rickey, please don't do this to me. I'm a white man, been living in Mississippi all my life. If you do this to me, you're going to force me to move out of Mississippi."

—Clay Hopper, Montreal Royals new manager and a cotton farmer, who worried when he learned he would have a black player on his team in 1946, to Branch Rickey

"Radio says that the Dodgers have hired a colored ballplayer. . . . The colored guy's a shortstop."

—Petty officer on a US Navy ship steaming home from Guam to midshipman Harold "Pee Wee" Reese, the Brooklyn Dodgers' Kentucky-born shortstop, October 1945

"The first thing I thought about when I heard about Jackie being signed was why does it have to be a shortstop, why does he have to be playing my position, why does he have to be after my job?"

—Pee Wee Reese, Dodgers shortstop and future Hall of Famer, quoted by Steve Garvey, *My Bat Boy Days,* 2008

"Suppose he beats me out. . . . I go back to Louisville. The people say, 'Reese, you weren't man enough to protect your job from a nigger.' . . . I mean if they said to me, 'Reese, you got to go over and play in the colored guys' league,' how would I feel? Scared? The only white. Lonely. But I'm a good shortstop and that's what I'd want 'em to see. Not my color. Just that I can play the game. And that's how I got to look at Robinson. If he's man enough to take my job, I'm not gonna like it, but dammit, black or white, he deserves it."

—Pee Wee Reese, Dodgers shortstop and future Hall of Famer, putting himself in Robinson's shoes, to Roger Kahn, *The Boys of Summer,* 1972

"I was fishing up in Burleigh Falls, Ontario, back in 1945 with my brother. We were at a store, and the radio was on, and the announcer said the Brooklyn Dodgers signed a black player named Jackie Robinson. I was holding my breath hoping that he wouldn't be an outfielder. When I heard he was going to be [an infielder] I felt a lot better."

—George Shuba, Dodgers outfield prospect in 1945, to Andrew Carter, *Orlando Sentinel,* March 4, 2006

"He's been signed for the Montreal club, and as long as he isn't with the Dodgers, I'm not worried."

—Dixie Walker, Dodgers outfielder, 1945

"Roy Campanella . . . told me he had just signed a contract to play with the Brooklyn Brown Dodgers. . . . Before I knew it, I signed a contract with Mr. Rickey. . . . A month or two went by. I saw the *New York Daily News* with the headline, 'Jackie Robinson Signed by Montreal Royals.' . . . I said to my wife, 'Maybe now there is a chance for me to play in the major leagues.' The next week . . . Mr. Rickey informed me that he really didn't want Roy and me to play for any Brooklyn Brown Dodgers. . . . That's when Roy and I found out we were going to be part of the Brooklyn Dodgers system."

—Don Newcombe, Newark Eagles pitcher who would sign with the Nashua, New Hampshire, Dodgers and, along with Roy Campanella, break the Class B color barrier in 1946, to Danny Peary, *We Played the Game*, 1994

"I was drafted and assigned to the Navy Stevedore Battalion . . . at Subic Bay in the Philippines. [When my white commanding officer] told me, 'I just thought you should know that the Brooklyn Dodgers have just signed Jackie Robinson,' . . . I thanked the officer and got on the bullhorn myself: 'Now hear this! Now hear this! The Dodgers just signed Jackie Robinson!' You should have heard the celebration. Halfway around the world from Brooklyn, we started hollering and shouting and firing our guns in the air. . . . It didn't matter who was first or which team had the courage; this was the first real step toward integration, toward equality, since maybe the Reconstruction . . . this was the dawning of a new era."

—Buck O'Neil, Kansas City Monarchs star who would be the first black scout and, in 1962, coach in the major leagues, *I Was Right on Time*, 1996

"I WAS BORN IN 1935, IN LACOOCHEE, FLORIDA, A SEGREGATED TOWN OF 500 PEOPLE. . . . TRANSITION WAS SLOW IN TERMS OF CIVIL RIGHTS. . . . I WAS THROWN IN JAIL ONCE BECAUSE I DIDN'T SAY, 'YES, SIR,' TO A POLICEMAN. . . . WE KNEW ABOUT JACKIE ROBINSON AND WHEN WE HEARD ON THE RADIO THAT HE SIGNED WITH THE DODGERS, EVERYBODY SPILLED OUT INTO THE STREETS AND THERE WAS A CELEBRATION."

—JIM "MUDCAT" GRANT, WHO BECAME THE AMERICAN LEAGUE'S FIRST STAR BLACK STARTING PITCHER BEGINNING WITH CLEVELAND IN 1958, TO DANNY PEARY, *WE PLAYED THE GAME*, 1994

"I hope he makes it, because if he does, I know I can."

—Sam Jethroe, Negro League star who would be signed by Branch Rickey in 1949 but debut in the majors with the Boston Braves in 1950

"Yes, it came as a surprise. I was delighted for Jackie, and it gave hope [that] he was going to open the door for other black players to follow. . . . There was a lot at stake. . . . I guess we knew better than anybody else what he was going to have to put up with."

—Monte Irvin, Negro Leagues star and future New York Giants Hall of Famer, to Donald Honig, *Baseball Between the Lines,* 1976

"I'm afraid Jackie's in for a whole lot of trouble."

—Buck Leonard, Negro Leagues star and future Hall of Famer

"[Owners] like Connie Mack in Philadelphia, [Clark] Griffith in Washington, [Frank] McKinney, who owned the Pirates, and [Sam] Breadon in St. Louis were calling him. 'Branch, you're gonna kill baseball bringing that nigger into baseball now,' they said."

—Mal Goode, first African American to hold a regular on-air job in the journalism field, to Harvey Frommer, *Rickey and Robinson,* 1982

"I concluded there would be no concerted effort to keep me out. Some men didn't object to my being signed with Montreal; others, though they disapproved, admitted they couldn't do anything about it."

—J. R., *Jackie Robinson: My Own Story,* as told to Wendell Smith, 1948

"W. G. Bramham, commissioner of minor league baseball, said today that Negro Jackie Robinson's contract with Montreal would be approved by his office, but he indicated in a statement that the signing of Negroes would prove harmful to the game. Bramham charged that it is the 'carpetbagger stripe of the white race,' which is retarding the Negroes. 'Why should we raid their ranks, grab a player, and put him, his baseball associates, and his race in position that will inevitably prove harmful?' Bramham said."

—United Press, October 25, 1945

"The Negro leagues are doing all right and Negro players should be developed and then remain as stars in their own league. A mixed [baseball] team differs from other sports because ball players on the road live much closer together. . . . I think Branch Rickey was wrong in signing Jackie Robinson and it won't work out."

—Rogers Hornsby, Hall of Famer from Texas, United Press, October 24, 1945

"PERSONALLY, I THINK IT'S THE WORST THING THAT CAN HAPPEN IN ORGANIZED BALL. I THINK A LOT OF SOUTHERN BOYS WILL REFUSE TO COMPETE WITH NEGROES IN BASEBALL, JUST AS THEY HAVE IN OTHER SPORTS."

—GEORGE DIGBY, RED SOX SCOUT, UNITED PRESS, OCTOBER 24, 1945

"In Kansas City, the Monarchs owners were blind-sided, and initially made noise in the press that they were owed some sort of compensation, and they'd be taking the matter up with baseball commissioner Happy Chandler. But saying anything short of full support of Jackie's signing was not a good look, and they quickly changed their tune."

—Aaron Stilley, talk at the Negro Leagues Baseball Museum in Kansas City, 2013

"Sorry my interview with the Associated Press relative to Jackie Robinson was misquoted, also misinterpreted. We would not do anything in any way to impede the advancement of any Negro ball player, nor would we do anything to keep any Negro ball player out of the white major leagues."

—Tom Baird, co-owner of the Kansas City Monarchs, who now regretted not having Robinson sign a formal contract, telegram to the *Pittsburgh Courier* that was relayed to the Dodger office, October 25, 1945

"Inasmuch as Rickey had long regarded Negro-league baseball as a racket, he simply ignored the Kansas City Monarchs' financial interest in Robinson, thereby establishing a precedent for other major league clubs. J. L. Wilkinson, the Monarchs' white owner, told the press that while he was entitled to some kind of compensation, he wouldn't protest to commissioner [Happy] Chandler."

—Charles C. Alexander, *Our Game*, 1991

"Commissioner Chandler tosses out protest of Negro leagues. It was scant consideration, in fact none at all, that the colored American and National Leagues got from Chandler's office when they squawked about Branch Rickey's 'grab' of shortstop Jackie Robinson from the Kansas City Monarchs."

—Shirley Povich, *Washington Post,* **November 14, 1945**

"The Negro Leagues were flourishing for a time, and it's ironic that Jack's being signed by the Dodgers signaled the demise of the Negro Leagues."

—Rachel Robinson, interview, *Scholastic* **magazine, February 11, 1998**

"Robinson was now a titanic hero to all Negroes, big and small and middle-class. His entry into organized baseball presaged, they believed, an approaching realization of their dreams of a better life at last. . . . Better days were ahead."

—A. S. "Doc" Young, *Ebony* **magazine, December 1968**

"When Robinson's signing was announced, the news was heralded in black newspapers and generally received positive reviews in national publications despite objections and attacks from predictable quarters. But Rickey and the Dodgers faced near-unanimous disapproval from the Organized Baseball establishment. After the initial furor died down, a campaign to downplay Robinson's talent and the import of the event began. The *New York Daily News* rated Robinson's chances of making the grade as 1,000 to 1."

—Rick Swaine, SABR Baseball Biography Project

"In November 1945, [the *Sporting News*] editorialized that if Robinson were six years younger and a different color, he might possibly rate a look in Class C ball."

—Frederick Turner, *When the Boys Came Back: Baseball and 1946,* **1996**

"Maybe I should buy a lot of cotton to stuff in my ears. I don't think I'll have to take anything I didn't have to take before but maybe there'll be more people ready to give it to me. . . . I realize what I'm going into. . . . I'm very happy for this chance and I'll do my best to make the grade."

—J. R. to Sergeant Bob Stone, *Yank, The Army Weekly,* **November 23, 1945**

"If Robinson makes good, the major-league teams may sign up other Negro players, many of who are of big-league caliber. Although some ballplayers and club owners have expressed disapproval, most of baseball seemed willing to give Robinson a fair chance."

—*Life* magazine, expressing a more optimistic attitude than most national publications that Robinson and other Negro League players were good enough to play in the majors, November 26, 1945

"Publicly, Negro League players had nothing but support and well wishes for Jackie. Many years down the line, Negro League players often stated that Jackie was not the best Negro League player at the time, but he was the right one to break the color line. I think that undersells just how fantastic Jackie played in 1945. . . . I think he was already an elite player in addition to having the right make-up to face the strain ahead. Perhaps those Negro leaguers that downplayed his performance in 1945 did so because he wasn't an established star. . . . But the established stars were on the wrong side of their primes."

—Aaron Stilley, talk at the Negro Leagues Baseball Museum in Kansas City, 2013

"When Jackie Robinson was chosen . . . [Satchel Paige] was bitter about it. 'That was my right,' he argued. 'Watching me made them think about Negroes in the majors. I am the one everybody says should be in the majors.' I think he was right, even though Jackie was indeed an excellent choice."

—Max Manning, Negro League pitcher, *Cult Baseball Players*, edited by Danny Peary, 1990

"How would you feel seeing a rookie selected? I was very happy for Jackie. I knew he would make it. But we could play, too. We knew that. Sometimes when I look back, it's very tough to take."

—Jimmie Crutchfield, Negro League veteran, quoted by Donn Rogosin, *Invisible Men*, 1983

"We all knew who Jackie was [in Alabama]. In fact, to us black ball players it seemed like a bigger breakthrough when . . . he signed to play for the Dodgers farm team in Montreal [than when he first played major league baseball]. . . . No Negroes . . . had ever been in the minor leagues, had ever played any organized ball."

—Willie Mays, fourteen-year-old in Alabama and future Negro League and major leaguer Hall of Famer, quoted by Allen Barra, *Mickey and Willie*, 2013

"Jackie Robinson's temper [in Venezuela] was a real problem for his friends. Due to his inability to cool it, we were worried about him making the grade [in the Dodgers organization]. . . . But things weren't always tense. We had a lot of good times, too. Campy and I were with Jackie when he bought the engagement ring in Caracas for Rachel."

—Quincy Trouppe, Negro League catcher, *20 Years Too Soon*, 1977

"By the time Jack returned from Venezuela [in January, Rachel] had paid for the wedding dress, the veil and two suits, and was ready to go to California for the wedding. . . . They left [New York] for California and the big church wedding to which they had agreed to please Mrs. Isum. After tedious rehearsals, the day came—February 10, 1946 [at the Independent Church in Los Angeles, presided over by the Reverend Karl Downs]. Nervous and uncomfortable in the fancy attire he had rented, Jack stood waiting at the altar for his bride, who looked regal and lovely in her satin dress. They got through the marriage vows as rehearsed (except for the usual bad moment when his old friend Jack Gordon, the best man, almost [couldn't find] the ring)."

—Carl T. Rowan, *Wait Till Next Year*, Carl T. Rowan with Jackie Robinson, 1960

"Jackie Robinson and his bride of a few weeks, the former Rachel Isum, left yesterday for the Sanford, Fla., spring training camp of the Montreal Royals, to which he has been assigned by the Brooklyn Dodgers. . . . After their wedding, the Robinsons honeymooned in San Jose and San Francisco."

—*Pasadena Star-News*, March 1, 1946

"In 1946, following a five-year long-distance courtship, and two weeks of marriage, we traveled to the segregated South for the first time. . . . We instinctively drew on our mutual love and trust to strengthen the bond between us. It was clear even then that we would need to transcend the immediate provocations of racism, and commit ourselves to higher goals. And so, in the first leg of our trip, when we were bumped from an airplane in Pensacola, Fla., [to make room for two white passengers] and boarded an empty bus to our destination, we moved to the back seat, as required by the driver, without outward protest. We contained the angry [retaliatory] feelings as they arose. I was particularly pained to see my assertive man functionally reduced to the status of the South's 'boy,' but I said to myself, 'Not for long.'"

—Rachel Robinson, who was introduced to Jim Crow laws and was "shocked by the legal discrimination where I had to use a drinking fountain labeled 'for Negroes only' or where I had to use a Negro women's bathroom in the airport," *New York Times* News Service, April 12, 1987

"ON MARCH 4, 1946, IN A PARK ON THE CORNER OF SOUTH MELLONVILLE AND CELERY THAT NO LONGER EXISTS, ROBINSON BEGAN HIS FIRST SEASON IN THE BROOKLYN DODGERS ORGANIZATION. HE ARRIVED AT THE FIELD IN SANFORD [FLORIDA] THAT MONDAY MORNING."

—ANDREW CARTER, SIXTY YEARS AFTER THE EVENT, *ORLANDO SENTINEL*, MARCH 4, 2006

"By the time Robinson reported to Sanford at the beginning of March, Rickey had also signed pitchers Roy Partlow and John Wright."

—Frederick Turner, about signings in addition to Roy Campanella and Don Newcombe, *When the Boys Came Back: Baseball and 1946*, 1996

"Baseball broke a precedent of long standing yesterday when shortstop Jackie Robinson and pitcher John Wright, two Negro athletes, reported for spring training with the Montreal Royals, Brooklyn's farm club in the International League."

—Small item in the *Orlando Sentinel*, March 5, 1946

"Robinson did not dominate the headlines [as the 1946 baseball season approached]. The excitement in the sports press concerned the first postwar season; besides, some considered Robinson a minor-league story; he was going to train with the Dodgers' farm club."

—Ira Berkow, *Red: A Biography of Red Smith*, 1986

"There were a couple of hundred men on the field when Robinson and Wright arrived, and most knew the moment was coming. . . . Everything stopped."

—Andrew Carter, *Orlando Sentinel*, March 4, 2006

"Suddenly I felt uncomfortably conspicuous standing there. Every single man on the field seemed to be staring at Johnny Wright and me."

—J. R., *Jackie Robinson: My Own Story*, as told to Wendell Smith, 1948

"I was relieved to see [Clay Hopper] stick out his hand [when Clyde Sukeforth introduced us], for even in those days great numbers of Southerners would under no circumstances shake hands with a Negro. After the introduction we made polite conversation."

—J. R., *Wait Till Next Year*, Carl T. Rowan with Jackie Robinson, 1960

"Duck!"

—J. R. to a reporter who asked what he'd do if a pitcher threw at him,
spring training, 1946

"I've gotten along with white boys at UCLA, at Pasadena, in high school and in the army. I don't see why these should be any different."

**—J. R., saying he expected to get along with his white teammates in Montreal,
to reporters, spring training, 1946**

"Jackie Robinson is face to face with his baseball destiny. The first boy of his race in 50 years to enter professional baseball that has been a white man's game ever since. . . . He's really on the spot. The future of the Negro in baseball is all bound up in Jackie's own destiny."

**—Harold Burr, adding to the pressure on Robinson, *Brooklyn Eagle*,
March 1, 1946**

"The Negroes at Sanford who came out to watch during . . . practice . . . cheered if I leaned to tie my shoe. Sure, it was embarrassing to me, and it seemed childish on the part of the Negroes, but I understood that my being on that field was a symbol of the Negro's emerging self-respect, of a deep belief that somehow we had begun a magnificent era of Negro progress, a period in which Negroes could walk onto a baseball field, or into another area of life, asking no quarter, no special concessions, and complete credibility with white men."

—J. R., *Wait Till Next Year*, Carl T. Rowan with Jackie Robinson, 1960

"Robinson had a support group with him when he arrived in Sanford. In addition to Wright he was traveling with his wife Rachel, and two black journalists from the *Pittsburgh Courier*, Wendell Smith and [photographer] Billy Rowe. While in Sanford, the group stayed in a two-story house at 612 S. Sanford Ave., a place owned by black [doctor] D. C. Brock."

—Andrew Carter, *Orlando Sentinel*, March 4, 2006

"Since black and white players couldn't stay together, Robinson and . . . Wright stayed at a home on Sanford Avenue, while the rest of the team stayed in a hotel."

**—Joel Schipper, reporter for Bright House Sports, mynews13.com,
February 7, 2014**

"My father owned the [Mayfair] hotel, and he couldn't allow him to stay there, or he would lose his license to have a hotel."

—Bill Kirchhoff, who was seven at the time, quoted by Joel Schipper, mynews13.com, February 7, 2014

"GET THOSE TWO BLACK BOYS OUT OF TOWN BEFORE MIDNIGHT OR WE WILL."

—UNNAMED SOURCE TO BRANCH RICKEY, A THREAT THAT PROMPTED RICKEY TO TELL WENDELL SMITH TO HURRY ROBINSON AND WRIGHT OUT OF SANFORD AND TAKE THEM TO THE DODGERS' FULL-TIME CAMP AT DAYTONA BEACH, MARCH 1946

"He had to be snuck out . . . with two Negro sportswriters, and when he called later he told us if they didn't get him out of there in time a gang was coming after him. 'I might have been lynched,' he said, and we just sat down and cried."

—Willa Mae Robinson Walker to Maury Allen,
Jackie Robinson: A Life Remembered, 1987

"What [the early difficulties] did for us was not only enlighten us and open our eyes to what things were going to be like, but it also mobilized a lot of fight in us. We were not willing to think about going back. It gave us the kind of anger and the rage to move ahead with real determination [and] because we were a newly married couple, I think it had a lot to do with quickly solidifying our marriage."

—Rachel Robinson to Jules Tygiel, *Baseball's Great Experiment,* 1983

"The rest of the team soon moved to Daytona and was quartered in a hotel on the ocean. Rae and I went . . . to the home of [Joe Harris, a prominent black druggist and politician], and Wright to the home of another Negro family. We disliked that distinction . . . but . . . Mr. Rickey had made it clear that . . . we would have to bear indignities and humiliations without complaint. He said that I would have to be 'a man big enough to bear the cross of martyrdom.' . . . It's not easy to be a martyr in this field of race relations. I remember . . . my mother had taught me that God made Negroes black as a challenge and that if we met that challenge it would make better people for us. I hoped that, somehow, I could meet the challenge . . . because so much more than my sensitivity was at stake."

—J. R., *Wait Till Next Year,* Carl T. Rowan with Jackie Robinson, 1960

"The Dodgers had divided their training base in the resort community into two camps. Ironically, the parent club worked out on the white side of town, while the Royals practiced in the black district. Local officials [including City Managar Tim Titus and Mayor William Perry] raised no objections to Robinson and training in Daytona Beach, but [because Jim Crow laws existed in the town] widespread speculation persisted that they would be barred from actual competition."

—**Jules Tygiel,** *Baseball's Great Experiment,* **1983**

"Several Montreal players, Southern and otherwise, resented Robinson because they believed the team would find a spot for him, which meant one fewer spot for them."

—**Chris Lamb,** *Blackout,* **2004**

"I was glad I played the outfield. . . . I always had the impression that [Robinson] had the attitude that he was better than us. He was almost cocky. Looking back at it now I guess he had to be that way. He was all business. Maybe he had to psych himself up all the time to make it through all that. Maybe he was so quiet because he didn't want to blow it."

—**Dave McBride, Montreal teammate,** *Daytona Beach News-Journal,* **June 29, 1987**

"I sort of keep to myself by habit. Even in the colored leagues I was that way."

—**J. R. to Bill Roeder,** *New York World-Telegram,* **July 3, 1947**

"When we finished practice, I'd go home and play cards with Smith, Rowe, and my wife. . . . There was only one Negro movie in town and the picture ran for three days. Consequently we'd see two pictures a week. Often there was absolutely nothing to do."

—**J. R.,** *Jackie Robinson: My Own Story,* **as told to Wendell Smith, 1948**

"I was thirteen years old when Jackie Robinson signed to play with Montreal. I was not aware that Jackie was going to be based in [my hometown of] Daytona Beach with the Montreal club. . . . Jackie coming down to Daytona made a definite impact on the lives of the blacks in my community. . . . I was awed by it all, and I prayed for him."

—**Ed Charles, future Kansas City Athletics and New York Mets third baseman, to Peter Golenbock,** *Bums,* **1984**

"The . . . Brooklyn brass shifted Robinson from shortstop to second base, and he began to encourage them with his performances on the field. Rickey's scouts had said Robinson's arm wasn't strong enough for shortstop but it was adequate for second base."

—A. S. "Doc" Young, about Robinson's permanent shift to second base during a period in which his arm ached so badly from trying to impress Hopper with strong throws that the manager even resorted to trying him at first base, *Ebony* magazine, December 1968

"I COULD HEAR [THE BLACK FANS] SHOUTING IN THE STANDS, AND I WANTED TO PRODUCE SO MUCH THAT I WAS TENSE AND OVER-ANXIOUS. . . . I STARTED SWINGING AT BAD BALLS AND DOING A LOT OF THINGS I WOULD NOT HAVE DONE UNDER ORDINARY CIRCUMSTANCES. I WANTED TO GET A HIT FOR THEM BECAUSE THEY WERE PULLING FOR ME SO HARD."

—J. R., WHO STRUGGLED WITH THE BAT EARLY IN THE EXHIBITION SEASON, QUOTED IN THE *PITTSBURGH COURIER*, APRIL 20, 1946

"It's do-gooders like Rickey that hurt the Negro because they try to force inferior Negroes on whites and then everybody loses. Take this guy Robinson. If he was white they'd have booted him out of this camp long ago."

—White reporter, after watching Robinson's struggles at bat and in the field during spring training, 1946

"Branch Rickey was acutely aware of such rumblings by newspapermen and by Montreal players, so he deserted the Dodger camp to keep a close eye on Robinson and his progress. He notified Rachel that it would be all right for her to attend practice sessions, hoping that her presence might inspire Robinson."

—Carl T. Rowan, *Wait Till Next Year,* Carl T. Rowan with Jackie Robinson, 1960

"A few days later, Robinson got his first hit of the spring. Rae was so delighted that she left the park early and went to agricultural school at Bethune-Cookman to pick some vegetables. . . . When she told faculty members that Jackie had gotten his first hit, they insisted on giving her a couple of chickens. . . . She . . . invited Smith, Rowe and other Negro newspaperman in for the celebration dinner."

—Carl T. Rowan, *Wait Till Next Year,* Carl T. Rowan with Jackie Robinson, 1960

"I couldn't have made it without her."

—J. R., about having Rachel in Florida with him during spring training in 1946, to Jack Sher, *Sport* magazine, October 1948

"So far it has been a real pleasure playing here with the fellows. Everyone has been so nice and they have given us help along the way. I did not expect any trouble but I also did not expect to be welcomed as I have. . . . We have met a couple that have resented us, but only a sharp eye could tell. All I can say is if we make the club, it will be on our own merits. . . . Our manager Clay Hopper has been very helpful and is giving us every chance possible."

—J. R., about trying to make the Montreal Royals in spring training, to former *Pasadena (JC) Chronicle* staffer Ralph Norton, excerpt from letter, March 12, 1946

"Mr. Rickey, do you really think a nigger's a human being?"

—Clay Hopper, Montreal Royals manager, asking a shockingly naive yet sincere question during an intrasquad game, to Branch Rickey, who didn't respond, spring training, 1946

CLASSIC MOMENT: MARCH 17, 1946, CITY ISLAND PARK, DAYTONA BEACH, FLORIDA

"In 1946, the Dodgers played their spring training home games at City Island Park in Daytona Beach, while . . . Montreal . . . worked out at Kelly Field. . . . On St. Patrick's Day, March 17, Jackie Robinson and the Royals came to City Island to face the Dodgers in the first spring training meeting of the two clubs. It would also be the first game Robinson played as a member of the Brooklyn organization, though Rickey would not attend, owing to the fact that the game was on a Sunday. Attending the match, however, were over 4,000 fans."

—Matt Rothenberg, manager of the Giamatti Research Center at the National Baseball Hall of Fame and Museum, Baseball Hall of Fame website, April 2, 2015

"There was an overflow crowd of Negro spectators—nearly 1,000—and the small Jim Crow bleacher section allotted to them was entirely inadequate, many of them standing out beyond the right-field foul line."

—Roscoe McGowan, *New York Times,* March 18, 1946

"A precedent for baseball training in the South was set today when the Dodgers played their Montreal International League farm club, with the minor leaguers having Jackie Robinson, Negro infielder, in their lineup. It was the first time a Negro player ever participated with whites in an exhibition game for which admission was charged in the state of Florida. The Dodgers won the game, 7–2."

—*Boston Globe,* **March 18, 1946**

"Jackie Robinson, the first boy of his race to play against a big league team south of the Mason and Dixon line, was on the spot yesterday when he shuffled out to cover second base for Montreal against the Dodgers. . . . The occasion passed off quietly with no demonstration. Robinson was booed mildly when he fouled out twice by the 2,500 white folks present."

—**Harold Burr, a respected journalist who worked far above the Mason-Dixon Line yet was not above using derogatory terms such as "boy" and "shuffled" when describing Robinson,** *Brooklyn Eagle,* **March 18, 1946**

"Robinson played the first five innings at second base and batted sixth in the order. He cleanly handled two chances in the field. Though he went 0-for-3 at the plate, Robinson did reach on a force play, stole second, and scored on catcher Ferrell Anderson's base hit. The crowd's reaction to Robinson's debut was mixed. The Associated Press reported that the African American fans applauded Robinson when he came up for the first time, but the white fans did not applaud until Billy Herman caught Robinson's foul fly. Both groups applauded Robinson in his other two at bats, though on those occasions, the *Brooklyn Eagle* claimed 'Robinson was booed mildly.' . . . Under the microscope for his first game, Robinson later said he was 'thinking so many other things he didn't know just what he was doing.'"

—**Matt Rothenberg, manager of the Giamatti Research Center at the National Baseball Hall of Fame and Museum, Baseball Hall of Fame website, April 2, 2015**

"Robinson Hitless"

—**Article headline that ignored the positives in Robinson's debut,** *Washington Post,* **March 18, 1946**

"Robinson Debut with Montreal Is a Flop at Bat"

—**Article headline,** *New York World-Telegram,* **March 18, 1946**

"The next day, Montreal and St. Paul faced off at Kelly Field, with the Royals taking a 1–0 decision. Robinson had three hits and African American pitcher John Wright pitched five innings for Montreal, allowing one run on five hits."

—Matt Rothenberg, manager of the Giamatti Research Center at the National Baseball Hall of Fame and Museum, about one of Robinson's few good games at the plate early in the exhibition season, Baseball Hall of Fame website, April 2, 2015

"One afternoon in Daytona, I was the lead-off hitter [for Montreal against Brooklyn] and quickly singled. Robinson came up next, laying down a sacrifice bunt and running to first. [Dodgers second baseman Eddie] Stanky, covering the sack, tagged him hard and jock-high. Robinson went down, taking a fist in the balls. He was mad as hell, you could see that, but Rickey had warned him, no fights. He got up, dusted himself off and said nothing. After the game, when he was resting, Stanky came over to apologize. He had been testing his temper, under orders from Rickey."

—Kermit Kitman, minor league outfielder, to Mordecai Richler, Canadian journalist and novelist, *The Ultimate Baseball Book*, edited by Daniel Okrent and Harris Lewine, 1979

"Branch Rickey sat in the stands at City Island park yesterday and watched his Dodgers of the future, temporarily in Montreal uniforms, out-hit, out-think and out-run a skeleton Broooklyn team for an easy 6–1 triumph over their big brothers. He was highly pleased with Jackie Robinson who looked like a pro for the first time this spring."

—Harold Burr, *Brooklyn Eagle*, April 3, 1946

"He'll make the Montreal team this year. And he definitely is a big league prospect."

—Branch Rickey, after Robinson had one of his best games of the spring, quoted by Tommy Holmes, *Brooklyn Eagle*, April 3, 1946

"[Brooklyn manager] Leo Durocher . . . made no bones about wanting Robinson as a player on his Dodger varsity from the very first moment he saw Jackie in spring training with . . . Montreal. . . . Money was the reason, pure and simple. . . . But Rickey . . . stuck to his carefully planned timetable: slow, slow, get the boy ready with a full year in the International League."

—Harold Parrott, Dodgers traveling secretary, *The Lords of Baseball*, 1975

"In Jacksonville, where the Royals were scheduled to play against the Jersey City Giants on March 23, the *Florida Times-Union*, the local newspaper, noted the possibility that Robinson would be in the lineup, marking 'the first time a member of his race had played with white ball players at a Jacksonville park.' . . . Outside the stadium [in Jacksonville], they found a large crowd awaiting them, but the park itself, wrote Wendell Smith, 'was as closed and quiet as a funeral parlor at three o'clock in the morning.' City officials had padlocked the gate and a contingent of city police barred further entry."

—Jules Tygiel, *Baseball's Great Experiment*, 1983

"The *Florida Times-Union* of Jacksonville imposed a veritable cover-up of the lockout controversy. On March 23 a small item announced the game cancellation but made no mention of the race issue. Two days before a second scheduled contest at Jacksonville, the paper reported that Robinson and Wright 'would not be available.' When officials blocked this game as well the *Times-Union* reinstituted the cloak of secrecy, noting the cancellation but offering no explanation. According to the city's foremost daily, the Jacksonville lockout, which had received widespread treatment in the national press, had not occurred."

—Jules Tygiel, *Baseball's Great Experiment*, 1983

"We ain't having Negras and white boys mix in this town. You can't change our way of livin'."

—Deland, Florida, policeman who halted an exhibition game being played between Montreal and Indianapolis and threatened to arrest Robinson unless he got off the field, March 1946

"In Deland, ninety-four blacks signed a letter appealing the city's action in barring Robinson and called for a second scheduled game to be allowed to occur. . . . The black protest fell upon deaf ears. The second game was transferred to Daytona Beach."

—Jules Tygiel, *Baseball's Great Experiment*, 1983

"[Baltimore Afro-American writer Sam] Lacy drove Robinson to a spring training game [April 7] in Sanford, Fla."

—DeWayne Wickham, about Robinson's return to the town he fled a month before, *USA Today*, April 29, 2013

"In Sanford, Florida, when Lacy and other black writers were turned back at the front gate, Robinson found a loose board in the outfield wall and helped the writers slip through into the ballpark."

—Jim Reisler, *Black Writers/Black Baseball*, 1994

"The Royals were scheduled to play the St. Paul Saints at Sanford, where townspeople had expelled Robinson and Wright earlier. . . . Robinson nervously took batting practice and, to everyone's surprise, appeared in the starting lineup. . . . As he returned to the dugout at the end of second frame, his reverie came to an abrupt end. . . . The chief of police walked on to the field and informed Manager Hopper that Robinson and Wright had to be removed from the ballpark."

—Jules Tygiel, *Baseball's Great Experiment*, 1983

"Jackie Robinson and John Wright go with the team, or there's no game."

—Hector Racine, Montreal club president, stating a new strategy after his integrated team had been turned away in a few Florida towns, quoted in the *Baltimore Afro-American*, April 20, 1946

"DON'T BRING THAT FELLOW OVER THERE, YOU'RE GOING TO HAVE A RACE RIOT."
—FRANK SHAUGHNESSY, PRESIDENT OF THE INTERNATIONAL LEAGUE, PRIOR TO ROBINSON'S FIRST OFFICIAL GAME IN THE MINOR LEAGUES FOR MONTREAL AT JERSEY CITY, TO BRANCH RICKEY, APRIL 17, 1946

"Frank, Robinson is going to play and I'll bet you everything I own or could borrow that when the game is over he'll be the most popular player in the ballpark."

—Branch Rickey, about Opening Day, to Frank Shaughnessy, April 17, 1946

CLASSIC MOMENT: APRIL 18, 1946, ROOSEVELT STADIUM, JERSEY CITY, NEW JERSEY

"We all sensed that history was in the making, that the long ban against Negro players was about to come crashing down, setting up reverberations that would echo across a continent and perhaps around the world."

—J. R. about his first minor league game at Jersey City on April 18, 1946, *Jackie Robinson: My Own Story*, as told to Wendell Smith, 1948

"This in a way is another Emancipation Day for the Negro race. A day Abraham Lincoln would like."

—Baz O'Meara, *Montreal Star*, April 1946

"Jackie Robinson was trying to hide his excitement, his nervousness, but those emotions betrayed him constantly as the time to begin the ball game approached. . . . Robinson was plain frightened. . . . Not of being hit or anything like that, but what gnawed at him most was the fear of failure. That frightened him terribly. He also feared for his wife, Rachel, sitting in the stands. He was afraid of the things she'd hear."

—Milton Richman, United Press, October 25, 1972

"At 3:04 that afternoon, Robinson came to bat in the top of the first inning [to an ear-splitting roar], feeling weak in his knees and stomach. Swinging with a full count, he dribbled a weak grounder to the shortstop who threw him out easily. When he batted again with two on and none out in the third inning, Jersey City expected him to bunt."

—Chris Lamb, *Blackout*, 2004

"[Warren] Swindell's first pitch was a fast one, letter-high down the middle. I swung with all my might and knew when the bat met the ball that I really had connected. As I dashed toward first, the roar of the crowd told me that this one was going all the way. It sailed more than 340 feet over the left field fence. I had hit my first homer and driven in my first three runs in organized baseball. I was so excited, so exhilarated, as I circled those bases that it seemed all the oxygen had left my brain and for a moment those stands were just a blur in front of me. As I crossed home plate two teammates were waiting to shake hands."

—J. R., on his historic second official minor league at-bat, *Wait Till Next Year*, Carl T. Rowan with Jackie Robinson, 1960

"I GOT LINED UP WITH JACKIE, HE CAME TOWARD THE PLATE AND HE HAD A BIG SMILE ON HIS FACE. I DID, TOO. I DIDN'T HAVE A PROBLEM WITH JACKIE AT ALL. WE WERE BALLPLAYERS. IT DIDN'T MATTER WHAT COLOR HE WAS. SHAKING HIS HAND AND CONGRATULATING HIM WAS JUST THE RIGHT THING TO DO."

—GEORGE SHUBA, ROBINSON'S MONTREAL ROYALS AND FUTURE DODGERS TEAMMATE, ABOUT THE FIRST KNOWN PHOTOGRAPH OF BLACK AND WHITE BALLPLAYERS CONGRATULATING EACH OTHER ON A BASEBALL DIAMOND

"In the fifth inning, Robinson dropped a bunt single, then stole second, and went to third on a ground out. When Jersey City brought in a new pitcher, Robinson unnerved him by sprinting up and down the third base line, forcing a balk that sent Robinson home with another run. Robinson had 4 hits in 5 at-bats, scored 4 runs, and stole 2 bases as Montreal won 14–1. 'The cold figures of the box score do not tell the whole story,' reported the *New York Times*, which [stated] Robinson had converted 'his opportunity into a brilliant triumph.'"

—Chris Lamb, *Blackout,* 2004

"I didn't appreciate it at the time. He bunted on me twice and I was playing him back and he beat my throw to first both times. I gave him a great introduction to organized baseball."

—Larry Miggins, New Jersey Giants third baseman, to Michaelangelo Conte, *Jersey Journal,* April 16, 2013

"Negro Jackie Robinson, the first of his race ever to play in modern organized baseball, was off to a sensational start today in his ambition to become in baseball what Joe Louis has been to boxing, Jesse Owens to track, Buddy Young to football, and Isaac Murphy is to racing."

—*Brooklyn Eagle,* April 19, 1946

"Almost everything he did was pure gold."

—Bill Mardo, the *New York Daily Worker,* April 19, 1946

"The most significant sports story of the century was written into the record books today as baseball took up the cudgel for democracy and an unassuming but superlative Negro boy ascended the heights of excellence to prove the rightness of the experiment. And prove it in the only correct crucible for such an experiment— the crucible of white-hot competition."

—Joe Bostic, *New York Amsterdam News*

"I guarantee that if Jackie Robinson hits homers and plays a whale of a game for Montreal, the fans will soon lose sight of his color."

—W. N. Cox, who showed there were liberal white sportswriters in the South who supported Robinson, *Norfolk Virginian-Pilot*, 1946

"In Montreal we lived in a French Canadian neighborhood. There we felt genuinely that few people thought we were intruding. Even the younger children, who had never seen Negroes before, didn't make us feel that we were different."

—Rachel Robinson, *McCall's* magazine, January 1951

"MONTREAL ADORED HIM, AS NO OTHER BALLPLAYER WHO HAS BEEN HERE BEFORE OR SINCE. NO SOONER DID ROBINSON REACH FIRST BASE, ON A HIT OR A WALK, THAN THE FANS ROARED WITH JOY AND HOPE, OUR HEARTS GOING OUT TO HIM AS HE DANCED UP AND DOWN THE BASE PATH, TAUNTING THE OPPOSING PITCHER WITH HIS ASTONISHING SPEED."

—MORDECAI RICHLER, CANADIAN JOURNALIST AND NOVELIST, *THE ULTIMATE BASEBALL BOOK*, EDITED BY DANIEL OKRENT AND HARRIS LEWINE, 1979

"Although his forty stolen bases (second best in the league), weren't a large number by earlier (or later) standards, what most impressed observers was his intrepidness—his ability to beat out bunts, stretch singles into doubles, upset pitchers by dancing up and down the basepaths, and generally demoralize opponents' defenses in ways that reminded a few old-timers of Ty Cobb. Robinson gave International League fans a sample of the speed and dash that characterized Negro-league play, even as those qualities had largely disappeared from white baseball."

—Charles C. Alexander, *Our Game*, 1991

"Robinson came from the Negro Leagues, but was not necessarily of the Negro Leagues. . . . He picked up his style from the Negro Leagues, but he also knew how to tailor it to [organized baseball]."

—William Rhoden, *Forty Million Dollar Slaves*, 2006

"Most of the older fellas, especially the pitchers, never thought [Jackie] would hit, because he was a lunger. They'd throw him fastballs inside, and he'd fight them off . . . but he could always hit the breaking ball, and he was . . . a better hitter with two strikes. The older guys didn't think he'd hit for average, but he had so much damn speed that you might hit him on the fist, but he'd hit a blooper over the infield for a base hit, and he'd get one hit bunting, and then he'd cream a couple of curveballs. And he did hit for average. He had a slow start, but . . . it turned out, he fit right in."

—Spider Jorgensen, Montreal Royals and future Dodgers third baseman, to Peter Golenbock, *Bums*, 1984

"[Jackie] was a great teammate but really had a tough time breaking in. Back then, Baltimore was still considered part of the South. We played there in the beginning of the season, and they wanted to know if we were really going to go out on the field with a black player. They didn't want to play the game. We said, 'Well, you don't have to play, but we're still going out there.'"

—Herman Franks, Montreal catcher and future major league player and manager, quoted by Benjamin Hill, mlb.com, September 19, 2006

"The night of the first game in Baltimore, Rae sat near the Dodger dugout. When the Montreal team took the field, a man sitting directly behind her shouted, 'Here comes that nigger son of a bitch. Let's give it to him now!' Rae cringed. In Florida people had called Robinson insulting names behind their hands, but in Baltimore they were openly shouting them. The man behind her and a companion of his continued to shout the loudest of all. . . . The racists were making derogatory remarks about Jackie's mother, his family, his color, his odor, and anything they could think of. . . . Only about 3,000 fans were attending [after] publicized threats that Baltimoreans would boycott the Orioles if they played against a Negro. . . . The boycott fear was short-lived. The next day, for an afternoon doubleheader, 25,396 fans (about 10,000 Negroes) jammed into the stadium."

—Carl T. Rowan, *Wait Till Next Year,* Carl T. Rowan with Jackie Robinson, 1960

"Tommy Thomas was the Baltimore manager, and he was anti-Robinson, and he'd have his pitchers knock Jackie down, and there'd be a lot of stuff coming from the bench. They called him 'black son of a bitch, black bastard.' And despite all of this, Jackie never said a word."

—Spider Jorgensen, Montreal Royals third baseman, to Peter Golenbock, *Bums,* 1984

"In Syracuse one day, the rival team let out a black cat from their dugout."

—*Time* magazine, about an ugly incident on April 25 at MacArthur Stadium after Robinson had grounded out against the Chiefs before 3,410 fans and Rachel Robinson, September 22, 1947

"I know that incident did happen."

—Rachel Robinson, dismissing those people who insisted for five decades that no black cat was thrown onto the field in Syracuse, at Hall of Fame, quoted by Bud Poliquin, *Syracuse Herald American,* June 15, 1997

"He'll do!"

—Paul Derringer, veteran Indianapolis Indians pitcher and former major leaguer, after Robinson twice got hits off him after being knocked down in a game in the former major leaguer's test of the black player's mettle, to Montreal manager Clay Hopper, 1946

"Pitchers commonly test young players by throwing at their heads, but in Robinson's case, the consequences of this test were magnified. In the eyes of many, not only was Robinson's personal courage in question, but that of all ballplayers of his race."

—Jules Tygiel, *Baseball's Great Experiment,* 1983

"He's been thrown at more than any batter in the league. If he hasn't been, there are a flock of pitchers in this league who have inexplicable lapses in control."

—Curt Davis, Royals teammate, 1946

"Larry MacPhail later admitted to Wendell Smith that he ordered pitchers on the Yankees' Newark farm team to throw at Robinson. One anonymous manager stated, 'I offered to buy a suit of clothes for any pitcher on our club who knocks him down.'"

—Jules Tygiel, *Baseball's Great Experiment*, 1983

"There's some of the boys [on the Royals] that were uptight a little because they were from the South. . . . As soon as he won his first ballgame for us, they started pulling for him, especially when he'd get knocked down at second base or [get] thrown [at] at the plate."

—Tom Tatum, Royals outfielder, to Jules Tiegel, *Baseball's Great Experiment*, 1983

"He still had that respect that maybe this [teammate] doesn't want to eat with me."

—Al Campanis, Royals shortstop and future Dodgers executive, about how he had to invite Robinson to eat with him so he wouldn't eat alone, to Jules Tiegel, *Baseball's Great Experiment*, 1983

"It wasn't a question of the players getting along with me. I was on the spot to see if I could get along with them. . . . It wasn't my privilege to make friends with [the Southern players] at first."

—J. R. to *Sporting News* publisher J. Taylor Spink, 1946

"Some of the Royals, Jackie sensed, 'felt funny' about him right up to the end of the season."

—Bill Roeder, *New York World-Telegram*, July 3, 1947

"No minor-league ballplayer has ever attracted the kind of national attention that was focused on Jackie Robinson. . . . Special charter trains came from Chicago [with fans who wanted] to see Robinson perform with his Montreal teammates at Buffalo. After virtually every game, swarms of kids and their parents begged for autographs."

—Harvey Frommer, *Rickey and Robinson*, 1982

"Almost everywhere the Royals went, he had to deal with hostile and often abusive white fans, pitchers who threw at his head, and base runners who came in with spikes high. Robinson took it and kept his temper under control, but teammate John Wright . . . couldn't endure the stress. Optioned to Three Rivers, Quebec, in the lower minors in May and subsequently released, Wright returned to the Homestead Grays, his prewar club. Pitcher Ray Partlow, another Negro Leaguer, also spent part of 1946 with Montreal, but by late summer he had followed Wright to Three Rivers."

—Charles C. Alexander, *Our Game*, 1991

"NOBODY KNOWS WHAT I'M GOING THROUGH THIS SEASON."
—J. R. TO ROYALS GENERAL MANAGER MEL JONES, 1946

"Yet, never once did he imagine quitting."

—Mel Jones, Montreal Royals general manager, quoted by Tom Meany, *Sport* magazine, January 1947

"By the end of July the Royals led the league by a dozen games. . . . Only Rae knew that Jackie was weary, bedraggled, worn out physically and mentally. . . . He was having trouble sleeping; he was nauseated; on many days he was unable to eat."

—Carl T. Rowan, *Wait Till Next Year,* Carl T. Rowan with Jackie Robinson, 1960

"Near the end of the season, my nerves were pretty ragged. I guess I hadn't realized I wanted to make good so badly. I sort of went to pieces."

—J. R. to Jack Sher, *Sport* magazine, October 1948

"Rachel got him away. . . . He loafed around, played a little golf, forgot for the time that baseball had become a life-or-death thing to him and his people."

—Jack Sher, *Sport* magazine, October 1948

"My wife . . . was . . . an inspiration."

—J. R., about Rachel Robinson, who thought Jackie's main problem was a stomach disorder, at a post-season testimonial dinner in Pasadena, November 7, 1946

"You see, Skipper, as soon as that doctor told me that I wasn't dying of anything horrible like cancer, that it was just my nerves, I was all right. I wasn't nervous anymore. So I'm ready to go."

—J. R., about why he was ready to return to the team so quickly,
Wait Till Next Year, Carl T. Rowan with Jackie Robinson, 1960

"Robinson is the greatest player in the game today. Whoever is playing the position he wants at Brooklyn had better move over, because Robinson is on his way."

—Hank DeBerry, New York Giants scout, 1946

"In the recent Newark series, he doubled in the ninth to win one game, saved another with a diving catch of a low line drive near first base when the bases were filled, doubled in the tenth to win a third game."

—Red Smith, *New York Herald Tribune,* August 4, 1946

"THERE DOESN'T SEEM TO BE ANYTHING HE CAN'T DO."
—DINK CARROLL, *MONTREAL GAZETTE,* AUGUST 8, 1946

"[Robinson] went on to lead the International League with a .349 batting average and tie for the leadership in runs scored."

—Charles C. Alexander, *Our Game,* 1991

"The first black in the International League in 57 years, he led . . . the Royals to a pennant by 19½ games."

—*The Ballplayers,* edited by Mike Shatzkin, 1990

"Between 1931 and 1975, a 'Junior' or 'Little' World Series often took place as a means to determine the best team in Minor League Baseball. Perhaps the most notable such series took place in 1946, when Jackie Robinson's International League champion Montreal Royals defeated the American Association's Louisville Colonels, four games to two. The first three games of the series were scheduled to be played in Louisville, a considerably more hostile area [than Montreal]. . . . Louisville's fans brought this unwelcoming attitude straight to the stadium."

—Benjamin Hill, mlb.com, September 19, 2006

"The Little World Series was special in that day. . . . It was a very exciting time, because of all the controversy surrounding Jackie being the first black player. Jackie didn't even have a place to stay [in Louisville]. There were no hotels that would take him, so they didn't even know whether or not they were even going to play. . . . I know he was a heck of a ballplayer. There was nothing delicate about him. He did everything rough and tumble, there was always dust. But he was very quiet, even with all the commotion around him."

—Al Brancato, Louisville Colonels infielder

"Everything he did, they booed him. I remember our pitcher Jim Wilson knocked him down, and the fans cheered. Robinson didn't seem to pay any attention to any of it."

—Otey Clark, Louisville Colonels pitcher

"The fans, nonetheless, may have had an effect on Robinson, as he went 1-for-10 over the three games in Louisville. The series then moved to Montreal, with the Colonels holding a 2–1 lead. There, Robinson found that the Royals' fans were livid over the rude welcome he had received in Louisville."

—Benjamin Hill, mlb.com, September 19, 2006

"All through that first game [at home] they booed every time a Louisville player came out of the dugout. I didn't approve of this kind of retaliation, but I felt a jubilant sense of gratitude for the way Canadians expressed their feelings."

—J. R.

"It was in that first game in Montreal that the series' momentum swung decisively in the Royals' favor. . . . In fact, it was Robinson himself who drove in the winning run in the 10th inning. In Game 5, he went 3-for-5 with a double, a triple, an RBI and two runs scored as the Royals won, 5–3. One day later, he collected two hits in the Royals' 2–0 series-clinching victory."

—Benjamin Hill, mlb.com, September 19, 2006

"When they won it, Jackie was accorded an emotional send-off unseen before or since in this city. First they serenaded him in true French Canadian spirit with 'Il a gagné ses Epaulettes,' and then clamored for his reappearance on the field. When he finally came out for a curtain call, the fans mobbed him. They hugged him, kissed him, cried, cheered and pulled and tore at his uniform while parading him around the infield on their shoulders. With tears streaming down his face, Robinson finally begged off in order to shower, dress, and catch a plane to the States. But the riot of joy wasn't over yet. When he emerged from the clubhouse, he had to bull his way through the waiting crowd outside the stadium. Thousands of fans chased him down Ontario Street for several blocks before he was rescued by a passing motorist and driven to his hotel."

—Dick Bacon, *Montreal Gazette,* 1978

"IT WAS PROBABLY THE ONLY DAY IN HISTORY THAT A BLACK MAN RAN FROM A WHITE MOB WITH LOVE, INSTEAD OF LYNCHING, ON ITS MIND."

—SAM MALTIN, *PITTSBURGH COURIER,* 1946

"He's ready. . . . [Robinson] . . . must go to the majors. He's a big-league ballplayer, a good team hustler, and a real gentleman."

—**Clay Hopper, Montreal Royals manager, at the conclusion of the 1946 season, to Branch Rickey**

"Jack found his own style, his own style of play. He found his place on the team . . . being in Montreal and doing well and being on a Championship team made him feel more secure about his place in baseball."

—**Rachel Robinson**

"My first year in organized baseball was probably the most crucial one of my life. . . . I learned a lot of things, the most important of which was that ball players—whether they came from the South or North—would accept me and play with me."

—**J. R., *Jackie Robinson: My Own Story,* as told to Wendell Smith, 1948**

"That summer and fall, after more than a decade of segregation, professional football welcomed its first black players: Marion Motley, Bill Willis, Woody Strode, and Kenny Washington. The latter two had been Robinson's teammates at UCLA, part of the Gold Dust Trio. Had he stuck with football, Robinson, too, might have been among professional football's first class of black athletes. But football had nowhere near the fan support that baseball had in the 1940s. On the gridiron, his impact on America's culture would have been negligible."

—Jonathan Eig, *Opening Day: The Story of Jackie Robinson's First Season*, 2007

"Even if I'd known that the barriers had broken down, I never would have played football; my legs and bones were not strong enough."

—J. R., *Black Sports Magazine*, March 1972

"Despite ambitious plans . . . the [two-year-old US League] continued to lag behind the [Negro National League] and [Negro American League] in player strength and was unable to attract substantial press or fan attention. . . . Several USL officials . . . attempted one final promotion: a post-season barnstorming tour featuring Jackie Robinson and other black minor leaguers. Financial problems, however, marred the trip, as Robinson not only failed to receive his promised fee, but ultimately lost more than $2,400 resulting from bounced checks. Hoping to recover his losses, Robinson subsequently enlisted the assistance of Thurgood Marshall and the NAACP, without apparent success. . . . The USL . . . quietly disbanded in 1946."

—Neil Lanctot, *Negro League Baseball*, 2004

"On October 23, a small crowd in San Francisco saw [Bob] Feller pitch a two-hitter and beat Robinson's team, 6–0. The next day in San Diego, Feller's team won, 4–2, as Musial singled to start a winning rally in the eighth."

—George Vecsey, about the first two games of a three-game exhibition series between the barnstorming Bob Feller's All-Stars and an all-black All-Star team with Satchel Page and Robinson, *Stan Musial*, 2011

"[ROBINSON] DIDN'T IMPRESS ME TOO MUCH WHEN I SAW HIM AT THE END OF '46, IN THE FALL. I FIGURED THIS GUY WOULDN'T . . . DO WELL IN THE BIG LEAGUES."

—STAN MUSIAL, CARDINALS OUTFIELDER AND FUTURE HALL OF FAMER

"Bob Feller's All-Stars defeated Jackie Robinson's All-Stars, 4–3, before a turnout of 12,140 fans at Wrigley Field [in Los Angeles] last night. Feller said aloha prior to his departure to Honolulu, hurling no-hit, no-run balls for the five innings he worked. He struck out 10 of the 15 men that faced him. Manager Leo Durocher was a spectator and watched closely the play of Jackie Robinson . . . who goes up with the Dodgers next season. Although held hitless in three attempts, Robinson turned in two spectacular plays in the fifth inning to rob Stan Musial and Jeff Heath of base hits."

—*Los Angeles Times,* **October 26, 1946**

"Brooklyn will have two or three other good infielders next year, but Jackie will get the job if he can outplay them. He is a great bunter. I'd say he's better than Shoeless Joe Jackson. And Robinson is a magnificent pivot man on double plays. . . . There isn't a finer gentleman on the Montreal ball club."

—Leo Durocher, Brooklyn Dodgers manager, indicating Robinson would be a Dodger in 1947 at a breakfast hosted by comedian Jack Benny at the Brown Derby in Los Angeles, *Pasadena Star-News,* **November 16, 1946**

"Star pitcher Bob Feller of the Cleveland Indians said that Robinson had 'football shoulders and couldn't hit an inside pitch to save his neck.'"

—Rick Swaine, SABR Baseball Biography Project

"What are football shoulders? . . . If it means muscle-bound, I don't have them. . . . If Feller said that about [my hitting], I wish he hadn't. . . . Feller only pitched against me twice, both in night games. You stand ten of us colored boys in a row at a night game, and Feller couldn't pick me out. He's quoted as saying I can't hit an inside pitch. Feller never threw me an inside pitch. He kept it outside after I leaned on one almost inside and pulled it into the bleachers foul by inches. . . . I faced him a third time in San Diego, where they have the worst lighting system in organized baseball. . . . Bob was really bearing down to top Satch. I never saw the third strike, nor did eleven others of us Royals who fanned. But Feller's team was worse, because old Satch struck out sixteen of his All-Stars. So on the strength of that, Feller is quoted as saying I won't make it."

—J. R., at the beginning of a long feud between Robinson and Feller, quoted by Arthur Mann, *Collier's* **magazine, March 2, 1946**

"ANYBODY WHO SAYS I CAN'T MAKE IT DOESN'T KNOW WHAT I'VE GONE THROUGH, AND WHAT I'M PREPARED TO GO THROUGH TO STAY UP."

—J. R., QUOTED BY ARTHUR MANN, *COLLIER'S* MAGAZINE, MARCH 2, 1946

"With the lone exception of Jackie Robinson's wrangling [loudly arguing balls and strikes] . . . at Los Angeles [playing for Chet Brewer's California Winter League team] there has been no evidence that any of the 1946 barnstormers behaved in a manner which would bring discredit to the game. But here, again, is an aspect which cannot be shrugged away."

—*Sporting News,* which had reacted negatively to Robinson's signing with the Dodgers, now singled him out for criticism of his character, November 6, 1946

"Robinson . . . in [October] 1946 . . . joined a racially integrated professional basketball team called the Los Angeles Red Devils. The [newly formed] Red Devils . . . were organized seeking to join the National Basketball League (NBL), which, in its merger talks with the NBA, wanted a West Coast franchise."

—Black Fives Foundation, January 31, 2008

"Sparked by Jackie Robinson, the Angelinos came through brilliantly in the debut last week. On Friday they trounced Sheboygan, 42–36, and on Saturday came back to win [against the Redskins] by a tight-fit margin, 39–38. Robinson accounted for 20 points in the two games; played splendidly throughout."

—*Los Angeles Times,* about Robinson leading a formidable Red Devils team that included future major leaguers George Crowe and Irv Noren, November 15, 1946

"The first player who I ever saw dunking as part of his game was Jackie Robinson."

—John Isaacs, New York Rens Hall of Fame basketball player

"When my wife gave birth to a bouncing baby boy [on November 18, 1946], we named him Jackie Jr. and vowed that we'd give him all the things we missed as a kid. My athletic career had been a full one, and I have enjoyed almost all of it. I hope my son will be an athlete, too. I am sure it will keep him out of trouble."

—J. R., having hopes for his son who would have a troubled life, *Jackie Robinson: My Own Story,* as told to Wendell Smith, 1948

"In Canada, Jackie Jr. was born, precious beyond belief."

—Rachel Robinson, *New York Times* News Service, April 12, 1987

"An article in the *People's Voice* newspaper [in 1946] said Jackie had agreed to become chair of the New York State Organizing Committee for United Negro and Allied Veterans of America and speak at one of the group's conferences in Harlem. The organization sought to help black veterans adjust to life after the war, although the increasingly suspicious FBI later described it as a communist front."

—Jonathan Eig, *Opening Day: The Story of Jackie Robinson's First Season,* **2007**

"I consider it a great honor. . . . The burning problems of discrimination in housing, employment, education and on-the-job training facing Negro veterans demand an immediate solution. I am happy to join Joe Louis, honorary national commander of UNAVA, in the fight to solve these problems."

—J. R., 1946

"Robinson was also identified in a newspaper article as a member of the advisory board for a new cultural center in Harlem. The center was created by the International Workers Order, a left-wing labor group with communist ties. . . . And in December of 1946, [Robinson] agreed to speak at a couple of fundraising events for the Detroit Committee to Fight Racial Injustice and Terrorism, another group that the government would later label subversive. Robinson canceled his appearance in Detroit at the last minute, perhaps on orders from Rickey, a staunch anticommunist."

—Jonathan Eig, *Opening Day: The Story of Jackie Robinson's First Season,* **2007**

"Paced by Jackie Robinson's 11 points, the Los Angeles Red Devils . . . defeated the San Diego Wizards, 44–34, at the Olympic Auditorium last night before a slim gathering of 400."

—*Los Angeles Times*, December 21, 1946

"There was a reasonable amount of publicity . . . yet the promoters took a real bath in this venture. Our games just didn't draw."

—J. R.

"Jackie Robinson left the Red Devils abruptly in January 1947. At the time, few knew why. Looking back, however, the reason was clear, and it had to do with the fact that Jackie parted ways with the Red Devils just after a Branch Rickey visit to Los Angeles."

—Black Fives Foundation

"That January at the baseball winter meetings at the Waldorf-Astoria in New York City . . . fifteen owners wearing expensive suits and pained expressions declared a need to continue the 'gentleman's agreement' that for sixty-two years had denied blacks equal opportunity to play in the majors. Yankee owner Larry MacPhail delivered an impassioned speech about why the Dodgers shouldn't be allowed to sign Jackie Robinson to a major-league contract for the coming season. Only Rickey spoke in favor of integrating baseball. The vote was 15–1."

—Tom Clavin and Danny Peary, about a vote the fifteen naysayers would swear never took place, *Gil Hodges,* 2012

"I made no comment. For one thing, the press didn't know about it and I didn't consider that [vote] an order, only an expression of sentiment. Naturally those fifteen fellows who had opposed Robinson in New York still opposed him, and me, too, but . . . when I became commissioner I [had] insisted they could not reverse any decision or judgment of mine. They didn't."

—Happy Chandler to Morris Siegel, *Washington Star,* October 27, 1972

"It was now up to commissioner Happy Chandler to make the final decision, knowing that if he let Robinson into the majors he wouldn't be reelected by the owners when his contract expired in 1951. The former governor and senator from Kentucky, wanting to 'face my maker with a clear conscience,' boldly opened the door for Robinson, suddenly placing Major League Baseball at the forefront of social change in the country."

—Tom Clavin and Danny Peary, *Gil Hodges,* 2012

"I HAD A ROLE IN ROBINSON'S BREAKING THE COLOR LINE JUST LIKE RICKEY, THOUGH RICKEY TRIED TO TAKE ALL THE CREDIT FOR THAT, AND IN THAT I WAS DISAPPOINTED. BUT I HAVE NOTHING TO BE ASHAMED OF. I HAD THE RESPECT OF THE RESPECTABLE PEOPLE IN BASEBALL, AND I PROTECTED THE INTEGRITY OF THEM AND THE GAME."

—HAPPY CHANDLER, BASEBALL COMMISSIONER, TO PETER GOLENBOCK, *BUMS,* 1984

"Robinson appeared likely to earn a promotion to Brooklyn in 1947. Anticipating a dramatic surge in black patronage at Dodger games, Branch Rickey met with several black leaders of Brooklyn in February and warned that inappropriate fan behavior might jeopardize Robinson's chances."

—Neil Lanctot, *Negro League Baseball,* 2004

"If Jackie Robinson does come up to the Dodgers, the biggest threat to his success, the one enemy most likely to ruin that success is the Negro people themselves. . . . We don't want premature Jackie Robinson Days or Nights. We don't want Negroes in the stands gambling, drunk, fighting, being arrested. We don't want Jackie wined and dined until he is fat and futile. . . . We don't want what can be another great milestone in the progress of American race relations turned into a national comedy and an ugly tragedy."

—Branch Rickey, excerpt from post-dinner speech to three dozen black civics leaders in New York, February 5, 1947

"The black elite subsequently launched a campaign advising black working-class fans to behave with restraint [at ballparks where Robinson played]."

—Neil Lanctot, *Negro League Baseball*, 2004

"Don't Spoil Jackie's Chances."

—Slogan adopted to encourage self-policing of black fans when watching Robinson play, 1947

"Mexican baseball had long provided off-season play for members of the Negro leagues, and now Jorgé Pasquel even began courting Rickey's pet project, Jackie Robinson."

—Frederick Turner, *When the Boys Came Back: Baseball and 1946*, 1996

"I believe in Mr. Rickey. I feel that if I'm good enough, I'll get my chance to play with the Dodgers."

—J. R., on why he wasn't tempted to play in Mexico for more money, quoted by Lester Bromberg, *New York World-Telegram*, February 26, 1947

"Because the Dodgers didn't want Jackie Robinson to be subjected to the same harassment he endured in Florida in 1946, and since the facility [Dodgertown] they were building for themselves in Vero Beach wouldn't be ready until 1948, Rickey accepted a lucrative offer to hold spring training in '47 in Havana, Cuba."

—Tom Clavin and Danny Peary, *Gil Hodges*, 2012

"Call the choice of Havana a decision made on behalf of Jackie and economics both."

—Buzzie Bavasi, a Dodgers jack-of-all-trades before becoming general manager in 1951

"While Robinson, Campanella, Newcombe, and Partlow stayed [as Sam Lacy, who was there in Havana in 1947, told me in 1997] at the Hotel Los Angeles—a fleabag that the *New York Sun* at the time described as a 'musty third-rate hotel'—[the] white Royals teammates stayed and trained at the Havana Military Academy on the outskirts of Havana. The Dodgers, meanwhile, stayed at the opulent Hotel Nacional."

—Cesar Brioso, Havana-born Florida sportswriter and editor, *Cuba Béisbol* blog, September 28, 2011

"Robinson was irate when he discovered that the segregation was due not just to Cuban customs but to arrangements made by the Dodgers. Rickey wanted no chance of racial incidents in the Dodger or Royal camp."

—Roberto González Echevarría, Yale professor and Cuban baseball historian, *Spring Training Magazine*, 1996

"TRAINING IN CUBA WAS TYPICAL OF THE METICULOUS PLANNING THAT BRANCH RICKEY DID IN SUPPORT OF THE BLACK PLAYERS WHO WERE PART OF THE TEAM THERE. BUT HAVANA WASN'T WHAT JACKIE AND THE OTHERS HOPED FOR. THEY WERE SURPRISED WHEN THEY GOT THERE AND FELT ALMOST BETRAYED BECAUSE THEY WERE KEPT SEPARATE."

—RACHEL ROBINSON, NOTING HER HUSBAND SUFFERED SEVERE STOMACH PAIN IN CUBA BECAUSE OF THE FOOD, TO DANNY PEARY, 2012

"Worse than the hotel was the fact that the four men had to eat in local restaurants, while the white players had kitchens and a cooking staff at their disposal. . . . Robinson . . . had to be treated for dysentery and was too weak to play in several of the Royals' exhibition games."

—Mary Kay Linge, *Jackie Robinson: A Biography*, 2007

"The Brooklyn bunch had blown into town surrounded by the hype of Jackie Robinson's possible move from the minor-league Montreal Royals' roster to the varsity. . . . Perhaps even more media attention spotlighted manager Leo Durocher's marriage to Hollywood starlet Laraine Day after a scandalous affair that titillated the tabloids."

—Roberto González Echevarría, Yale professor and Cuban baseball historian, *Spring Training Magazine*, 1996

"The *Afro-American* very closely covered Jackie Robinson's progress through . . . his spring training in 1947 with the Brooklyn Dodgers. Sam Lacy, the paper's sports editor, was sent to Havana, Cuba . . . to interview Robinson. In March 1947 the paper ran a three-part series, 'This Is My Story' by Jackie Robinson as told to Sam Lacy. . . . Lacy, in his column, 'Looking Them Over,' reported that Robinson had 'a swell chance' to make the Dodgers. He was a second baseman, but with the talented and scrappy Eddie Stanky a Dodger fixture at that position, he was tried a first base where he excelled."

—Hayward Farrar, *The Baltimore Afro-American, 1892-1950*, 1998

"Mr. Rickey had some kind of pipe dream that as soon as the [Dodgers] players recognized how much Jackie could help us, they were going to demand that he be brought up. What happened was exactly the opposite . . . when early in the spring we went to Panama for a weekend series against a squad of Caribbean All-Stars."

—Leo Durocher, Dodgers manager, *Nice Guys Finish Last*, 1975

"Dixie Walker was 'The People's Cherce,' the most popular player in Brooklyn when Jackie Robinson joined the Dodgers in 1947. He also was the most vocal in his opposition to playing with blacks. Walker was one of several Dodgers from Southern states with concerns over Robinson's joining the club, and attempted to start a petition [while the team was in Panama]. Walker sought Southern allies and turned to reserve catcher Bobby Bragan, pitcher Dixie Howell, and second baseman Eddie Stanky."

—Matt McHale, *Pasadena Star-News*, April 10, 1987

"I ORGANIZED THE PETITION IN 1947, NOT BECAUSE I HAD ANYTHING AGAINST ROBINSON PERSONALLY OR AGAINST NEGROES GENERALLY. I HAD A WHOLESALE HARDWARE BUSINESS IN BIRMINGHAM AND PEOPLE TOLD ME I'D LOSE MY BUSINESS IF I PLAYED BALL WITH A BLACK MAN. THAT'S WHY I STARTED THE PETITION. IT WAS THE DUMBEST THING I DID IN ALL MY LIFE. . . . I AM DEEPLY SORRY."

—DIXIE WALKER, DODGERS OUTFIELDER, TO ROGER KAHN, 1976

"Walker was optimistic about his petition until he was rebuffed by one of his closest friends, shortstop Pee Wee Reese, a native of Louisville, Kentucky."

—Matt McHale, *Pasadena Star-News*, April 10, 1987

"I looked at it and I just flatly refused. I just said, 'Hey, look man, I just got out of the service after three years. I don't care if this man is black, blue, or what the hell color he is. I have to play baseball.' I wasn't trying to be the Great White Father. I just wanted to play ball."

—Pee Wee Reese, Dodgers shortstop and future Hall of Famer, who admitted he had never yet shaken a black man's hand, to Peter Golenbock, 1983

"Reese . . . hadn't forgotten the contributions of black soldiers during the war and refused to add his name, leading to a wave of rejections. [Duke] Snider, who idolized Robinson when he was a multisport star at UCLA, didn't sign."

—Roger Kahn

"Reese was a more important player at the time, but [Gil] Hodges said no, too. [Carl] Furillo [from Reading, Pennsylvania] said sure. He later recanted but still got unfairly portrayed as a racist when he wasn't. With Gil there was no black and white. If you were a teammate who played hard to win, no one was more loyal than Gil Hodges."

—Roger Kahn to Tom Clavin, *Gil Hodges,* Tom Clavin and Danny Peary, 2012

"Ironically, the leak about the planned revolt came from a Southerner, Kirby Higbe, of South Carolina. Higbe had a few too many beers one night, and he began feeling uncomfortable about the conspiracy. He revealed the plot to one of Mr. Rickey's aides and Mr. Rickey put down the rebellion with steamroller effectiveness. . . . He found out who the ringleaders were—Hugh Casey, a good relief pitcher from Georgia; . . . Bobby Bragan, a respected catcher [of Alabama]; Dixie Walker of Alabama; and Carl Furillo [of Pennsylvania]. . . . The ringleaders were called in individually and Mr. Rickey told each one that . . . he would carry out his plan, regardless of protest. Anyone not willing to have a black teammate could quit."

—J. R., *I Never Had It Made,* as told to Alfred Duckett, 1972

"Mr. Rickey came right to the point. 'I understand that there's a conspiracy going on around here to get Robinson off the club and that you're part of it.' 'I'm not part of any conspiracy,' I said. 'And if there is one going on, I don't know anything about it. But I do know there is some resentment. . . . I'd just as soon be traded.'"

—Bobby Bragan, Dodgers catcher and future major league manager, to Donald Honig, *The Man in the Dugout,* 1977

> **"I DON'T CARE IF THE GUY IS YELLOW OR BLACK, OR IF HE HAS STRIPES LIKE A F*****G ZEBRA. I'M THE MANAGER OF THIS TEAM AND I SAY HE PLAYS. WHAT'S MORE, I SAY HE CAN MAKE US ALL RICH. AND IF ANY OF YOU CANNOT USE THE MONEY, I WILL SEE THAT YOU ARE ALL TRADED."**
>
> **—LEO DUROCHER, DODGERS MANAGER, TO HIS PLAYERS, PRESEASON 1947**

"The petition itself was a challenge, but it was a challenge for Rickey, not for Jackie Robinson. You paid attention to some of the more outspoken players, like Dixie Walker, and others who wanted a way to get out of Brooklyn and had to be traded. But I wouldn't say that at that point Jack was looking at his teammates and saying, 'These are my friends and are the ones who are going to be good to me, and those are the ones that are going to undermine me.'"

—**Rachel Robinson to Danny Peary, 2012**

"Early in 1947, the Brooklyn Dodgers played an exhibition game in Puerto Rico. I saw Jackie Robinson as he arrived at the ballpark in a car. . . . Because I was [only nine] and it was getting late, I didn't get to stay for the game. But I did get to shake his hand."

—**Orlando Cepeda, San Francisco Giants outfielder and Hall of Famer,**
Baby Bull, **1998**

"That man there will make it possible for others like us to play in the major leagues. If you play in the majors one day, it will be because of [Jackie Robinson]."

—**Orlando Cepeda Sr., who was a huge star in his native Puerto Rico but never wanted to play in the United States because of the racial strife, to Orlando Jr., spring training, 1947**

"[Rickey's] plan was to allow the Dodgers' veterans to gradually get used to having Jackie around and to see for themselves what an asset he would be to their pennant prospects. . . . Rickey scheduled [an] exhibition series between the Dodgers and the Royals to showcase Robinson's skills, and Jackie dominated the contests with a .625 batting average [and seven stolen bases]."

—**Rick Swaine, SABR Baseball Biography Project**

"Robinson was magnificent against Dodgers pitching, but he didn't sway anyone opposing him."

—**Tom Clavin and Danny Peary,** *Gil Hodges*, **2012**

"A five-run outburst in the fifth inning that gave the Dodgers their eighth victory in ten starts against their Montreal farm team's cousins by the score of 6–3, also threatened to remove Jackie Robinson's much-discussed chances from promotion to the Brooks from the realm of speculation. The Negro star, again playing first base for the Royals, was knocked out when Bruce Edwards slid hard back to the bag as Robinson was reaching for a high throw from Jack Jorgensen. Robinson lay on the ground as players from both teams and Doc Wendler rushed to his aid. After Jackie had been fanned for a bit by [Montreal shortstop] Al Campanis he arose and walked slowly off the field."

—Roscoe McGowan, *New York Times*, April 5, 1947

"Five days before the 1947 opener, Manager Leo Durocher was expected to announce Robinson as his first baseman. But that day, Durocher was suspended for one year by Commissioner Albert 'Happy' Chandler [for allegedly consorting with gamblers]."

—Matt McHale, *Pasadena Star-News*, April 10, 1987

"Now I will have to make the announcement directly."

—Branch Rickey to Robinson, April 10, 1947

SIX

The Pioneer

"The Brooklyn Dodgers today purchased the contract of Jackie Roosevelt Robinson from the Montreal Royals."

—Dodgers official announcement, which was typed and handed out by Arthur Mann to the press at Ebbets Field during an exhibition game in which Robinson and the Royals defeated the Dodgers 4–3, April 10, 1947

"Thanks, I'll need it."

—J. R. to his Montreal teammates, who wished him good luck, April 10, 1947

"Jackie Robinson, 28-year-old infielder, yesterday became the first Negro to achieve major-league baseball status in modern times. His contract was purchased from the Montreal Royals of the International League by the Dodgers and he will be in a Brooklyn uniform at Ebbets Field today, when the Brooks oppose the Yankees in the first of three exhibition games over the weekend."

—Louis Effrat, *New York Times*, April 11, 1947

"You're on this ball club and as far as I'm concerned that makes you one of twenty-five players on my team. . . . I want you to know I don't like it. I want you to know I don't like you."

—Eddie Stanky, Dodgers second baseman, to Jackie Robinson, who thanked him for being upfront, April 1947

"When Jackie Robinson was promoted from Montreal to Brooklyn . . . Roy Campanella was promoted from Nashua to Montreal. With him there, I was left behind to pitch another year in Nashua. . . . Because of Mr. Rickey's stair-step procedure for getting blacks to the big leagues I couldn't move up to Montreal with Roy already there."

—Don Newcombe, Nashua pitcher, to Danny Peary, *We Played the Game*, 1994

"When it was announced the Dodgers had purchased Robinson's contract just prior to the 1947 season, I . . . wasn't sure Robinson would turn out to be a good major league player . . . and even if he did, I couldn't picture a parade of other Negro leaguers marching into the majors on his heels. It's a ticklish point, but the general view of white players . . . was that African American players weren't as good as they turned out to be. . . . I think most of us didn't believe they were equal to us as players . . . or . . . nearly as competitive as we were. That was really a mistaken impression. I can't fathom why I didn't equate talent with being competitive."

—**Ralph Kiner, Pirates outfielder and Hall of Famer,** *Baseball Forever,* **2004**

"Elston was eighteen years old . . . the day he heard the news on the radio. . . . In 1947, if you were young, black, and loved baseball, there was no better news. Even in St. Louis, they were dancing in the streets. Suddenly everyone wanted to become the next Jackie Robinson."

—**Arlene Howard, widow of Elston Howard, who became the first black player on the Yankees in 1955,** *Elston and Me,* **2001**

"The movement [to curtail unruly behavior by black fans at ballparks that began in February] spread to other cities after Robinson [officially] joined the Dodgers. . . . The issue of improper public behavior soon dominated the editorial and sports columns of black newspapers, featuring stern warnings to potential transgressors."

—**Neil Lanctot,** *Negro League Baseball,* **2004**

"[On] April 11, I was walking south on Bedford Avenue on my way to Erasmus Hall High School, where I was a freshman. As I passed Martense Street, a young black man in a later model car stopped and, in a distinctive voice, asked me, 'Excuse me, fella, which way to Ebbets Field?' I replied, 'Keep going about a dozen blocks up Bedford. You can't miss it.' As he thanked me, I realized it was Jackie Robinson. He was to play as a Dodger for the first time that afternoon in an exhibition game against the Yankees. . . . When I told the story in the school lunchroom that day, a few black kids came over and shook my hand."

—**Robert Gruber, a Brooklyn Dodgers fan who got an MA in journalism, excerpt from paper presented at the Jackie Robinson anniversary conference, Long Island University, Brooklyn Campus, April 1997**

"I FINALLY GOT DRESSED AND LOOKED AT MYSELF IN THE MIRROR. I WAS WEARING A BRAND NEW UNIFORM—NUMBER 42."

—J. R., *JACKIE ROBINSON: MY OWN STORY,* **AS TOLD TO WENDELL SMITH, 1948**

"The Brooklyn Dodgers had just blasted the New York Yankees, 14–5, in the first of a three-game exhibition series, and now the players on both teams were rushing madly for their respective dugouts to avoid the maddening throngs. . . . 'Grab Jackie Robinson,' cried a hysterical woman standing on top of the Dodger dugout. 'Don't let him get away before I get his autograph.' Now the maniacs were leaping over the box seat rail and trying to force their way past a squadron of policemen. . . . They held the line, and now Jackie Robinson was safe in the clubhouse. . . . When he finally reached the street, he was mobbed again. . . . They almost pulled his clothes off him."

—**Wendell Smith,** *Pittsburgh Courier,* **April 19, 1947**

"It was postwar. We couldn't get any housing. We were strangers in the city. We didn't have much money. We could afford only one room in the Hotel McAlpin in Manhattan. . . . There was a cafeteria on a side street. One of us would mind the baby, and the other would go out and eat."

—**Rachel Robinson to Harvey Frommer,** *Rickey and Robinson,* **1982**

"When Rachel Robinson had difficulty hailing a cab in Manhattan to take her to Ebbets Field [to see Jackie debut] on Opening Day, she learned something black New Yorkers had known for years—and know still today—about the city's taxi drivers."

—**Jonathan Eig,** *Opening Day: The Story of Jackie Robinson's First Season,* **2007**

CLASSIC MOMENT: APRIL 15, 1947, EBBETS FIELD, BROOKLYN, NEW YORK

"Triumph of Whole Race Seen in Jackie's Debut in Major League Ball"

—**Headline in the black-owned** *Boston Chronicle,* **about Robinson's historic major league debut against the Boston Braves, April 15, 1947**

"April 15 was a perfect day for baseball, with blue skies, a soft breeze, and just
enough chill in the air to remind fans that a long season of baseball lay ahead.
Soon the fans would arrive in Flatbush, catching their first glimpse of Ebbets Field,
a bird's nest of brick and steel tucked inside one square city block. All of Brooklyn's
ethnic groups converged. . . . By one estimate, nearly three-fifths of the fans were
black. . . . But the most stunning thing was that only [26,623] fans came through
the gates—2,000 fewer than on Opening Day in 1946, and 5,000 fewer than the
ballpark's capacity. . . . Many fans were concerned that Robinson's presence would
set off more than the usual number of skirmishes."

—Jonathan Eig, *Opening Day: The Story of Jackie Robinson's First Season,* 2007

"Robinson posed for pictures on the dugout steps with the rest of the Dodger
infield, John 'Spider' Jorgensen [who borrowed Robinson's fielder's glove to play
third], Pee Wee Reese, and Eddie Stanky. . . . [Then] the men went about . . .
loosening their arms and fielding some ground balls."

—Jonathan Eig, *Opening Day: The Story of Jackie Robinson's First Season,* 2007

"JACKIE IS VERY DEFINITELY BRUNETTE."
—RED BARBER, DODGERS BROADCASTER, INTRODUCING THE FANS TO THE NEWEST DODGER OVER WHN, APRIL 15, 1947

"I became the first pitcher to face Jackie Robinson. We knew he was going to play
although they hadn't announced it, which may be why there were over 6,000 empty
seats at Ebbets Field. . . . There were no incidents or mischief during the game,
which is why nobody remembers who pitched to Robinson. He played first base and
batted second. In his first at-bat in the first inning, I threw him a low curveball."

—Johnny Sain, Boston Braves pitcher, to Danny Peary, *We Played the Game,* 1984

"Jackie slapped a grounder to shortstop [Dick Duller] and was called out in one of
those bang-bang plays. Instinctively he turned to argue with the umpire. Suddenly,
the combativeness oozed out of him. He walked away. . . . Jackie had the character
to follow the blueprint of the master plan."

—Arthur Daley, *New York Times,* October 26, 1972

"He went 0 for 3, but reached on an error on a sacrifice bunt and then scored. I lost
the game 5–3."

—Johnny Sain, Boston Braves pitcher, to Danny Peary, *We Played the Game,* 1984

"Yes, I was nervous. But it wasn't nerves that stopped me from getting any hits. Johnny Sain . . . threw just about the best curve ball I've seen."

—J. R.

"Sam Lacy . . . took a seat opposite the Dodger dugout in order to provide his readers an inning-by-inning account of Robinson's seating choice and facial expressions. Throughout most of the game, the story said, Robinson sat next to [temporary manager Clyde] Sukeforth, like a new kid at school sticking close to the teacher, although at times he was joined by Pete Reiser, catcher Bruce Edwards, or Tom Tatum, the part-time outfielder who had been his teammate at Montreal. At other times he sat alone. In the bottom of the seventh, after he scored the winning run, according to Lacy, Robinson allowed himself a yawn."

—Jonathan Eig, *Opening Day: The Story of Jackie Robinson's First Season,* 2007

"The debut of Jackie Robinson was quite uneventful."

—Arthur Daley, underestimating the game's drama and significance and not mentioning Robinson until the second column of his story, *New York Times,* April 16, 1947

"[ROBINSON'S] ARRIVAL IN BROOKLYN WAS A TURNING POINT IN THE HISTORY AND THE CHARACTER OF THE GAME; IT MAY NOT BE STRETCHING THINGS TO SAY IT WAS A TURNING POINT IN THE HISTORY OF THIS COUNTRY. I THINK I FAILED TO UNDERSTAND, TO APPRECIATE REALLY, THE BURDEN ROBINSON WAS CARRYING ON HIS SHOULDERS."

—RED SMITH, *NEW YORK TIMES,* 1956

"In this historic opening game against the Boston Braves, a dignified and heroic descendant of American slaves and sharecroppers who wore Number 42 on his Dodger uniform played first base in one of the sacred spaces of American culture. More even that either Abraham Lincoln and the Civil War, or Martin Luther King, Jr., and the Civil Rights movement, Jackie Robinson graphically symbolized and personified the challenge to the vicious legacy and ideology of white supremacy in American history."

—Cornel West, African American socialist philosopher, author, activist, and professor, Introduction, *I Never Had It Made,* Jackie Robinson as told to Alfred Duckett, 1972

"The decision to play Jackie Robinson in 1947 fit in with the larger shifts that were concurrently under way. . . . Robinson's entry into the major leagues in April was preceded in March by the Truman Doctrine and followed in June by the Marshall Plan. . . . Six days before . . . the Congress of Racial Equality (Core) sent 'freedom riders' to the South to test the previous year's decision of the Supreme Court against segregation in interstate bus travel."

—**Joram Warmund,** *Jackie Robinson: Race, Sports and the American Dream,* **edited by Joseph Dorinson and Joram Warmund, 1998**

"I believed that the single most important aspect of Jack's presence was that it enabled white baseball fans to root for a black man, thus encouraging more whites to realize that all our destinies were inextricably linked."

—**Rachel Robinson,** *Jackie Robinson: An Intimate Portrait,* **1996**

"There is no greater figure in terms of impact on social history than Jackie Robinson. . . . He really broke the color line for mainstream America."

—**Christopher Moore, historian and author,** *Jackie Robinson: My Story* **(documentary), 2003**

"He was history's man. Nothing less. Though he came to the nation disguised as a mere baseball player, he was, arguably, the single most important American of that first post war decade. . . . What made him so important was the particular moment when he arrived and the fact that he stood at the exact intersection of two powerful and completely contradictory impulses, one the impulse of darkness and prejudice, the other the impulse of idealism and optimism, the belief in the possibility of true advancement for all Americans in this democratic and meritocratic society."

—**David Halberstam, author and historian, excerpt from original essay** "**History's Man,**" *Jackie Robinson: Between the Baselines,* **edited by Glenn Stout and Dick Johnson, 1997**

"In the first game Jackie Robinson played, I pinched hit for Dixie Walker. Base hit to right. I sent the clippings to my mother and I wrote that it wasn't only a colored person's first game in the big league, it was also her son's."

—**Duke Snider, Dodgers outfielder and future Hall of Famer, to Roger Kahn,** *The Boys of Summer,* **1972**

"My thoughts are on Jackie Robinson today, my birthday. I was born in Harlem the day after Jackie's first major league game across the river in Brooklyn's Ebbets Field. . . . I have always considered it a gift that I slipped into the world just at that moment."

—Kareem Abdul-Jabbar, basketball Hall of Famer and author, April 16, 1989

"Robinson's first major league hit came in the next game, a 12–6 rout of the Braves. It was also a bunt—but a clean bunt single rather than a sacrifice."

—David Falkner, about Robinson's first hit off Glenn Elliot,
***Great Time Coming,* 1995**

"There's good reason I remember [Robinson's] first home run. It came [off Dave Koslo] in the Polo Grounds on April 18, but we won 10–4 and I hit 2 homers, one a grand slam, and drove in 6 runs. That was the biggest offensive output of my career."

—Bill Rigney, Giants shortstop and future manager, about Robinson's first game against the New York Giants and suit-clad Burt Shotton's first game as Dodgers manager, to Danny Peary, *We Played the Game,* 1994

AN EARLY TEST

"The most significant event of the year was Jackie Robinson integrating baseball. Some of the clubs wanted to strike before he came in. . . . The Phillies had a meeting at which Skeeter Newsome got up and said, 'Men, you can't strike.' And we voted against striking. A few voted [in favor of a] strike."

—Andy Seminick, Phillies catcher, about his team's decision to play games at Ebbets Field April 22, 23, and 24, to Danny Peary, *We Played the Game,* 1994

"As Robinson dug his cleats into the back of the batter's box, a torrent of foul language, harsher than anything Robinson had heard in his professional baseball career, poured from the Phillies dugout."

—Jonathan Eig, about the Phillies' first game in Brooklyn on April 22,
***Opening Day: The Story of Jackie Robinson's First Season,* 2007**

"All the talking for the Phillies was done . . . by their Southern-born and bred manager, Ben Chapman, and at no time in my life have I ever heard racial venom and dugout filth to match the abuse that Ben sprayed on Robinson that night. . . . Chapman sang this hate song almost alone at first, but soon he picked up an infantile chorus behind him on the bench."

—Harold Parrott, Dodgers traveling secretary and publicist in 1947,
The Lords of Baseball, **1976**

"We don't want you here, nigger."

—Words from the Phillies dugout

"The Phillies mentioned Robinson's lips, thick skull, and sores and diseases his teammates and their wives would likely contract by associating with him. . . . Even the veterans of the game had never heard anything like the insults hurled at Robinson. . . . Chapman, the Alabama-born manager of the Phillies, was leading the cry and had reportedly ordered his players to join him. They would incur fines if they didn't obey, some players later recalled."

—Jonathan Eig, *Opening Day: The Story of Jackie Robinson's First Season,* **2007**

"They're waiting for you in the jungles, black boy!"

—Words from the Phillies dugout, April 22, 1947

"The Philadelphia Phillies dugout pointed their bats like guns at Robinson to mock him for the death threats he was receiving."

—Gavin Evans and Jack Erwin, complexsports.com, April 11, 2013

"Hey, nigger, why don't you go back to the cotton field where you belong?"

—Words from the Phillies dugout

"Meanwhile, there wasn't a peep out of Robinson."

—Harold Parrott, Dodgers traveling secretary and publicist in 1947,
The Lords of Baseball, **1976**

"Hey, snowflake, which one of the white boys' wives are you dating tonight?"

—Words from the Phillies dugout

"I'D GET MAD. BUT I'D NEVER LET THEM KNOW IT."
—J. R., *TIME* MAGAZINE, SEPTEMBER 22, 1947

"For one wild and rage-crazed minute I thought, 'To hell with Mr. Rickey's noble experiment.' I thought what a glorious, cleansing thing it would be to let go. To hell with the image of the patient black freak I was supposed to create. I would throw down my bat, stride over to the Phillies dugout, grab one of those white sons of bitches and smash his teeth in with my despised black fist. Then I could walk away from it all."

—J. R., who kept his cool in the Dodgers' 1–0 victory, but years later admitted how he really felt about the verbal abuse from Chapman and his players, *I Never Had It Made,* as told to Alfred Duckett, 1972

"I felt sure that Chapman would tone down his attacks [against Robinson] the second night, perhaps after some discreet hints from his embarrassed superiors. But no, Ben raved on without a letup."

—Harold Parrott, Dodgers traveling secretary, *Lords of Baseball,* 2001

"I saw enough to make me sick and upset. They would lift up their arms and make believe they were smelling and that there was a stink. They yelled about black cats being Jackie's relatives."

—Lee Scott, reporter for the *Brooklyn Times,* to Harvey Frommer, *Rickey and Robinson,* 1982

"Listen, you yellow-bellied cowards, why don't you guys go to work on somebody who can fight back? There isn't one of you who has the guts of a louse."

—Eddie Stanky, Dodgers second baseman, who by directing his tirade toward the Phillies dugout proved Rickey's contention that the mistreatment of the passive Robinson would make even his Southern teammates come to his defense, 1947

"In the third game of the series [which was swept by Brooklyn], Chapman called in sick, letting one of his coaches take over for him in the dugout. But the storm over his behavior didn't end. In the days and weeks ahead, fans and sportswriters weighed in on whether Chapman had a right to harass Robinson. The *Sporting News* noted that all ballplayers face insults."

—Jonathan Eig, *Opening Day: The Story of Jackie Robinson's First Season,* 2007

"There is not a man who has come to the big leagues since baseball has been played who has not been ridden."

—Ben Chapman, who claimed he threw insults at every player of every ethnicity as a strategy for unnerving them, 1947

"Ballplayers who don't want to be in the same ball park with Robinson don't belong in the same country with him."

—Walter Winchell, America's most popular journalist, giving strong support to Robinson and condemning all those like Chapman, 1947

"[The insults] didn't really bother me."

—J. R., in his always positive Wendell Smith–ghosted *Pittsburgh Courier* column, April 1947

"The black press did a real job of letting readers know about the race baiting which had taken place. The publicity in the press built so much anti-Chapman public feeling that the Philadelphia club decided steps must be taken to counteract it. Chapman met with representatives of the black press to try to explain his behavior."

—J. R., *I Never Had It Made,* as told to Alfred Duckett, 1972

"Lee Handley, Ben Chapman's third baseman, later made it a point to seek out Robinson. He said quietly, 'I'm sorry. I want you to know that stuff doesn't go for me.' Handley was the first opposing major leaguer to treat Robinson as a man. Robinson remembered Lee Handley . . . for the rest of his life."

—Roger Kahn, *The Era,* 1993

"Right now I am somewhat of a slump but I am not worried (much). I have gone 0–13 and my average has really hit rock bottom .273 but I am sure they will start falling again."

—J. R., to former *Pasadena (JC) Chronicle* staffer Ralph Norton, excerpt from letter, May 5, 1947

"Jackie . . . felt that Shotton supported him. During [Robinson's] first batting slump, Shotton left him in the lineup and made no comments."

—Robert A. Moss, fan of his hometown Brooklyn Dodgers, who grew up to be a prominent chemist, excerpt from paper presented at the Jackie Robinson anniversary conference, Long Island University, Brooklyn Campus, April 1997

"We just couldn't get him to take a normal cut at the cripples they were getting him out on. Time after time we gave him signals to hit the 3-and-1 pitch, but very often he didn't even swing. Guess he had too much on his mind."

—Burt Shotton, Dodgers manager

"Robinson's Job in Jeopardy"

—Headline, after Robinson, who went 0-for-20 before doubling in his first at-bat that day and then—after four days of rainouts that allowed his sore shoulder to heal—came alive with the bat, *New York Sun*, May 1, 1947

"Outside of baseball everything is OK. My wife and baby are fine and we now have an apartment, even though we have to share it with the owner."

—J. R. to Ralph Norton, excerpt from letter sent to St. Louis from 526 MacDonough Street in Brooklyn, May 5, 1947

"Jackie's intensity melted when he walked in the door [of their apartment on MacDonough Street], happy to be with his family, happy to have shelter from a world that expected him to be perfect all the time, a credit to his team and his race."

—Jonathan Eig, *Opening Day: The Story of Jackie Robinson's First Season*, 2007

"In our household, from the beginning of our marriage, there were self-imposed taboos against angry outbursts. I never, ever, heard Jack utter a profane word at home throughout his life. . . . However, I learned that there were no such constraints in the baseball clubhouse; Jack was reported to be quite a regular fellow there."

—Rachel Robinson, *Jackie Robinson: An Intimate Portrait*, 1996

"I never missed a home game, and Jackie would look for me in the stands. I would try to communicate with him through the airwaves mentally."

—Rachel Robinson to Danny Peary, 2012

> "I FELT I NEEDED TO BE THERE TO WITNESS AND SHARE IN WHAT WAS HAPPENING TO JACK. AS WE TRAVELED BACK TO MACDONOUGH STREET FROM THE BALLPARK, WE DISCUSSED THE DAY'S EVENTS. WE VENTED OUR ANGER AND FRUSTRATION AND SHARED THE JOY AND EXCITEMENT OF WINNING A GAME OR A NEW SUPPORTER. BY THE TIME WE GOT HOME, JACK COULD ENTER IN RELATIVE PEACE."
>
> —RACHEL ROBINSON, *JACKIE ROBINSON: AN INTIMATE PORTRAIT*, 1996

"She's been the most important and helpful and encouraging person I've ever known in my life."

—J. R., about Rachel Robinson, quoted by Jack Sher, *Sport* magazine, 1948

A CARDINALS CONSPIRACY UNCOVERED

"[*New York Herald Tribune* sportswriter Stanley] Woodward broke the sensational story that several players on the St. Louis Cardinals had planned to organize a boycott of the Dodgers because of Robinson's appearance [at Ebbets Field May 6–8]."

—Ira Berkow, *Red: A Biography of Red Smith*, 1986

"A National League players' strike instigated by some of the St. Louis Cardinals against the presence in the league of Jackie Robinson, Negro first baseman, has been averted temporarily and perhaps permanently quashed. In recent days, Ford Frick, president of the National League, and Sam Breadon, president of the St. Louis club, have been conferring with St. Louis players. . . . The strike, formulated by certain St. Louis players, was instigated by a member of the Brooklyn Dodgers, who has since recanted. . . . The story is factually and thoroughly substantiated. The St. Louis players will unquestionably deny it. We doubt, however, Frick and Breadon will go that far."

—Stanley Woodward, *New York Herald Tribune*, May 9, 1947

"Brooklyn was, after all, Robinson's home turf. It made more sense, the conspirators decided, to wait until May 20 when the Dodgers played their opening game at Sportsman's Park in St. Louis. [Dixie] Walker said he might go on strike himself then and enlist some other Dodgers to join. It began to look as though on the sixth of May seven Cardinals and several key Dodgers would refuse to take the field with Jackie Robinson. Nor did the scheme stop there. Some Phillies might join the strike. [Philadelphia's racist manager] Ben Chapman did not stand alone. The best pitcher in baseball, Ewell 'the Whip' Blackwell of Cincinnati, didn't care for integration. He could be recruited. As the Cardinals traveled the circuit, the rednecked ballplayers began loosely to organize a league-wide strike."

—**Roger Kahn,** *The Era,* **1993**

"If you do this (strike) you will be suspended from the league. You will find that the friends you think you have in the press box will not support you, that you will be outcasts. I do not care if half the league strikes. Those who do it will encounter quick retribution. All will be suspended and I don't care if it wrecks the National League for five years. This is the United States of America and one citizen has as much right to play as another. . . . You will find if you go through with your intention that you have been guilty of complete madness."

—**Ford Frick, National League president, letter to the St. Louis Cardinals to prevent a strike by players who didn't want to play on the same field as Robinson, May 1947**

"Frick was proclaimed a hero. . . . Woodward's story was praised far and wide as one of the most important pieces of journalism ever to grace a sports page. But in the days after the *Herald Tribune* story appeared, and for years to come, players up and down the Cardinal roster denied any conspiracy. They denied everything in the story, in fact. Breadon labeled the Woodward article 'ridiculous.' Manager Eddie Dyer called it 'absurd.' Burt Shotton didn't believe it either."

—**Jonathan Eig,** *Opening Day: The Story of Jackie Robinson's First Season,* **2007**

"As for the Cardinals—and this is important to me—some of the world champions didn't like it, but *none* conspired to strike against Robinson. The team, many of them still my friends, received an unfair rap."

—**Bob Broeg, long-time writer for the** *St. Louis Post-Dispatch,* **who always insisted there was no strike conspiracy,** *Bob Broeg: Memories of a Hall of Fame Sportswriter,* **1995**

"You don't always lynch a man by hanging him from a tree. There is a great lynch mob among us and they go unhooded and work without the rope. . . . They lynch a man with a calculated contempt, which no court of law can consider a crime. Such a venomous conspiracy is the one now trying to run Jackie Robinson out of organized baseball. It does not go for all the ball players and not even all the St. Louis Cardinals, some of whom are accused of trying to arrange a strike to protest against the presence of a Negro in the big league. But such a state exists and we should all be ashamed of it, not only those connected with the sport, but anyone who considers this his country. . . . Baseball is supported by the people and I have heard them demand justice for Robinson. If their applause is any indication, they ask that Robinson be accepted as an athlete and is entitled to the right to be judged by the scorer's ledger and not by the prejudices of indecent men."

—**Jimmy Cannon,** *New York Post,* **May 13, 1947**

"The National League stands firmly behind Jackie Robinson."

—**Ford Frick, quoted in** *Sporting News,* **May 1947**

"Rickey was motioning for me to pick up the extension phone. 'Herb Pennock is calling from Philadelphia,' he whispered. 'I want you to hear this.' '[You] just can't bring the nigger here with the rest of your team, Branch,' I heard Pennock [the suave, silver-thatched general manager of the Phillies] saying, 'We're not ready for that sort of thing yet. We won't be able to take the field against your Brooklyn team if that boy Robinson is in uniform.' 'Very well, Herbert,' replied the always-precise Rickey. 'And if we must claim the game nine to nothing, we will do that, I assure you.'"

—**Harold Parrott, Dodgers traveling secretary and publicist in 1947,**
The Lords of Baseball, **1976**

"Our players often weren't told what was going on. When we went to Philadelphia on the first road trip, the bus picked us up at the train depot and stopped at the Benjamin Franklin Hotel. After a few minutes we were told that we were going directly to the ballpark and not checking in. After the game, we checked into the Warwick Hotel, a much plusher place. . . . (Only forty years later would I learn that the Benjamin Franklin Hotel had turned us away because of Robinson.)"

—**Spider Jorgensen, Dodgers third baseman, recalling the beginning of Robinson's**
first road trip with the Dodgers to the City of Brotherly Love, to Danny Peary,
We Played the Game, **1994**

"They fooled me. I thought it would be St. Louis and *Cincinnati*."

—J. R., being sarcastic about being denied a room at the Benjamin Franklin in
Philadelphia, Time magazine, September 22, 1947

"Happy Chandler wrote [Phillies manager Ben] Chapman and warned him there must be no repetition of what had taken place in Brooklyn. The next time the Dodgers met the Phillies, in Philadelphia [for a four-game series May 9–11], Robinson and Chapman posed together for a spurious picture. Presumably, Chandler and Ford Frick, National League president, had ordered the photo to offset bad publicity from the previous Dodgers-Phillies series."

—Tim Cohane, *Look* magazine, January 6, 1948

"It was Herb Pennock . . . who asked me to have a picture made with Robinson because the *New York Times* had requested it. I didn't ask for it 'to save my job.'"

—Ben Chapman, Phillies manager, to Wayne Martin, *Sporting News*,
March 24, 1973

"Local photographers and newspapermen engineered a meeting between Robinson and Chapman, with the two posing together in front of the Philadelphia dugout in apparent good nature. In the view of one veteran ball player, who need not be named, the good nature was hardly real."

—Roscoe McGowan, *Sport* magazine, September 1947

"Chapman allegedly refused to shake Robinson's hand in the picture (and vise versa for Robinson), so the two posed holding a bat."

—Joe Vallee, philly2philly.com, April 15, 2013

"I swear I never thought I'd see ol' Ben eat s**t like that."

—Dixie Walker, quoted by Harold Parrott, *The Lords of Baseball*, 1976

"It was one of the most painful moments ever. Deep in my heart, I couldn't forgive Chapman and the Phillies for what they did."

—J. R.

"Players would get on him more than any other player in baseball. I don't think white players worried about losing their jobs to black players if Robinson succeeded. Some were just concerned about the ending of segregation. Some players were staunch rednecks. And some fans were hostile. There was fear of someone being hurt, shot. . . . In Philadelphia, the park wasn't far from the black community and blacks filled the stands to see him. We thought of white players being shot by black fans and Robinson being shot by white fans. In Shibe Park we had to go through the crowd to get into our clubhouse and get to the field. For the visitors' clubhouse, they had to go under the stands and through a hallway. We had tight security."

—Andy Seminick, Phillies catcher, to Danny Peary, *We Played the Game,* 1994

"We had clubhouse meetings about Robinson. . . . He played first that year so players couldn't try to take him out sliding into second. . . . We'd still say, 'Try to get him!'"

—Del Ennis, Phillies outfielder, to Danny Peary, *We Played the Game,* 1994

"May 9, 1947—In his first game outside of New York City, Jackie Robinson has two hits and scores twice in the Dodgers 6–5 loss to the Phillies. After the game, the Dodgers give their young first baseman a vote of confidence by selling Howie Schultz, Robby's back up, to the Phils for $50,000. On May 10, Branch Rickey [will announce] he's giving up his attempts to pry [star first baseman] Johnny Mize away from the Giants."

—*The Baseball Chronology,* edited by James Charlton, 1991

"Learning to play first base and trying to break into the big leagues at the same time was probably the biggest problem of my career. . . . I never thought I'd be successful."

—J. R., *Jackie Robinson: My Own Story,* as told to Wendell Smith, 1948

"It is my belief that Robinson is a big leaguer of ordinary ability. . . . It is a tribute to his solidness as a man that he hasn't fallen apart as a ball player. Less heart has burned better ball players out of the big leagues."

—Jimmy Cannon, who didn't yet understand that Robinson's talent matched his heart, *New York Post,* May 13, 1947

"Jackie had a spot on the right side [of the clubhouse at Ebbets Field], a little two-by-four. It was not as large as the other lockers of the regulars on the Dodgers. He was really almost all by himself on the other side of the clubhouse. I guess it was because we had a few guys from the Deep South and Rickey wanted to keep them apart. . . . The only fellows who spoke to him in real conversations were Pee Wee Reese and Gil Hodges, and they became good friends. Jackie would go out and take practice and go into this little cubicle when the game was over and get dressed. He wouldn't say a word, and then he'd go about his business."

—Lee Scott, reporter for the *Brooklyn Times,* about Robinson's first locker, to Harvey Frommer, *Rickey and Robinson,* 1982

"HE IS THE LONELIEST MAN I HAVE EVER SEEN IN SPORTS."
—JIMMY CANNON, *NEW YORK POST,* MAY 13, 1947

"It's isn't too tough on me. I have played with white boys all my life. But they hadn't played with a Negro before, and it sure was rough on them."

—J. R. to his high school coach, about his Dodgers teammates' slow acceptance of him, excerpt from letter, 1947

"Robinson was rarely seen in public off the field. He stayed in his hotel room even for meals. I remember it was considered a momentous event when he came down to the Kenmore dining room and had breakfast at the same table with a teammate named Don Lund."

—Bill Roeder, *New York World-Telegram and Sun,* January 8, 1957

"When I [was traded] to Brooklyn in May, Jackie would not take a shower with the other players. He always waited and he showered last. . . . Most of the old Dodgers ignored me, when I came over from Pittsburgh, like I didn't belong. I said to Jackie, 'You know, they're treating you a little like they're treating me and, hey, we're *both* members of this team. Jackie, let's go shower together. If those Southern guys don't want to be in a shower with you—with you and me, Jackie—let 'em get the hell out."

—Al Gionfriddo, Dodgers five-feet-six outfielder who arrived in a deal for pitchers Kirby Higbe of South Carolina and Cal McLish of Oklahoma—who had opposed Robinson's signing in spring training—and would forever be known for robbing Joe DiMaggio of an extra base hit in the '47 World Series, to Roger Kahn, *The Era,* 1993

"Al Gionfriddo had a hearts game going in 1947 and Jackie was in it and they asked and I said, 'Yeah, I'll play.' Somebody said to me, 'Damn. How can you sit and play cards with *that* guy?' I said, 'What the hell's wrong with playing with a guy on your own team?'"

—**Pee Wee Reese to Roger Kahn,** *The Boys of Summer,* **1972**

"For Robinson, each game was not just a battle but a crusade. . . . His teammates would watch him come into the locker room . . . and prepare himself emotionally as he pulled up his long blue socks and laced his shoes. . . . His mood darkened. He made little or no effort to find friends among his teammates. . . . He withdrew, even at times from his wife."

—**Jonathan Eig,** *Opening Day: The Story of Jackie Robinson's First Season,* **2007**

"He was the kind of person who, if he had things bothering him, he'd be unusually quiet. He was not stormy and he wasn't tearful. He wasn't shaky. Just very quiet. You had a feeling that he was figuring it out. . . . I learned that about him in those early days. Let him work that out quietly on his own."

—**Rachel Robinson to Jonathan Eig,**
Opening Day: The Story of Jackie Robinson's First Season, **2007**

CLASSIC MOMENT: MAY 13, 1947, CROSLEY FIELD, CINCINNATI, OHIO

"After Robinson arrived [in Cincinnati], the abuse began with hate mail and death threats. The bigots threatened to kill Robinson's wife, Rachel, and kidnap his newborn son, Jack Jr."

—**Matt McHale,** *Pasadena Star-News,* **April 10, 1947**

"We are going to kill you if you attempt to enter a ball game at Crosley Field."

—**Anonymously written threat received by Robinson when he arrived in Cincinnati, April 1947**

"There had been a sack of mail for Robinson at our hotel, and I went through it the morning we hit town. Three of the letters contained threats that Jack would be shot in his tracks if he dared take the field. I handed these over to the FBI, which . . . searched every building that overlooked [Crosley Field] and would afford a sniper a shot at Number 42. Usually I didn't show Robbie the hate mail . . . but this time I had to warn him, and I could see he was frightened. I passed the word to Pee Wee, who was the captain, and to a couple of the other solid players on the club."

—Harold Parrott, Dodgers traveling secretary, *The Lords of Baseball*, 1976

"The record for our National Anthem they played that day had the sound of bombs bursting in air, and the thought occurred to me that that precise moment would have been the ideal cover for gunfire. . . . But we got through that all right, and through the top of the first, too, in which Jackie was the third out. The crowd was still buzzing from its first look at the black man in action when our team ran onto the field from the first-base dugout. Reese stopped at first for a few last-second words with Robbie. As he hid his mouth behind his gloved left hand the way ballplayers talk, Pee Wee put his right arm around Robinson's shoulders. The silence that hit those stands where the fans had been buzzing a second before was truly deafening. Their boy had put his arm around a nigra!"

—Harold Parrott, Dodgers traveling secretary, *The Lords of Baseball*, 1976

"REESE RESPONDED TO VILE RANTINGS FROM A CINCINNATI FAN BY WALKING OVER TO ROBINSON ON THE FIELD AND CASUALLY DRAPING HIS ARM AROUND JACKIE."

—LESTER RODNEY, SPORTS EDITOR OF THE *NEW YORK DAILY WORKER*, EXCERPT FROM PAPER PRESENTED AT THE JACKIE ROBINSON ANNIVERSARY CONFERENCE, LONG ISLAND UNIVERSITY, BROOKLYN CAMPUS, APRIL 1997

"Robbie told me later that that gesture by Reese was the first big breakthrough and meant as much to him as any single bit of approval or acclaim that was to come to him in the ten years that followed. . . . Well, it drove the Cincinnati players right through the ceiling, and you could have heard the gasp from the crowd as he did it."

—Rex Barney, quoted by Peter Golenbock, *Bums*, 1984

"You can hate a man for many reasons; his color isn't one of them."

—Pee Wee Reese, Dodgers shortstop and future Hall of Famer, telling reporters why he openly put his arm around Robinson's shoulder

"Many people insisted that Reese was making a public gesture to show he had accepted Jackie, thus paving the way for other Dodgers to do the same. That's funny because Pee Wee said the gesture was something he hadn't given any thought to. . . . It never was said that Pee Wee Reese was the protector of Jackie Robinson. Jackie didn't need any goddamn protector. He needed somebody to understand. Pee Wee understood, or tried to."

—Don Newcombe, Nashua pitcher, to Danny Peary, *We Played the Game*, 1994

"Pee Wee kind of sensed the sort of helpless, dead feeling in me and came over and stood beside me for a while. He didn't say a word, but he looked over at the chaps who were yelling at me and just stared."

—J. R., quoted by Arnold Rampersad, *Jackie Robinson: A Biography*, 1997

"I saw the [Robinson-Reese] incident in Cincinnati. . . . That kind of drama, how do you measure it?"

—Lester Rodney, founding sports editor of the *New York Daily Worker*, who was on the only road trip the *Daily Worker* permitted him to take that year

"Rodney said he would kick himself years later for not writing about what he had seen. But no one else wrote about it either; not in New York, not in Cincinnati, not in white papers, not in black—not in 1947. In fact, the *New York Post* called Robinson 'the toast of the town' after that game and the *Cincinnati Enquirer* reported that he was 'applauded every time he stepped to the plate.' Robinson, in his weekly column, called his visit to Crosley field 'a nice experience.' . . . In the days and weeks after the game, no newspaper stories placed Robinson and Reese together on the diamond. No photos of the incident were ever identified. . . . In a book written many years later, Robinson . . . set the drama in Boston in 1948."

—Jonathan Eig, dismissing the famous story as being partly fiction, *Opening Day: The Story of Jackie Robinson's First Season*, 2007

"There were times when I went over to talk to him on the field thinking that people would see this and figure we were friends and this might help Jack. And there were times when he was on his own."

—Pee Wee Reese to Roger Kahn, *The Boys of Summer*, 1972

ROBINSON AND GREENBERG: A COMMON BOND

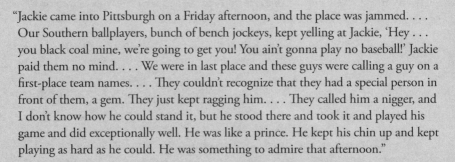

"Jackie came into Pittsburgh on a Friday afternoon, and the place was jammed. . . . Our Southern ballplayers, bunch of bench jockeys, kept yelling at Jackie, 'Hey . . . you black coal mine, we're going to get you! You ain't gonna play no baseball!' Jackie paid them no mind. . . . We were in last place and these guys were calling a guy on a first-place team names. . . . They couldn't recognize that they had a special person in front of them, a gem. They just kept ragging him. . . . They called him a nigger, and I don't know how he could stand it, but he stood there and took it and played his game and did exceptionally well. He was like a prince. He kept his chin up and kept playing as hard as he could. He was something to admire that afternoon."

—**Hank Greenberg,** *Hank Greenberg: The Story of My Life,*
edited by Ira Berkow, 1989

"That afternoon, Hank Greenberg . . . was disappointed that his own manager, Billy Herman, had told his pitchers to throw at Robinson if the count ran to three-and-oh. . . . In [that] game, Robinson bunted and sped for first. Pirates pitcher Ed Bahr fielded the ball but hurried his throw wide of the bag. Hank reached out his mitt and collided with Robinson. The ball eluded Hank. Jackie stumbled and fell. The crowd hushed. Black men were not supposed to smash into white men, especially aging superstars. Many critics of the Robinson experiment anticipated just such a moment to touch off a race riot."

—**John Rosengren, author of** *Hank Greenberg: The Hero of Heroes,*
to Bruce Markusen, *Detroit Athletic Co. Blog,* **June 12, 2013**

"The next time Jackie came down to the sack, Hank said, 'I forgot to ask you if you were hurt in that play.'"

—**Associated Press, May 17, 1947**

"You're doing fine. Keep your chin up."

—**Hank Greenberg to Robinson, quoted by Robinson,** *Pittsburgh Courier,*
May 24, 1947

"Knowing Robinson had been the lightning rod for wretched behavior from opposing players, Hank made a point of giving him words of encouragement. I watched them closely as they spoke quietly and later learned Hank told him, 'I know what you're going through. I went through it as a Jewish ball player [in the 1930s with the Detroit Tigers]. Just hang in there and you're going to be all right.' Afterward Jackie said that Hank was the first opposing player to offer support and acknowledged it meant a great deal to him. Hank even asked him out to dinner in that conversation. Robinson turned him down because he didn't want Hank to be put on the spot, but they remained friends."

—Ralph Kiner, Pittsburgh outfielder and future Hall of Famer who was the 1947 NL co-home run champion, *Baseball Forever*, 2004

"I HAD FEELINGS FOR HIM BECAUSE THEY HAD TREATED ME THE SAME WAY. NOT AS BAD, BUT THEY MADE REMARKS ABOUT MY BEING A SHEENIE AND A JEW ALL THE TIME."

—HANK GREENBERG, *HANK GREENBERG: THE STORY OF MY LIFE*, EDITED BY IRA BERKOW, 1989

"Class tells. It sticks out all over Mr. Greenberg."

—J. R., Associated Press, May 17, 1947

"In a way it was sad that he was so educated because [it] made it difficult for him to accept a role of a subhuman being in a world where he felt he was an equal. . . . Jackie had it tough, tougher than any ballplayer who ever lived."

—Hank Greenberg, *Hank Greenberg: The Story of My Life*, edited by Ira Berkow, 1989

"We were always friends after that [conversation at first base], even though he was in the National League and I went back to the American League as a club executive after that season."

—Hank Greenberg, *Hank Greenberg: The Story of My Life*, edited by Ira Berkow, 1989

"He was going to be in Wrigley Field for the first time. . . . I had to see Jackie Robinson, the man who was going to somehow ruin baseball, so . . . another kid and I started walking to the ball park early. . . . By noon, Wrigley Field was almost filled. The crowd outside spilled off the sidewalk and into the streets. . . . I had never seen anything like it . . . a record, more than 47,000. . . . In 1947, few blacks were seen in downtown Chicago, much less up on the white North Side at a Cub game. That day, they came by the thousands, pouring off the north-bound Els and out of their cars. . . . Robinson came up in the first inning. I remember the sound. . . . They applauded, long, rolling applause. . . . Robinson didn't get a hit or do anything special, although he was cheered on every swing and every routine play."

—Mike Royko, about Robinson's debut in Chicago's Wrigley Field on May 18, 1947, in a 4–2 Brooklyn victory in which he which he went 0-for-4 with an error, *Chicago Daily News*, October 25, 1972

"ROBINSON PLAYED FIRST AND EARLY IN THE GAME A CUB STAR HIT A GROUNDER AND IT WAS A CLOSE PLAY. JUST BEFORE THE CUB REACHED FIRST, HE SWERVED TO HIS LEFT. AND AS HE GOT TO THE BAG, HE SEEMED TO SLAM HIS FOOT DOWN HARD AT ROBINSON'S FOOT. IT WAS OBVIOUS HE WAS TRYING TO RUN INTO HIM OR SPIKE HIM. ROBINSON TOOK THE THROW AND GOT CLEAR AT THE LAST INSTANT. I WAS SHOCKED. THE CUB, A HOME-TOWN BOY, WAS MY BIGGEST HERO. IT WAS NOT ONLY AN UNHEROIC STUNT, BUT IT SEEMED A RUDE THING TO DO IN FRONT OF PEOPLE WHO WOULD CHEER FOR A FOUL BALL. . . . I DIDN'T KNOW THAT, WHILE THE WHITE FANS WERE RELATIVELY POLITE, THE CUBS AND MOST OTHER TEAMS KEPT UP A STEADY STREAM OF RACIAL ABUSE FROM THE DUGOUT."

—MIKE ROYKO, *CHICAGO DAILY NEWS*, OCTOBER 25, 1972

"Somewhere between Chicago and St. Louis, Robinson and Smith got word that they might not be welcome at the Chase Hotel, where the rest of the Dodgers planned to stay. . . . May 20, Robinson checked into the Deluxe Hotel, where the manager of the hotel turned over the keys to his own Cadillac, and told Robinson to use it as much as he liked."

—Jonathan Eig, *Opening Day: The Story of Jackie Robinson's First Season*, 2007

"Poor Jackie had to go to the other hotel. That's pretty hard to live with. But that never changed his personality or his thoughts about the game. When the game started, that first pitch he was all ball player and all man."

—Eddie Stanky, Dodgers second baseman

"Robinson was cheered each time he went to bat and the Dodgers as a team received more vocal encouragement than they usually got at Sportsman's Park."

—St. Louis Post-Dispatch, about Robinson's first game in St. Louis before a crowd of 16,249, the largest for a weekday day game that season at Sportsman's Park, including an estimated six thousand African Americans, May 22, 1947

"In the top of the first inning [of the Dodgers' lone game in St. Louis in May], Robinson showed patience, working a walk from Harry 'the Cat' Brecheen, the Cards' best pitcher, and went to third on a single by Reiser. When Carl Furillo cracked a ground ball to first, Stan Musial grabbed it and stepped on the bag. . . . He could see that Robinson was staying put, so he . . . threw to second, hoping to catch Reiser there for the double play. When Musial pivoted, Robinson, taking a chance, broke for home, scoring the first run of the game. . . . Robinson went hitless in the game, but his aggressive base-running in the first inning proved important as the Dodgers won it, 4–3."

—Jonathan Eig, *Opening Day: The Story of Jackie Robinson's First Season*, 2007

"Pitchers hit Robinson with fastballs six times in his first thirty-seven games. Once a week he had to take a 90-mile-an-hour baseball in the ribs or in the arm. And he was agile. He was hard to hit. If Robinson complained, no one heard him. He played the game."

—Roger Kahn, *The Era*, 1993

"No pitcher ever made me back up. *Not one.* And they all tried."

—J. R. to Roger Kahn, *The Boys of Summer*, 1972

"I don't know how he took it, to be frank. . . . I remember guys from other teams kidding Jackie. 'Hey, you have your watermelon today?' Or somebody trying to stick the baseball in his ear. Or yelling, 'You black bastard!' . . . Terrible. . . . He had to block all that out, block out everything but this ball that is coming in at a hundred miles an hour. . . . To do what he did has got to be the most tremendous thing I've ever seen in sports."

—Pee Wee Reese to Roger Kahn, *The Boys of Summer*, 1972

"Plenty of times, I wanted to haul off when somebody insulted me for the color of my skin, but I had to hold onto myself. I knew I was a kind of experiment. If I blew my top right in the beginning, when some people were just waiting for trouble, the whole thing might blow up. If I lost my chance—the whole thing was bigger than me—the Negro might lose his chance, too."

—J. R. to Jean Evans, *New York Post*, September 20, 1947

"I'll never forget how frightened I was for Jackie Robinson, how we were frightened because we knew that if he made the normal mistakes that any ballplayer made it would be a reflection on his race. We felt, oh God, he must perform magnificently or those white players will scorn him."

—Lena Horne, famed singer from Brooklyn, Sunday supplement *PM*, 1947

"I think every black person in the country held his breath hoping Jackie would succeed."

—K. C. Jones, fifteen-year-old Texan who would become a basketball
Hall of Famer, *Rebound*, 1986

"He felt disappointed at times, disillusioned, frustrated, down. But he would pick himself up. He was very resilient, very determined and really stubborn. . . . He was going to make it work."

—Rachel Robinson

"Whatever obstacles I found made me fight all the harder. But it would have been impossible for me to fight at all, except that I was sustained by the personal and deep-rooted belief that my fight had a chance. . . . My fight was against the barriers that kept Negroes out of baseball. This was the area where I found imperfection, and where I was best able to fight. And . . . it was my faith in God that sustained me in my fight."

—J. R., recorded essay, Edward R. Murrow's radio series *This I Believe*, 1952

"WE USED TO READ THINGS IN THE PAPER ABOUT THE HATE MAIL AND PEOPLE TRYING TO GET HIM OUT OF BASEBALL, AND THE PHONE WOULD RING AND WE WOULD BE AFRAID TO PICK IT UP. WE USED TO THINK IT WOULD BE A CALL FROM SOMEBODY SAYING JACKIE WAS DEAD. JACKIE'S MAMA WAS SCARED ALL THE TIME, BUT SHE WOULDN'T REALLY EVER LET ON. SHE JUST PRAYED HE WOULD BE ALL RIGHT AND SHE TRUSTED IN GOD. . . . THERE WERE LOTS OF TIMES WE JUST THOUGHT HE SHOULD COME HOME AND COACH AT A BLACK SCHOOL AND BE DONE WITH IT. BUT THAT WASN'T JACK. HE WAS DETERMINED TO DO IT SO HE DID IT."

—WILLA MAE ROBINSON WALKER TO MAURY ALLEN,
JACKIE ROBINSON: A LIFE REMEMBERED, 1987

"In a very real sense, black people helped make the experiment succeed. . . . It was one thing for me out there on the playing field to be able to keep my cool in the face of insults. But it was another for all those black people sitting in the stands to keep from overreacting when they sensed a racial slur or an unjust decision. They could have blown the whole bit to hell by acting belligerently and touching off a race riot. That would have been all the bigots needed to set back the cause of progress of black men in sports another hundred years. . . . But this never happened."

—J. R., *I Never Had It Made,* **as told to Alfred Duckett, 1972**

"I live in a small all-Negro town. We go to Memphis for all our amusements, but there is no greater thrill than a broadcast of the Dodgers baseball game. . . . Right now the farmers are gathering [at the store] for your game this afternoon."

—**Bernice Franklin, owner of a general store in Tyronza, Arkansas, and one of countless blacks across the country who became Dodgers fans, 1947**

"After just one road trip, I saw the quality of Jackie the man and the player. I told Mr. Rickey I had changed my mind and I was honored to be a teammate of Jackie Robinson."

—**Bobby Bragan, Dodgers catcher and a signer of the petition, mlb.com, 2005**

"Nobody ever came to the big leagues under less favorable circumstances, and he handled himself beautifully and he played like a demon. He was one of the greatest ballplayers ever to come down the pike."

—**Bobby Bragan, Dodgers catcher and future major league manager, to Donald Honig, The Man in the Dugout, 1977**

"[Robinson] has finally become relaxed and is playing the kind of ball that earned him his major league chance."

—**Burt Shotton, Dodgers manager**

J. R. NOTE: In April, Robinson's 0-for-20 slump resulted in a .225 average, but he batted .284 in May and, buoyed by a career-high twenty-one-game hitting streak, hit a robust .377 in June to erase all doubts that he was a worthy major leaguer.

"The time has come to recognize Jackie Robinson . . . as a major league ballplayer who has come through under extreme pressure to become an important factor in the Dodgers' rise to the National League lead."

—Associated Press, during Robinson's twenty-one-game hitting streak, June 27, 1947

"I don't think anyone in that league or ours had any idea that when put to the test [Robinson] had the ability to become such a tremendous all-around player. . . . A fire raged inside him constantly, and that was so clear to everyone."

—Ralph Kiner, Pirates outfielder and Hall of Famer, *Baseball Forever,* 2004

"Fans, black and white, were learning to recognize his tics—the way he held his bat high and wiped his hands on his pants between pitches, the way he seemed to swing down on the ball, as if to pound it into submission. Robinson's steady play [with his average over .300 in early June] was keeping the Dodgers in the pennant hunt, and it even earned him his first endorsement opportunity. Bond Bread . . . reportedly offered him five hundred dollars to pose for pictures that would run in some city newspapers."

—Jonathan Eig, *Opening Day: The Story of Jackie Robinson's First Season,* 2007

"My favorite at 'home plate' is that good Bond Bread. It tastes grand and packs lots of energy!"

—J. R., product endorsement on the back of thirteen promotional Robinson trading cards distributed with loaves of Bond Bread, 1947

"The Rickey policy . . . of attempting to keep Robinson out of the limelight has cost the player a great deal of money. Until almost midseason Jackie has been denied the privilege of endorsing any product . . . nor was he allowed to appear on radio programs. . . . One exception for radio was made early in the year when Jackie was a guest on *Information Please,* all profits from that appearance going to a Negro college fund."

—Roscoe McGowan, *Sport* magazine, September 1947

"When Jackie Robinson joined the Dodgers in 1947, there was no better player in the league. He was the toughest out and there would be no better competitor during my career. . . . All professional ballplayers had to admire him. We all kept an eye on him, watching his progress. It didn't matter if we rooted for him to make it, which many of us did, because he was going to make it in spite of everything."

—Bill Rigney, Giants shortstop and future manager, to Danny Peary, *We Played the Game,* 1994

"IT WAS NAIL-BITING TIME. IF JACKIE HAD NOT BEEN ABLE TO STAND UP UNDER THE PRESSURE, I DON'T KNOW . . . WHERE IT WOULD HAVE GONE FROM THERE. BUT HE WAS A GREAT BALLPLAYER, A DYNAMIC BALLPLAYER, AND EVERY DAY THAT HE PLAYED HE PUSHED THAT DOOR OPEN JUST A LITTLE WIDER FOR THE REST OF US WHO WERE WAITING TO GET THROUGH."

—MONTE IRVIN, TWENTY-SEVEN-YEAR-OLD OUTFIELDER IN THE NEGRO LEAGUES WHO SIGNED WITH THE NEW YORK GIANTS IN 1949 AND BECAME A HALL OF FAMER, TO DONALD HONIG, *BASEBALL BETWEEN THE LINES*, 1976

"I was happy when Jackie Robinson broke the major league color barrier because it opened the doors for Latin players, as well as American blacks."

—Chico Carrasquel, the first Venezuelan shortstop in the majors with the 1950 White Sox and the first Latin American to start in the All-Star Game, to Danny Peary, *We Played the Game*, 1994

"I became one of the stars in Cuba and was signed to a contract by the New York Cubans in the Negro National League. . . . When Jackie Robinson signed to play in the major leagues, many players in the Negro Leagues thought they had the opportunity also. I wanted to play in the major leagues and prove that I was one of the best ballplayers."

—Minnie Minoso, who, after debuting with the Indians in 1949, would become the first Latin American star in the major leagues playing for the White Sox, to Danny Peary, *We Played the Game*, 1994

"Before 1947, I had three guys I could talk about in the major leagues—Ted Williams, Stan Musial, and Joe DiMaggio—but from then on, I had Jackie. When Jackie played for Brooklyn that year, I knew I had a chance to play in the majors, too. All I had to do was keep playing, keep playing, and wait for my chance."

—Willie Mays, New York Giants outfielder beginning in 1951 and future Hall of Famer

"By the time the Dodgers visited St. Louis on June 12, several Cardinals made a point of welcoming Robinson as the Dodgers took the shortcut from their clubhouse to the field through the Cardinals' dugout. . . . The Cardinals were on their best behavior for a while."

—George Vecsey, *Stan Musial*, 2011

"You get him mad, he'll beat you by himself. So I told my players to take it easy."

—Eddie Dyer, Cardinals manager, to St. Louis sportswriter Bob Broeg,
June 12, 1947

"[What] a swell bunch of fellows. They treated me so nice I was actually surprised."

—J. R., about Stan Musial, Joe Garagiola, and the rest of the Cardinals on the
Dodgers' June visit to St. Louis, to Wendell Smith, *Pittsburgh Courier*, June 1947

"Jackie Robinson's little-known role as a columnist for the *Pittsburgh Courier* . . .
[was] one prong of a . . . public relations campaign by ['Robinson Says' ghostwriter
Wendell] Smith designed to ensure Robinson's success with the Dodgers and
to leave no doubt in anyone's mind that [he] belonged in Brooklyn. . . . The
persuasive goals of the column perhaps explain why Robinson's accounts lack any
real indication of the horrors of that first season or of the real possibility that he
could fail. . . . The column's wide-eyed enthusiasm celebrated his introduction
to the Dodgers' clubhouse [and] both Robinson and Smith eagerly praised the
Cardinals in June. . . . Robinson's columns for the rest of the season followed
suit, focusing on the action on the field rather than relations with teammates or
experiences in ballparks on the road."

—Brian Carroll, associate professor in Department of Communication
at Berry College, *Journalism History* journal, Fall 2011

"I was with the Cubs, and . . . Bobby Sturgeon was . . . a utility infielder . . . and
when Jackie first came up, Sturgeon said, 'I'll get that son of a bitch.' So Jackie
got on in the third inning and [then] the ball was hit to the second baseman, Don
Johnson, and Johnson made a quick relay, and Sturgeon [playing short] didn't even
try for the double play. He threw the ball right into Jackie's chest. Jackie didn't say
a word. . . . About six weeks later, we came to Brooklyn. . . . Jackie got on base,
and on the first pitch, he takes off, and Sturgeon was playing short, and Jackie
didn't slide. He threw a block at Sturgeon and knocked him halfway into left field.
Busted two of his ribs. Jackie didn't say a word, and neither did Sturgeon. That was
a ballplayer retaliating in his own way."

—Russ Meyer, who would pitch for the Cubs and Phillies before joining the
Dodgers, to Peter Golenbock, *Bums*, 1984

"According to Robinson, the only club he has to 'look out for' is Chicago. . . .
In a recent series Len Merullo, Cub [first-string] shortstop, roughed Robinson
unnecessarily. 'I'm pretty sure Merullo is looking for trouble,' Jackie said."

—Bill Roeder, *New York World-Telegram*, July 3, 1947

"Possibly [Robinson's] most outstanding feat was the occasion against the Chicago Cubs [on June 18] when . . . Jackie broke from first base as Gene Hermanski bunted. As the pitcher threw out Hermanski, Jackie went past second, and on to third as he saw Stan Hack drawn off the base. The throw to Hack was hurried and Robinson blazed for the plate. He crossed it safely for a most amazing running exhibition."

—Excerpt from bio sketch on back of Swell Sports Thrills baseball card, number three, 1948

"At Forbes Field in Pittsburgh, there were about thirty thousand in the stands for a night game [on June 24, 1947]. Close to a third of them were black. The score was tied 2–2 [in the fifth inning], with Robinson on third base. Fritz Ostermueller was the pitcher. Dancing off the base, Robinson ran down the third-base line about ten yards toward home plate, and then ran back to third. [Ostermueller] turned his head and went into the full-wind up position. Jack broke for home and stole it. . . . Robinson's steal gave the Dodgers a . . . victory."

—Harvey Frommer, about Robinson's first steal of home in the major leagues, *Rickey and Robinson*, 1982

"In the years to come, the steal of home would become Robinson's calling card. He would pull off the trick nineteen times in his career. . . . But for Robinson, it wasn't the quantity that counted so much as the style. . . . The play meant a great deal to Robinson, and even more to his fans. It spoke of both the fearlessness with which he carried himself and the fear he inspired. . . . The steal of home was his special weapon, the switchblade in his pocket."

—Jonathan Eig, *Opening Day: The Story of Jackie Robinson's First Season*, 2007

"Robinson was a topic of conversation among players throughout his first year. . . . The veterans would say, 'He has a lot to learn,' as they did with all rookies. We would mostly talk about his running. He was the first of many Negro leaguers who would bring an exciting run-through-the-base style of baseball to the National League."

—Ralph Kiner, Pirates home-run champion and future Hall of Famer, *Baseball Forever*, 2004

THE MOST DARING BASERUNNER SINCE TY COBB

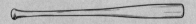

"You've heard all those stories about Ty Cobb? Well, that's the closest thing to Ty Cobb I ever saw. Jackie Robinson."

—Cy Perkins, Phillies coach who had played against Cobb

"Robinson is closer to [Ty] Cobb in his baseball technique than any of the modern players. There have been base runners since Ty and before Jackie who upset pitchers, but nobody since Cobb, except Robinson, who upset entire ball clubs."

—Tom Meany, *Sport* magazine, 1949

"He dances and prances off base, keeping the enemy's infield upset and off balance, and worrying the pitcher. The boys call it 'showboat baseball.' He is not, in his first year, the greatest baserunner since Ty Cobb, but he is mighty good. Cobb made a practice of coming in with spikes aimed at anyone brave enough to get in his way. It wouldn't have been politic for Jackie to do it that way very often. Robinson's base running, which resembles more the trickiness of 'Pepper' Martin, is a combination of surprise, timing and speed. Says Jackie: 'Daring. . . . that's half my game.'"

—*Time* magazine, September 22, 1947

"If he was a runner at first and a sacrifice was in order, I never saw him go to second and stop, he would keep right on going to third. It got to the point where [Jackie would] bunt, and the third baseman would field it, and he'd stand there and hold it to stop him from going to third. . . . He'd get on first and take such a big lead that the pitcher would throw to first, and he'd go to second. . . . His first fifteen to twenty feet was the quickest you've ever seen. I've seen him round first base after a hit to right field, and the right fielder would bluff a throw back to first base, and he'd go right into second. And so the fans . . . would go wild . . . because they knew he was going to do something."

—Rex Barney, Dodgers pitcher, to Peter Golenbock, *Bums*, 2000

"FOR THOSE WHO WATCHED ROBINSON IN ACTION, IT WAS WORTH EVERY CENT THEY PAID. AT TIMES, THE STYLE WITH WHICH HE PLAYED APPEARED TO BE A CASE OF TRICK PHOTOGRAPHY. HE WAS AN ILLUSIONIST IN A BASEBALL UNIFORM, A MAGICIAN ON THE BASE PATHS. THE WALKING LEADS, THE FOOTBALL-LIKE SLIDES, THE CHANGE-OF-PACE RUNS—ALL WERE A PART OF ROBINSON'S APPROACH TO THE GAME."

—HARVEY FROMMER, *RICKEY AND ROBINSON*, 1982

"He was on first one time, and there was a pickoff play, and the ball got away and rolled not more than six feet from me. He saw where the ball was a split second before I did, and that's all he needed. By the time I picked it up I didn't even have a play at second on him. That's how quick he was. Unbelievable reflexes. And alert, always alert."

—**Elbie Fletcher, Pirates first baseman, to Donald Honig,** *Baseball When the Grass Was Real*, 1975

"Breaking, Robinson reached full speed in three strides. The pigeon-toed walk yielded to a run of graceful power. He could steal home, or advance two bases on someone else's bunt, and at the time of decision, when he slid, the big dark body became a bird in flight. Then, safe, he rose slowly, often limping, and made his pigeon-toed way to the dugout."

—**Roger Kahn,** *The Boys of Summer,* 1972

"The focus of the game had to do with the fear of his stealing. It doesn't tell you how many pitchers threw fastballs rather than curves, keeping him on, to guys who could hit the fastball. And it didn't matter what base he was on. . . . And once in a while he'd steal home with the Dodgers five runs ahead, and he would stick it to you."

—**Roger Kahn, to Peter Golenbock,** *Bums,* 1984

"The rundown was his greatest play. Robinson could start so fast and stop so short that he could elude anyone in baseball, and he could feint a start and feint a stop as well."

—**Roger Kahn,** *The Boys of Summer,* 1972

"He was the only player I ever saw in a rundown who could be safe more often than out. He ran as if his head was on a swizzle, back and forth, back and forth, until he could get out of it."

—**Bobby Bragan, Dodgers catcher**

"Jackie was so quick, so elusive, that even seasoned major league players looked like inept amateurs trying to catch him. Then, most often, Jackie would find a way to weave and dodge all tags and arrive safely on the base."

—**Carl Erskine, Dodgers pitcher,** *Carl Erskine's Tales from the Dodger Dugout,* **2000**

"Even when Robinson was caught off base, he was dangerous. Opposing players used to say that trying to catch him was like trying to bottle mercury."

—**Harvey Frommer,** *Rickey and Robinson,* **1982**

"Robinson could make a rundown play into an Agatha Christie mystery—will he or won't he? He would dash around until he escaped the rundown and allowed his base-running mates to move up. His steals of home were breathtaking and his fake steals, as he charged down the line at third base, would electrify that gang of faithful fans at Brooklyn's Ebbets Field."

—**Maury Allen,** *Baseball's 100,* **1981**

"I was playing second base this day and Jackie, on third, made a feint as if to break for the plate. I cocked my arm but before I could even throw, he . . . was sliding across with a run."

—**Hank Aaron, Braves future Hall of Famer and the majors' all-time home run and RBI leader, quoted by Red Foley,** *New York Daily Mirror,* **October 28, 1972**

"Jackie Robinson was the best base runner I ever saw, not only when stealing bases but also taking the extra base. He had such great instincts, and if you made any kind of mistake on him in the outfield, like double-pumping or not throwing the ball correctly, he would take advantage of that."

—**Hank Aaron,** *The Tim McCarver Show*

"He was fantastic on the bases. He could make a good rifle arm look bad. If you threw behind him, to first, on that big turn of his, he'd be standing on second base, smiling."

—**Billy Martin, Yankees second baseman and future manager, quoted by Dick Young,** *New York Daily News,* **July 19, 1977**

"Robinson could steal a base any time he wanted. When Bob Rush pitched, I said, 'Why don't we just put Robinson on third base and get it over with?' Because with Rush pitching, he'd steal second and third on two pitches. With his first step he was going full blast."

—Hank Sauer, Cubs outfielder, to Danny Peary, *We Played the Game*, 1994

"He sent them running to their rule books after executing one of his unpredictable gambits. In the top of the ninth inning against the Cubs, with the score tied 1–1, he worked the count to three and two and then walked. While the Chicago catcher was disputing the base on balls with the umpire, Robinson loped down to first base, touched it, and then dashed to second and slid in safely. A lengthy argument followed, but there was nothing in rule book against stealing second on a walk. Robinson moved to third on a sacrifice, and then a sacrifice fly brought him home. His alert steal won the game for the Dodgers."

—Harvey Frommer, *Rickey and Robinson*, 1982

"ROBINSON MAY HAVE BEEN THE MOST EXCITING PLAYER OF ALL-TIME; HE WAS A DEADLY BATTER, A GREAT CLUTCH HITTER, A MARVELOUS SECOND BASEMAN, AND THE MOST THRILLING BASERUNNER THE GAME HAS EVER SEEN."

—MAURY ALLEN, *BASEBALL'S 100*, 1981

"With Red Barber calling the action in 1947, Robinson came to life for fans in the best possible way. When he finally started to hit, he became a hero, his color not a factor. In person, Robinson could be irritating. He was standoffish at times. But over the radio, he was all action."

—Jonathan Eig, *Opening Day: The Story of Jackie Robinson's First Season*, 2007

"I didn't actually attend a ball game until the middle of that 1947 season. It was a night game at Ebbets Field, and the Dodgers were playing the Giants. . . . Jackie Robinson was conspicuously dark among all the white players, but what you soon fixed on was his quickness and grace, in the field and at bat. Baseball, I saw, was a kind of ballet, with continually improvised movements, and Robinson was its premier danseur. His stance at the plate was deep, the bat held high. He'd rub one hand on his hip, then grip the bat again, and I wondered if this was a nervous habit, if he was only wiping off his sweaty palm. After he reached base, with a hard line drive to left, he dodged and danced and bluffed going, to the crowd's delight and the pitcher's distraction. And he eventually did steal second, running swiftly in his distinctive, pigeon-toed gait, then sliding in to just beat the throw. So this was baseball!"

—Hilma Wolitzer, novelist, remembering a seminal day of her youth,
***Cult Baseball Players*, edited by Danny Peary, 1990**

"If Jackie Robinson was the ideal man to break the color line, Brooklyn was the ideal place."

—Bill Veeck Jr., Cleveland Indians owner who signed black ballplayers in the late forties, including Larry Doby, Satchel Paige, Minnie Minoso, and Luke Easter

"The Dodgers had no national appeal without Brooklyn. Brooklyn was the essential, perfect, diverse place for Jackie Robinson's courageous destruction of many of the bigoted myths about race. And for many people, and more than a few even today, part of Brooklyn's essence was the Dodgers."

—Thomas Oliphant, *Praying for Gil Hodges*, 2005

"Before each game, white kids stood on the sidewalks around Ebbets Field selling pins that read 'I'm Rooting for Jackie Robinson.' After each game Robinson would dash from the stadium to the subway to avoid the mobs of autograph hunters. . . . In Brooklyn he was doing fine."

—Jonathan Eig, *Opening Day: The Story of Jackie Robinson's First Season*, 2007

"I always thought of Brooklyn as special. Jack said that also. Brooklyn fans were incredible in terms of their interest and their support, and their willingness to come back even when things weren't going well. There was such tremendous pride demonstrated to us. You'd feel it, and hear it when people talked, and see it with the large attendance. There was an increase in the number of black fans that attended, so it enriched the fan base for us, certainly."

—Rachel Robinson to Danny Peary, 2012

"Which one is Jackie?"

—**Ignorant new white baseball fan**

"The signing of [Larry] Doby by Cleveland is a good thing for everybody. . . . I'm glad to know another Negro player is in the majors. I'm no longer in there by myself. I no longer have the feeling that if I don't make good it will kill the chances of other Negro players. . . . We'll try to act and play in such a way that the owners will sign Negro players."

—**J. R., writing in his Wendell Smith–ghosted column about the American League's first black player,** *Pittsburgh Courier,* **July 1947**

"The only difference between what I went through and what Jackie went through in 1947 is that Jackie deservedly got all the publicity, because he made it possible for me to be part of it. . . . I'm not knocking the media for writing only about Jackie because there was no need to write about me having a tough time, too, when it's assumed I'm going through the same situation. In fact one of the reasons I admired Jackie is that from my own experiences, I knew what he was going through without Jackie having to tell me. We weren't going to stay in certain hotels or eat in certain restaurants, but Jackie and I had no need to talk about that stuff, so [when we'd see each other] we'd talk most about which players were riding him, and I'd tell him the players who gave me a tough time."

—**Larry Doby, Indians outfielder and future Hall of Famer who broke the color barrier in the American League on July 5, 1947,** *The Tim McCarver Show*

"Jackie Robinson went through a lot. We all went through a lot. It wasn't easy being a black man in America in 1947."

—**Larry Doby to Maury Allen,** *Jackie Robinson: A Life Remembered,* **1987**

"One of the things he was very clear about was that being first was wonderful, but it didn't mean anything unless there was a second and a third and a fourth."

—**Rachel Robinson, quoted by Kevin Baxter,** *Los Angeles Times,* **November 17, 1996**

"If he wanted to, Mr. Rickey could have cornered the Negro market. He not only had Jackie but had the inside track on fellows like Monte Irvin and Larry Doby, too. But he decided that other ballclubs interested in acquiring Negroes should get a chance at them. That's how Bill Veeck was able to bring Doby to Cleveland and Irvin eventually became a star with the Giants."

—**Mickey McConnell, scout and aide to Branch Rickey, quoted by Red Foley,**
New York Daily Mirror, **October 28, 1972**

"The two pioneers—Robinson and Rickey—could . . . take heart from the slowly growing acceptance of other Negro players that summer. All told, sixteen black men appeared in organized ball during 1947, about half of them on minor-league clubs of the Brooklyn organization."

—**Robert Peterson,** *Only the Ball Was White,* **1970**

"Dan Bankhead, who was purchased from Memphis, Tennessee, was brought up by the Dodgers [on August 26] to become the first black pitcher in major league history. . . . He was a pretty good pitcher who struck out a lot of batters, but I think he was brought in mostly as a companion for Jackie . . . the only black player in the league. The American League's first black was former Newark Eagles star Larry Doby, who joined the Indians in July. Then the St. Louis Browns brought up Hank Thompson and Willard Brown. All these men were talented, but it says something that only Jackie Robinson had a good year in 1947."

—**Don Newcombe, Nashua pitcher, to Danny Peary,** *We Played the Game,* **1994**

"If they only knew how much I was pulling for these guys to make good!"

—**J. R., annoyed that fans compared him to the blacks who came to the majors after him as if they were rivals, to Jack Sher,** *Sport* **magazine, October 1948**

"Any resentment that anybody had [before about his signing] left them because it soon became apparent that there wasn't any way we were going to win without Jackie. . . . And I'll tell you, Jackie won the respect of everybody by sheer guts and ability."

—**Bobby Bragan, Dodgers catcher and future major league manager, to Donald Honig,** *The Man in the Dugout,* **1977**

"The Dodgers have accepted him so placidly that Robinson admits he is surprised. . . . 'They all try to help me. Eddie Stanky is always showing how to play hitters and . . . Dixie Walker . . . took the trouble to explain to me when to bunt and when to swing away. No matter what you might have heard, Dixie has been fine with me.'"

—**Bill Roeder, passing on Robinson's rosy midseason report,** *New York World-Telegram,* **July 3, 1947**

"Robinson was then very cautious in his relations with most of his teammates, and especially with Southerners, and he did not speak unless spoken to. . . . Jackie told me some years afterward, Walker did speak to him. The two of them happened to be standing on the sidewalk in front of the Hotel Kenmore in Boston . . . and Walker volunteered some batting tips that helped Jackie break a slump."

—**Bill Roeder,** *New York World-Telegram and Sun,* **January 8, 1957**

"I think in 1947, I was on base three times when Walker hit a home run. But I never stopped to home plate and offered a hand. Why not? I thought Walker would not take my hand. Then we would have had the beginnings of an incident."

—**J. R., in response to those who believed he didn't shake Walker's hand as a vengeful protest against bigotry, to Roger Kahn,** *Rickey & Robinson,* **2014**

"For all his fiery nature, Jack never was a vengeful man."

—**Roger Kahn,** *Rickey & Robinson,* **2014**

"[Beginning] on July 22 in Cincinnati . . . for twelve days and nights . . . the team put together a thirteen-game winning streak. Robinson in that stretch scored sixteen runs (a whopping 21 percent of the team's total), banged thirteen hits, walked nine times, hit two home runs, yet his name never appeared in a *Daily News* headline or in the first paragraph of a story. . . . While on the road in July, [Dick] Young did find time to bang out a couple of feature stories, one of them about the contenders in the National League for the Rookie of the Year award. Even then, he managed to slight Robinson, rating his teammate Spider Jorgensen as the top candidate. . . . Young never revealed his feelings, but all season long he avoided writing meaningfully about Robinson."

—**Jonathan Eig,** *Opening Day: The Story of Jackie Robinson's First Season,* **2007**

"I am positive that Dick wrote the way he did because he didn't particularly like me."

—**J. R., who would always have a complex, difficult relationship with the** *Daily News'* **Dodgers beat writer, Dick Young**

"Some reporters write nice things about me and mean them, and others write nice things and don't mean them. I can always tell."

—J. R., 1947

"This summer of our Lord 1947, the Dodgers are doing right with Jackie Robinson at first. . . . And maybe if the Dodgers win the pennant, a hundred years from now history will be grinning."

—Langston Hughes, African American poet, fiction writer, columnist, and social activist, *Chicago Defender,* 1947

"Just when the Dodgers thought they had locked up the pennant, the Cardinals went on a terrific run, closing the gap [to five games]. Their sluggers Enos 'Country' Slaughter and Stan Musial were slugging again. . . . The Cardinals came to Brooklyn saying they needed to win at least three of four [August 18–20]. . . . In the first game, the Cards sent Howie Pollet to the mound. . . . [Batting second, Robinson] hit a high fastball . . . into the left-field bleachers, for his ninth homer of the season. . . . In the fifth, Pollet . . . lost connection with the strike zone, walking Stanky and Robinson to open the inning. The Dodgers scored five runs and cruised to the win."

—Jonathan Eig, *Opening Day: The Story of Jackie Robinson's First Season,* 2007

"[Enos] Slaughter hit a grounder to Robinson, who decided not to try to force Musial at second but instead stepped on first base for the sure out. However, as Robinson turned to check on Musial at second, Slaughter's spikes raked down against the back of his right leg, just above the heel. Robinson jumped around in pain before seeking treatment from the trainer, Harold Wendler."

—George Vecsey, about a controversial spiking that occurred in the eleventh inning on August 20, 1947, as the Cards won 3–2 to split the four-game series, *Stan Musial,* 2011

"[That was] one of the lousiest things I've seen in baseball."

—Eddie Stanky, Dodgers second baseman, August 1947

"I've never deliberately spiked anyone in my life. Anybody who does don't belong in baseball. It was an accident, pure and simple. I hope it is not serious."

—Enos Slaughter, Cardinals outfielder and future Hall of Famer, Associated Press, August 21, 1947

"This veteran had sped across first base perhaps five thousand times in his 10-year career without disabling anybody."

> —**Harold Parrott, Dodgers traveling secretary in 1947,** *Sporting News,*
> **February 3, 1973**

"In St. Louis, Robinson got spiked again. Catcher Joe Garagiola almost tore one of his shoes off. He didn't get cut this time. But he had to go to the dugout for a new shoe. When he got up to bat, Umpire Beans Reardon asked him: 'Did you get cut?' 'No, I didn't,' Robinson said. Then he added, nodding toward Garagiola, 'But it wasn't his fault I didn't.' Garagiola came back at him, and they jawed at each other."

> —**Tim Culhane, about Robinson being confrontational for a rare time in 1947 during the crucial series against the Cardinals,** *Look* **magazine, January 6, 1948**

"For a moment, it looked like the men might fight. But Clyde Sukeforth, the Brooklyn coach, rushed from the dugout to pull Robinson away. When the game resumed, Robinson swung at a belt-high fastball and popped out to end the inning. The fracas with the Cardinal catcher made an angry man of Robinson— never a good thing for Dodger opponents. In his next trip to the plate, Robinson . . . banged it deep into the left-field seats to tie the score."

> —**Jonathan Eig, about the Dodgers' 4–3 victory,** *Wall Street Journal,*
> **March 31, 2007**

"I CAN HARDLY WAIT FOR AN UMPIRE TO THROW ME OUT OF A GAME BECAUSE THAT'LL SHOW THAT I'M BEING TREATED LIKE EVERYBODY ELSE."
—J. R. TO JIM BECKER, ASSOCIATED PRESS, 1947

"Burt Shotton managed the Dodgers for the season of 1947. He was always kind and helpful to me and a great man to work for."

> —**J. R., about the manager who took the Dodgers to the World Series but, unlike Durocher might have, didn't take the spotlight off Robinson,** *Jackie Robinson: My Own Story,* **as told to Wendell Smith, 1948**

"[Shotton] simply ignored the terrible racial tension tormenting Jackie Robinson."

> —**Roger Kahn,** *The Era,* **1993**

"The coming of Jackie Robinson brought a seething turbulence that was waiting to explode. Shotton saw to it that serious internal trouble didn't break loose."

—**Red Barber, Dodgers broadcaster,**
1947: When All Hell Broke Loose in Baseball, **1982**

"If you were Jackie Robinson, you would probably feel a twinge of loneliness once in a while. On train trips you might play a game of hearts now and then with three other ballplayers who look upon you as just a nice kid. But mostly you'd sit and stare out the window. Occasionally you might eat at the same hotel dining room table with another Brooklyn player. But mostly you'd eat by yourself. The games of hearts, and the infrequent meals with a teammate, along with the conversation in the clubhouse, would make up most of your social contacts with the older Dodgers. You would be among them, rather than of them."

—**Roscoe McGowan, who, despite Robinson's traveling all year with Wendell Smith, restated Jimmy Cannon's supposition that the black rookie was the loneliest man in baseball,** *Sport* **magazine, September 1947**

"In 1947, Jack wasn't looking for people to come pat him on the back, or have a Coke with him. Socializing was not that important to him. I think given the climate and the forces that were not in favor of integration, what he was looking at then was how he could contribute to the team as a player, and his welfare was secondary. Because he knew that he was a good player, he understood that he could hold his own on the team and be part of a winning process."

—**Rachel Robinson to Danny Peary, 2012**

"He knew that if he made a mistake in 1947 and that safety valve on his emotions shot off, Branch Rickey would call the whole thing off. Were it not for a beautiful woman named Rachel Robinson, his wife, he would have exploded. He had to keep everything inside of him because, like the rest of us, he felt obligated to Rickey. Jackie wasn't the type who could do that. I know it took a toll on him."

—**Don Newcombe, Nashua pitcher, to Danny Peary,** *We Played the Game,* **1994**

"MY WIFE HAS MEANT EVERYTHING TO ME. SHE HAS INSPIRED ME ALL THE TIME, PUSHING ME ON, ENCOURAGING ME WHEN THINGS LOOKED BLACK, AND ALWAYS ASSURING ME THAT I COULD DO ANYTHING ANY OTHER BALL PLAYER COULD. I DO NOT BELIEVE I COULD HAVE MADE THE GRADE WITHOUT HER HELP."

—J. R., *JACKIE ROBINSON: MY OWN STORY,* **AS TOLD TO WENDELL SMITH, 1948**

"Sometimes I must reinforce my belief that it was a collaboration between Jackie and Branch, a pairing of two men who needed to respect and trust each other so that they could make it work. They talked sporadically, usually about something that was coming up that they had to plan together. It was frequent at certain stages, early on in particular, and it was in person. Jack would go to his office. Occasionally, I would be invited to sit in and observe. I loved seeing Jackie and Branch together."

—Rachel Robinson, about how Rickey helped Robinson through difficult times, to Danny Peary, *Gil Hodges,* Tom Clavin and Danny Peary, 2012

"Wives aren't allowed to travel with the team. Jackie and his wife, Rachel, preferred long-distance telephoning to writing. On the Dodgers' last road trip, they ran up a $28 phone bill in two weeks."

—Tim Culhane, *Look* magazine, January 6, 1948

"Fortunately for Robinson, Rickey ruled out all personal appearances at banquets and socials during the season. This allowed Jackie to spend evenings at home with Rachel and one-year-old Jackie Jr."

—Tim Culhane, *Look* magazine, January 6, 1948

"Jackie lives [with Rachel] a long way from Harlem's high life, in a five-room, second-floor on Brooklyn's MacDonough Street, in a Negro neighborhood. His name is not on the door, and he knows few of his neighbors. How he feels about them shows through the guarded brevity of his speech, which sometimes carries a suggestion of dryness."

—*Time* magazine, September 22, 1947

"I don't want to bother with too many people who want to be my relatives."

—J. R., quoted about his decision to keep to himself, *Time* magazine, September 22, 1947

"Playing in more games than any other Dodger in 1947, Robinson scored more runs than any other teammate, stole more bases than any other player in the National League, and wound up with a batting average of .297. . . . It was an extraordinary season for a man playing under unimaginable pressure."

—Harvey Frommer, *Rickey and Robinson,* 1982

"Jackie's nimble/Jackie's quick/Jackie's making the turnstiles click."

—Wendell Smith, *Pittsburgh Courier* sportswriter and Robinson's ghostwriter and companion during the 1947 season, 1947

"Jackie Robinson has pulled about $150,000 extra admissions this season."

—*Time* magazine, September 22, 1947

"Wherever Jackie played, he drew large crowds. He became the biggest attraction in baseball since Babe Ruth. Robinson put serious money into the pockets of every National League owner."

—Red Barber, making a claim about Robinson's drawing power that would be argued about for decades, Dodgers broadcaster, *1947: When All Hell Broke Loose in Baseball*, 1982

"It is regularly written that Jackie Robinson . . . was a boon to attendance at Ebbets Field. In 1946, the all-white Brooklyn Dodgers drew 1,796,824 at home. With Jackie Robinson in 1947, the integrated Dodgers drew 1,807,526. The difference, about 11,000 spectators, works out to 150 fans a game."

—Roger Kahn, *The Era*, 1993

"IN ROBINSON'S INITIAL SEASON, THE BROOKLYN DODGERS SET ROAD ATTENDANCE RECORDS IN EVERY NATIONAL LEAGUE PARK, EXCEPT CINCINNATI'S CROSLEY FIELD."

—LARRY LESTER, BASEBALL HISTORIAN, LARRYLESTER42.COM

"In 1947, Brooklyn went 90–64, going 52–25 in the friendly confines of Ebbets Field, to win the pennant by 5 games over the Cardinals. . . . They clinched on September 22, and the celebration continued on the twenty-third, when 'Jackie Robinson Day' was held at Ebbets Field and he received a car and entertainer Bill 'Bojangles' Robinson presented Jackie with an inscribed gold wristwatch from Tiffany's. The Robinsons also received a television, cash, and other gifts."

—Tom Clavin and Danny Peary, *Gil Hodges*, 2012

"That was one of the most touching moments of Jack's career . . . to see Mother right there in the middle of the ceremony and all the accolades."

—Mack Robinson to Harvey Frommer, *Rickey and Robinson*, 1982

"I am sixty-nine years old, but I never thought I would live to see the day when I would stand face to face with Ty Cobb in Technicolor."

—Bill "Bojangles" Robinson, famed African American entertainer who, in 1935, with Shirley Temple, performed the first interracial dance in film history in *The Little Colonel*, September 23, 1947

"I thank you all. . . . I especially thank the members of the Dodgers who were so cooperative and helpful in helping me improve my game."

—J. R., acknowledging his teammates at Jackie Robinson Day, September 23, 1947

"Among those gathering near home plate to honor him was Dixie Walker."

—Tom Clavin and Danny Peary, *Gil Hodges*, 2012

"Me being a Southern boy and raised in the South, it wasn't easy for me to accept. At that time I was resentful of Jackie and I make no bones about it. But he and I were shaking hands at the end."

—Dixie Walker, Dodgers outfielder

"No other player on this club, with the possible exception of Bruce Edwards, has done more to put the Dodgers up in the race than Robinson has. He is everything Branch Rickey said he was when he came up from Montreal."

—Dixie Walker, Dodgers outfielder, quoted by Harvey Frommer, *Rickey and Robinson*, 1982

"Walker forgot all about his objections. Here was a cracker from the South who hated everything black, but he changed when Jackie helped him get into the World Series and make some extra money."

—Don Newcombe, Nashua pitcher, to Danny Peary, *We Played the Game*, 1994

"I wasn't traded; I stayed with the club all year, and we won the pennant and got into the World Series. . . . Being Jackie's teammate was one of the best breaks I ever got. Watching what he had to go through . . . helped make me a better, more enlightened man, and it helped me to have a future in baseball as a manager . . . of other black players. . . . It was a breakthrough for me."

—Bobby Bragan, Dodgers catcher and future major league manager, to Donald Honig, *The Man in the Dugout*, 1977

"I had started the season as a lonely man, often feeling like a black Don Quixote tilting at a lot of white windmills. I ended it feeling like a member of a solid team. The Dodgers were a championship team because all of us had learned something. I had learned how to exercise self-control—to answer insults, violence, and injustice with silence—and I had learned how to earn the respect of my teammates. They had learned that it's not skin color but talent and ability that count. Maybe even the bigots had learned that, too."

—J. R., *I Never Had It Made,* as told to Alfred Duckett, 1972

"I was told . . . when I was a rookie ball player that the only way I was going to succeed was if my teammates picked up the ball and carried it. They did."

—J. R., *This Week* magazine, October 12, 1969

J. R. NOTE: Jackie Robinson became the first African American to be on the cover of the national weekly magazine *Time*, on its September 22, 1947 issue. In May 1950, he would be the first African American on the cover of *Life* magazine.

"On September 26, the sidewalks on Flatbush Avenue were packed as a seventeen-car motorcade proceeded to Borough Hall. There [twenty-seven] Dodgers received watches, praise, and cheers, and a teary Jackie Robinson and Dixie Walker spoke gratefully about the support they had from the best fans in the world."

—Tom Clavin and Danny Peary, *Gil Hodges,* 2012

"[After the] ticker-tape parade . . . he received the [first-ever National League] Rookie of the Year award from J. G. Taylor Spink, the owner of the *Sporting News.* As he accepted it, close observers could see the tears in Robinson's eyes."

—Peter Golenbock, excerpt from paper presented at the Jackie Robinson anniversary conference, Long Island University, Brooklyn Campus, April 1997

"Robinson was rated and examined solely as a freshman player in the big leagues—on the basis of his hitting, his running, his defensive play, his team value. The sociological experiment that Robinson represented, the trail-blazing that he did, the barriers he broke down did not enter into the decision."

—J. G. Taylor Spink, editor of the *Sporting News,* explaining why Robinson was chosen by the paper as the 1947 National League Rookie of the Year

"But there ought to be another citation for Jackie Robinson, based on the very factors with which *Sporting News* did *not* concern itself. Not only did Jackie prove himself to be a great baseball player, he also established the Negro in Major League Baseball. That achievement took more than fine playing. It took courage, self-control, and the ability to take punishment for the sake of a long-range objective."

—Jean Evans, *New York Post,* September 20, 1947

"We had a 1936 Ford and that's the car we still had in 1947 when Jack played for Brooklyn and five of us drove cross-country to see him play."

—Mack Robinson about how Jackie's family always drove to New York to watch him when he played in the World Series, to Maury Allen, *Jackie Robinson: A Life Remembered,* 1987

"ON SEPTEMBER 30, 1947, THE YANKEES SQUARED OFF AGAINST THE DODGERS. IT WAS THE FIRST WORLD SERIES A BLACK MAN EVER PLAYED IN."
—HARVEY FROMMER, *RICKEY AND ROBINSON,* 1982

"We knew the Dodgers had outstanding, hustling players like Pee Wee Reese and Jackie Robinson. And Rex Barney was one of the fastest pitchers I have hit against. But we weren't worried about them."

—Billy Johnson, Yankees third baseman, to Danny Peary, *We Played the Game,* 1994

"At the beginning of the World Series of 1947, I experienced a completely new emotion, when the National Anthem was played. This time, I thought, it is being played for me, as much as for anyone else. This is organized Major League Baseball, and I am standing here with all the others; and everything that takes place includes me."

—J. R., recorded essay, Edward R. Murrow's radio series *This I Believe,* 1952

"When I stood near home plate with the Dodgers and Yankees as Guy Lombardo's band played the National Anthem before the game, it was the biggest moment of my life."

—J. R., quoted by columnist and Pirates home-run champion Ralph Kiner, *Pittsburgh Press,* June 5, 1952

"The Dodgers made it clear they figured I was the weak link on our club. They had good speed in fellows like Jackie Robinson and Pee Wee Reese and Pete Reiser, and they had the guts to use it. They came right out and said they were going to run on me, and then they went ahead and did it."

—Yogi Berra, Yankees catcher and future Hall of Famer, *Yogi,* 1961

"Robinson flashed the razzle-dazzle style that had boggled National League pitchers all season. He walked in the first inning, and then stole second. He walked again in the third inning. This time, his dancing moves off first base so unnerved Yankee pitcher Spec Shea that he balked Robinson to second base."

—Harvey Frommer, *Rickey and Robinson,* 1982

"In the sixth game [on October 5] . . . Robinson, always a zealous player, strayed a little beyond zealotry and threw a rolling football block on Phil Rizzuto when the little Yankee shortstop had gotten out of the baseline after completing a double play. There was a little booing, and then the incident, like the inning, was over."

—Heywood Hale Broun, sportswriter and broadcaster, *Cult Baseball Players,* edited by Danny Peary, 1990

"I feel real sorry about hurting Rizzuto. He's the last guy in the world I'd want to take a shot at, him being so small and such a nice guy. When the play happened I went right back to the dugout, but on the bases later on I told him I was really sorry."

—J. R., upset about upending Rizzuto with a hard slide into second base during the Dodgers' Series-tying Game 6 victory, quoted by Bill Roeder, *New York World-Telegram,* October 6, 1947

"Later in the game, [Joe] DiMaggio hit a routine grounder to Pee Wee Reese, who threw over to Robinson, an inexperienced first baseman who put his right foot across the bag, an invitation to a legal and painful spiking, which DiMaggio managed to avoid with a sideways leap."

—Heywood Hale Broun, sportswriter and broadcaster, *Cult Baseball Players,* edited by Danny Peary, 1990

"I thought about [stepping on Robinson's foot] running down to first base, and then it occurred to me that Phil's an Italian, I'm an Italian, and Robinson is black, and I didn't want them to think it was the guineas against the niggers. If Phil was black or Robinson Italian, I guess I would have done the spiking."

—Joe DiMaggio, Yankees outfielder and future Hall of Famer, to Jimmy Cannon,
***New York Post*, September 30, 1947**

"We had it all the way. We just wanted to give 'em a thrill."

—J. R., making a tongue-in-cheek comment to reporters after Dodgers pinchhitter Cookie Lavagetto amazingly hit a two-run double with two outs in the bottom of the ninth inning to break up Bill Bevens' no-hit bid and beat the Yankees 3–2, to even up the Series at two games apiece, October 3, 1947

"It seemed to me that whenever I looked up out of the dugout during the Series, kids were hanging over the roof asking for autographs."

—J. R., *Jackie Robinson: My Own Story*, as told to Wendell Smith, 1948

"As the Yankees burst onto the field to celebrate [their 5–2 victory in Game 7], the Dodgers slipped quietly off. . . . After the players were all inside, Rickey closed the door and spoke to the team for about fifteen minutes. He said he was proud. He said the men had accomplished a great deal. He said he expected the Dodgers to be even better in 1948. But he made no mention of their greater triumph, [the] acceptance of Jackie Robinson. That wasn't the time or place to speak of moral victories."

—Jonathan Eig, *Opening Day: The Story of Jackie Robinson's First Season*, 2007

"We lost. We got no alibis. We'll get them next year."

—J. R. to reporters, October 6, 1947

"Robinson's seven hits tied him with Reese for the club leadership for the Series. He also played errorless ball in the field and stole two bases. [But] at bat, his performance overall was disappointing."

—Harvey Frommer, about Robinson's .259 average for the seven games,
***Rickey and Robinson*, 1982**

"It was a pleasure to play with you. Thanks for all you've done for me."

—J. R. to his teammates as they came over to him after the World Series, ending his remarkable rookie season, October 6, 1947

> **"WE WON THAT SERIES, BUT WE KNEW THAT WITH ROBINSON IN BROOKLYN, WE'D BE FACING THE DODGERS LOTS OF TIMES IN THE FUTURE."**
>
> **—YOGI BERRA, YANKEES CATCHER**

"Jackie Robinson, star Negro baseball player of the Dodgers, will appear in the film 'Courage' to be made by the Producers Releasing Corp. It was announced today."

—United Press, October 6, 1947

J. R. NOTE: Jackie Robinson's movie acting career hit a snag, resulting in Robinson filing a suit that wouldn't be settled until early 1954. On January 5, 1954, the Associated Press reported: "Jackie Robinson . . . received an award of $14,500 in Brooklyn Supreme Court yesterday in an action brought against a movie producer. . . . Mr. Robinson testified that he had signed a contract with Mr. [Jack] Goldberg in October 1947, to make a movie for $12,500. He said he had gone to Hollywood in January 1948, waiting around for several days, but made no picture, although he had been assured that a story was being developed. The court's verdict includes interest." Robinson would get the chance to star in a movie in 1950, playing himself in a biopic.

"I know that after the 1947 season . . . Rachel took Jackie away on a luxury liner, on an ocean cruise for three weeks, because she was afraid he was going to lose his mind."

—Don Newcombe, Nashua pitcher who would be the first great black starting pitcher in the majors beginning in 1949, *Jackie Robinson: My Story* **(documentary), 2003**

"[Bob] Elliott, 31-year-old third baseman of the Boston Braves, today was designated the Most Valuable Player of the National League for 1947. A committee of 24 did the picking for the Baseball Writers Assn. of America. . . . Jackie Robinson . . . landed fifth place . . . and beat out the home-run slugging [Ralph Kiner]."

—Dan Daniel, *New York World-Telegram*, November 20, 1947

"Jackie Robinson, baseball's rookie of the year, opened a week's engagement at the Million Dollar Theater yesterday."

—*Los Angeles Times,* **about the last leg of Robinson's four-city post-season vaudeville tour, following appearances at the Apollo Theater in New York City, Howard Theatre in Washington, DC, and Regal Theater in Chicago, November 19, 1947**

"He had no business in vaudeville, but the money was too good to resist: three thousand dollars a week plus a percentage of the gate. . . . The critics hated it. Robinson stood before the audience in a suit and tie for about eight minutes, answering prearranged questions. . . . On tour, Robinson attended one honorary banquet after another. He would eat a big dinner, receive a trophy, say a few words and sit down for dessert."

—**Jonathan Eig,** *Opening Day: The Story of Jackie Robinson's First Season,* **2007**

"We ate like pigs."

—**J. R., who put on thirty pounds during the offseason,** *I Never Had It Made,* **as told to Alfred Duckett, 1972**

"His [World Series] share was $4,081.19. His regular season salary was $5,000, four weeks of vaudeville brought him $10,000 and he stood to make about $12,000 from a movie. An autobiography and other items may earn him another $5,000. He hopes to save enough from all this to insure Jackie Jr.'s future."

—**Tim Culhane,** *Look* **magazine, January 6, 1948**

— SEVEN —

Transcending Sports

"In 1948 I expect to earn much more than $5,000 from the Dodgers. I've got to make it quick, because I'm 28, older than most people think. The story about me quitting after three years was wrong. I hope I've got six years of big-league ball ahead."

—J. R. quoted by Tim Culhane, *Look* magazine, January 6, 1948

"The Brooklyn Dodgers will offer Jackie Robinson a 'substantial increase' in salary for the 1948 season and hope to be able to 'announce their 1948 manager before the close of the Major League Baseball meetings on December 10, President Branch Rickey said yesterday."

—Associated Press, November 27, 1947

"For all his great play and success as a box-office attraction, baseball's pioneer was still just a second-year man in Rickey's mind. . . . Rickey offered $12,500 and refused to go higher. Robinson was angry. Rachel was angrier. . . . Yet Robinson, beholden and grateful to Rickey, accepted the offer and told reporters he was satisfied."

—Jonathan Eig, *Opening Day: The Story of Jackie Robinson's First Season*, 2007

"[Billy] Cox became a Dodger [on December 8, 1947], arriving from Pittsburgh along with pitcher Preacher Roe in one of the greatest one-sided deals of all-time. [Former Dodger and future manager] Gene Mauch . . . was also included [with Cox], and Brooklyn sent Dixie Walker and pitchers Hal Gregg and Vic Lombardi to the Bucs. Had not Walker been such a vocal critic of Jackie Robinson's color, the deal would never have come off. Later Dixie would tell me how much he regretted his own thinking; but I would thank him for giving me the joy of seeing Billy Cox play third on a daily basis."

—Larry King, television host and author, *Cult Baseball Players*,
edited by Danny Peary, 1990

"Rickey produced the letter Walker had written during spring training [asking to be traded because of Robinson], failing to mention that Walker had asked for it back [and Rickey refused]. . . . Walker met with Rickey after the 1947 season to ask for a raise. Rickey countered by proposing to cut Dixie's salary from $23,000 to $15,000. . . . Dixie objected . . . and [again] asked to be traded. . . . Rickey [who remembered being hung in effigy by Dodgers fans after he traded the popular Dolph Camilli in 1943] 'knew he'd take a lot of heat if he traded [Walker because of a salary dispute],' [his brother] Harry Walker said. Rickey's solution was to release the letter [and imply Walker had just written it]."

—Larry Powell, offering an alternate version of why Walker was traded, *Southern Cultures* magazine, Summer 2002

"ROBINSON TRAILED ONLY BING CROSBY IN A YEAR-END NATIONAL POPULARITY POLL. VIRTUALLY THE ENTIRE BLACK POPULATION OF AMERICA BECAME DODGER FANS."

—*THE BALLPLAYERS*, EDITED BY MIKE SHATZKIN, 1969

"[In September] Robinson [had received] a pro basketball offer from the Canton Cushites, an all-black team that featured future Football Hall of Fame member Marion Motley and Larry Doby. He declined that offer, but did sneak in 2 games with the professional all-black Detroit Wolverines."

—Black Fives Foundation, about Robinson continuing to play his favorite sport, January 31, 2008

"Now there is a communistic effort to get credit for 'forcing' us to sign Robinson, but I warn you to be on your guard against that thing. . . . Four National League clubs have put out feelers for Robinson—one asking if we were interested in trading him, another asking that he be included in a deal we were making, another asking if we knew where it could find a Negro star, and another showing a decided interest in him."

—Branch Rickey, Dodgers owner and a staunch Republican, giving a speech at the annual football dinner at the Negro college Wilberforce State University in Ohio, February 17, 1948

"Spring training began [in] February in Santo Domingo. Cuba flunked the test of being a friendly site for black ballplayers, and the baseball-crazy Dominican Republic was given an opportunity to do better. Jackie Robinson and Dan Bankhead (who had been disappointing as the majors' first black pitcher in 1947) stayed with the rest of the team at the Hotel Jaragua, and [Roy] Campanella stayed with the Montreal team at a swanky hotel in San Cristobel."

—Tom Clavin and Danny Peary, *Gil Hodges,* **2012**

"Leo Durocher returned from his one-year suspension to manage the Dodgers. . . . Laraine Day came down with Leo, and all the players really liked her. . . . When Robinson came to spring training, Leo got after him in person and in the press to lose some of the weight he gained doing banquets in the off-season. Jackie weighed well over 200 pounds and looked like a balloon. . . . The two of them got after each other pretty good and I think the resentment lasted."

—Spider Jorgensen, Dodgers third baseman, to Danny Peary,
We Played the Game, **1994**

"[Robinson] came to camp hog fat, and I let him know I was unhappy with him, the same as I would have done with anybody else. What really made me mad was that he kept insisting he wasn't overweight. When I finally was able to get him on the scales, the needle went to 216 pounds. The previous year he had come in at 195. 'Not overweight?' I hollered."

—Leo Durocher, *Nice Guys Finish Last,* **1975**

"Durocher ordered Robinson to put on a tan rubber shirt that covered the entire upper body and arms. He stationed Robinson between first and second and hit ground balls to Robinson's right and left. The temperature on the Caribbean field approached 90 degrees. . . . Durocher's ringing voice kept bawling, 'Move it, fat boy, move it.'"

—Roger Kahn, *The Era,* **1993**

"I was wrong to report overweight, but Durocher was wrong to humiliate me, every day, in front of the other ballplayers, in front of the rookies, in front of the sportswriters. To tell the truth, I hated the loud-mouthed bastard."

—J. R.

"Durocher was surprised to learn that his favorite player, Eddie Stanky, was on the trading block. Without consulting his manager, Rickey had decided to move Robinson to second base, his position at Montreal, making 'the Brat' expendable. Stanky was sent to the Braves on March 6. As a result, Durocher seemed to deliberately antagonize Rickey."

—Tom Clavin and Danny Peary, *Gil Hodges,* 2012

"By the time the Dodgers broke camp at Santo Domingo, Robinson had lost fifteen pounds. He remained ten pounds overweight. And he and Durocher were locked in a blood feud that lasted for six years."

—Roger Kahn, *The Era,* 1993

"I was 14 years old when I first saw Jackie Robinson. It was the spring of 1948, the year after Jackie changed my life by breaking baseball's color line. His team, the Brooklyn Dodgers, made a stop in my hometown of Mobile, Ala., while barnstorming its way north to start the season, and while he was there, Jackie spoke to a big crowd of black folks over on Davis Avenue. I think he talked about segregation, but I didn't hear a word that came out of his mouth. Jackie Robinson was such a hero to me that I couldn't do anything but gawk at him."

—Hank Aaron, future career home-run and RBI king and Hall of Famer, *Time* magazine, June 14, 1999

"Not surprisingly, African Americans would continue to gravitate toward Robinson and other black players in Organized Baseball during 1948. . . . Reflecting his massive appeal, black newspapers in 1948 featured an array of advertisements for Robinson products, including photographs, books, Dodger hats, and a publication containing 'Every Hit—Error—Run—Stolen Base—Homer of Jackie Robinson.' Robinson also gained continuous mainstream exposure through endorsement deals and media profiles."

—Neil Lanctot, *Negro League Baseball,* 2004

"For a treat rather than a treatment, I recommend Old Gold cigarettes."

—J. R., a nonsmoker, quoted on the back of Old Gold cigarettes promotional baseball card, 1948

"Brooklyn opened [the 1948 season] against the Giants at the Polo Grounds. Robinson, batting in the leadoff spot, had only one hit in five at-bats, but it was the key blow in Brooklyn's 7–6 win. . . . Robinson was playing his first major league game at second base that afternoon."

—**Lyle Spatz, baseball historian, excerpt from paper presented at the Jackie Robinson anniversary conference, Long Island University, Brooklyn Campus, April 1997**

"The Brooks started poorly. They dropped four of their first seven games against their Eastern rivals, without any Dodger pitcher lasting the full distance. Durocher was an impatient loser. . . . To change a loser to a winner, Durocher reasoned, change a player in the lineup. . . . He . . . benched Jackie Robinson in Boston [indicating] that [his] poor condition was the cause. With Robinson out of the lineup, the Dodger attack sputtered to a new low. The Braves, with Bill Voiselle firing a three-single game, blanked them 5–0. Durocher was frantic. He had played the weak-hitting Gene Mauch in Robinson's place. Now he wanted to switch Billy Cox from third base to second, and put Spider Jorgensen on third. . . . Billy quietly jumped the club and [temporarily] returned home to Harrisburg, Pennsylvania."

—**Dick Young, about Durocher losing control of his team, *Roy Campanella*, 1952**

"The incident Robinson remembers best as illustrating [Pee Wee] Reese's innate decency occurred in Boston . . . shortly after Jackie was shifted to second base. The Boston bench jockeys decided that rather than give Robinson the works, they would goad Reese [about his playing with a black teammate]. . . . For a while Reese ignored the calls. . . . As the calls got louder, however, he strode over to Robinson and put his arm around his shoulder. They talked for a minute in buddy-buddy fashion . . . and the Braves' players fell silent. . . . That ended the race heckling."

—**Carl T. Rowan, about an incident many believe is the basis for the more famous but perhaps fictional story of Reese silencing hecklers in Cincinnati in 1947 by putting his arm around Robinson's shoulders, *Wait Till Next Year*, Carl T. Rowan with Jackie Robinson, 1960**

"It made sense for Robinson to move to second because when he had played there with me in Montreal, he had been much more relaxed than at first base. He had very good hands and rarely booted anything hit his way. Robinson would have an even better year at the plate—he led the team in RBIs—and would also make more contributions as a fielder and as a vocal infield leader. Robinson was much more demonstrative."

—**Spider Jorgensen, Dodgers third baseman, to Danny Peary, *We Played the Game*, 1994**

"IN 1948, ROBINSON WOULDN'T TAKE AS MUCH ABUSE AS HE HAD AS A ROOKIE. NOW HE'D TALK BACK TO UMPIRES AND TALK BACK TO PLAYERS, JUST LIKE OTHER PLAYERS WOULD. HE WAS A TOUGH COOKIE."

—ANDY SEMINICK, PHILLIES CATCHER, TO DANNY PEARY,
WE PLAYED THE GAME, 1994

"In 1948, everyone went after Robinson at second base on force plays. He had one rhythm and it was easy to time him. He took more knocks than Carter had liver pills. But Robinson was agile and strong and avoided getting hurt. He'd also retaliate, using his spikes when he came down on runners and sliding into infielders who had slid hard into him."

—Del Ennis, Phillies outfielder, to Danny Peary, *We Played the Game*, 1994

"We had been told [by Phillies manager Ben Chapman] to slide hard into him as often as we could. . . . I slid into him this one time and really cut him badly. The trainer rushed out second base, and I could see he was bleeding the same color blood as me. I just stood there and felt ashamed of myself, like a real jerk. There was no reason for that. It wasn't part of baseball. The next game we played I walked over to him and apologized for cutting him and told him that it wouldn't happen again. It never did."

—Richie Ashburn, Phillies rookie outfielder and future Hall of Famer from Nebraska who never saw an African American until he was eighteen, to Maury Allen, *Jackie Robinson: A Life Remembered*, 1987

"I heard Chapman and a couple of our Southern players get on Jackie when I first came up. I think it was because he was killing us. One time Chapman was yelling at him, and Jackie came over to our bench after the inning, stuck his face in Chapman's face and said, 'Now let's see how tough you are.' Chapman never moved. Jackie was a big guy, an intimidating presence, and not too many guys wanted to challenge him directly."

—Richie Ashburn, Phillies center fielder and future Hall of Famer, about his manager, who would be fired during the 1948 season, to Maury Allen, *Jackie Robinson: A Life Remembered*, 1987

"He was still a reasonably quiet young man at that stage [but] as the season progressed he became more and more combative. . . . I told him, 'There's a certain percentage of pitchers that are knocking you down because of your color. . . . But I got to . . . say they're pushing you back, most of them, because you're a great athlete and they're afraid of you.'"

—**Leo Durocher, Dodgers and Giants manager in 1948,**
Nice Guys Finish Last, **1975**

"Jack was never told by Branch Rickey that it was a two-year trial. The media had decided that. . . . I thought . . . Rickey would expect Jack to say, 'The conditions are such [now] that I can be myself and not do any damage to the experiment.' Jack changed by the second year; he was no longer taking anything from other players. He'd also now argue with umpires, and I'd try to tell him mentally not to get kicked out of the game because foremost I was a fan who wanted the Dodgers to win."

—**Rachel Robinson to Danny Peary,** *Gil Hodges,*
Tom Clavin and Danny Peary, 2012

"Having served out a year in silence, Jackie apparently felt that he had earned the right to assert himself. Before I left, he was asserting himself with a vengeance. I had no way of knowing that he was the kind of player who—like me—had to be diving and scratching and yelling to be at his best. Maybe he resented my trying to keep a rein on him more than he'd have resented it from anybody else."

—**Leo Durocher, Dodgers and Giants manager in 1947,**
Nice Guys Finish Last, **1975**

A NEW ALLY

"I was a kid pitcher with Fort Worth, a Double A Dodger farm team. . . . I started and pitched well [against the Dodgers in spring training] even though we lost. After the game, Jackie Robinson came over to our bench. He said, 'Young man, I hit against you today. I just want to tell you, with that stuff, you're not going to be in this league very long.' Later in the 1948 season, I was called up to the Brooklyn Dodgers. At Forbes Field in Pittsburgh, the first player to greet me was Jackie Robinson, who put out his hand and said, 'I told you so. You couldn't miss.' He reached out to me in friendship."

—Carl Erskine, Dodgers pitcher from 1948 to 1959, excerpt from paper presented at the Jackie Robinson anniversary conference, Long Island University, Brooklyn Campus, April 1997

"[At Ebbets Field in 1948,] I came out of the Dodger clubhouse after a game and stopped to chat with some of the wives. Among them was Rachel Robinson with Jackie Jr. This was a protected area inside wrought-iron fencing, so the fans were pressing against the fence, peering in as the players came out of the clubhouse. The next day, Jackie came to my locker and said, 'I want to thank you for what you did yesterday. . . . You stopped out there in front of all those fans and talked with Rachel and little Jack.' I said, 'Hey, Jackie, you can congratulate me on a well-pitched game, but not for that.' That was just a natural thing for me to do."

—Carl Erskine, Dodgers pitcher, *Carl Erskine's Tales from the Dodger Dugout*, 2000

"I'll never forget Carl Erskine and how he came to symbolize, at least for me, what a Christian is supposed to be. If Rae or just a Negro friend of mine was around, Carl was never too busy to stop and chat. In difficult times, he seemed by instinct to know the right thing to say. There was no condescension, no conscious effort to be nice, about him. I got the feeling that because of his religious principles and upbringing, race truly meant nothing to Carl."

—J. R., *Wait Till Next Year*, Carl T. Rowan with Jackie Robinson, 1960

"Whenever Jack came to the mound, he always gave me the feeling he knew I could do the job. . . . Times when I wasn't sure I could do it myself, he seemed to be."

—Carl Erskine to Roger Kahn, *The Boys of Summer*, 1972

"Now here's what bothers me. He wins a game. We go to the next town. We're all on the train, a team. But leaving the station, he doesn't ride on the team bus. He has to go off by himself. He can't stay in the same hotel. But I didn't do anything about it. Why? Why didn't I say, 'Something's wrong here. I'm not going to let this happen. Wherever he's going, I'm going with him.' I never did. I sat there like everybody else, and I thought, 'Good. He's getting a chance to play major league ball. Isn't that great?' And that's as far as I was at the time."

—**Carl Erskine to Roger Kahn,** *The Boys of Summer,* **1972**

"It would be Jackie Robinson, the most venerated of the black major leaguers, whose criticisms would prove most damaging [to the Negro Leagues]. After relating to a reporter in February 1948 that 'Negro baseball needs a housecleaning from bottom to top,' Robinson articulated his views more formally in a June article in *Ebony* entitled 'What's Wrong with Negro Baseball.' . . . Robinson's assessment of black baseball . . . demonstrated little sympathy for the previous decades of [financial] struggle to establish the industry [in which blacks could make a living] and largely failed to acknowledge . . . black baseball had achieved a great deal despite substantial odds. . . . The Robinson article and its aftermath dealt yet another heavy blow to black baseball, whose fortunes continued to decline in 1948, particularly in the East."

—**Neil Lanctot,** *Negro League Baseball,* **2004**

"Robinson is where he is today because of organized colored baseball. . . . An apology is due the race which nurtured him—yes, the team and league which developed him."

—**Effa Manley, owner of the financially struggling Newark Eagles and later the first woman inducted into the Baseball Hall of Fame,** *Our World* **magazine, August 1948**

"After Jackie [integrated the majors, the segregated] Negro Leagues was a symbol I couldn't live with anymore."

—**Sam Lacy, who, in 1948, became the first black member of the Baseball Writers Association, fifty years before becoming the first black journalist inducted into the Hall of Fame**

"[Gil Hodges] was switched [from catcher] to first base as a desperation move in June 1948 [when Roy Campanella was brought up from St. Paul to stay]. . . . Durocher switched Hodges abruptly, so abruptly that there wasn't even a first baseman's glove available for him. Gil had to use one of Jackie Robinson's old ones until it was fairly certain that Hodges was on the bag to stay."

—Harold Rosenthal, about Hodges's permanent move to make room for Roy Campanella to catch for the Dodgers, *Baseball Is Their Business,* 1952

"I NEVER SAW A BALLPLAYER WHO COULD DO ALL THE THINGS JACKIE COULD. HE COULD THINK SO MUCH FASTER THAN ANYBODY I EVER PLAYED WITH OR AGAINST. HE WAS TWO STEPS AND ONE THOUGHT AHEAD OF ANYONE ELSE."

—ROY CAMPANELLA, AN INSTANT STAR AND THE MAJOR LEAGUES' FIRST BLACK CATCHER IN 1948 AND A FUTURE THREE-TIME MVP FOR BROOKLYN AND HALL OF FAMER

"Jackie Robinson and Roy Campanella have the trail cleared ahead of them. Both can hit as well as play their positions with great versatility. Both are team players, a rare combination of talents, and in addition, they occupy the singular role of Negroes sparking the morals of white players."

—Dan Burley, *New York Amsterdam News,* June 5, 1948

"Robinson . . . squabbled in the clubhouse with his manager. Since their confrontation in the spring over Robinson's weight, things hadn't improved. Robinson was hitting over .320, but Durocher didn't think he was igniting the offense as he did in '47 and going all out for him . . . and at times he'd bench Robinson for Eddie Miksis, displeasing Rickey. . . . Attendance for home games was way down from 1947, and [Dodgers co-owners] Walter O'Malley and John L. Smith were blaming Durocher's poor public image and his team's lackluster performance. . . . In a bizarre series of events, Rickey fired Durocher and rehired Burt Shotton, and Giants owner Horace Stoneham fired [beloved manager Mel] Ott and, with Rickey's blessing, hired Durocher."

—Tom Clavin and Danny Peary, *Gil Hodges,* 2012

"Leo is a wonderful manager and that statement you read about my being happy to see him go was absolutely untrue. . . . Shotton is the sort of man you love to play for. What I like about him is the way he gets everything over to you in that quiet, confident voice, without hurting your feelings. . . . I think my type of player probably does better under a calmer man, such as Burt Shotton, but that isn't a criticism of Leo Durocher, who was wonderful to me and a fine manager."

—J. R. to Jack Sher, *Sport* magazine, 1948

"Late in July, when the Dodgers caught fire and traveled from seventh to second place, it was the big bat of Jackie Robinson, booming out hits day after day, driving in runs and sparkplugging the team. . . . The majority of fans along the Gowanus Canal will tell you that as Robinson goes, so go the Dodgers."

—Jack Sher, *Sport* magazine, October 1948

"Although Jackie Robinson has yet to throw his first punch in the big leagues, and may never do so, he [now] seems to enjoy rhubarbs. . . . The emotions he kept bottled up last year have gone on public display. Twice within the last few days Jackie has 'had words' with an opponent, once with Bob Rush, a Cub pitcher, and yesterday with Virgil (Red) Stallcup, Cincinnati shortstop. Another time recently he kicked a glove into right field in anger at an umpire's decision."

—Bill Roeder, *New York World-Telegram*, August 9, 1948

"I learned that as long as I appeared to ignore insult and injury, I was a martyred hero to a lot of people who seemed to have sympathy for the underdog. But the minute I began to answer, to argue, to protest, the minute I began to sound off—I became a swellhead, a wise guy, an uppity nigger. When a white player did that, he had spirit. When a black player did it, he was 'ungrateful,' an 'upstart,' a 'sorehead.'"

—J. R., quoted by Peter Golenbock, *Bums*, 1984

"Jackie Robinson always wanted to be treated as 'just another ballplayer' and he had passed another milestone today. In the game with the Pirates last night Jackie was tossed out by an umpire for the first time in his three seasons in organized ball. Butch Henline, the Pirate umpire, ejected Bruce Edwards, Robinson, and Clyde Sukeforth when the Brooklyn bench persisted in taking issue with his balls and strikes."

—*New York World-Telegram*, August 25, 1948

"On August 29, Robinson hit for the cycle against the St. Louis Cardinals, in a 12–7 Dodger win. He homered, tripled, doubled, and after flying out, he singled."

—Larry Lester, baseball historian, about the first game of a doubleheader sweep that brought Brooklyn to within half a game of Boston, larrylester42.com

"Behind [Warren] Spahn and [Johnny] Sain, Boston raced to its first pennant since 1914. . . . The Dodgers slipped to third place, a game behind St. Louis. . . . Robinson had a decent [second] year, batting .296 with twelve home runs and twenty-two stolen bases. . . . Carl Furillo officially led the team in hitting with a .297. It was the first time that neither the Dodgers nor the Giants could boast having a regular hitting .300 since 1907!"

—Marvin A. Cohen, *The Dodgers-Giants Rivalry 1900–1957*, 2000

"Jackie Robinson has been signed by station WMCA to do a six-day-a-week early evening sports [radio] show, it was announced today. The Dodger second sacker will start in early November [and continue until Robinson reports to spring training in March]."

—*New York World-Telegram*, about *The Jackie Robinson Sports Show*, September 28, 1948

"With Jackie Robinson as an added starter, Bob Lemon leads his All-Stars against Satchel Paige and the Kansas City Royals . . . this afternoon at 2:30 at Wrigley Field in a winter baseball exhibition."

—*Los Angeles Times*, October 31, 1948

"Jackie Robinson has just come off a barnstorming trip through the Deep South, the Southwest and the Pacific Coast, and his one observation is: 'It pays.' The Dodgers' second baseman picked up a check which exceeded the winning World Series share of the [victorious] Cleveland [Indians] regulars. With Robinson was Roy Campanella on a team of Negro all-stars. . . . The two Dodgers played eighteen games . . . and now they are back in town doing YMCA work at the Harlem branch. . . . Robinson also does a sports broadcast now each weekday at 7:15, which is indicative of how ballplayers are branching out nowadays."

—Herbert Goren, *New York Sun*, November 1948

"A free trip to the Rose Bowl game is being offered in connection with *The Jackie Robinson Show*. . . . The contest is a variation of the popular giveaway programs and involves the identity of the 'Mystery Singing Athlete.'"

—*New York World-Telegram*, December 22, 1948

"The Dodgers were going on a bus trip and Jackie said, 'Rachel isn't feeling well. Would you call on her and see how she's doing?' I said, 'Have no fear.' I drove over to see her. At the time, they had only one child, Jackie Jr., who I absolutely adored and would hold in my lap at ball games in Brooklyn. I took him and went to the store and got chicken soup and other groceries and brought it to her."

—Joan Hodges, about a kind act she did in Vero Beach during spring training in 1949 that received condemnation from some of the other Dodgers' wives, to Danny Peary, *Gil Hodges*, Tom Clavin and Danny Peary, 2012

"It was spring training in 1949, and there was a little get-together in the clubhouse with the guys who had been there a while, and Jackie said, 'I realize there are some people here who don't like me. I don't like them any more than they like me. I know there are a lot of players in the league who have knocked me down, spiked me, done these things to me, and I put up with it. . . . And from this point on, I take nothing from no one, on this team or on any other team, not from umpires or anyone else.' . . . From 1949 on he was what he wanted to be."

—Rex Barney, Dodgers pitcher, to Peter Golenbock, *Bums,* 1984

"Robinson not only told his teammates how he felt, but he was brave enough to announce it publicly. He was quoted as saying, 'They better be rough on me this year, because I'm gonna be rough on them.' For that statement, Commissioner Happy Chandler called him into his office. Proving he intended to fight back, Robinson responded . . . by asking whether Chandler would have said anything had it been Ty Cobb or any white player making the statement."

—Peter Golenbock, *Bums,* 1984

"Not being able to fight back is a form of severe punishment. I was relieved when Mr. Rickey finally called me into his office and said, 'Jackie you're on your own. You can be yourself now.'"

—J. R., about Rickey formally telling Robinson prior to the 1949 season that he no longer had to restrain himself, *I Never Had It Made,* as told to Alfred Duckett, 1972

"I told Mr. Rickey that if a pitcher hits me intentionally with a fastball, his ass belongs to me. And if a second baseman strikes me intentionally, his ass belongs to me."

—J. R.

"IT'S TRUE I'VE BEEN THE LABORATORY SPECIMEN IN A GREAT CHANGE IN ORGANIZED BASEBALL."

—J. R., JULY 1949

"I once put my freedom into mothballs . . . accepted humiliation and physical hurt and derision and threats to my family in order to do my bit to help make a lily white sport a truly American game. Many people approved of me for that kind of humility. For them, it was the appropriate posture for a black man. But when I straightened up my back so oppressors could no longer ride upon it, some of the same people said I was arrogant, argumentative and temperamental. What they call arrogant is confidence. What they call argumentative, I categorize as articulate. What they label temperamental, I cite as human."

—J. R. to literary agent Michal Hamilburg, excerpt from letter, October 10, 1970

"You'll be a 20-year man in Class D."

—J. R., needling pitcher Chris Van Cuyk because the Dodgers farmhand had been needling Robinson after he booted a ground ball in an intrasquad game, March 30, 1949

"You do a lot of talking, Chris. Why don't you do a little talking off that mound and see what happens?"

—J. R. challenging pitcher Chris Van Cuyk, March 30, 1949

"He's been trying to make a fool of me, so I just reared back and fired one at him."

—Chris Van Cuyk, Dodgers farmhand about how he responded to Robinson, March 30, 1949

"Infuriated . . . after the game Jackie accosted Van Cuyk, in the presence of a group of spectators, describing in lurid detail the unpleasantry he would have performed if [Van Cuyk] had hit him. Van Cuyk took this calmly. Later he said he did not want to stir things up any further, and that he was already embarrassed by Robinson's language in front of the mixed crowd."

—Bill Roeder, describing an incident that got a lot of media attention, *New York World-Telegram*, March 11, 1949

"I think you would be smarter to continue acting in the same manner you did during your first year in baseball."

—Happy Chandler, MLB commissioner, to Robinson,
who had no intention of following this advice, March 1948

"Mr. Robinson is called on the carpet and is defending himself once again . . . to imply that the press has been unjust and unfair to him. This it seems is time for someone to remind Mr. Robinson that . . . if it had not been for the press—the sympathetic press—Mr. Robinson would have probably still been tramping around the country with a Negro team. . . . We do not know whether he was right or wrong in the conflict with Chris Van Cuyk. We hope he was justified in saying the things he is reported to have said."

—Wendell Smith, who possibly had a falling out with Robinson because of the
mistakes (including the misspelling of Jackie's mother's name) in the Robinson
autobiography on which he collaborated, about Robinson's dismay that the press
took Van Cuyk's side in their dispute, *Pittsburgh Courier*, March 19, 1949

"Jackie Robinson's complaint about treatment of Negro fans, at games here [at Holman Stadium in Vero Beach], should be filed not with the community but with the Brooklyn ball club, which must have been aware that the rigid Jim Crow laws would be in effect but chose to train [t]here anyway. The charge is that the Negro customers are permitted only 100 seats, though there are empty seats in the white sections."

—*New York World-Telegram*, about Vero Beach, March 21, 1949

"The usual 'Jim Crow twist' was given reverse English when Brooklyn visited [Beaumont, Texas] for the first game of the spring exhibition tour. . . . Instead of barring the Dodgers' colored players from the clubhouse, Stuart Stadium officials 'suggested' that Jackie Robinson and Roy Campanella use the players' quarters at the park and the rest of the team dress at their hotel. . . . It so happened that the unfinished dressing room floor was covered with mud and water, shower facilities were incomplete and the place was entirely devoid of window covering."

—Sam Lacy, *Baltimore Afro-American*, April 9, 1949

ROBINSON'S RETURN TO GEORGIA

"I will play baseball wherever my employers, the Brooklyn Dodgers, want me to play."

—J. R., about upcoming exhibition games in his native state, Georgia,
***The Jackie Robinson Show*, January 1949**

"Klan Quiet as Jackie, Roy Take Field in Georgia"

—Title of article about how Robinson and Campanella were scheduled to play in the first mixed-race baseball games in Macon and Atlanta despite warnings from the Ku Klux Klan, *New York World-Telegram*, April 7, 1949

"Jackie showed me the letters he got. In Atlanta the Klan said they would shoot him if he played. During warmup I said, 'Jack. Don't stand so close to me today. Move away, will ya?' It made him smile."

—Pee Wee Reese to Roger Kahn, *The Boys of Summer*, 1972

"I was nervous when I reached Macon. But when two white girls rushed up to me at the airport and wanted my autograph—I knew everything was going to be all right."

—J. R. to Harold Burr, *Brooklyn Eagle*, April 1949

"The Georgia folk took Jackie Robinson in stride, and vice versa, and indications are that's the way it will be in Atlanta too. No one seems to be excited about the first appearance of a Negro in mixed competition. A morning paper was on the streets here without a line about Robinson. . . . Jackie needs no publicity, though, and the Atlanta people expect to do 15,000, 10,000, and a record 25,000 in the three Brooklyn games. The crowd at Macon was 6,436, overflow and a park record. [In the Dodgers' 11–2 victory,] Robinson obliged with three hits [and Carl] Furillo and Duke Snider banged home runs against the Peaches."

—Bill Roeder, *New York World-Telegram*, April 8, 1949

"DEFINITELY SEE THAT CAMPANELLA AND ROBINSON COME TO PLAY."

—MARTIN LUTHER KING JR., BAPTIST MINISTER FROM ATLANTA WHO WAS INSPIRED BY THE PIONEER BLACK PLAYERS IN HIS CIVIL RIGHTS ACTIVISM DURING THE 1950S AND 1960S, TO BRANCH RICKEY, 1949

"When we got to Atlanta we went to Dr. King's house and had dinner with him and stayed with him just about the entire trip. He told us, 'Don't worry about these threats. You carry on as you've been doing. That's the greatest thing for our country.' At the ballpark we couldn't totally dismiss the threats from our minds. They wouldn't let blacks sit in the grandstand. They made 'em all sit on the banks of the outfield with a cushion. . . . I told Jackie jokingly, 'You've got it made. You're playing second base. All you have to do is run into center field, and you'll be safe. I have to run all the way from home plate.'"

—**Roy Campanella, Dodgers catcher and future Hall of Famer, about games in which both black and white fans cheered the Dodgers' black players, to Peter Golenbock, *Bums*, 1984**

"I went to Atlanta, Georgia, to play in an exhibition game. On the field, for the first time in Atlanta, there were Negroes and whites. Other Negroes, besides me. And I thought: 'What I have always believed has come to be.'"

—**J. R., recorded essay, Edward R. Murrow's radio series *This I Believe*, 1952**

"[The Yankees] completed the exhibition season with a three-game series against the Brooklyn Dodgers in Yankee Stadium and Ebbets Field. . . . The Yankees lost all three games. . . . Jackie Robinson . . . taunted Allie [Reynolds, the Yankees ace,] several times in the third game. Robinson took huge leads at third base twice and glared at Allie, as if to say he could steal home anytime he wanted to. After the games Stengel was mad regarding Robinson stealing bases at will against the Yankees."

—**Royse Parr and Bob Burke, *Allie Reynolds: Super Chief*, 2002**

"HE STOLE EVERYTHING OUT THERE HE WANTED TODAY SO HE MIGHT HAVE STOLEN YOUR JOCKS AS WELL."

—CASEY STENGEL, YANKEES MANAGER, TELLING HIS TEAM TO CHECK THEIR LOCKERS TO SEE IF ROBINSON'S THIEVERY DIDN'T JUST TAKE PLACE ON THE BASES, SPRING TRAINING, 1949

"Stengel disliked Robinson, although not with the intensity with which Robinson disliked him. . . . His distaste for Robinson—or Robi'son, as he always pronounced it—may have been racial at heart (if not overt, than at least latent), but in retrospect it seems to have been caused more by professional jealousy. Robinson was awfully good, precisely the talented all-around player that Stengel admired and would love to have had on his own team."

—Robert Creamer, *Stengel: His Life and Times*, 1984

"On April 19, before 34,530 boisterous fans at Ebbets Field, Branch Rickey announced the lineups. . . . Shotton's starters would be everyday players all year, with the exception of leftfielder Cal Abrams. Hodges at first, Robinson at second, Reese at short, Cox at third, Furillo in right, Snider in center, and Campanella behind the plate would be Dodgers fixtures through 1954. . . . The Dodgers thrilled the home fans by crushing the Giants 10–3. . . . Campanella hit a 3-run homer . . . while Robinson, who would bat fourth all year, and Furillo had solo shots against Larry Jansen."

—Tom Clavin and Danny Peary, *Gil Hodges*, 2012

"Jack talked about how he admired and liked Gil [Hodges]. . . . Joan and Gil and Jack and I, not often and not many times, got together for dinner or something like that. It was when we lived in Brooklyn, as they did. I felt close to them as a couple. Joan and I sometimes sat together at the games, that kind of thing. As with Pee Wee, Jack could count on Gil to do his part in building unity for a winning team, and help him with his part. Jack celebrated the power of the entire infield, and working together with Gil and Pee Wee and having success at that."

—Rachel Robinson to Danny Peary, *Gil Hodges*,
Tom Clavin and Danny Peary, 2012

"I give [Gil Hodges] strong credit for Jackie Robinson's success. Pee Wee Reese gets identified with Jackie because they were the second-short combination. But on the other side of Jackie, Gil Hodges played and Gil was a peacekeeper. Everybody respected Gil, teammates and opponents alike. He was strong, and he subdued several confrontations before they really got started that evolved around Jackie in those early years."

—Carl Erskine, Dodgers pitcher, to Randy Harris, *Baseball Digest* magazine, February 1995

"I was recalled by the Dodgers in late May. . . . I was reunited with Roy and got to play with Jackie Robinson for the first time."

—Don Newcombe, Dodgers pitcher whose fastball, size, and intimidating demeanor made him the ace of the Dodgers staff as a rookie, to Danny Peary, *We Played the Game,* 1994

"May 16, 1949—Boston's Earl Torgeson, who separated his shoulder when he attempted to block Jackie Robinson on a double play . . . will be operated on [today] and will be sidelined several months.

"May 21, 1949—The Dodgers break up a tight game with an 8-run 9th to trim the Cardinals, 15–6. Pee Wee Reese scores 5 runs and Jackie Robinson has 6 RBIs.

"May 30, 1949—Jackie Robinson hits a 13th-inning HR to give the Dodgers a 2–1 game one win at the Polo Grounds. The Giants take the nightcap, 7–4, and the Leo Durocher-Robinson feud is fueled when Robby steals second during a timeout for a pitching change. He has to return to first and Leo gives him the 'swollen head' gesture."

—*The Baseball Chronology,* a two-week sampling of May 1949 highlights that showed some diverse ways Robinson impacted games, edited by James Charlton, 1991

"A name-calling exchange between Jackie Robinson and Schoolboy Rowe, precipitated when Rowe urged his [Phillies] teammate, Ken Heintzelman, to 'throw at' Robinson, resulted in a brief rhubarb near the end of the Phillies-Dodgers game at Ebbets Field last night."

—*New York World-Telegram,* July 6, 1949

"I was witness to a splendid first game [in person, on July 8, 1949]. Not only did the Dodgers win 4–3, but my hero, Jackie Robinson, ignited the Dodger offense in the second inning when he walked, stole second, went to third on an errant pickoff throw, and scored on an infield hit. Watching him on the base path, with his long leads, his feints toward second, and his needling of the pitcher, kept me on the end of my seat. . . . I knew that Jackie's baserunning was part of his mystique . . . but to see him in person, through my own eyes instead of Red Barber's, was thrilling. 'As long as he got on base,' was our ritual refrain, 'he was going to do something to bring himself home.' The game at Ebbets Field was a first not only for me, but the sport of baseball as well. When Giant batter Henry Thompson stepped up to bat against Dodger rookie Don Newcombe, it was the first time that a black pitcher faced a black batter in a major-league game."

—Doris Kearns Goodwin, young Dodgers fan who became a famous historian, about the historic game in which Henry Thompson and Monte Irvin broke the color barrier for the New York Giants, *Wait Till Next Year,* **1997**

"[There will be] no fewer than seven Dodgers on the National League squad for the 16th All-Star game at Ebbets Field next Thursday. . . . Jackie Robinson and Pee Wee Reese were mandated for the starting lineup by the 4,637,743 fans, from Coast to Coast, who participated in the three weeks' poll which ended last Thursday. . . . Noteworthy among the many interesting facets of the All-Star selections is the presence of four Negro players among the 50. . . . It will be the first participation by Negro players in the All-Star game. The Nationals three are Robinson, Newcombe, and Campanella, all Dodgers, while the American Leaguer is Larry Doby, Cleveland outfielder. Jackie will be the only Negro in action when the game gets under way."

—Dan Daniel, about the groundbreaking All-Star Game in which Robinson started and scored three of the National League's seven runs in a losing effort, *New York World-Telegram,* **July 7, 1949**

"The three of us became the first blacks to make the All-Star team [with Larry Doby playing for the American League], which was a thrill . . . but how could they have left Jackie off the team in 1947 and 1948? Of course they couldn't have had [the 1949] All-Star Game in Brooklyn and not have the three of us."

—Don Newcombe, Dodgers pitcher, to Danny Peary, *We Played the Game,* **1994**

"On the home front we were making progress as well. In July 1949, we moved into the first place we had of our own, a two-bedroom apartment on the second floor of a house on the corner of Tilden Avenue and 53rd Street in Flatbush. The move meant that we had decided to make New York our home. . . . Even in this predominantly Jewish neighborhood, we heard rumors of a petition being circulated to prevent our black landlady from purchasing the house we were to live in. By this time we were used to brushing off such cowardly tactics and we settled in, happy to have our lives under our control at last."

—Rachel Robinson, *Jackie Robinson: An Intimate Portrait,* 1996

THE PAUL ROBESON DILEMMA

"Two years [after he entered the majors]—as the anti-red McCarthyite madness was reaching fever pitch—Branch Rickey persuaded a dubious Jackie to appear before the House Un-American Activities Committee [on July 18, 1949] to contest Robeson's suggestion at a Paris Peace Conference that it would be unthinkable for America's blacks to ever go to war against the Soviet Union that supposedly had erased racial discrimination."

—Bill Mardo, activist sports and political writer for the *New York Daily Worker,* excerpt from paper presented at the Jackie Robinson anniversary conference, Long Island University, Brooklyn Campus, April 1997

"Actually, he was shy about testifying. . . . Jack's first reaction was that he should stick to baseball. . . . But Branch Rickey convinced him that it would mean more coming from 'just' a baseball player."

—Rachel Robinson, *McCall's* magazine, June 1951

"Rae and I remembered how, as children, we had thrilled to Robeson's success, had hummed the tunes made famous by his booming bass-baritone voice. Now a white man from Georgia [Representative John S. Wood, chairman of HUAC] was asking me, a 'refugee' from Georgia, to denounce Robeson, who spoke from a well of bitterness that few white people ever would understand. Thus white Americans would not understand my dilemma, or that of any Negro faced with the task of passing judgment on Robeson. . . . What added to our mental strain was the messages from people we respected, some urging me to testify, others insisting that I tell the Un-American Activities Committee to 'go to hell, where it most likely was conceived.' Negroes warned that I should beware of letting myself be used in 'that old white man's plan to divide and conquer.'"

—J. R., *Wait Till Next Year*, Carl T. Rowan with Jackie Robinson, 1960

"Branch Rickey urged both Robinson and my father to testify against Robeson at a committee hearing. Robinson agreed—a decision he would always regret—and my dad declined. Years later, Paul Robeson Jr. would tell me with touching sincerity how deeply his father appreciated my dad's refusal to denounce him. My father told me, 'White people will use you to attack other blacks, be careful of that. . . . I respect Mr. Rickey, but why should I denounce Paul Robeson? I told Mr. Rickey I'm a baseball player and I don't need to get into politics.'"

—Roy Campanella II, *Cult Baseball Players*, edited by Danny Peary, 1990

"I knew that many Negroes welcomed Robeson's remarks, not because of disloyalty, or of any tender feelings toward the Soviet Union, but because they feared that white America would never grant the Negro a position of equality simply out of a sense of justice and decency. . . . I could not help but sense the irony of the fact that I, a Negro once court-martialed for opposing Army Jim Crow, should now be asked to pledge the Negro's loyalty to the Army, to the nation's military ventures."

—J. R., *Wait Till Next Year*, Carl T. Rowan with Jackie Robinson, 1960

"It did not seem right to me that . . . anyone should become so filled with despair as to say that fifteen million Negroes had given up on America."

—J. R., stating his rational for testifying before HUAC, *Wait Till Next Year*, Carl T. Rowan with Jackie Robinson, 1960

"If Mr. Rickey at that time had asked me to jump headfirst off the Brooklyn Bridge, I would have done it."

—J. R., to writer Howard Fast when he asked Robinson why he had testified, at Roger Kahn's book party for *The Boys of Summer*, 1971

"I was asked to testify in Congress as a loyalty witness. They wanted me to voice my feelings—as an American Negro—about my country. Between us, Rickey and I must have spoken to fifty people as we tried to frame my beliefs in the best possible phrases. The words weren't quite right until Rickey remembered Lester Granger, whom he'd met at a dinner of the Urban League. . . . Among the three of us we worked out a speech that perfectly express my views."

—J. R., as columnist for his own magazine, *Our Sports* magazine, June 1953

"Then he and I took it home and talked it over many times, making revision after revision. Even going down in the train [to Washington], we went over it again."

—Rachel Robinson, *McCall's* magazine, June 1951

"With movie and television cameras grinding away and the committee room packed, [Robinson] made it clear that he believed black Americans had real grievances, and 'the fact that it is a communist who denounces injustice in the courts, police brutality, and lynching when it happens doesn't change the truth of his charges'; racial discrimination in America was not 'a creation of communist imagination.' Robeson had written Robinson just before his HUAC appearance to warn him that the press had 'badly distorted' his remarks in Paris, and Robinson commented that 'if Mr. Robeson actually made' the statement ascribed to him about American blacks refusing to fight in a war against Russia, it 'sounds very silly to me. . . . He has a right to his personal views and if he wants to sound silly when he expresses them in public, this is his business and not mine. He's still a famous ex-athlete and great singer and actor.'"

—Martin Duberman, *Paul Robeson,* 1989

"White people must realize that the more a Negro hates communism because it opposes democracy, the more he is going to hate the other influences that kill off democracy in this country—and that goes for racial discrimination in the Army, segregation on trains and buses, and job discrimination."

—J. R., whose appearance gave symbolic legitimacy to HUAC and was a terrible blow to Robeson (someone who had fought for the integration of organized baseball), but allowed him to speak out about the racial discrimination in America that both men were combating, testimony before the House Un-American Activities Committee, July 18, 1949

> **"JACKIE—EVER THE MILITANT—TURNED HIS TESTIMONY INTO MORE OF A VIGOROUS ASSAULT AGAINST AMERICAN RACISM THAN AN ALL-OUT ATTACK AGAINST ROBESON."**
>
> —BILL MARDO, ACTIVIST SPORTS AND POLITICAL WRITER FOR THE *NEW YORK DAILY WORKER*, EXCERPT FROM PAPER PRESENTED AT THE JACKIE ROBINSON ANNIVERSARY CONFERENCE, LONG ISLAND UNIVERSITY, BROOKLYN CAMPUS, APRIL 1997

"[HUAC chairman Georgia Representative John S.] Wood wasn't there because he didn't want to call Jackie 'Mister Robinson.'"

—Paul Robeson, singer, actor, athlete, and civil rights activist, July 20, 1949

"Mr. Robeson does his people great harm in trying to line them up on the communist side of [the] political picture. Jackie Robinson helped them greatly by his forthright statements."

—Eleanor Roosevelt, former first lady, who was one of many who believed Robinson's testimony was patriotic, syndicated "My Day" column, November 2, 1949

"The *New York Times* put Robinson's testimony on page one . . . and for good measure ran an editorial the same day declaring, 'Mr. Robeson has attached himself to the cause of a country in which all men are equal because they are equally enslaved.'"

—Martin Duberman, *Paul Robeson*, 1989

"Jackie Robinson had batted 1,000 percent in this game."

—*New York Amsterdam News*, a black paper that backed Robinson's testifying against Robeson, July 23, 1949

> **"BUT BLACK REACTION, IN FACT, WAS FAR FROM UNANIMOUS. . . . OPINION WAS BOTH CONGRATULATORY AND CONDEMNATORY."**
>
> —MARTIN DUBERMAN, *PAUL ROBESON*, 1989

"It was very hurtful to see Jackie Robinson be made to attack Paul Robeson, whom many of us loved so dearly."

—Oscar Peterson Jr., renowned jazz pianist,
Speak of Me As I Am (British documentary), 1998

"The *Times* printed the full testimony of Jackie Robinson, but had no report of the press conference held by Robeson to answer the baseball player's testimony."

—Philip S. Foner, *Paul Robeson Speaks,* 1978

"I have nothing but the deepest respect for Jackie Robinson, and I brook no quarrel with him. It's an insult to Jackie and myself and the people in our race to have the committee invite us to testify. The committee's shenanigans are a definite menace."

—Paul Robeson, singer, actor, athlete, and civil rights activist who would be blacklisted and then have his passport revoked for his communist affiliation, directing his anger at HUAC rather than Robinson at a rally sponsored by the Civil Rights Congress, quoted by the *New York World-Telegram,* July 21, 1949

"We cannot forget that John S. Wood, chairman of the committee, once called the Ku Klux Klan an American institution. Why then should Negroes pick this type of committee to express their loyalty? . . . It should be clear that Robinson, by appearing before this committee, has performed a profound political act that has aided those who would enslave the Negro."

—Paul Robeson, to reporters, 1949

"I am not going to permit the issue to boil down to a personal feud between me and Jackie. To do that, would be to do exactly what the other group wants us to do."

—Paul Robeson, although he considered Robinson's testimony to be a "disservice" to the black community, 1949

"On August 27, 1949, on the lovely Peekskill picnic grounds thirty miles north of New York City, yesterday's 'Militia Mentality' maniacs acted out their own version of Hitler's storm troopers on [Paul Robeson's] fans [that] had come upstate for an annual Robeson concert. . . . Robeson's music sheets [were] fed into the fires that were started with the wood chairs of the stunned concert goers. Burning crosses blazed a few feet from the stage. People were stoned mercilessly. Cars were overturned. Blood stained the grass. And it was just one day after that horror,

I firmly believe, that Jackie Robinson began to see Robeson for what he really represented and for what a giant target he had become for the witch-hunters and racist thugs of his time."

—Bill Mardo, activist sports and political writer
for the *New York Daily Worker*, April 1997

"Paul Robeson should have the right to sing, speak, or do anything he wants to. . . . It's Robeson's right to do or be or say as he believes. They say here in America you're allowed to be whatever you want. I think those rioters ought to be investigated, and let's find out if what they did is supposed to be the democratic way of doing things. . . . Anything progressive is called communism."

—J. R., who, although a staunch anticommunist himself, was horrified by
newspaper accounts of the Peekskill mob action, to Bill Mardo,
New York Daily Worker, August 29, 1949

"The very same newspapers that had salivated over Jackie's political differences with Robeson at the House hearings—the very same wire services that had relayed to newspapers all over American the minor critique of Robeson at the House hearings— somehow 'missed' Jackie's passionate defense of Robeson's rights just five weeks later!"

—Bill Mardo, activist sports and political writer for the
New York Daily Worker, April 1997

"Robinson [lamented] his testimony against Paul Robeson in front of the House Un-American Activities Committee in 1949. Robinson never outwardly expressed regret—he was too tough and had too much pride—but after twenty years he came to recognize that [they had the same commitment to their race]."

—Howard Bryant, *Shut Out: The Story of Race and Baseball in Boston,* 2002

"The salient fact of my life and Paul's life were the same. We were black men in a bigoted white society. I was only 30, I wish I hadn't made that talk."

—J. R. to Roger Kahn, quoted by Kahn, *Los Angeles Times*, September 22, 1996

"In those days I had much more faith in the ultimate justice of the American white man than I have today. I would reject such an invitation if offered now. . . . I have grown wiser and closer to the painful truths about America's destructiveness. And I do have increased respect for Paul Robeson who, over the span of twenty years, sacrificed himself, his career, and the wealth and comfort he once enjoyed because, I believe, he was sincerely trying to help his people."

—J. R., *I Never Had It Made,* as told to Alfred Duckett, 1972

"The Dodgers' hotel in St. Louis is the Chase. On arrival in that city, the white ballplayers take cabs in one direction and the colored in another. [In] September, when the Brooks went into St. Louis for their final crucial series with the Cardinals . . . four of us squeezed into a third-class hotel in the colored section, Jackie and Campy having to put up together. Newcombe, who was slated to pitch the next day, spent the night trying to sleep in a room located directly over a constantly screeching jukebox. I fitted myself into a basement room the size of an overfed telephone booth."

—Sam Lacy, about the night prior to Robinson and Campanella going hitless in the first game of a doubleheader to the Cardinals and Newcombe taking the 1–0 loss, *Baltimore Afro-American,* April 1, 1950

"A great to-do arose when Bill Stewart threw Robinson out of the first game [of a doubleheader] while the [first-place] Cards were in the winning rally in the ninth [with two outs]. [With the game scoreless] Stewart called a ball [on starter Don Newcombe] on what the Dodgers felt was a third strike to Enos Slaughter. A few minutes later, during a mound consultation, Robinson gripped his throat as much as to tell Stewart he had choked."

—*New York World-Telegram,* September 22, 1949

"Jackie made us better because of his ability and made us closer because of his suffering. The Dodgers helped make him a major leaguer, and he helped make us champions."

—Duke Snider, Dodgers outfielder and future Hall of Famer, crediting Robinson for the Dodgers edging the Cardinals by one game to capture the 1949 NL pennant, *The Duke of Flatbush,* 1988

"[AT PENN STATION] 25,000 CHEERING, JUMPING DODGER FANS WERE THERE TO GREET TRAIN 229, AND 75 EXTRA POLICE OFFICERS WERE ON DUTY. THE CROWD WENT SO BONKERS WHEN THEY SAW JACKIE, THEIR NEW BATTING CHAMPION, THAT HE BECAME SEPARATED FROM HIS WIFE RACHEL AND THE POLICE HAD TO RESCUE HIM FROM THE MOB."

—DUKE SNIDER, *THE DUKE OF FLATBUSH,* 1988

"Jackie Robinson led the National League with a .342 batting average and had . . . 203 hits . . . the first time that a Brooklyn batter had collected 200 hits . . . since . . . 1930. Robinson added 124 RBIs [and led] the National League in stolen bases with thirty-seven."

—Marvin A. Cohen, *The Dodger-Giants Rivalry 1900–1957,* 2000

"Joe DiMaggio . . . gets the applause of the nation's ball fans as 'the greatest baseball player in the game today.' He is the winner in a coast-to-coast survey just completed by the American Institute of Public Opinion. . . . Ted Williams of the Boston Red Sox and Jackie Robinson of the Dodgers get the next largest number of votes. . . . Then come[s] Stan Musial, star of the St. Louis Cardinals."

—George Gallup, director of the American Institute of Public Opinion, October 1, 1949

"[Casey] Stengel prepared us for the 1949 World Series quite simply. He said, 'Go get 'em!' I'd have to say that Jackie Robinson and Pee Wee Reese were the keys to the Dodgers. Reese had a good Series, but our pitchers pretty much stopped Robinson from getting on base. Pitchers dominated the first three games."

—Gene Woodling, Yankees outfielder, to Danny Peary, *We Played the Game,* 1994

"You'll see some more of that. Berra claims he has a good arm but he'll have to show us. Why, Pee Wee and I stole those bases without even getting a good jump on the pitch."

—J. R., saying the Yankees' young but confident catcher Yogi Berra hadn't the arm to challenge him or Reese on stolen base attempts, quoted by Bill Roeder, *New York World-Telegram,* October 1, 1947

"Right down the middle! Right down the blankety-blank middle and he doesn't get a strike on it. You can't tell me that wouldn't have made a difference. Now he has to get the curve over the plate. With a one and one count he doesn't have to come in there with it."

—J. R., about how umpire Cal Hubbard's missed call on a 1–0 pitch by Don Newcombe in the bottom of the ninth inning forced the Dodgers ace to throw a 2–0 pitch over the plate (which Robinson believed was why Tommy Henrich was able to smash a homer and win Game 1 of the 1949 World Series, 1–0), to reporters, October 5, 1949

"I lost my head. We were beaten legitimately and I thought that all in all Hubbard called a good game."

—J. R., offering a public apology rather than be fined by Happy Chandler for claiming the umpire's bad call cost the Dodgers a loss in Game 1, October 6, 1949

"Elwood (Preacher) Roe of Ash Flat, Ark., ace lefthander of the Dodgers, today achieved a rare shutout feat against the Yankees in the second game of the World Series. The Dodgers won by 1 to 0 and tied the classic. . . . Roe's associate heroes were Jackie Robinson, who organized the scoring array with a double and Gil Hodges, who drove him in with a single."

—Dan Daniel, *New York World-Telegram*, October 6, 1949

"Jackie Robinson was on third, and he was just about the best base runner I've ever seen. He could get away from a standing position in a flash; by his second or third stride he was going at full speed. I'd never pitched with him on base before and I was going into a full windup. But his movements were distracting to me . . . so I decided I had better . . . work from a stretch position. . . . Robinson had broken my concentration. I was pitching more to Robinson than I was to Hodges, and as a result I threw one up into Gil's power and he got the base hit that beat me. . . . I think that was the only mistake I made in that game."

—Vic Raschi, Yankees pitcher, to Donald Honig, *Baseball Between the Lines*, 1976

"Both the Yankees and Dodgers won 97 games and clinched pennants on the last day of the season. The Dodgers were a much better team in 1949 . . . with Jackie Robinson at second and Gil Hodges at first. But we also had improved and beat them in just 5 games."

—Billy Johnson, Yankees third baseman, to Danny Peary, *We Played the Game*, 1994

"Rookie Roy Campanella . . . was four for fifteen; Robinson was three for sixteen; Hodges was four for seventeen; and Don Newcombe lost two games."

—John Leonard, *The Ultimate Baseball Book*, edited by Daniel Okrent and Harris Lewine, 1979

"Jackie Robinson's great [barnstorming club] was asking ticket prices of $1.50, $1.30, $1.65, and 35 cents to see his black against black games that starred Buck Leonard, Roy Campanella, and Don Newcombe, as well as Larry Doby. (An upper reserved seat at the Polo Grounds, home of the New York Giants, cost $1.75 in 1949.) The team, ending with a record of 25–6 . . . as the *Sporting News* reported, drew more than 240,000, or 8,275 per game."

—**Thomas Barthel,** *Baseball Barnstorming and Exhibition Games,*
1901–1962, **2007**

"Once and for all, Rickey killed that persistent rumor about his selling Robinson to the Braves or any other club."

—**Dan Daniel,** *New York World-Telegram,* **October 30, 1949**

"Once a writer came up and said I better start saying thank you if I wanted to be Most Valuable Player. I said if I have to thank *you* to win MVP, I don't want a f***ing thing. And I didn't thank him, and I won it."

—**J. R. to Roger Kahn,** *The Boys of Summer,* **1972**

"Jackie Robinson of the Dodgers, batting champion and second base spark of a pennant winner, has been elected Most Valuable Player in the National League. . . . Twenty-four members of the Baseball Writers Assn., three from each city in the circuit, acted as a committee. . . . On a point basis, with 14 for first, nine for second on down to one for tenth, Robinson [who received twelve first-place votes] led by 38 with a final total of 264 to 226 for [the Cardinals' Stan] Musial. [Also from the Cardinals, Enos] Slaughter with 181 was third and Pittsburgh's Ralph Kiner, the home run king and runs batted in leader, was fourth with 133. [Pee Wee] Reese, Dodger captain and shortstop partner of Robinson's in a fine double play combination, drew a fifth place total of 118 points."

—*New York Post,* **about Robinson becoming the first black to be voted MVP,**
November 18, 1949

"I buried my disappointment [about losing the pennant] that winter by occupying myself with underprivileged kids in the Harlem YMCA. Together with Jackie Robinson, I spent a lot of time with these youngsters teaching them good sportsmanship and good citizenship, as well as supervising their sports activities. Jackie and I would make appearances in public schools all over the city and speak to the youngsters. We had baseball clinics after school and on Saturday."

—**Roy Campanella,** *It's Good to Be Alive,* **1959**

"JACKIE ROBINSON, NEGRO SECOND BASEMAN OF THE BROOKLYN DODGERS, TODAY RECEIVED THE ANNUAL GOLD AWARD OF THE GEORGE WASHINGTON CARVER INSTITUTE FOR THE YEAR'S OUTSTANDING CONTRIBUTION TO THE BETTERMENT OF RACE RELATIONS."

—NEW YORK WORLD-TELEGRAM, DECEMBER 14, 1949

"When Robinson returned to Pasadena . . . Mayor Warren Dorn gave a dinner in his honor. The [*Pasadena*] *Star-News* did not cover it."

—Pasadena Star-News, **April 7, 1987**

"Did You See Jackie Robinson Hit That Ball?"

—Title of hit song, Woodrow Buddy Johnson and Count Basie, 1949

"In the summer of 1949, Robinson [had] syndicated a serialized newspaper autobiography circulated in conjunction with [the forthcoming] release of *The Jackie Robinson Story*, a movie in which he played himself."

—Carl E. Prince, *Brooklyn's Dodgers,* **1996**

J. R. NOTE: In 1950, the newest edition of the *Columbia Encyclopedia,* the largest single-volume reference work of its kind in the world, was issued for the first time since 1935. Among the new subjects mentioned to promote the giant work were rockets, Mao Tze-tung, the United Nations, and Jackie Robinson.

"[The first *Jackie Robinson* 10c] comic was published in 1950. . . . The abuses he endured are addressed in a vague, sanitized way in the comic book, which mostly covers his minor league career and his call-up to the Dodgers. . . . Brief reference is made to 'the Jim Crow code.' The words 'race' and 'racist' are never used. Instead, the words 'scheming foes,' 'sinister plotters,' and 'Jackie's enemies' are used to describe the abusers, virtually implying that there were only a handful of bad apples who made his life unpleasant. . . . The comic includes a couple of scenes of the famous meeting between Robinson and Dodger President Branch Rickey. . . . Surely [Rickey] used stronger language than, 'As a Negro, Jackie, You'll have to take a lot of insults and gaff! You think you can do it?'

[One] page . . . informs us that in Montreal, 'Jackie even received a few threatening letters!' These too, probably contained stronger words than 'Jack Robinson: Don't try to play ball here! —A Friend.' The comic . . . does spend several frames describing Robinson's base running heroics, [but] not even one frame on Robinson's major league debut game on April 15, 1947 . . . instead concentrating on a game a few days later in which he got his first . . . home run, 'a death blow to intolerance which kept Negroes out of organized baseball for 70 years!' Why were the sharp edges of reality so blunted in this comic book?"

> **—Catherine Keen, archivist, National Museum of Natural History blog, June 3, 2013**

"Salary Demands Hint Deal for Jackie"

> **—Headline, indicating Branch Rickey would rather trade Robinson to the Braves than pay him the $50,000 he was asking for, *New York Daily News***

"EVERYTHING WAS NEGOTIATED BETWEEN JACKIE AND MR. RICKEY EXCEPT JACK'S SALARY. . . . WHAT RICKEY OFFERED YOU WAS ALL YOU WERE GOING TO GET. . . . THAT WAS THE ONLY ASPECT OF THE RELATIONSHIP THAT WAS DISAPPOINTING."

—RACHEL ROBINSON, ABOUT JACKIE ACCEPTING A $35,000 CONTRACT, ALTHOUGH JOE DIMAGGIO WAS BEING PAID $100,000 BY THE YANKEES, TO PETER GOLENBOCK, *BUMS*, 1984

"With all the incentives of a growing family, [Jack and I] took money carefully saved from each paycheck in 1948 and 1949 and purchased and extensively renovated an English Tudor house in St. Albans, Long Island. For the first time we had a backyard, a play area, sweeping lawns, old oak trees, and space, just as we'd had during our California childhoods. The neighborhood was in the process of changing to predominantly black, but at that point it was still racially mixed. . . . The greatest thrill of this peaceful period was the birth of Sharon [on January 13, 1950]. . . . I had longed for a girl as the second child."

> **—Rachel Robinson, *Jackie Robinson: An Intimate Portrait*, 1996**

"AFTER ROBINSON'S GLORIOUS 1949 SEASON, SCREENWRITER LAWRENCE TAYLOR WROTE A MOVIE SCRIPT FOR *THE JACKIE ROBINSON STORY.* IT WAS REJECTED BY SEVERAL STUDIOS. NO ONE WAS WILLING TO TAKE A CHANCE ON A FILM WITH A BLACK HERO. EAGLE-LION FINALLY PICKED UP THE PROJECT AND SENT A COPY TO BRANCH RICKEY. HE PLEDGED COOPERATION IF THE SCRIPT WERE REVISED TO INCLUDE MORE OF THE HARDSHIPS THAT JACKIE HAD ENDURED. EVERYONE AGREED THAT NO ONE COULD PLAY THE ROLE OF JACKIE ROBINSON AS WELL AS ROBINSON HIMSELF. THREE WEEKS OF PRODUCTION TIME WERE ALLOTTED FOR THE LOW-BUDGET FILM. NEAR THE END OF PRODUCTION, THEY SHOT DAY AND NIGHT. . . . RICKEY WAS COOPERATIVE BUT ADAMANT THAT HIS STAR BALLPLAYER NOT MISS A SINGLE MINUTE OF SPRING TRAINING."

—HARVEY FROMMER, *RICKEY AND ROBINSON,* 1982

"Either on orders by higher-ups or by his own volition, Jackie Robinson has gone on a rigid diet in an effort to pare off at least 14 pounds from his 210-pound frame."

—Joe Reichler, about Robinson being in excellent shape when he arrived at spring training, *Los Angeles Times,* March 13, 1950

"Before the 1950 season began, league president Ford Frick, in an unprecedented announcement, selected one player, Robinson, to receive a public warning against rough baserunning."

—Lester Rodney, sports editor of the *New York Daily Worker,* excerpt from paper presented at the Jackie Robinson anniversary conference, Long Island University, Brooklyn Campus, April 1997

"In 1950, as the defending National League champions, [the Dodgers] drew the largest opening crowd (29,074) ever to see the Phillies at Shibe Park. Philadelphia won, 9–1, behind Robin Roberts, with Robinson scoring the Dodgers' only run."

—Lyle Spatz, baseball historian, excerpt from paper presented at the Jackie Robinson anniversary conference, Long Island University, Brooklyn Campus, April 1997

J. R. NOTE: On April 16, 1950, Robinson appeared as a mystery guest on the popular TV game show *What's My Line?* Over the years, he'd appear on many other television programs, including *The Ed Sullivan Show* several times, *Tonight!* in 1955, *I've Got a Secret* in 1957, *Person to Person* in 1957, *Jack Paar* in 1960, *Mike Douglas* in 1962, *Merv Griffin* in 1965, *David Frost* in 1969, *Sesame Street* in 1970, and *Dick Cavett* in 1972. Most often he was interviewed, but in the late fifties he would be the interviewer on his syndicated radio show, *Jackie Robinson Radio Shots*. Subjects for three-minute interviews included Branch Rickey, Satchel Paige, entertainers Johnny Mathis and Ed Sullivan, and General Omar Bradley.

"For a young man of 31 he's not doing so bad: present salary from the Brooklyn Dodgers is at least $35,000 a year, and he is getting $30,000 plus 15 percent of the profits, for the new Hollywood movie based on his life."

—*Life* **magazine, for which Jackie Robinson became the first African American to appear on the cover, May 10, 1950**

"What is surprising . . . in this new film . . . is the sincerity of the dramatization and the integrity of Mr. Robinson playing himself. Too often, in films of this nature about sports figures, fanciful or real, the sentiments are inflated and the heroics glorified. Here the simple story of Mr. Robinson's trail-blazing career is re-enacted with manifest fidelity and conspicuous dramatic restraint. And Mr. Robinson, doing that rare thing of playing himself in the picture's leading role, displays a calm assurance and composure that might be envied by many a Hollywood star."

—**Bosley Crowther, America's most influential film critic, who praised the box-office hit,** *New York Times,* **May 17, 1950**

"I dare say the movie folk and even Jackie Robinson himself, aren't going to like me for saying this, but following the dictates of an honest reporter, I'm forced to say *The Jackie Robinson Story* . . . is full of fictitious sequences, all uncalled for . . . and worst of all, it is dishonest."

—**Sam Lacy, one of many to criticize the low-budget biopic and Robinson's performance,** *Baltimore Afro-American,* **June 17, 1950**

"Jack and I [had] rehearsed his lines at night [in Hollywood]. . . . I marveled at his memory and amazing self-confidence before the camera, and I loved watching Ruby Dee [who played me and became a lifelong friend] and Louise Beavers [who played Mallie Robinson], the pros, work. *The Jackie Robinson Story* was a scantily researched low-budget film. . . . However, the very fact that Jack played himself made it a classic of sorts. . . . For me, it brought back painful memories. . . . Jack himself watched quietly. . . . I'm sure he felt that even a 'B' film heightened the awareness of the general public to his struggle."

—**Rachel Robinson,** *Jackie Robinson: An Intimate Portrait,* **1996**

"In 1950, and the years to come, Jack battled with umpires over matters not simply of judgment but of ethics, in his growing belief that the umpires, all white, were abusing their power in order to put him in his place."

—**Arnold Rampersad,** *Jackie Robinson: A Biography,* **1997**

"I HAVE NO DOUBT THAT THAT THERE ARE SOME UMPIRES IN THE NATIONAL LEAGUE WHO ARE 'ON' ME."

—J. R., QUOTED BY A. S. "DOC" YOUNG, *GREAT NEGRO BASEBALL STARS AND HOW THEY MADE THE MAJOR LEAGUES,* 1953

"The first black player was termed shrill and irritating. Several umpires took their cue from the league officials, who singled out Robinson for censure."

—**Lester Rodney, sports editor of the** *New York Daily Worker,* **excerpt from paper presented at the Jackie Robinson anniversary conference, Long Island University, Brooklyn Campus, April 1997**

"[Robinson] was the most difficult ballplayer I had to deal with as an umpire. Jackie was one of those players who could never accept a decision."

—**Jocko Conlan,** *Jocko,* **Jocko Conlan and Robert W. Creamer, 1967**

"[Not] well known was the outspoken dislike Conlan had for Jackie Robinson, whom he admired as a player but despised personally for the obscene language and antagonistic attitude he said Robinson directed toward him as an umpire. It is an understatement to say that Jackie and Jocko did not get along."

—**Robert W. Creamer, afterword,** *Jocko* **(30th anniversary reprint), Jocko Conlan and Robert W. Creamer, 1997**

"Jocko Conlon called a third strike on Robinson, who walked away silently. Conlon turned and called out, 'It was right over the middle.' Robinson took the bait, wheeled and disagreed. Out of the game. Out with him went two batting streaks. He had hit safely in sixteen straight games, and had reached base in fifty-five straight. Nobody in the press box could remember an umpire so blatantly provoking a player into ejection."

—Lester Rodney, sports editor of the *New York Daily Worker*, about an incident on July 2, 1950, with an umpire Robinson felt was targeting him because he was black, excerpt from paper presented at the Jackie Robinson anniversary conference, Long Island University, Brooklyn Campus, April 1997

"There is no question in my mind that the umpires are picking on Robinson."

—Clyde Sukeforth, Dodgers coach, 1950

"At the All-Star break, [Brooklyn's] record stood at 39–32, four games behind the Phillies. . . . Dodgers All-Stars were starters Jackie Robinson and Roy Campanella, Duke Snider, Pee Wee Reese, [Gil Hodges], and Don Newcombe . . . in one of the most memorable summer games. Ralph Kiner's homer in the top of the ninth tied the score 3–3, and Red Schoendienst's blast in the fourteenth won it for the National League, 4–3."

—Tom Clavin and Danny Peary, *Gil Hodges*, 2012

"Again we had a strong offense. Jackie, Duke Snider and Carl Furillo batted over .300, and Roy, Snider, and Gil Hodges each hit over 30 homers. In August, Hodges hit 4 homers and a single in a game against the Braves. Nobody could hit like the Dodgers."

—Don Newcombe, Dodgers pitcher, about a strong Dodgers team that would battle down to the wire for the NL pennant with the young Philadelphia Phillies, "the Whiz Kids," to Danny Peary, *We Played the Game*, 1994

"New York Giants owner Horace Stoneham was deciding where to send his nineteen-year-old phenom from the Negro Leagues, Willie Mays. . . . Willie's departure from the [Birmingham] Black Barons was a severe blow [to the Negro Leagues]. In . . . 1950, he was far from the best-known black player in the country and far from the biggest star to emerge from black ball. But he was one thing that Jackie Robinson, Roy Campanella, Satchel Paige, Larry Doby, and Monte Irvin were not—young. . . . It was the main reason he would hit the major leagues with such enormous impact a year later."

—Allen Barra, *Mickey and Willie*, about the player who would make the Giants' offense as formidable as the Dodgers', 2013

"It means nothing to me. I just play ball."

—J. R., pretending not to be affected by the power struggle for Dodger ownership that would lead to Branch Rickey's departure at the end of the 1950 season and Walter O'Malley's long rule, Associated Press, September 22, 1950

"Robinson knew full well that the departure of Branch Rickey from Brooklyn in October 1950 would cost him his best friend and supporter in the front office. . . . It was not long before Walter O'Malley's criticisms of Robinson as 'a prima donna and a Rickey man' were widely known."

—Lee Lowenfish, baseball historian and author, excerpt from paper presented at the Jackie Robinson anniversary conference, Long Island University, Brooklyn Campus, April 1997

"The news that Branch Rickey would be leaving the Dodgers at the end of the 1950 season hit me hard."

—J. R., expressing his real feelings about knowing Rickey was being pushed out of the organization by Walter O'Malley, *I Never Had It Made*, 1972

"Richie [Ashburn, the Phillies' center fielder] threw a one-hopper to [catcher] Stan Lopata and [trying to score the pennant-winning run with no outs in the bottom of the ninth, Cal] Abrams was out by fifteen feet. It wasn't even close. The runners had moved up, so now it was men on second and third and one out and Robinson was up. [Phillies manager Eddie] Sawyer came out and said put Robinson on. Which made sense."

—Robin Roberts, Phillies pitcher and future Hall of Famer, about the Dodgers and Phillies being tied 1–1 with one out in the tenth inning in the season finale, with the winner capturing the pennant, to Donald Honig, *Baseball Between the Lines*, 1976

"The decision was mutual. . . . Robinson was an extremely dangerous hitter; in that situation you were better off with him on first base than at the plate."

—Eddie Sawyer, Phillies manager, to Donald Honig, *The Man in the Dugout*, 1977

"So we walked Jackie to load the bases. . . . My first pitch [to Furillo] was eye-high, but I got away with it because Carl popped it straight high up. The next batter was Hodges and he hit an easy fly to right field."

—Robin Roberts, Phillies pitcher and future Hall of Famer, on the key outs that sent the game to determine the pennant into extra innings, to Donald Honig, *Baseball Between the Lines*, 1976

"After we beat [Brooklyn] in the final game of the 1950 season to win the pennant [on Dick Sisler's three-run homer off starter Don Newcombe in the tenth inning], I was exhausted, having pitched three times in five days. I was sitting by my locker, really whipped, when I felt someone tug on my shoulder. It was Jackie, who came into our clubhouse and went to every guy and shook his hand. . . . For him to do that just shows you what kind of person he was. He was a marvelous player and tough competitor who anyone would love to have on his team. But he also was a beautiful person."

—Robin Roberts, Phillies pitcher and Hall of Famer, *The Tim McCarver Show*

"National League fielding averages for 1950 . . . gave to the Dodgers top ranking as a team and at three positions . . . Gil Hodges established his supremacy among first basemen with .994. Jackie Robinson copped the second sackers with .988, and Billy Cox's .957 was good enough for leadership among third basemen."

—Dan Daniel, *New York World-Telegram and Sun,* **December 20, 1950**

"After the Trenton Giants ended their season, Willie Mays . . . joined a team of professionals Piper Davis had put together for a barnstorming tour, and two of the best players, Hank Thompson and Monte Irvin, would soon be Willie's teammates on the New York Giants. They played several games against integrated teams whose rosters included the Brooklyn Dodgers' Pee Wee Reese, Gil Hodges, and Jackie Robinson, who also acted as manager. Willie had several opportunities to talk to Jackie but shied away nearly every time."

—Allen Barra, *Mickey and Willie,* **2013**

"When [journalist Paul Hemphill and I] got him talking [one afternoon in February 2006 in Alabama], Mays recalled being too shy to talk to Jackie Robinson, but how encouraging Jackie was about Willie's chances to make it in the big leagues."

—Allen Barra, *Mickey and Willie,* **2013**

"Before a game in Meridian, Mississippi, I was standing around the batting cage looking and learning as usual, when Jackie Robinson walked up to me. 'Young man,' he said, 'I've been watching you, and you really pull that inside pitch. You hit very well.' It was the greatest compliment I had ever had from a super star."

—Ernie Banks, Kansas City Monarchs shortstop who would become a Chicago Cubs Hall of Famer, about playing for and against Jackie Robinson's Major League All-Stars, *Mr. Cub,* **1971**

"Jackie grew pretty tired barnstorming, playing in one town and then taking a long automobile ride to the next. . . . He met his wife at Jacksonville when it was over and they took a plane for a vacation in Puerto Rico and the Dominican Republic."

—**Harold Burr,** *Brooklyn Eagle,* **November 21, 1950**

"My problem is not to so much to take weight off as to keep it off. . . . I'm on a diet and it's easy enough to give up sweets and starches. But I'm a sucker for hot bread. . . . I'm planning to work out at the Harlem Y. . . . We organize group games up in Harlem and play 'em with the kids, handball and basketball, mostly. I expect to run in the gym and spend plenty of time in the sweat room. I'm looking forward to a good year. I feel I'm just about ready to hit my peak."

—**J. R. to Harold Burr,** *Brooklyn Eagle,* **November 21, 1950**

"The two Rickeyphiles [who new majority owner Walter] O'Malley detested were Red Barber and Jackie Robinson. From the day he took over, O'Malley made both feel unwanted."

—**Peter Golenbock, about O'Malley taking over the Dodgers after Rickey's resignation on October 26,** *Bums,* **1984**

"AS SOON AS O'MALLEY TOOK OVER THE PRESIDENCY OF THE CLUB, HE MADE IT CLEAR THAT HE WAS ANTI-RICKEY. . . . HE KNEW THAT I FELT VERY DEEPLY ABOUT MR. RICKEY, AND, CONSEQUENTLY, I BECAME THE TARGET OF HIS INSECURITY."

—J. R., *I NEVER HAD IT MADE,* AS TOLD TO ALFRED DUCKETT, 1972

"Any changes Brooklyn makes must be with a view to recapturing attendance. This must be kept foremost in mind in naming the new manager [to replace Burt Shotton]. My Flatbush underground agents tell me Pee Wee Reese won't get the job, and that Jackie Robinson can be had in a trade, provided a stick-out pitcher is included. The new Brooklyn brass feels the roster is disproportionately weighted with Negroes and it is agreed that Robinson, though the club's most trenchant hitter, can be replaced at less risk than Campanella, Newcombe, or Bankhead."

—**Joe Williams, casually making jarring statements,**
New York World-Telegram and Sun, **November 6, 1950**

"It is certainly tough on everyone in Brooklyn to have you leave the organization but to me it's much worse, and I don't mind saying we (my family) hate to see you go but realize that baseball is like that and anything can happen. It has been the finest experience I have had being associated with you, and I want to thank you very much for all you have meant not only to me and my family but to the entire country and particularly members of our race. I am glad for your sake that I had a small part to do with the success of your efforts and must admit it was your excellent guidance that enabled me to do it."

—**J. R. to Branch Rickey, excerpt from letter, November 1950**

RICKEY ON ROBINSON

"There was never a man in the game who could put mind and muscle together quicker than Jackie Robinson."

—**Branch Rickey**

"He's a Methodist. I'm a Methodist. . . . And God's a Methodist. We can't go wrong."

— **Branch Rickey, quoted, *42* (movie), 2013**

"Adventure. Adventure. The man is all adventure. I only wish I could have signed him five years sooner."

—**Branch Rickey, quoted by Roger Kahn, *The Boys of Summer*, 1972**

"A man of principle. A moral man. I had to get a man who could carry the burden on the field. I needed a man to carry the badge of martyrdom."

—**Branch Rickey**

"Surely God was with me when I picked Jackie. I don't think any other man in the Negro race or any other race could have done what he did those first two or three years. He really did understand the responsibility he carried. . . . Then he had the intelligence of knowing how to handle himself. Above all, he had what the boys call guts, real guts."

—**Branch Rickey**

"The fact that you wrote the letter, and particularly the things you said in it, not only meant very much to me, and was . . . deeply appreciated, but it also revealed why you have come to so much deserved distinction. I hope the day will soon come when it will be entirely possible, as it is entirely right, that you can be considered for administrative work in baseball, particularly in the direction of field management. . . . It would be a great pleasure for me to be your agent in placing you in a big job after your playing days are finished. Believe me always."

—**Branch Rickey, who might have made Robinson the Dodgers' player-manager if he weren't forced to move to the Pirates, to Robinson, excerpt from letter, December 31, 1950**

EIGHT

A Ballplayer Who Couldn't Be Silenced

"Jackie Robinson, my husband, is a hero to many people because he is a famous baseball player. He's a hero to me because he has handled one of the most difficult problems in human relations with restraint and dignity. By doing this he has helped the status of Negroes everywhere."

—**Rachel Robinson, giving a rare interview to a national magazine,**
McCall's **magazine, 1951**

"The most luxurious possession, the richest treasure anybody has, is his personal dignity."

—**J. R.**

"Professional baseball players do not have prolonged careers. . . . Jack . . . is 31, and . . . has one main ambition for when his baseball career is over. He wants to work with boys. . . . He believes that a keen interest in athletics helps a boy keep his balance, prevents juvenile delinquency. Jack may be proof of that. . . . If we knew more about the future, we'd like to have lots of children. But right now our house is just the perfect size for [the four of] us and just big enough to put up an occasional California relative."

—**Rachel Robinson,** *McCall's* **magazine, 1951**

"Off-seasons he has two interests—his wife and children in St. Albans, Queens, and a YMCA in Harlem. A board member and paid director, he turns in his salary to the 'Y.' He also personally raised $9,000 last year. . . . He rejected a major liquor distributor's offer of a post unless it was on his terms—the right to warn children against drinking."

—**United Press, May 12, 1951**

"In those early years you could purchase a television set from Jackie Robinson in Rego Park, Queens. He worked during the off-season for salary and commission three nights a week at the Sunset Appliance Store."

—Harvey Frommer, *Rickey and Robinson,* 1982

"In a special news conference . . . Dodger star Jackie Robinson announced his acceptance of the post of manager of the proposed 'Jackie Robinson Garden Apts.' in Brooklyn. The Dworman Company, builders of 215 Montague Street, Brooklyn, have applied for FHA aid in building a 'low cost housing project' in the vicinity of the Belt Parkway, which will house between 2,000 and 3,000 families."

—*New York Age*, about one of Robinson's several attempts over the years to provide affordable housing to low-income families, February 24, 1951

"Growing up in Washington, DC, I . . . never ran into things like I saw in Vero Beach when I went to Dodgertown in the spring of 1951 to begin my professional career. . . . I went to Holman Stadium to see the Dodgers play their exhibition game. . . . I had to go down the right field line in the section [where t]here was a big sign: 'Colored Only.' . . . Then I went to where the restrooms were and went in without looking over the door. . . . I got run out of there. Then I looked up and I saw it again: 'Colored Only.' . . . A couple of years after that, Jackie Robinson complained about those signs. He put up a fuss and eventually the Dodgers took them down at Dodgertown. . . . That was a big deal for me because it was Jackie Robinson who did it."

—Maury Wills, Dodgers star shortstop in the early sixties, *On the Run,* 1991

"Duke Snider and Gil Hodges have the power to turn a game upside down without notice, but even so Jackie Robinson looms as the key man in any strategy designed to bring pitching and hitting closer together. He's the one player on the team—in the league, in fact—who is just as dangerous on base as at bat. Last year he wasn't in shape. He didn't run. And it's not too severe a criticism to say he cost the Bums the pennant. This spring Robinson is streamlined. . . . If Robinson elects to play all-out baseball . . . he will help the Bums' pitching simply by driving the enemy pitchers crazy with his frenzied fakes and exasperating calisthenics on the lines."

—Joe Williams, about Robinson, whose stolen base total would rise from 12 in 1950 to 25 in 1951, *New York World-Telegram and Sun,* April 7, 1951

"On Opening Day [April 17, 1951], Robin Roberts beat Brooklyn easily, 5–2. . . . The only bright spot [for the Dodgers] was the performance of Jackie Robinson, who went two for four and accounted for half the Dodger runs with a homer."

—Peter Williams, professor and baseball author, excerpt from paper presented at the Jackie Robinson anniversary conference, Long Island University, Brooklyn Campus, April 1997

"The great Dodger-Giant inter-borough rivalry began . . . on April 20, in the Polo Grounds. . . . Robby had another good day for the Bums, going two-for-four . . . and batting in two. Brooklyn won it, 7–3. They won again the next day, again by 7–3, and it was a fine game for Jackie, who came up in the fourth with Duke Snider on and his team behind by one, and hit a 400-foot drive into the upper-left-field stands. The game was tied . . . after seven, but the Dodgers scored 3 in the eighth. Robinson . . . doubled Snider home and then took off for third, drawing a wild throw from catcher Wes Westrum that allowed him to keep coming and score."

—Peter Williams, professor and baseball author, April 1997

"I'm not blind to the fact that certain umpires are out to get me. Anything I do they'll give me the worst of the breaks. I know what I'm up against. I'm doing my best to stay out of trouble. But no matter what anybody says, I think I know what's going on."

—J. R., soon after a squabble with umpires Babe Pinelli and Dusty Boggess at Ebbets Field, quoted by Dick Young, *New York Daily News*, April 14, 1951

"Don't be a sucker, a fall guy. Organized dope rings—real bums—are out to make a slave of you. . . . The kid who takes dope has as much chance of survival as the swimmer who fights a strong current wearing handcuffs. . . . Authorities should move in sufficient numbers of police to rid East Harlem of every dope pusher. . . . I'll certainly do anything in my power to lend a hand. If groups need my help, I'll be available on any off-day of the Dodgers' schedule."

—J. R., who spoke often against drugs, including at several performances of an open-air drama, *Dope*, which was sponsored by the East Harlem Protestant Parish and performed by local actors in vacant lots in the drug-troubled neighborhood, *New York World-Telegram and Sun*, April 26, 1951

CLASSIC MOMENT: APRIL 30, 1951, EBBETS FIELD, BROOKLYN, NEW YORK

"Jackie Robinson was a pioneer, but identification as a reformer is a role he has not sought and does not relish when it comes to him. He feels it has come and he must see it through even at the risk of his reputation, his body, his wealth and against the advice of his wife. It is the way the Dodger second baseman explains his aggression in the explosive incident at Ebbets Field Monday night when he pushed a bunt down the first base line and deliberately charged Sal Maglie as the Giant pitcher fielded it in foul territory."

—Milton Gross, *New York Post*, May 2, 1951

"I did it because of the bean ball throwing. It's got to stop before somebody gets really hurt. . . . I don't believe fans come to ball parks to . . . see fights, but this business of maliciously throwing at the batter's head has got to be stopped. [Larry] Jansen hit me with a pitch on Sunday. The mark's still there. Maglie had thrown one at me on the previous pitch. I made up my mind to do something to protect myself and the other fellows. I set out to create enough of a disturbance to make Ford Frick step in and stop this thing. The rule book specifically says the umpires must take action on bean balls. Not one of them has moved. I don't care if I'm fined but I'm telling you I bunted and ran into Maglie deliberately to bring this whole thing to a head."

—J. R. to Milton Gross, *New York Post*, May 2, 1951

"I told Jackie Maglie had denied throwing at him."

—Milton Gross, *New York Post*, May 2, 1951

"I suppose it's my fault. Every time something happens I pick up a paper and I'm at fault. If Maglie didn't throw at me then his catcher thought differently. After the bunt I came back to the plate and picked up my bat and [Wes] Westrum said, 'Sal wasn't throwing at you. You've been wearing us out. He was just brushing you back.' That's too fine a difference for me."

—J. R. to Milton Gross, *New York Post*, May 2, 1951

"It was a bush trick, period."

—Leo Durocher, Giants manager, about Robinson bunting so he could run into Maglie, May 1, 1951

"If I'm bush, Durocher made me that way. He taught it to me [when he was the Dodgers manager]. Right here in this clubhouse he used to tell us every day, 'If they throw one at your head don't say anything. Push one down and run right up his neck.' . . . Ask Jansen. He doesn't want to [throw at a hitter] but he does it because he's ordered to [by Durocher]. . . . I hope what I did helps stop it. I don't want to have to do it again but if I have to I will."

—J. R. to Milton Gross, *New York Post*, May 2, 1951

"Jackie, a great competitor has all the right in the world to 'invite' a pitcher to take his medicine on the baseline. . . . No less equal is the right of the pitcher to drive back from the plate such devastating hitters as Robinson. . . . The pitch is a part of the game, from time immemorial, and no panty-waists of today can ever change it, as long as pitchers work. But Robinson is right on his bunt. That is the hitter's retort to the pitcher. It is traditional and legitimate. The panty-waists forget that baseball is not only the most scientific and enduring game of ball but that it is also a contact game. That is the point, oddly, on which Durocher and Robinson would eagerly agree."

—Joe King, taking both sides in the dispute, *New York World-Telegram and Sun*, May 2, 1951

"I told Bavasi that if Brooklyn could not control it, I could and I can."

—Ford Frick, NL president, who claimed he had heard accusations about Robinson "umpiring" but nothing from umpires about bean balls, May 2, 1951

"I have no reason to be dissatisfied with Jackie Robinson, his conduct on the field or his spirit. . . . He has the full support of this organization."

—Walter O'Malley, Dodgers owner, defending Robinson to Frick, May 2, 1951

"Jackie Robinson willingly and deliberately endangered his body, his reputation and his pocketbook to goad Ford Frick, president of the National League, to step in and stop the bean ball war that has developed between the Giants and Dodgers. Apparently the stakes aren't high enough, Robinson's expenditure of all he holds dear has failed. Instead, it has been disclosed that Frick warned Robinson early this week to stop his umpire-baiting or face suspension. . . . [Robinson] alone should not be censured. . . . If Robby is punished, Durocher, Dressen, Frick and his umpires should be, too."

—Milton Gross, one of the few reporters in the city before the arrival of the *Herald Tribune's* Roger Kahn in 1952, who was often supportive of Robinson, *New York Times*, May 3, 1951

"JACK, SOME GUYS ARE THROWING AT YOU BECAUSE YOU'RE BLACK. BUT OTHER GUYS ARE THROWING AT YOU BECAUSE THEY PLAIN DON'T LIKE YOU."
—PEE WEE REESE TO JACKIE ROBINSON, THROUGHOUT HIS ENTIRE CAREER

"Maglie hated Robinson. . . . With Jackie, the feeling was mutual. Sal always pitched him high and tight—brushed him back or knocked him down—then curved him low and outside. That's what everybody tried to do, of course. The difference was that Maglie did it successfully. With everybody else, to throw close to Robinson was to make him a better hitter. . . . Sal was the one pitcher we had who could get him out consistently. Jackie just couldn't do a thing with him."

—Leo Durocher, Dodgers and Giants manager in 1947,
***Nice Guys Finish Last*, 1975**

"Contrary to popular belief (and personal memory) he . . . hit very well against Maglie, batting a solid .310 against the Dodgers' chief tormentor."

—Lyle Spatz, baseball historian, excerpt from paper presented at the Jackie Robinson anniversary conference, Long Island University, Brooklyn Campus, April 1997

"Jackie used to needle me a lot. He didn't say anything to me, but he would come out in the paper with it. Every time I would beat him, he would say that I was cheating or scratching the ball or something, which was not true. . . . I didn't get mad. . . . I'd just bear down more, and if I saw him quiet and not making too much of a ruckus, I let him alone. . . . I never woke him up, because he could beat you by himself."

—Sal Maglie to Peter Golenbock, *Bums,* 1984

"By 1951, one thing was clear: Robinson had become one of the most 'controversial' characters in baseball, and the reason had been shifted from the obvious and now discredited issue of the color of his skin to that of his temperament. He was being branded a pop-off, a troublemaker. . . . This led Robinson to develop some extremely sharp opinions about the caliber of men who write about Major League Baseball."

—Carl T. Rowan, *Wait Till Next Year,* Carl T. Rowan with Jackie Robinson, 1960

"One sportswriter who consistently ignored the pressures Jackie was under was Dick Young [Dodgers beat writer for the *Daily News*]. Young had been Robinson's primary champion prior to his coming to the Dodgers, but Young could not abide the fact that Robinson preached racial politics. Young felt ballplayers should keep politics to themselves and talk baseball. Robinson refused to accept that. He insisted on expressing his views on social issues. Friction resulted."

—Peter Golenbock, *Bums,* 1984

"I was all for Jackie. But he thought everything that happened to him was because of his color. Racism was sometimes a crutch for Jackie. I can understand it, but that doesn't make it right."

—Dick Young

"I used to think he was a nice guy personally, and I knew he was a good sportswriter. As time went by, Young became in my book, a racial bigot. . . . Although he seemed to stand up for me occasionally in later years, he often seemed to use his column to attack me, and the relations between us have often been strained."

—J. R., *I Never Had It Made,* as told to Alfred Duckett, 1972

"If you can't tell the truth, don't write."

—J. R. to Dick Young

"The Dodgers, with seven players, dominate the [National League All-Star] team. The fans selected Gil Hodges, Jackie Robinson and Roy Campanella, and [Phillies manager Eddie] Sawyer added [Preacher] Roe, [Don] Newcombe, Pee Wee Reese, who had been beaten by Alvin Dark, and Duke Snider."

—Dan Daniel, *New York World-Tribune,* July 3, 1951

"Detroit's Briggs Stadium was the site for some of the biggest All-Star Game fireworks ever as the two squads combined to slam six homers. The National League attack featured big flies from Stan Musial, Bob Elliott, Gil Hodges and Ralph Kiner. . . . The Senior Circuit showed some capability for 'little ball,' too [in its 8–3 victory] as Jackie Robinson laid down a perfect squeeze bunt [single to score Richie Asburn with two outs in the seventh inning]."

—mlb.com

"By July 3, [the Dodgers] were five and a half up on the Giants. . . . Then at Ebbets Field on July 3, they began [a] three-game series with the Giants, starting with a doubleheader. The first game went into extra innings. Finally, in the eleventh, Bobby Thomson homered to put his team ahead, 5–4, and things looked bad for the locals—until, in the bottom half, Jackie Robinson did these things: he singled Snider home with the tying run; he took second after a bad throw by [Monte] Irvin . . . ; he took third when a rattled Giant catcher [Ray Noble] threw a pickoff attempt into center field; and then he scored on a squeeze. Brooklyn, 6–5. After this, the Giants seemed to throw up their hands."

—Peter Williams, professor and baseball author, on how Robinson ignited a three-game sweep of the Giants to put the Dodgers up by a more comfortable 7½ games, excerpt from paper presented at the Jackie Robinson anniversary conference, Long Island University, Brooklyn Campus, April 1997

"HE BEAT ME A THOUSAND TIMES IN A THOUSAND WAYS. GETTING A BASE HIT, MAKING A PLAY, MAKING THE DOUBLE PLAY, HITTING THE HOME RUN, STEALING A BASE, STEALING HOME, UPSETTING MY PITCHER WITH HIS ANTICS ON THE BASES."

—LEO DUROCHER, GIANTS MANAGER,
NICE GUYS FINISH LAST, 1975

JACKIE AND LEO: AN INTENSE RIVALRY

"My part in the signing of Jackie Robinson was zero. I read about it in the paper like everybody else. I never even saw him play until he came to spring training in Havana [in 1947]."

—Leo Durocher, *Nice Guys Finish Last,* 1975

"Durocher loves to win. He makes all of us want to break our backs for him. The way he sometimes talks to us in the clubhouse before a game is absolutely inspirational."

—J. R. to Jack Sher, *Sport* **magazine, 1948**

"Durocher was accused of associating with mobsters and was suspended from baseball for the 1947 season. . . . Had Durocher remained as manager, Robinson would have had as fierce an ally as there was in all of baseball. With Durocher's banishment, the rookie was pretty much on his own."

—Peter Golenbock, excerpt from paper presented at the Jackie Robinson anniversary conference, Long Island University, Brooklyn Campus, April 1997

"You want a guy that comes to play. But [Robinson] didn't just come to play. He came to beat you. He came to stuff the damn bat right up your ass."

—Leo Durocher, quoted by Roger Kahn, *The Boys of Summer,* **1972**

"Durocher . . . is a unique kind of manager. In 1954 he did the best job of anyone. When Leo is winning he has a knack of getting something out of a club that makes it go a little bit farther. [In 1955] the Giants were not going well, and Leo is not a good manager when a club's going that way."

**—J. R., article titled "Why Can't I Manage in the Majors?",
as told to Milton Gross, 1956**

"Mr. Rickey might not have been willing to say that Jackie had the ability to make a bad situation worse, but I don't think he would have said that Jackie ever went out of his way to make it any better, either."

—Leo Durocher, 1975

"Durocher, who at the time was managing the Giants, was a great target for at least two of our players, Jackie Robinson and Don Newcombe. Of course, Leo was a master at superlatives and eloquent profanity, so there were some classic exchanges."

—Carl Erskine, *Carl Erskine's Tales from the Dodger Dugout,* **2000**

"We were always giving it to each other back and forth, because by then he had become as bad as me."

—Leo Durocher, *Nice Guys Finish Last,* **1975**

"I kept trying to find some way to upset him, anything to get his mind off the game. Even at the end, when he had become a third baseman, I'd be standing alongside him in the coaching box and I'd yell, 'Hit one down to Fatso, here. Old Fatso won't bend over.' And sure enough, someone would hit the ball down there and he'd make the goddamnest play you ever saw, and then he'd look at me and laugh, you know, and then he'd walk up there and hit one."

—Leo Durocher, *Nice Guys Finish Last,* 1975

"Hey, Leo, is that Laraine's perfume you're wearing?"

—J. R., a first-rate heckler directing one of his typical insults at Giants manager Leo Durocher, quoted by Durocher, *Nice Guys Finish Last,* 1975

"I asked Jackie how he handled [Leo Durocher once calling him an SOB] and he told me that he called him one, too. [I said,] 'That makes you both even, you can go on from there.'"

—Happy Chandler, baseball commissioner

"He knew that whatever I might yell at him, I admired him as a ballplayer and as a competitor. He was a Durocher with talent."

—Leo Durocher, *Nice Guys Finish Last,* 1975

"IF I HAD TO GO TO WAR I'D WANT HIM ON MY SIDE."

—LEO DUROCHER

"I would not say he's the best manager in the big leagues, but he's not the worst, either. In fact, you'd have to put him very high. He knows baseball, despite his personality problems."

—J. R., not giving Durocher, manager of the Cubs, the highest evaluation, February 13, 1971

"The Dodgers winning attitude is what I remember most. . . . Reese was the on-field leader. Hodges, Snider and Robinson were all leaders. . . . [Robinson] had a lot of inner strength and wasn't afraid to speak his mind. He had friends other ballplayers didn't have—politicians, Edward R. Murrow. He was a fine guy. I know he was unhappy that Branch Rickey had left and he didn't care much for Walter O'Malley, but he still hit .338 in 1951 and drove in about 90 runs. He also was an excellent second baseman."

—Rube Walker, Dodgers catcher beginning in 1951, to Danny Peary,
We Played the Game, 1994

"GIVE ME FIVE PLAYERS LIKE ROBINSON AND A PITCHER AND I'LL BEAT ANY NINE-MAN TEAM IN BASEBALL."

—CHARLIE DRESSEN, DODGERS MANAGER

"Dressen was his favorite manager. He appreciated what Jack could do for the team, not just for himself. Dressen always treated him as someone who was necessary to the process of the team winning and also someone who was capable of producing for him."

—Rachel Robinson to Danny Peary, 2012

"I can say nothing but the best of Charlie Dressen. . . . Charlie would help his worst enemy on the ball club, if the guy could help him win. . . . I know that Charlie doesn't think of himself personally when it comes to winning ball games. He loves to be responsible for success—but then, who doesn't? He is the ball player's best friend, because he fights for the player's rights."

—J. R., *Baseball Has Done It*, 1964

"I didn't blame Charlie for losing [the pennant to the Giants]. I blame myself and the other Dodgers. When our August lead was eleven games I decided that the pennant was in, that we'd break even, pick up a game here and there and finish breezing. So I quit the line-up for a minor operation. In September we had the habit of looking over our shoulders at the scoreboard to see what the Giants were doing, and forgetting to play the team on the diamond. And when the Giants came roaring on, we panicked."

—J. R., *Baseball Has Done It*, 1964

"When I became a New York Giant in 1951 and saw the money I was making, I said to myself, 'Boy, when I see Jackie, I'm going to thank him, even though he's not going to know what I'm talking about. I'm going to thank him because he took such a beating for two years without saying anything—he just played ball so I could play ball.'"

—**Willie Mays, Giants' 1951 Rookie of the Year outfielder and future Hall of Famer,** *The Tim McCarver Show*, **May 16, 2010**

"Prior to yesterday's doubleheader with Cincinnati, the Dodgers star received letters that threatened his life. The Cincinnati ball club also received letters which threatened to take care of Robinson during the game. Police searched Crosley Field and the immediate area around the ball park and expressed the opinion the letters were the work of a 'crank.' Robinson was the most unconcerned guy in the house. He ripped a three-run homer to help Brooklyn win the first game, 10–3, and got one-for-two in the nightcap to help the Dodgers win that one, 14–4."

—**United Press, May 21, 1951**

"Pee Wee Reese used to tell me he hated to go to Cincinnati because he had to face his family, everybody from Louisville was there. They'd all bug him about me, and he'd say, 'Look, have you ever met him?' and introduce me. Overall, there was nobody like Pee Wee for me. . . . [Another] time in Cincinnati when all our white players got letters saying if they don't do something, the whole team will be black and they'll lose their jobs, Pee Wee got on the bus and brought it up and we started discussing it and pretty soon we were all laughing about it. Pee Wee was the captain, he knew how to handle everything."

—**J. R., quoted by Dave Anderson,** *New York Times,* **December 5, 1971**

"In Ebbets Field last night, after the 4–3 Dodger win over the Phils . . . cops . . . moved before both dressing rooms as the game ended, to guard against a renewal of the tiff between [Phils' pitcher] Russ Meyer, and [Jackie] Robinson. . . . Meyer, the bad boy of the league who had alleged to have reformed, blew his top in the eighth as Robinson scored the winning run. With Robinson on third, Carl Furillo missed the pitch on a squeeze-play sign. . . . Jackie was hung up between third and home—apparently a dead duck. Robinson achieved amazing feats of agility as Andy Seminick, catcher; Puddinhead Jones, third baseman; Gran Hamner, shortstop; and Meyer tried to run him down. . . . As Jackie made his final essay towards the plate, Jones threw to Meyer, who dropped the ball. Meyer . . . by this time did not care whether he had the ball. He bumped the Dodger second baseman. . . . Larry Goetz, plate umpire, immediately declared Robinson safe because of obstruction. Meyer continued to bump Robinson. They stood nose to nose again after Jackie crossed the plate. . . . They agreed to meet beneath the stands. Both bench teams, on the alert, piled down en masse, leaving a bewildered group of competitors on the field. . . . No blow was struck. Goetz went below-decks, too, and earned an umpire's gold star for handling the whole deal. . . . Meyer came into the Dodger dressing room and apologized to Robinson. Jackie replied, 'It was my fault, too.'"

—Joe King, *New York World-Telegram and Sun,* June 1, 1951

"In 1951, Robinson, making the first of several attempts at establishing himself as a businessman, opened the Jackie Robinson Clothing Store in central Harlem. The idea was to sell a line of inexpensive men's apparel [with his name on the label]. But a nearby chain store easily undersold him, and his store did not outlast his playing career."

—David Falkner, *Great Time Coming,* 1995

"JACKIE ROBINSON MADE A PROMISE TO 14-YEAR-OLD JOHNNY NAGELSCHMIDT AT COOPERSTOWN, NY, AND KEPT IT WITH INTEREST. THE YOUNGSTER HAD APPROACHED THE BROOKLYN SECOND BASEMAN AT THE ANNUAL BASEBALL SHRINE EXHIBITION WITH THE ATHLETICS AND ASKED FOR HIS AUTOGRAPH ON A CRUMPLED SCORECARD. AS LEAGUE RULES FORBID SUCH AUTOGRAPHS, JACKIE SORROWFULLY DECLINED, BUT TOOK THE LAD'S ADDRESS. THE YOUTH RECEIVED A BALL, WITH THE SIGNATURES OF THE ENTIRE BROOKLYN SQUAD AND A NOTE."

—*SPORTING NEWS,* AUGUST 22, 1951

"In Boston, after the Dodgers lost a tight game late in 1951 on an umpire's decision [by Frank Dascoli on a play when Robinson threw the ball to Campanella in time, but the runner was ruled safe], one player [pitcher Preacher Roe] kicked in the base of the door to the umpires' dressing room. Jack, who didn't do it, was blamed by a Boston newspaper man and the story was carried by wire services. Next day when Robinson asked for an explanation, the reporter told him: 'Sorry, but I was right on deadline. Didn't have time to check.'"

—Roger Kahn, about an incident that led to Robinson and Campanella being fined **$100 each and Roe getting off with a $50 fine,** *New York Herald Tribune,* **August 29, 1954**

"The next day there was a brief story with a tiny headline saying that 'Robinson denies he kicked door in.' The writer still didn't have the honesty and guts to run this information as a correction, to concede that *he* was wrong, that he had written the story only on the basis of hearsay. . . . Saying that 'Robinson denies it' would still leave millions of Americans assuming that he was right but that I was a liar in denying it. . . . I gave a lot of thought to suing that guy and his newspaper."

—J. R., *Wait Till Next Year,* Carl T. Rowan with Jackie Robinson, 1960

"A big game I'll always remember was the final game of the 1951 season at Connie Mack Stadium, when we played the Dodgers, who needed a victory to tie the Giants in the pennant race. I had pitched Saturday, but [Phillies manager] Eddie Sawyer brought me into the game in the eighth inning, which is when Brooklyn scored three times to tie the score, 8–8. In the top of the eleventh inning, the Dodgers had the go-ahead run on second with two outs. . . . I got Jackie out that time."

—Robin Roberts, Phillies pitcher and Hall of Famer, *The Tim McCarver Show*

CLASSIC MOMENT: SEPTEMBER 30, 1951, CONNIE MACK STADIUM, PHILADELPHIA, PENNSYLVANIA

"Don Newcombe, the sixth pitcher Manager Chuck Dressen had tossed into the game, had the bases filled and two out in the twelfth when a hit would have sent the Dodgers tumbling into the most disastrous flag loss in National League history. Eddie Waitkus apparently had made that hit."

—Roscoe McGowan, *New York Times,* October 1, 1951

"Eddie Waitkus, dangerous and left-handed . . . with Robinson shifted over toward first, didn't pull. He hit a low-hard line shot straight up the middle. Somewhere, somehow, out of the shadows and floodlights of later afternoon, Robinson literally flew into the picture."

—David Falkner, *Nine Sides of the Diamond,* 1990

"He flings himself headlong at right angles to the flight of the ball, for an instant his body is suspended in midair, then somehow the outstretched glove intercepts the ball inches off the ground. He falls heavily, the crash drives an elbow into his side, he collapses . . . stretched at full length in the insubstantial twilight, the unconquerable doing the impossible."

—Red Smith, *New York Times,* October 1, 1951

"Umpire Lon Warneke's arm went up signaling the saving put out. Robbie fell hard on his shoulder and collapsed after tossing the ball weakly toward the infield. Anxious Dodgers clustered around the second baseman and several minutes later he rose groggily and walked slowly and uncertainly toward the dugout, while fans in every part of the stands rose and cheered."

—Roscoe McGowan, *New York Times,* October 1, 1951

"I was on third base. . . . I saw Jackie dive for it, get it and then throw it back over his head. I still to this day think he trapped that ball, and he knew it, and in desperation was trying to get a force play at second. . . . I've always wondered why Jackie, if he'd caught it on the fly for the third out, tried to throw the ball to second. Years later I met him at some function or other and I said, 'Jackie, did you really catch that ball?' He laughed and said, 'What'd the umpire say?'"

—Robin Roberts, Phillies pitcher and Hall of Famer, to Donald Honig, *Baseball Between the Lines,* 1976

"Leaning on coach Jake Pitler, Robinson slunk to the dugout where 'Doc' Wendler waved under his nostrils a cotton ball soaked in ammonia. Robinson revived and in the thirteenth trotted to his position."

—Joshua Prager, *The Echoing Green,* 2006

"[Robin] Roberts set the Dodgers down in the thirteenth and had retired Pee Wee Reese and Duke Snider on pop-ups in the fourteenth when Robinson came to the plate. Roberts got one ball and one strike on Robby, then Jack swung with all his power and the ball sailed high into the upper left field stands. Jackie trotted slowly around the bases and was overwhelmed by the entire Brooklyn team as he approached the dugout."

—Roscoe McGowan, *New York Times,* October 1, 1951

"IT WASN'T ANY SURPRISE THAT ROBINSON HIT THE HOMER. HE ROSE TO THE OCCASION MANY TIMES. HE HAD ALREADY SAVED THE GAME."

—ANDY SEMINICK, PHILLIES CATCHER, TO DANNY PEARY,
WE PLAYED THE GAME, **1994**

"Jackie Robinson made the most vital put-out of his career in the twelfth inning today, then hit the most important home run of his life in the fourteenth to give the embattled Dodgers a 9–8 triumph over the Phils and put the Brooks into a pennant play-off with the Giants. Two more dramatic events probably never have been seen in such a ball game, and the record Shibe Park crowd of 31,755—thousands of them from Brooklyn—reacted accordingly."

—Roscoe McGowan, *New York Times,* **October 1, 1951**

"In the first game [of the best-of-three playoffs between the Dodgers and Giants], there were a number of brushback pitches thrown by the Giants' Jim Hearn and the Dodgers' Ralph Branca. But there was only one hit batsman, Monte Irvin, the National League's RBI champion in 1951. Sure enough, two at-bats later, Irvin homered. Bobby Thomson had touched Branca for a 2-run homer earlier in the game, so Irvin increased the [Giants'] lead to 3–1. That was the final score of the first baseball game ever telecast coast-to-coast. . . . In the second game . . . the cocky rookie [Clem Labine, the Dodgers' best reliever] exhibited remarkable poise [as a starter] in a do-or-die game, limiting the Giants to 6 hits in a 10–0 victory. He was backed by homers from Robinson, Walker [who was filling in for the hobbled Campanella], Hodges, and [Andy] Pafko."

—Tom Clavin and Danny Peary, *Gil Hodges,* **2012**

"We're all tired. You've got two more innings to go—six outs. You just go out there and pitch."

—J. R. to Don Newcombe after the seventh inning in the final game of the playoffs, resulting in the tired starter staying in and taking a 4–1 lead into the bottom of the ninth, October 3, 1951

"[In the deciding game, with the Dodgers leading 4–2 in the bottom of the 9th inning but with two Giants on base, reliever] Branca's first pitch to Thomson was a fastball for a strike. . . . So Ralph threw the same pitch. And Bobby was ready for it, and he whacked it. . . . We were stunned for a moment. Nobody said anything, nobody moved, even though we saw that the ball had gone into the stands. . . . Then it struck us: we'd won. It sank in. We began jumping up and down and yelling. . . . And then pandemonium broke loose throughout the whole ballpark. One thing I'll always remember though: Jackie Robinson was standing there watching Bobby circle the bases, making sure he touched each one."

—**Monte Irvin, New York Giants outfielder and future Hall of Famer, describing the most famous homer in history, to Donald Honig,** *Baseball Between the Lines,* **1976**

"I was in the clubhouse looking out the window at the field when Thomson hit the pennant-winning 3-run homer off Branca. 'The Shot Heard Around the World!' 'The Miracle of Coogan's Bluff.' . . . After the game Jackie Robinson and a few other Dodgers congratulated us."

—**Bill Rigney, Giants shortstop and future manager, to Danny Peary,** *We Played the Game,* **1994**

"Bad as we felt, after it was all over, you couldn't help feeling how thrilled [Thomson] must be, and what a great thing it was in baseball."

—**J. R.**

"We had plans to go out with some friends but after the game we cancelled the entertainment and my wife and I had dinner alone then saw a movie."

—**J. R., about what he called "my biggest disappointment," quoted by guest columnist and Pirates' home run champion Ralph Kiner,** *Pittsburgh Press,* **June 5, 1952**

"THE DODGERS DIDN'T LOSE THE PENNANT, THE GIANTS WON IT."

—J. R., ABOUT THE ARCHRIVALS WHO OVERCAME A THIRTEEN AND A HALF–GAME DEFICIT TO THE DODGERS IN AUGUST BY GOING 39–8 DOWN THE STRETCH, 1951

"When Walter O'Malley announced in the clubhouse after the playoffs with the Giants that Dressen would be back, we all cheered."

—**J. R.**

"Jackie Robinson of the Dodgers, greatest all-around athlete in UCLA history, will serve as Grand Marshal at the school's 25th homecoming week celebration Nov. 2–3. Robinson is the first athlete ever accorded the honor. He is now on a baseball barnstorming trip in the South but he notified graduate manager William Ackerman he would be here for the celebration."

—Associated Press, October 22, 1951

"Jackie Robinson traveled his way south and west. . . . Promoter Ted Worner said that this year's tour did not draw as well as the 1949 and 1950 jaunts by Robinson, and that the overwhelming majority of attendees were Negroes."

—Thomas Barthel, *Baseball Barnstorming and Exhibition Games, 1901–1962,* 2007

"A growing number of African Americans shared sportswriter John I. Johnson's belief that 'there is no place in the nation for teams blocked off in racial groups.' By 1951, Sam Lacy criticized Jackie Robinson for continuing to participate in post-season barnstorming with a traditional all-black unit, while Wendell Smith condemned a proposed benefit game featuring major league players on two teams divided along racial lines."

—Neil Lanctot, *Negro League Baseball,* 2004

"Campanella really deserves every honor he can get. He kept us in the pennant race, both with his glove and his fine defensive work. He's a hard worker and I think he's the best catcher in baseball."

—J. R., who finished sixth in the NL MVP vote about Campanella winning the award for the first of three times in five years, Associated Press, November 1, 1951

"As a direct result of Robinson's baseball achievements, the National Broadcasting Company named Jackie 'Director of Community Activities'. . . making him NBC's first Negro exec."

—*Focus* magazine, July 1952

"[At Grossinger's in the Catskills that winter] Jackie and Rachel wanted to go skating so they came with me. We were putting on the skates and Jackie said, 'I'll race you for five bucks.' I said, 'Gee, Jack, I didn't know you skated.' He told me he had never been on skates in his life. [Having skated all my life] I told Jackie there was no way he could beat me. Jackie looked at me very seriously and said: 'Maybe you'll beat me, but that's how I'm going to learn.'"

—Vin Scully, Dodgers broadcaster, quoted by Bob Raissman, *New York Daily News,* April 6, 1997

"[Blackened out name] who has furnished reliable information in the past, stated that the Committee to End Discrimination in Levittown, New York, announced that Jackie Robinson, famous Dodger baseball star, told the committee he would cooperate with them to end discrimination in Levittown, New York, and offered them assistance in the matter."

—Item added to Jackie Robinson's FBI file, February 15, 1952

"Walter O'Malley revealed today that he had discussed the managership of the Montreal Royals with Jackie Robinson, offering the Negro sensation a crack at the job 'when his playing days are terminated. . . . Jackie told me that he would be both delighted and honored to tackle this managerial post. I warned him that first he would have to prove himself a handler of men—and white men at that. He told me that he always had a soft spot in in his heart for Montreal.' . . . 'It's like a wonderful dream,' Robinson told O'Malley."

—Larry O'Brien, about an offer that neither Robinson nor O'Malley discussed during the latter part of Robinson's playing career, *Montreal Star,* March 24, 1952

"Jackie Robinson and I became friends in the spring of 1952, friends almost by default. He was 33 years old and already heroic and despised. Walter O'Malley, the president of Robinson's employer, the Brooklyn Dodgers, warned me that 'this Robinson is the most shameless publicity seeker I've ever met.' Alvin Dark, shortstop for the New York Giants, said Robinson 'reminds me of Hitler.' . . . There were no women baseball writers in press boxes during the 1950s, nor any blacks. Bigotry—ol' boy bigotry; that sum-buck is too *uppity* bigotry—was the order of that journalistic day. . . . In that setting and given my background, a close friendship probably was inevitable. . . . He hated anti-Semitism just as he hated prejudice against blacks—without qualification and from the gut."

—Roger Kahn, Jewish Dodgers beat writer for the *New York Herald Tribune* beginning in 1952, *Journal of Blacks in Higher Education,* Winter 1996/1997

"Robinson was used commercially [by the Dodgers during the spring]. His visit to a Southern city stirred scuffles for reserved seats among whites. Black crowds lined up early on the morning of each game, struggling for places in the narrow colored section (reserved seats were not available). When you barnstormed with the Robinson Dodgers, you always covered sold-out games. . . . He was earning his annual salary, which never exceeded $40,000, before the season began."

—Roger Kahn, *The Boys of Summer,* 1972

"I DON'T MIND THE BOOING. WHAT GOT ME WAS WHEN SOME OF THEM STARTED TO HOLLER, 'HIT HIM IN THE HEAD.' THAT'S THE KIND OF THING THAT MAKES ME MAD. THESE CRACKPOTS ARE STILL FIGHTING THE CIVIL WAR."

—J. R., ABOUT PLAYING AN EXHIBITION GAME IN MOBILE, ALABAMA, QUOTED BY BILL ROEDER, *NEW YORK WORLD-TELEGRAM AND SUN*, APRIL 6, 1952

"In Tampa, Florida, Ben Chapman [whose racist remarks from when he was the Phillies manager in 1947 and 1948 weren't forgotten by Robinson] . . . was coaching third for the Reds in this exhibition game and we throw the ball around the infield and my throw goes to Jack pretty hard and he looks at me and makes a little motion shaking his hand. Ben Chapman hollered, 'Hey, Pee Wee. Don't throw it too hard to little Jackie now. You're liable to hurt his little hand.' Jack comes across from second base, walked right in front of me, almost to third and said, 'Look, Chapman, you son of a bitch. You got on me for two years and I couldn't say a word. Now you open your mouth to me one more time during this game, I'm gonna . . . kick the shit out of you.' . . . Chapman did not say another word. Chapman was rugged, but you better believe Robinson would have been something in a fight."

—Pee Wee Reese to Roger Kahn, *The Boys of Summer*, 1972

"Back in those days, club management had a very cozy relationship with the newspaper writers who covered the team. Not coincidentally, once Rickey left and friction developed between Robinson and O'Malley, Robinson's relationship with the New York media—particularly Dick Young of the *New York Daily News*—grew increasingly inflamed. Whether it was Jim Crow living arrangements at hotels or school desegregation in the South, Robinson had an opinion and wasn't afraid to express it. He believed his newfound outspoken nature didn't conform to O'Malley's perception of what a Negro ballplayer should be."

—Steve Garvey, a five-year-old Tampa boy in 1952 who became a Brooklyn bat boy in Florida in 1956 and Los Angeles Dodgers star first baseman from 1969 to 1982, *My Bat Boy Days*, 2008

"I knew what O'Malley's problem was. To put it bluntly, I was one of those 'uppity niggers' in O'Malley's book."

—J. R., *I Never Had It Made*, as told to Alfred Duckett, 1972

"O'Malley . . . accused Robinson of faking an injury to miss a 1952 exhibition game, leading to a meeting between O'Malley, Robinson, and his wife, Rachel. O'Malley added fuel to the fire by also reprimanding Robinson for complaining about being assigned to a different hotel than the rest of the team."

—Steve Garvey, future Los Angeles Dodgers star first baseman,
My Bat Boy Days, 2008

"It doesn't strike me as fair to have people who are sitting in comfort in an air-conditioned hotel lecture me about not complaining."

—J. R. to Walter O'Malley, during spring training meeting, 1952

"You know, Mr. O'Malley, bringing Jack into organized ball was not the greatest thing Mr. Rickey did for him. In my opinion, it was this: having brought Jack in, he stuck by him to the very end. He never listened to the ugly little rumors like those you have mentioned to us today."

—Rachel Robinson, putting O'Malley in his place,
during spring training meeting, 1952

"In 1952, the Dodgers opened at Boston in what would be the Braves' final year in that city. The game drew only 4,694 fans. . . . Brooklyn opened with a 3–2 victory behind veteran left-hander Preacher Roe. . . . Sam Jethroe's leadoff homer in the third had given Boston a 1–0 lead, but in the fifth . . . singles by Gil Hodges, Carl Furillo and Billy Cox and walk to Robinson [gave] them a run and left the bases loaded. . . . Campy lined [Warren] Spahn's first pitch to right field to score Furillo and Cox and put the Dodgers ahead to stay. . . . Besides his walk, Robinson had a fourth-inning single."

—Lyle Spatz, baseball historian, excerpt from paper presented at the Jackie
Robinson anniversary conference, Long Island University,
Brooklyn Campus, April 1997

"With the 1950 loss on the last day of the regular season, and the horrible [1951] play-off loss, the Dodgers were bound together in some mystical way. Dick Young, the clever writer for the *Daily News* . . . suggested the Dodgers were a bunch of chokers, the most vile description of a sports team. It was an insult that galled Robinson more than any of the others. His entire aura was as a winner. While Roy Campanella . . . was always certain there would be another day, Robinson never seemed sure."

—Maury Allen, *Jackie Robinson: A Life Remembered,* 1987

"Warren Giles, [new] president of the National League, has warned the Dodgers and particularly Jackie Robinson to mind their manners on the bench. The warning was by a letter, which Giles sent to Charlie Dressen on Wednesday afternoon, in between two night games the Dodgers played the Reds. . . . Giles . . . said he would not stand for the kind of bench jockeying, which he said he had heard the Dodgers direct at plate umpire Frank Dascoli in the first game. Giles mentioned hearing such terms as 'wop' and 'dago.' He said that Robinson's behavior was more offensive than that of the other Brooklyn players. Robinson was enraged. . . . He angrily told Giles that he hadn't done it. 'How can you say I called that man a wop?' . . . 'Well, you were hollering, weren't you?' Giles said. 'Yes, but I never called him any names.'"

—**Bill Roeder,** *New York World-Telegram and Sun,* **May 9, 1952**

"At the request of Jackie Robinson's business manager, the Dodgers are seeking a retraction from Warren Giles . . . who recently criticized Robinson's bench behavior. . . . Robinson, after telling Giles personally that he had not done any name calling, wanted to let the matter drop. But his manager felt that the slap by Giles might have a harmful effect on Jackie's sources of income outside of baseball, such as endorsements."

—*New York World-Telegram and Sun,* **May 12, 1952**

"A third child and second son, named David, was born to the Robinsons on May 14 and Jack responded with a triumphantly aggressive game that brought the team back to first place. The Chicago Cubs led Preacher Roe, 1–0, when Willard Ramsdell hit Robinson with a knuckleball. That loaded the bases in the fourth inning. A walk and ground out scored two runs. Now Robinson led away from third as Roe, whose lifetime batting average was .110, stepped in to bat. . . . With the count three balls and one strike, Robinson burst for home and did not stop. Ramsdell's hip-high fast ball had him cleanly beaten. Robinson sprang into a slide; it seemed as though he would crash into Bob Pramesa, the Cub catcher. But that was a final feint. As Jack slid, he hurled his body *away* from Pramesa, and toward first base. Only his right toe touched home plate. Pramesa lunged and tagged the air. . . . The Cubs did not challenge after that."

—**Roger Kahn, about Robinson stealing home to celebrate the birth of his second son,** *The Boys of Summer,* **1972**

"My biggest thrill [my rookie year] was the day I walked into Ebbets Field and saw that I had a locker next to Jackie Robinson. We became good friends. Robbie was the leader of the Dodgers and everyone looked up to him. He was no longer in his prime, but he was still the best ballplayer on the club. There were a lot of great players on the Dodgers, but he was the one who got it started. He was an inspirational player, a gung-ho guy, the best competitor I ever saw. I didn't see anger in him, except when . . . opponents tried to upset him. That made him a much better player."

—**Ben Wade, Dodgers pitcher, to Danny Peary,** *We Played the Game*, **1994**

A PEERLESS COMPETITOR

"Above all else, I hate to lose."

—**J. R.**

"In modern times there has never been a more passionate competitor than Robinson. He made every play as if it were a crucial one and ran just as hard on a ball hit back to the pitcher as he did on one that bounced off the fence."

— **Jimmy Cannon,** *New York Post*, **July 22, 1962**

"I would have to say that of all the fellows I played with, Jackie had to be the greatest competitor."

—**Spider Jorgensen, quoted by Bob Anderson,** *New York Daily News*, **October 25, 1972**

"He's the greatest competitor I have ever known."

—**Duke Snider, quoted by the Associated Press, October 25, 1972**

"I used to watch Robinson get into uniform. Jack would joke and kid and talk about the racetrack. But as he pulled on the Brooklyn shirt and the blue Brooklyn stirrups and the Brooklyn pants and the blue Brooklyn cap, he just got more and more serious. He was putting on his game face. Jack had a helluva game face: take no prisoners."

—Duke Snider

"Duke. Home to first base. That's ninety feet. Not seventy-five."

—J. R., telling Duke Snider to run out grounders at full speed

"Jackie is the greatest competitor I ever faced."

—Bobby Thomson, Giants outfielder from 1946 to 1953, to Pat Williams,
How to Be Like Jackie Robinson, **2005**

"He could beat you with a home run, he could beat you with a single or double, he could beat you with a bunt, he could beat you with a stolen base, he could beat you so many ways it was unbelievable."

—Don Zimmer, Dodgers infielder

"He would disrupt the game. He would drive you crazy."

—Frank Torre, Milwaukee Braves first baseman

"Jackie Robinson was one of the fiercest competitors I've ever played with or against."

—Tommy Lasorda, Dodgers pitcher

"He was a great competitor who could do it all. He was a great player, a manager's dream."

—Leo Durocher

"Jackie was probably as fine a baseball player as I ever saw. Sometimes he looked a little stiff and awkward out there . . . but what a base runner, what reflexes, and what a competitor!"

—Robin Roberts, Phillies pitcher and Hall of Famer, to Donald Honig,
Baseball Between the Lines, **1976**

"I don't try so hard to win because I'm a Negro. I try to win because that's the way I am. I hate to lose, even more when I'm playing cards with my wife."

—J. R. to Roger Kahn, *New York Herald Tribune*, August 29, 1954

"I played tennis, Ping-Pong, and gin rummy with Robinson and in friendly games, too, it was 'take no prisoner.'"

—Roger Kahn, *Journal of Blacks in Higher Education*, Winter 1996/1997

"IT KILLS ME TO LOSE. IF I'M A TROUBLEMAKER, AND I DON'T THINK THAT MY TEMPER MAKES ME ONE, THEN IT'S BECAUSE I CAN'T STAND LOSING. THAT'S THE WAY I AM ABOUT WINNING—ALL I EVER WANTED TO DO WAS FINISH FIRST."

—J. R.

"He made everybody around him play just a little bit better and a lot harder than they could play. Even in batting practice, he could make his teammates bear down and perform beyond their peaks."

—Hank Aaron, Braves outfielder and Hall of Famer, *The Tim McCarver Show*

"I have never seen a competitor like Jackie. After the game was over you could not talk to him. It was like he was still in the game. Everything he had in him had been drained out of him."

—Roger Craig, Dodgers pitcher from 1955 to 1961, to Pat Williams,
How to Be Like Jackie Robinson, 2005

"In my mind he was the greatest athlete ever to play Major League Baseball. . . . He was certainly the greatest competitor I ever saw."

—Ralph Kiner, Pirates' seven-time home-run champion and future Hall of Famer,
The Tim McCarver Show

"Jackie came running out [after I crashed into the wall at Ebbets Field after catching a line drive]. He turned me over to see if the ball had dropped out of my glove."

—Willie Mays

"His locker was where all the action was. He was friendly toward the media, and all the reporters came up to him before and after games. It was interesting to sit there and listen to him and then get up the next morning and not find one thing in the paper that you heard him say."

—**Ben Wade, Dodgers pitcher, to Danny Peary,** *We Played the Game,* **1994**

"Because he was so often quoted and misquoted, Jackie never missed reading any edition of the seven New York newspapers."

—**Carl Erskine, Dodgers pitcher,**
Carl Erskine's Tales from the Dodger Dugout, **2000**

"It was an incredibly talkative locker room. Campanella was talking all the time. Robinson was talking. Pee Wee liked to talk. Snider, my god. There were areas of static in the locker room. There was Reese who had a captain's chair. Everybody else had a stool. . . . Hodges . . . and Jackie lockered next to each other and he enjoyed Jackie but there wasn't back and forth between them. Sometimes Gil just burst out laughing at something Jackie or Campy said, but it wasn't like he had a comeback."

—**Roger Kahn, who, in 1952, began a two-year stint as the Dodgers beat writer for the** *New York Herald Tribune,* **to Tom Clavin,** *Gil Hodges,* **Tom Clavin and Danny Peary, 2012**

"There were several card games going on all the time. Reese, Hodges, Snider and Jackie played cards, mostly bridge. Clyde King, Billy Cox, and Carl Erskine liked bridge, too. . . . We couldn't do it every day, but after a game some of us would park at a service station in back of right field. And there'd be a hell of a crowd every time we went out. Reese, Jackie, and the others would sign autographs. I think everyone in Brooklyn identified with the Dodgers—we symbolized the 'city.'"

—**Rube Walker, Dodgers catcher, to Danny Peary,**
We Played the Game, **1994**

"The biggest improvement [for Negro players] has been in the social relationship between white and Negro players. . . . Now I sit down with the boys over cards, or Campy does, or Newcombe, and nobody gives it a second thought. It's just natural. I start a game, and other men join me. I'm asked—and I sit in. That's a far cry from 1947. Off the field, social relationships are not unusual. . . . I go to dinners with other Dodgers, play golf, get invited out with my wife. . . . White Southerners, by their associations with Negro players, have learned to respect them, just as all the Dodgers have learned to respect Campanella, Newcombe, and me. Some of them seem to realize that what they may have believed about Negroes all their lives is just false."

—J. R., interview, *Focus* magazine, July 1952

"There were people who became friends, but there wasn't much socializing outside the clubhouse between black players and white players. It just rarely was done in those days. We didn't get upset that we weren't part of things. The team would get together for a social event, and we would go, and we'd enjoy that. But we had other friends, and we had family, and we had our place in our own community, so it wasn't essential for them to come home with us."

—Rachel Robinson to Danny Peary, 2012

"We had lost the 1951 pennant in an upsetting way, but in 1952 . . . we held off the Giants by 4 games. We won the pennant with our best pitcher, Don Newcombe, in the army. . . . Probably our key addition was Joe Black, a big right-handed reliever, who, like his name, was black. Dressen used him all the time and he won 15 games and saved about the same number. . . . Hodges led our team with over 30 homers and 100 RBIs, but Robinson, Furillo, [Andy] Pafko, Campy, and . . . Snider provided a great deal of power. And we had our usual outstanding defense."

—Rube Walker, Dodgers catcher, to Danny Peary, *We Played the Game*, 1994

"The Dodgers signed me, and I was sent to Montreal. Jackie had played there and a lot of people thought I looked like Jackie. Then I was bought up to Brooklyn, and I roomed with Jackie for a while."

—Joe Black, Dodgers reliever who'd be voted 1952 NL Rookie of the Year, to Maury Allen, *Jackie Robinson: A Life Remembered*, 1987

"HE SAID, 'MAN, YOU'RE BIG. CAN YOU FIGHT?' I SAID YES, AND HE SAID, 'WELL, WE'RE NOT GOING TO.' THEN HE TOLD ME WHAT TO EXPECT. THAT SHOCKED ME. FIVE YEARS LATER, I THOUGHT THE WAR WAS OVER. IT WASN'T. . . . HERE'S A GUY WHO COULD . . . ACCEPT THE SLINGS AND SLURS AND NOT GET ANGRY. . . . HE WAS FIGHTING THE FIGHT ALL THE TIME, AND IT WASN'T JUST FOR JACKIE ROBINSON. IT WAS FOR ALL OF US."

—JOE BLACK, DODGERS RELIEVER, *ONEONTA (NY) DAILY STAR*, JUNE 13, 1997

"I remember one time we walked on the field and some loudmouth started yelling at him from the stands, 'Hey, Jackie, king of the niggers, hey Jackie.' Then he was screaming all kinds of vile things at him. Jackie just stared straight ahead, but you knew he was burning inside. . . . On a close pitch, if Jackie got the call the fans would scream, 'Nigger lover, nigger lover' at the umpire."

—**Joe Black, Dodgers reliever, to Maury Allen,**
Jackie Robinson: A Life Remembered, **1987**

"Jackie had more confidence in his ability than any player I ever saw. He helped me a great deal that way. He just told me I was better than the hitter. Pretty soon I began believing it."

—**Joe Black, Dodgers reliever, to Maury Allen,**
Jackie Robinson: A Life Remembered, **1987**

"We had three leaders on the Dodgers. Pee Wee was the mother hen. Campy was the jocular one. Jackie made you play."

—**Joe Black, quoted by Phil Pepe,** *New York Daily News,* **July 20, 1972**

"The Dodgers had one of the best defensive infields in the game, if not the best. I said to Joe Black, how is this different from the Negro League? And he said, 'Well, the hitters are better, and you notice those guys behind me, they can pluck them.' Hodges, Cox, Reese, Robinson, where can you find an infield like that? Everybody's an all-star defender. Robinson one year made [only] five errors at second base. Reese was a wonderful shortstop. Cox in my mind was the best third baseman I ever saw. And except for that one goddamn ball that got off Hodges's glove before Bobby Thomson's homer in the 1951 playoff, I don't remember him making a bad play. He was always there with a quick tag on a pick or a throw."

—**Roger Kahn, Dodgers beat writer for the** *New York Herald Tribune,*
to Tom Clavin, *Gil Hodges,* **Tom Clavin and Danny Peary, 2012**

"Making that double play, they didn't move [Jackie]. He'd get over that damn bag. He didn't care how big you were, how hard you slid. He challenged you and he had those big legs and, playing alongside him seven, eight years, I don't remember seeing this guy knocked down. He didn't fear *anything*."

—Pee Wee Reese, about his partner in the Dodgers' peerless double play combination, to Roger Kahn, *The Boys of Summer,* 1972

"Robinson's toughness made him almost immune to injury. Billy Herman, the great second baseman, once told me that Robinson was the only second baseman he ever saw who made no effort to get out of the path of oncoming baserunners who were intent on breaking up double plays by hitting him before he could throw to first. He just stood there and let those base runners bounce off him. If I tried that I'd get killed.'"

—Larry Claflin, *Boston Herald,* October 26, 1972

"I'm sitting in my hotel and the phone rings and it's Jackie. And he said, 'Did you hear what went on last night?' Stanky was calling to him, 'Hey, porter, get my bags,' and holding up shoes and asking him to shine them. 'I've been in the league seven years. I don't think I should have to take this shit.' I said I agree with him. 'Want me to write it?' He said, "Why do you think I'm calling?" So I wrote it. . . . I went to Stanky the next day and he said, 'Are you Robinson's little bobo? I didn't hear anything out of line. I heard 'black bastard' and 'nigger' plenty of times, but that's not out of line.'"

—Roger Kahn, about Cardinals manager Eddie Stanky, to Tom Clavin, 2012

"The flare-up of racial intolerance, with Jackie Robinson and pitcher Joe Black the alleged targets of an unidentified Cardinal player, which occurred in the first game of the recent four-game series in St. Louis . . . probably can be listed as a closed incident. The following night Fred Saigh, Cardinals owner, called Robinson over to his box, where the two men talked for a few minutes, then shook hands. . . . Saigh told Robinson . . . that if any remarks had been offensive to Robby and Black, he (Saigh) wanted to apologize. Saigh further expressed his admiration for Robinson as a player and man."

—Roscoe McGowan, *New York Times,* June 18, 1952

"Speaking of tantrums, Jackie Robinson seems to be improving by leaps and bounds in this phase of his play. His more recent outbursts have shown unexpected freshness and originality, especially in the clutch. It was a fine, zestful well-rounded sort of rage that sent Jackie to the showers in Cincinnati yesterday, and it may be that we have the new umpire to thank, Augie Guglielmo, for encouraging Robinson and the Dodgers as a group to blow their tops more often and more appealingly. Guglielmo called a man safe at second when Robinson thought he had him out, and Jackie put on a show. . . . Jackie slammed the ball to the ground, followed it with his glove, jumped up and down several times, shouted, shook his head, walked around with his hands on his hips and punted the glove 50 feet. Guglielmo put him out of the game for tossing ball and glove."

—Bill Roeder, being sarcastic about Robinson's ongoing conflicts with umpires,
***New York World-Telegram and Sun,* July 18, 1952**

"Jackie Robinson, Dodger infielder who was fined $75 by umpire Larry Goetz in Boston last Thursday, and who refused to pay unless he got a hearing, will be heard by Warren Giles, National League president. . . . The fining incident stemmed from a 6–4 Dodger loss in 11 innings, in which [Boston Braves shortstop Johnny Logan], who scored the winning run, was awarded first when hit by a pitched ball. Roy Campanella argued against the ruling and was fined $100. Jackie's fine came as a result of a conversation with Umpire Goetz immediately after the game."

—*Philadelphia Inquirer,* September 8, 1952

"Jackie Robinson could be perverse even when he was right. Edward R. Murrow used his television show to assault segregation from time to time, and Robinson of course approved. But the Dodger was anticommunist, and he did not like Murrow's television denunciation of Senator Joseph McCarthy. When Dodger public relations director Irving Rudd brought Murrow to the Dodger locker room in 1952, he was told off by [Mike Gavin of the *New York Journal-American*] for bringing a 'Red' around. . . . Robinson, according to the Dodger public relations man, at that point said, 'Irving, any time Edward R. Murrow wants to enter the Dodger locker room, dugout or anyplace else, he's my guest.' 'It got quiet fast,' according to Rudd. Robinson, who agreed with his teammates on the evils of communism, nevertheless deliberately elevated the tension level in the clubhouse to make a political point larger than baseball."

—Carl E. Prince, *Brooklyn's Dodgers,* 1996

"ROBINSON DID NOT MERELY PLAY AT CENTER STAGE. HE WAS CENTER STAGE; AND WHEREVER HE WALKED, CENTER STAGE MOVED WITH HIM."

—ROGER KAHN, *THE BOYS OF SUMMER*, 1972

"Robinson first met Richard Nixon during the 1952 Republican National Convention [held July 7–11] in Chicago. Introduced by Harrison McCall, a prominent Republican from California, Nixon shared his memory of the first time he had encountered Robinson—at a 1939 football game between UCLA and the University of Oregon. According to McCall, 'Nixon then proceeded to describe an unusual play which occurred in that game and Jackie Robinson recalled immediately the play . . . and proceeded to explain to Nixon the reason in back of the play.' . . . Neither Robinson nor Nixon would forget."

—**Michael G. Long, about the genesis of Robinson's odd camaraderie with the soon-to-be vice president and future president, *First Class Citizenship*, 2007**

"By September 3, the Dodger lead over the Giants had dropped to five games. In almost empty Braves Field, Boston moved five runs ahead, then the big hitters rallied, tying the score in the fourth inning. . . . The game stayed tied until the eighth inning. Then Robinson hit a grounder which the Boston second baseman threw wildly. Robinson never broke stride, and slid safely into third. . . . Snider bunted at Ed Mathews, the third baseman. Mathews charged and Robinson charged with him, staying one step behind. Mathews gloved the ball. He glanced back at Robinson, who stopped short. He threw to first. As Mathews released the baseball, Robinson sprinted home. He scored the winning run, with a long graceful slide."

—**Roger Kahn, *The Boys of Summer*, 1972**

"I certainly might, there's no getting around it. There are a lot of things causing [me to consider] it and well, I feel that this thing that has happened with umpires is going to be one of the things if I do."

—**J. R., angry about being fined $75 by NL president Warren Giles after a run-in with an umpire and hinting he may quit baseball at the end of the season because of the frequency of such incidents, WNBC radio recap program *Hy Gardner Calling*, September 12, 1952**

"Just say I'm considering it. I'm talking it over with my wife, but there's a good chance I'll stay in baseball."

—**J. R., about whether he'd call it quits because of umpires, to a reporter, *New York Herald Tribune*, September 12, 1952**

"Jackie is too much of a team man to be serious. Let's just chalk it up to pennant fever and consider the incident closed."

—Walter O'Malley, Dodgers owner, about Robinson saying he might retire, quoted by Roger Kahn, *New York Herald Tribune,* **September 13, 1952**

"We'll take those Yankee bastards."

—J. R., about the World Series after the Dodgers captured the pennant by beating the Phillies, September 23, 1952

"I looked at [the Yankees lined up] at third base and there's . . . not a dark face. Then you look at first base—Charlie Dressen, Cookie Lavagetto, Jake Pitler, and Jackie Robinson, Pee Wee Reese, Duke Snider, Gil Hodges, Roy Campanella, Carl Furillo, Preacher Roe, and I found myself saying, 'Thank God for the United States where you have a chance to make your dreams come true. Here I am, man, in the W-o-o-o-rld Series and nobody can do anything 'till I throw this baseball.'"

—Joe Black, Dodgers reliever who, as a starting pitcher, became the first black to win a World Series game, beating the Yankees 4–2, quoted by Martha Jo Black and Chuck Shoffner, *Joe Black: More Than a Dodger,* **2015**

"Game Two, however, was a dispiriting 7–1 thrashing of Carl Erskine. . . . The third game [was] in the Bronx and won 5–3 by Preacher Roe. . . . Going into the ninth inning, Pee Wee Reese and Jackie Robinson each singled and then executed a . . . double steal of second and third. With Roy Campanella at bat, a pitch from reliever Tom Gorman got past the normally flawless Yogi Berra, and both Reese and Robinson raced home."

—Thomas Oliphant, about how in Game 3, Robinson, who had scored the tying run on Andy Pafko's sacrifice fly in the eighth, scored the final run all the way from second on Berra's passed ball, *Praying for Gil Hodges,* **2005**

"We expected to win the Series. And that was the year [Bob] Kuzava beat us. Jesus. Jimmy Christmas. I want to throw up. We used to eat left-handers alive. But those were the kinds of things that happened against the Yankees. . . . Dressen said we were the worst club he ever managed for scoring a run from third. . . . [With two outs in the seventh inning of Game 7 and with the Yankees ahead 4–2,] Robinson hit a ball off his fists with the bases loaded. . . . It was the same old thing that plagued us."

—Carl Erskine, Dodgers pitcher, to Peter Golenbock, *Bums,* **1984**

"Most accounts of the Dodger disaster focus on the third out of the inning, but according to the Duke Snider the second out (which he made) was just as important. . . . The count went full and Snider fouled off more than one pitch after that. In the end, though, Kuzava threw him a fastball low and outside, which Snider more reached for than swung at, popping up to Gil McDougald at third. Two outs; Jackie Robinson coming up. This time Kuzuva threw a fastball inside."

—Thomas Oliphant, *Praying for Gil Hodges,* 2005

"Nobody told me [Kuzuva] could break it off that good."

—J. R., who remembered the pitch being a breaking ball

"Now, you are gonna ask me why I left in the left-hand fella [Kuzava] to face the right-hand fella [Robinson], who makes speeches, with bases full. Don't I know percentages and et cetera? The reason I left him in is the other man [Robinson] has not seen hard-throwing left-hand pitchers much and could have trouble with the break of a left-hander's hard curve, which is what happened."

—Casey Stengel, Yankees manager, quoted by Roger Kahn, *The Era,* 1993

"The ball was hit above a kind of no-man's land between the pitcher's mound and first base. With Billy Martin playing deep at second, the ball was hit over an area where it wasn't clear who should come over and catch it. In fact, both Kuzava and the Yankee first baseman, Joe Collins, appeared frozen. Eventually, the ever-hustling Martin began to run—and run and run and run. He caught the ball near the mound no more than six inches off the ground, saving at least two runs and the game. Kuzava's next two innings were almost climactic."

—Thomas Oliphant, about the Yankees clinching the World Series with a Game 7 victory, *Praying for Gil Hodges,* 2005

"Mantle beat us. He was the difference between the two clubs. They didn't miss DiMaggio. It was Mickey Mantle who killed us."

—J. R. to the press about the young slugger who batted .345 with ten hits, including two home runs, in the 1952 World Series, October 1952

"AFTER THE GAME, JACKIE ROBINSON CAME INTO OUR CLUBHOUSE AND SHOOK MY HAND. HE SAID, 'YOU'RE A HELLUVA BALLPLAYER AND YOU'VE GOT A GREAT FUTURE.' I THOUGHT THAT WAS A CLASSY GESTURE, ONE I WASN'T THEN CAPABLE OF MAKING. I WAS A BAD LOSER. . . . I HAVE TO ADMIT, I BECAME A JACKIE ROBINSON FAN ON THE SPOT. . . . HERE WAS A PLAYER WHO HAD WITHOUT DOUBT SUFFERED MORE ABUSE AND MORE TAUNTS AND MORE HATRED THAN ANY PLAYER IN THE HISTORY OF THE GAME. AND HE HAD MADE A SPECIAL EFFORT TO COMPLIMENT AND ENCOURAGE A YOUNG WHITE KID FROM OKLAHOMA."

—MICKEY MANTLE, *ALL MY OCTOBERS*, 1994

"To make the experience even more dispiriting, this was the World Series when Gil Hodges famously didn't hit—not once in twenty-one times at bat. . . . Hodges, Robinson, Furillo, Campanella and Pafko came up 116 times and got just fourteen hits."

—Thomas Oliphant, *Praying for Gil Hodges*, 2005

WHEN HONESTY WASN'T NECESSARILY THE BEST POLICY

"[On November 30, 1952] I appeared on a television program, *Youth Wants to Know*, and became involved in one of the biggest blowups of my career. A girl asked me if I felt that the New York Yankees were discriminating against Negroes. . . . I felt that I couldn't answer that girl dishonestly so I said that I'd . . . found the players to be real sportsmen and gentlemen . . . but that if she was referring to the Yankee management and the fact that the Yankees were the only New York team without a Negro on the squad, then I did feel the Yankees were guilty of discrimination. The next day, to my great amazement, a press hurricane had blown up. The Yankees' public relations staff really must have gotten busy; writers who covered the Yankees were devoting reams of copy to stories under big headlines, crying, 'Robinson Accuses Yankees of Prejudice,' followed by bitter denials by [GM] George Weiss of the Yankees. . . . Only one newspaperman, Milton Gross of the *New York Post*, bothered to telephone me to ask what I really had said, why I had said it, and what I meant."

—J. R., *Wait Till Next Year*, Carl T. Rowan with Jackie Robinson, 1960

"He was asked a direct question on a radio program. His statement was treated by many newspapers as a pure and simple pop-off. There's a considerable difference."

—**Roger Kahn,** *New York Herald Tribune,* **August 29, 1954**

"There are thousands upon thousands of people in Harlem who feel the same way."

—**J. R., continuing to criticize the Yankees for not bringing up black minor leaguers (including Puerto Rican Vic Power, who had batted .331 for the Yankees' Triple A Kansas City Blues but was kept there for another year), December 1952**

"Jackie Robinson . . . criticized the Yankees for not bringing up a black player. They brought up my white teammates . . . but not me. I think they were waiting for my skin to turn white."

—**Vic Power, Kansas City Blues star whose reward for batting .331 and .349 was to be traded by the Yankees to the Philadelphia Athletics for several white players on December 16, 1953, to Danny Peary,** *We Played the Game,* **1994**

"He accused the Yankee organization of being bigots, which of course they were. . . . The Yankees didn't bring a black to New York until [1955]. . . . But the Yankees quickly denied Robinson's charges and accused Robinson of being a troublemaker."

—**Peter Golenbock,** *Bums,* **1984**

"He was excoriated in the national press as a 'soap box orator' and a 'rabble rouser' who should limit his activities to 'ball playing' instead of being a 'crusader.'"

—**William C. Kashatus,** *Jackie and Campy,* **2014**

"Suddenly, I was deluged with mail, the great majority of it unsigned, filled with vicious, insulting remarks, most of them referring to my racial ancestry. Some letters were stuffed with newspaper clipping about Negroes involved in crimes, with penciled notations such as: 'Do you blame a nice clean organization like the Yankees for trying to avoid this?'"

—**J. R.,** *Wait Till Next Year,* **Carl T. Rowan with Jackie Robinson, 1960**

"When the Yankees complained, Ford Frick, commissioner of baseball, summoned me to his office. A lot of people assumed that he reprimanded me, but all he said was, 'Always be sure of one thing. When you believe you're right and you come out swinging, make sure you're swinging a heavy bat and not a fungo.'"

—**J. R., writing a three-part series,** *Look* **magazine, February 1955**

"JACK TOOK THOSE RISKS BECAUSE HE ALWAYS THOUGHT HE WAS RIGHT. EVEN WHEN HE WAS WRONG, HE FELT HE WAS RIGHT. HE USED HIS ATHLETICS AS A POLITICAL FORUM. HE NEVER WANTED TO RUN FOR OFFICE, BUT HE ALWAYS WANTED TO INFLUENCE PEOPLE'S THINKING."

—RACHEL ROBINSON TO PETER GOLENBOCK, *BUMS*, 1984

"I notice in a recent issue of *Our World* magazine that some folks think you're too outspoken. Certainly not many of our folks share that view. They think like you that the Yankees, making many a 'buck' off Harlem, might have had a few of our ball players just like Brooklyn. . . . Maybe these protests around you, Jackie, explain a lot of things about people trying to shut up those of us who speak out in many other fields. . . . People who 'beef' at those of us who speak out, Jackie, are afraid of us. Well, let them be afraid. I'm continuing to speak out, and I hope you will, too."

—Paul Robeson, open letter to Jackie Robinson, *Freedom* magazine, April 1953

"Jackie Robinson, signed, sealed and delivered for 1953, says that he should last through the 1954 season before hanging up his spikes. . . . Robinson, by the admission of Dodger veep Buzz[ie] Bavasi, is the highest paid player on the Brooklyn roster. It is believed that the figure is $35,000. Shortstop Pee Wee is next at $32,000. Catcher Roy Campanella . . . will draw $25,000."

—Barney Kremenko, *New York Journal-American,* January 13, 1953

"Thanks to Jackie Robinson and Branch Rickey and everybody who came after them, the Kansas City Monarchs were no longer the be-all and end-all for a Negro ball player. Monarchs' shortstop Ernie Banks, who signed with the Cubs in 1953, was the last of the great players produced in the Negro Leagues. . . . By 1953, only the Monarchs, the Memphis Red Sox, the Birmingham Black Barons, and the Indianapolis Clowns persisted."

—Janet Bruce, *The Kansas City Monarchs,* 1985

"I was traded from the Phillies to the Dodgers. Jackie was the first guy up in the clubhouse in Vero Beach. He held out his hand in front of everyone and said, 'Russ, we've been fighting one another—let's fight the other teams together now.'"

—Russ Meyer, Dodgers pitcher from 1953 to 1955, to Harvey Frommer, *Rickey and Robinson,* 1982

"It wasn't easy to break into the Dodgers' lineup, but Junior Gilliam came up from the minors and immediately became our second baseman, moving Robinson. . . . He was a nice, quiet young black man from Tennessee who fit right in. Jackie and Campy looked after him."

—**Rube Walker, Dodgers catcher, about Robinson's new roommate, to Danny Peary,** *We Played the Game,* **1994**

"Jackie told Junior what he was supposed to do as a human being, a person, a player. And not to do Uncle Tom 'Yes, sir! No, sir!' shit. Instead it was, 'Act like a champion, carry yourself like a professional.' Jackie nursed Gilliam along so that he overcame his shortcomings and became a star player himself."

—**Don Newcombe, Dodgers pitcher, to Danny Peary,** *We Played the Game,* **1994**

"I'll have to admit that Junior covers more ground than I could cover."

—**J. R., 1953**

"They decided that [Junior] Gilliam will play second and Robinson will play third and they will bench Billy Cox. . . . I had coffee after a game with Billy and Preacher Roe, and suddenly Cox said to me, 'What do you think about Gilliam?' I said, 'I think he's a pretty good ballplayer.' And Billy said, 'How would you like a nigger to take your job?' And Preacher said, 'It's alright to have them in the game but now they're taking over.' And it went on and on. And so without using their names, I wrote what I thought was a clever lead: While Charlie Dressen fiddles with the Dodger infield, Billy Cox burns. The AP picked it up, and suddenly, my racial stuff is in every paper in the country. . . . [Mike Gavin of the] *Journal-American* stole Robinson's byline: 'No Dissension on Dodgers by Jackie Robinson.'"

—**Roger Kahn, about the biggest story of spring training, to Tom Clavin, 2012**

"Junior had a world of talent [and] was voted Rookie of the Year, following in the footsteps of Jackie, Don Newcombe, and Joe Black."

—**Rube Walker, Dodgers catcher, to Danny Peary,** *We Played the Game,* **1994**

"Jackie Makes Third Base Look Hard"

—Article title about Robinson's early struggles to learn a new position in spring training, *New York World-Telegram and Sun,* April 9, 1953

"Brooklyn's opponent in the 1953 opener was the Pittsburgh Pirates, the first time in history that these long-time National League rivals had ever met on Opening Day. . . . Brooklyn won 8–5. . . . Robinson . . . singled in the fourth, coming home on Campy's [three-run] homer, and singled again in the fifth. He scored his second run of the game on Don Thompson's fly ball."

—Lyle Spatz, baseball historian, excerpt from paper presented at the Jackie Robinson anniversary conference, Long Island University, Brooklyn Campus, April 1997

"I asked [Dressen] if I could go out [to left field]. It must have been a month ago when I first spoke to him about it and after a while he took me up on it and started working me out there in practice. . . . I could see the outfield wasn't going too good and meantime Cox [at third] was hitting and Gilliam [at second] was doing all right. . . . I worked out there quite a bit before [Charlie] used me there."

—J. R., insisting it was his idea to be moved from third base to left field, quoted by Bill Roeder, *New York World-Telegram and Sun,* May 27, 1953

"Right on schedule the Dodgers moved into first place and Charlie Dressen hopes to stay in front the rest of the year with the same lineup that [has] produced the 10-game winning streak. In other words, Dressen believes he can go along with Jackie Robinson in the outfield, and, frankly, that comes as a great surprise to the writer. For one thing, it means that Robinson, who used to be regarded as a brilliant fielder, apparently has reached the point where he is being carried almost entirely for his hitting and base running. . . . Robinson climbed back over .300 with five hits in the double-header [sweep of Pittsburgh], and he says he's glad to be in the outfield without letting it affect his hitting because that seems to give the Dodgers their strongest lineup, leaving room as it does for Billy Cox, Junior Gilliam, and Gil Hodges in the infield [with Pee Wee Reese]."

—Bill Roeder, *New York World-Telegram and Sun,* June 1, 1953

"When Robinson played left field, the Dodgers fielded a starting lineup with an all-star at each of the eight positions. . . . In the outfield, Robinson hit .329 and drove in ninety-five runs, [center fielder] Snider hit .336, hit forty-two home runs, and drove in 126 runs, and [right fielder] Furillo hit a league-leading .344, with ninety-two RBIs."

—**Peter Golenbock,** *Bums,* **1984**

"It looks like the Dodgers have finally found a home for Jackie Robinson, out in left field. . . . In two months, he has played in three different spots, none of them the position he handles best [second base], and he has taken this shuffling without complaint and without letting it affect his hitting and baserunning. As usual, in fact, he has been the steadiest attacking player in the lineup . . . and he is still the one that a pitcher least likes to see in a tough spot. Lately he has been extra hot, with 12 hits in the last 19 at-bats."

—**Bill Roeder,** *New York World-Telegram and Sun,* **June 11, 1953**

"Robinson would play in almost 200 games in the outfield over his final four seasons, and hit better in that position than in any other, a resounding .342."

—**Lyle Spatz, baseball historian, April 1997**

J. R. NOTE: Was it destiny or coincidence that Jackie Robinson was given Number 42 when he joined the Dodgers? Numerologists might be able to explain why Number 42 batted .342 when he led the NL in hitting in 1949; .342 as an outfielder, his highest career average at any position; .342 against the Pirates, his highest career average against any team; and .342 in Pittsburgh's Forbes Field, his highest career average at any ballpark. All impressive numbers for the man who was elected to the Hall of Fame at the age of forty-two.

"Robinson [was on a] quiet quest to find backers for a magazine that would cover what the mainstream press did not. That was what led to his . . . asking me to develop [and ghostwrite his column and write my own for] *Our Sports*. . . . His manner was alive with excitement and enthusiasm. . . . But the magazine was doomed from the start. Major advertisers . . . discounted the Negro market in those days, and without major advertising a mass-market magazine cannot survive. . . . We marched fearlessly into hot-button issues. The silence of the mainstream press proved fatal. *Our Sports* did not survive the season."

—Roger Kahn, about, as the cover stated, *The Great New Negro Sports Magazine*, which debuted in May 1953 but lasted only five issues, *Rickey & Robinson*, 2014

"When Mr. Rickey left Brooklyn, I was well up in the $30,000 class [in salary]. President O'Malley and the rest of the current Dodger management are a fine group of men—but they aren't paying me a cent more than Mr. Rickey did in his last year in Brooklyn. I'm as good now as I was then and I'm older. As a rule, if a player doesn't slump, he gets raises as he gets older."

—J. R., as owner and columnist, *Our Sports* magazine, June 1953

"There are thoughtless and stupid people in every business and baseball is no exception."

—J. R., after a melee that was caused by Campanella charging the mound after Milwaukee Braves pitcher Lew Burdette tossed insults and bean balls at him, to reporters, August 3, 1953

"What are the people in the stands trying to prove with their treatment of Campanella and Robinson—that Milwaukee is a citadel of white supremacy."

—Tommy Holmes, about how the fans in the Braves' new home city booed the Dodgers' black players, *Brooklyn Eagle*, 1953

"The Cards were in town for a three-game series. The opener [on August 30], with Robinson playing on a bad leg, was a landmark game. . . . During the first six innings of a close game, [Cardinals manager Eddie] Stanky very crudely mimicked an ape in the visitor's dugout at Ebbets Field . . . whenever Robbie came to bat. . . . Robinson led off the seventh [and] fanned, as [the Dodgers' most famous fan Hilda] Chester led a localized round of booing directed at Stanky. . . . Eight Dodgers would bat and six would score before Robinson made the second out of the inning again by striking out. Six more Dodgers would score before the inning was over, breaking the game open and winning by a humiliating 20–4."

—Carl E. Prince, *Brooklyn's Dodgers*, 1996

"Jackie had one of his biggest nights. He got the hit that opened the way to the 1–0 rout, then he beat the Cards practically by himself in the second game, with two homers that won it by 7–4. But in the middle of it he was hearing boos [from Dodgers fans]. The fans let him know they didn't like it when he kept insisting that a drive by Duke Snider . . . should have been called a homer. The umpire ruled that it hit the fence, and Snider had to settle for two bases. . . . Snider didn't say anything, although he revealed later that he thought the ball went into the stands. . . . Many of the fans sided with [Cards catcher] Del Rice who got tired of the delay and told Robinson, who was due at bat, to get in there and hit. Jackie told Rice to mind his own business and they seemed ready to square off until Eddie Stanky ran from the dugout and pushed them apart. . . . Every time Robinson came up thereafter the boos trailed him into the batter's box. Jackie had to break up the game to silence the hecklers. With the score tied and a man on second in the eighth, the Cards risked trouble by walking Snider and pitching to Robinson, who responded by hitting his second homer."

—**Bill Roeder,** *New York World-Telegram and Sun,* **July 18, 1953**

"Dear Mr. Robinson, [FBI deletion] was warned *not* to win the pennant. But he did anyhow, and he won't be in St. Luis. Well that's bad cause *you* are going to get it. Remember what happened to Arnold Shuyster in Brooklyn in 1952? Well Wed. nite Sept. 15 you *die*. No use crying to the cops. You'll be executed gangland style as Busch Stadium."

—**"Dodger Hater," crank letter, September 15, 1953**

"The Dodgers [who have clinched the pennant] beat Pittsburgh, 5–4, with Carl Erskine very sharp. . . . Just for fun Jackie Robinson played shortstop. He has now whirled right around the infield this season, with stops at third, first, second, and short, but [in the World Series] he'll still be the leftfielder against the Yankees."

—**Bill Roeder,** *New York World-Telegram and Sun,* **September 23, 1953**

"An experienced outfielder would have gone back to the fence. I trailed the ball instead. I didn't think it was going that far and I kept drifting back with it. By the time I got there it was going into the stands. If I'd been there in time I wouldn't even have had to jump for it."

—J. R., taking the blame for not catching Billy Martin's seventh-inning homer off Preacher Roe that tied the score and set the stage for Mickey Mantle's game-winning two-run homer in the next inning that put the Yankees up 2–0 in the World Series, quoted by Bill Roeder, *New York World-Telegram and Sun*, October 1, 1953

"I always enjoyed those series because of Jackie Robinson. . . . See there was a black lawyer by the name of Walter Gordon out in California that helped my mother when I was a kid, and he also helped Jackie, so when we played against Jackie in the Series, I always wanted to show that I was a better second baseman. That was my real challenge. And I always wanted to outhit him, and I always outplayed him."

—Billy Martin, quoted by Peter Golenbock, *Dynasty*, 1975

"Back from the dead yesterday [after two losses at Yankee Stadium], came Carl Erskine, Jackie Robinson, and Roy Campanella . . . driving the Brooklyn Dodgers to their first 1953 World Series victory [in Game 3], a bitterly earned 3-to-2 triumph over the New York Yankees. . . . A crowd of 35,270 fans [was the] largest ever to squeeze its way into Ebbets Field for a Series contest. . . . Robinson, the power behind the first two runs, and Campanella, who powered home the winning run with an eighth-inning homer off Vic Raschi, made amends for weaknesses in the first two games. But Erskine . . . held center stage. . . . The soft-spoken twenty-six-year-old Hoosier, a twenty-game winner for the Dodgers this season, struck out fourteen Yankees, a [Series] record. Four times he struck out Mickey Mantle, Yankee centerfielder."

—Roger Kahn, *New York Herald Tribune*, October 3, 1953

"The fourth game pitted Whitey Ford against Billy Loes. . . . On this day the character outpitched the perfectionist. The Dodgers scored three runs in the first inning [and] tied the series at two games each with a 7–3 win. In the ninth the Yankees had the bases loaded with two outs when Mantle singled to left field for the final Yankees run, but when Martin tried to score from second on the hit, left fielder Robinson pegged home perfectly on one bounce, and catcher Campanella registered the final out of the game with a crashing tag against Martin's forehead."

—Peter Golenbock, *Dynasty*, 1975

"[In] Game Six [with New York up three games to two], the Yankees got to Carl Erskine early—three runs in the fourth inning. . . . The Dodgers got one of the runs back on a classic bit of Jackie Robinson daring. With one out [in the sixth inning] he doubled off Whitey Ford and then promptly stole third, coming home on a ground ball out by Campanella. . . . The Dodgers were just two outs from the end of the season when Carl Furillo lined an outside pitch [thrown by Allie Reynolds] into the right-field seats for the [two-run] homer that tied the game. . . . [In] the bottom of the ninth . . . Martin['s] record-tying twelfth hit of the Series [off Clem Labine] was a 'bleeder' . . . through the middle of the Dodger infield into center field. Hank Bauer scored the winning run less than ten minutes after Carl Furillo's home run."

—Thomas Oliphant, about the Yankees' 4–3 victory that gave them five consecutive world championships, *Praying for Gil Hodges*, 2005

"I'D TRADE EVERY F***ING HIT IF WE COULD HAVE WON."
—J. R., WHOSE .320 AVERAGE IN THE SERIES WAS FOR NAUGHT, OCTOBER 5, 1953

"Over [Robinson's] first seven years in the majors, he ranked fourth [in the National League] . . . in batting average, he ranked second in runs scored, and he ranked first in stolen bases."

—Steve Hirdt, executive vice president of Elias Sports Bureau, TV special *The Lineup: New York's All-Time Best Baseball Players*, MSG Network, 2010

"Before Robinson's debut [in 1947], no player in the history of the white major leagues had ever had more than six '12–12' seasons—that is, seasons in which he hit at least 12 home runs and stole at least 12 bases—in his entire career. Robinson broke that record [in 1953] by accomplishing this feat in each of his first seven years in the league. He demonstrated that power and speed were not mutually exclusive, and his example set the tone for the Dodgers. . . . From 1949 through [1953] the Dodgers led the National League in both home runs and steals every year."

—David Shiner, dean of Shimer College and writer, excerpt from paper presented at the Jackie Robinson anniversary conference, Long Island University, Brooklyn Campus, April 1997

A BOLD BUT BOTCHED ATTEMPT TO BREAK DOWN RACIAL BARRIERS

"A few days after the Series . . . Jackie Robinson's All-Stars barnstorming tour [commenced]. Beginning in Baltimore on October 9 and concluding in Houston on November 1, it was intended by Robinson to be a groundbreaking tour in which an integrated team would travel through the South and Southwest. Four white players were on Robinson's roster: [Gil] Hodges, [Ralph] Branca [now on Detroit], St. Louis Browns' second baseman Bobby Young, and star Indians third baseman Al Rosen, who would hurt his back and leave the tour early. Among the black players were Robinson, Athletics pitcher Bob Trice, Indians first baseman Luke Easter, and Dodgers farmhands Charlie Neal and Maury Wills."

—**Tom Clavin and Danny Peary,** *Gil Hodges,* **2012**

"[Jackie] asked Gil and me because we were very close to him. We played all-black local teams and other barnstorming teams. We realized it was a gambit for integration."

—**Ralph Branca, to Danny Peary,** *Gil Hodges,* **Tom Clavin and Danny Peary, 2012**

"Robinson's tours in 1950 and 1953 were close to identical. . . . True, Jack had replaced Florida games with games in Mexico, but the trip did not avoid the Deep South. The barnstorming organizers were Lester Dworman, a money man from New York, and Ted Worner again assigned as promoter. (Worner was the promoter for all five of Jack's tours.)"

—**Thomas Barthel,** *Baseball Barnstorming and Exhibition Games, 1901–1962,* **2007**

"I accepted Ted Worner's offer this year when he agreed to pay me well."

—**J. R.,** *New York Age,* **December 1953**

"The historic team's first game was in Baltimore, October 9, a 6–2 win over a Negro League all-star outfit before 1,500. . . . The next game in Wilmington, Delaware, ended in a 4–4 tie, but at Myers Field in Norfolk, Virginia, Robinson's integrated squad won 11–3 before 3,700 in a game that saw first baseman Gil Hodges pitch three innings."

—**Thomas Barthel, about the beginning of the 1953 barnstorming tour that would travel to North Carolina, Chattanooga, and Birmingham on October 18,** *Baseball Barnstorming and Exhibition Games, 1901–1962,* **2007**

"[Ted] Worner had been assured that there would be no trouble in Birmingham."

—J. R., *New York Age,* December 1953

"Police Commissioner Eugene Connors . . . said . . . an all-Negro team would be all right [to play here but] Birmingham has a city ordinance which prohibits 'mixed athletic events.'"

—*Washington Post*, **anticipating that when Robinson brought his integrated team to play in Birmingham, he risked arrests by a police commissioner who would be known nationwide as "Bull" Connors in May 1963 when hoses and attack dogs were used against unarmed protest marchers in his city, October 9, 1953**

"The tour went well until it arrived in Birmingham . . . where there was [still] a city ordinance forbidding mixed athletic events. If Hodges, Branca, and Young played, *they* would be arrested. Rather than cancel the game, Robinson and . . . Worner agreed to have the white players sit in the stands and watch. . . . The Birmingham police were serious about arresting Caucasian players who suited up with Robinson's All-Stars, as was demonstrated when the officers charged into the dugout to arrest Robinson's replacement. They left red-faced and rednecked when they discovered Willie Mays wasn't white. . . . Willie Mays, home in Alabama while on leave [from the army], filled in. The same thing happened in Memphis, where the All-Stars played the Indianapolis Clowns."

—**Tom Clavin and Danny Peary,** *Gil Hodges,* **2012**

"Concerning the October 21 game at Martin Stadium in Memphis . . . Hodges, Young, and Branca [were] introduced from the stands during the game but . . . the 5,600 fans watched only Robinson and [Luke] Easter as major league players, Robby's team winning 10–4."

—**Thomas Barthel,** *Baseball Barnstorming and Exhibition Games, 1901–1962,* **2007**

"Robinson was vilified and defended in the black and political press across the country for agreeing to sit the white players after bringing them into the two cities that he knew had ordinances against mixed sporting events."

—**Tom Clavin and Danny Peary,** *Gil Hodges,* **2012**

"Jackie Disgraces the Race"

—**Title of op-ed piece,** *Chicago Defender,* **October 1953**

> "WE THINK JACKIE OWES AN APOLOGY TO EVERY WHITE MEMBER OF HIS SQUAD FOR THE EMBARRASSMENT HE SUBJECTED THEM TO. WE FEEL THAT JACKIE SHOULD ALSO APOLOGIZE TO EVERY REAL AMERICAN WHO IS FIGHTING AGAINST RACIAL DISCRIMINATION IN THIS COUNTRY."
>
> —*CHICAGO DEFENDER*, EXCERPT FROM OP-ED, OCTOBER 1953

"Cancel or Challenge"

—Title of editorial, *Birmingham World*, October 1953

"It's up to Jackie Robinson and his promoters to cancel the scheduled engagement or challenge the 'unconstitutional' sports segregation ordinance which will force him to bench his three white players. Branch Rickey set a bold precedent by introducing Negro players to the major leagues. He stood up and fought, by-passing cities which were not enlightened enough to permit fair competition. Has Jackie Robinson forgotten this? . . . Money is not as precious as a good name. Is Jackie Robinson going to let Branch Rickey down? Is he coming to Birmingham to give aid and comfort to bigotry?"

—*Birmingham World*, excerpt from editorial, October 1953

"Robinson has been the central figure in a startling case of Southern discrimination against white ballplayers. . . . Possibly there were valid reasons impelling Robinson to set aside his principles and go through with the Birmingham engagement, without Hodges, Branca and Young. Considering his past-performance sheet, however, the reasons are difficult of explanation. From here it looks as though he blew a great chance to make a big score for tolerance."

—Red Smith, not differentiating between Robinson's *practicing* bigotry by deciding on his own without provocation to keep his white players on the bench and cancel if they refused—which did not happen—and *not challenging* bigotry so that his white players wouldn't be arrested because he forced them to play, *New York Herald Tribune*, October 26, 1953

"Isn't it amazing that so many swivel chair analysts can expect Jackie Robinson to go into two cities like Birmingham and Memphis and change conditions in one day when thousands of Negroes living there every day can do nothing."

—Luix V. Overbea, trailblazing journalist for the Associated Black Press and one of Robinson's most influential defenders, October 1953

"Everyone knows how I feel about discrimination. [But] I was just a hired hand on the barnstorming tour."

—J. R., *New York Age*, December 1953

"Jack said at the time that he would not take responsibility for the fact the three white players didn't play. That's because he was not . . . the one who decided who played. Later on, he thought about it, and he began to feel that he should have been more vocal about it, seeing to it that they played, or, if they couldn't play, taking steps to make sure that no one played. He felt he could have been more helpful in that situation. He wouldn't have liked it if it had been the reverse, three black players on a white team. It had to be considered a negative experience for him because his objectives were not met."

—Rachel Robinson to Danny Peary, 2012

"A ban against mixed competition was in effect and a group of Birmingham citizens were battling to get it removed. They asked me not to disobey the law—a disturbance I would stir up and would hurt their cause. 'If you don't upset the apple cart right now,' they told me, 'we'll be able to get rid of this Jim Crow ordinance next year.'"

—J.R, writing a three-part series, *Look* magazine, February 1955

"When Birmingham ended [temporarily] its racial sports ban four months later, Robinson could have been given more credit."

—Tom Clavin and Danny Peary, *Gil Hodges*, 2012

"Play continued in . . . Arkansas, as well [as] Louisiana and Texas. On November 7, 1953, in Mexico City, Jack's team played before 13,000 in Parque Delta when they faced the Mexico City Aztecas of the Winter Baseball League. In sum, the barnstorming team's record, traveling from Baltimore to Mexico City was 23–7–1."

—Thomas Barthel, *Baseball Barnstorming and Exhibition Games, 1901–1962*, 2007

"I'd like to see Jackie Robinson picked to manage the Dodgers for these reasons: 1. Robinson has good baseball sense. . . . 2. He is a leader. . . . 3. He is familiar with the team. . . . 4. He has 'winningness.' . . . 5. This one is strictly shop. Robinson is good copy because he talks, and as a manager he'd have even more to say. With Robinson managing against Durocher, the baseball writers would have a field day."

—**Bill Roeder, among those at his paper saying who they'd pick to replace Charlie Dressen after he was fired for demanding a multiyear contract as Dodgers manager,** *New York World-Telegram and Sun,* **November 12, 1953**

"I've known him just a bit down there at Vero Beach. He seems like a decent sort of guy and I'm tickled to death to see him get the opportunity. I figured it would be a man from the organization and I'm glad they're doing it that way."

—**J. R., saying kind words about new Dodgers manager Walter "Smokey" Alston, not realizing they would have a shaky relationship, to Bill Roeder,** *New York World-Telegram and Sun,* **November 24, 1953**

"EVER SINCE LAST SPRING JACKIE ROBINSON AND HIS WIFE, RACHEL, HAVE BEEN LOOKING FOR A HOME IN THE COUNTRY. . . . THE BROKERS IN WESTCHESTER COUNTY AND SUBURBAN CONNECTICUT HAVE LONG LISTS OF AVAILABLE PROPERTIES. BUT NONE, SO FAR, HAS BEEN FOR SALE TO THE DODGERS' STAR AND HIS FAMILY. NOT OF COURSE, THAT ANYONE WOULD THINK OF USING THE UGLY WORD 'DISCRIMINATION.' NO, INDEED. PROPERTY OWNERS AND REAL ESTATE BROKERS IN THREE WELL-BRED COMMUNITIES JUST EXPLAIN POLITELY: 'YOU WOULDN'T BE HAPPY HERE.'"

—NANCY SEELY, *NEW YORK POST,* NOVEMBER 23, 1953

"A reporter from the *Bridgeport Herald* was writing a story on housing discrimination, and caught wind of [the Robinsons'] difficulty buying a house. The reporter called Rachel and interviewed her. She believed the brokers had tipped him off, trying to create the impression she was causing trouble. Once the story ran, Dick and Andrea Simon stepped in. Dick co-founded Simon & Schuster publishing company; their daughter Carly became a famous singer-songwriter. They invited Rachel, local clergy, and real estate agents to their home in North Stamford, Conn., to talk about helping the Robinsons. After the gathering, Rachel, Andrea, and a real estate broker looked at property."

—**New England Historical Society, website, February 19, 2014**

"[There] was a moving moment at a dinner [for the Anti-Defamation League of B'nai B'rith] in Washington [November 23] 1953. As Jack entered the dining room, President Dwight D. Eisenhower descended from the dais and met him in the middle of the room. Jack described this gracious gesture as 'a great experience,' in one of the several letters that he and the president exchanged in the wake of this meeting and the violence in Little Rock [in 1957]."

—**Rachel Robinson,** *Jackie Robinson: An Intimate Portrait,* **1997**

"Dear Mr. President: I want to take this opportunity to let you know how very much it meant to me to be able to meet you briefly at the dinner in Washington Monday night. It was a great privilege for me to appear on a program in which the President of the United States took part. It was equally great for me to experience the warmth and sincerity of your handshake in the midst of such an illustrious group of Americans. My wife and I will always remember our experience that night. It is events like this that make us certain our faith in democracy in indeed justified."

—**J. R., letter to President Dwight D. Eisenhower, November 25, 1953**

"Thank you very much for your nice note. In answer, may I say only that you represent to me and to many Americans one more evidence that our democracy, in which we have so much pride, is indeed in our country a workable, living ideal. All of us are grateful to you for the courage on your part required to demonstrate this."

—**President Dwight D. Eisenhower to Robinson, excerpt from letter, November 30, 1953**

— NINE —

From the Spotlight into the Twilight

"I've reached the stage where it's just too tough to keep on going. Actually, I'm in the best shape this spring that I have been for several years. But it meant that I had to diet all winter long. And my legs and body are starting to feel the wear and tear."

—J. R., on why he hoped to quit at the end of the 1954 season no matter how well he did, Associated Press, March 3, 1954

AT ODDS WITH ALSTON

"I felt I was stepping into an unusual situation. . . . Charlie [Dressen] . . . had just won two [pennants]. . . . But [what] made it a little easier for me was that there were seventeen guys on that club who had been with me in the minors—guys like Campanella, Newcombe, Carl Erskine, Clem Labine, and a lot of others. . . . Another thing . . . was that I got an awful lot of help and cooperation from Pee Wee Reese, Gil Hodges, and Roy Campanella. . . . We also had guys like Duke Snider, Carl Furillo, Billy Cox, and Jackie Robinson. That was a hell of a team."

—Walter Alston, former Montreal manager who began a twenty-two year stint as Dodgers manager beginning in 1954, to Donald Honig, *The Man in the Dugout*, 1977

"Robinson in his day was a great baseball player, perhaps one of the greatest all-around athletes there has ever been. There's no doubt when I took over in 1954 that it wasn't the same Jackie Robinson. . . . He was still a fine, fine baseball player—one who was terribly intimidating in almost any situation. But he . . . was thirty-five years old and had lost some of his speed [although] none of his skills. . . . He was an inspiring player, a born leader who could literally lift a team. . . . If ever a man came to play the game of baseball Jackie Robinson did."

—Walter Alston, *A Year at a Time,* 1976

"I guess I had a problem or two with Robinson when we first went to spring training. I think he was kind of testing me out a little bit. We'd be doing calisthenics, and he'd stop on the side to talk to a writer or someone. This went on for two or three days, and I talked to him about it. I think he just wanted to see what I'd take and what I wouldn't."

—Walter Alston to Donald Honig, *The Man in the Dugout,* 1977

"Then during one of our early exhibitions I rested Jackie to get a long look at some of the young fellows. He was supposed to be on the bench in case he was needed. The next thing I realized, he was out in the bullpen chatting with a writer. . . . The next day I called a clubhouse meeting. Explained the rules. . . . Jackie had a habit of talking to others during clubhouse meetings and when I made points about the bench and writers he talked back a little. Our conversation got a little rough. . . . I do know that there was an inference that if Robinson wanted to test me man-to-man that was OK with me. Roy Campanella . . . helped calm the storm."

—Walter Alston, about almost having a physical confrontation with Robinson prior to an exhibition game in Louisville, *A Year at a Time,* 1976

"When are you guys going to grow up? We came here to play ball not fight each other."

—Roy Campanella, Dodgers catcher and future Hall of Famer, to Robinson and Alston, April 1954

"I had to let him know that I would treat him fairly, no more and no less than any other ballplayer. Who he was or how good he was never entered my mind. It smoothed out all right with Jackie, and I think the longer we worked together, the better we got along."

—Walter Alston to Donald Honig, *The Man in the Dugout,* 1977

"I don't know what the hell that man is trying to do. Upset us all?"

—J. R., one of several Dodgers who was offended when Alston said everybody had to fight for their jobs, 1954

"Jack missed Dressen. He didn't want him to go in the first place, so he may not have been receptive to Walter Alston. Alston had a different personality than Dressen. He was quieter and less expressive. And probably not a good manager. Jack was a very good judge of that. So they just didn't work together, and from the beginning, didn't like each other very much."

—Rachel Robinson to Danny Peary, 2012

"[Alston] had a gut conviction that I resented his having taken Dressen's job."

—J. R.

"ALSTON . . . SAW ROBINSON AS A THREAT TO HIS AUTHORITY. IN '54, THE TWO MEN SILENTLY FOUGHT FOR CONTROL OF THE DODGERS. ROBINSON BITCHED THAT ALSTON LOST HIS COOL UNDER PRESSURE, AND HE WOULD RAIL AT WHAT HE SAW AS 'BONEHEAD JUDGMENTS' DURING GAMES. SOME OF THE OTHERS GRUMBLED ABOUT ALSTON, BUT ROBINSON, WHOSE EMOTIONS WERE ALWAYS CLOSE TO THE SURFACE, LET ALSTON KNOW THAT HE DIDN'T THINK MUCH OF HIM AS A MANAGER."

—PETER GOLENBOCK, *BUMS*, 1984

"Alston made his big-league debut at the Polo Grounds against a Giants club that would replace the Dodgers as the National League champions and then sweep the Cleveland Indians in the World Series. They would be led all season, as they were [Opening Day], by Willie Mays, back after a two-year hitch in the Army. Mays' sixth-inning home run . . . broke a 3–3 tie as the Giants won 4–3 behind Sal Maglie and Marv Grissom. Robinson was in left field. Jim Gilliam . . . was at second base, and Billy Cox, in his final season in Brooklyn, was at third. . . . Robinson had one hit in three at-bats while Maglie was on the mound, a sixth-inning single."

—Lyle Spatz, baseball historian, excerpt from paper presented at the Jackie Robinson anniversary conference, Long Island University, Brooklyn Campus, April 1997

"When I returned from the service, I joined a rotation that was completely different. Preacher Roe and Ralph Branca were both gone, and now Carl Erskine was the top veteran and Johnny Podres, Billy Loes, and Russ Meyer filled the other slots. . . . Jackie Robinson was still hitting .300, but was no longer playing every day. Now Walt Alston more often played him the outfield or at third than second. Second now belonged to Jim Gilliam. . . . I didn't socialize with Jackie because he lived on Long Island and I lived in New Jersey."

—Don Newcombe, Dodgers pitcher, to Danny Peary, *We Played the Game*, 1994

"Reese's and Hodges' lockers form a triangle with Snider's. Add Erskine and Robinson right alongside, and you have the core of the room. Tucked in between the two pillars and Robinson's locker is the big steamer trunk, filling up all the extra space. It is the all-purpose card table. There will usually be a game of bridge or hearts going on, with Jackie—always the competitor—noisily involved."

—Sandy Koufax, rookie Dodgers pitcher and future Hall of Famer getting his first impression of his team's locker room, *Koufax*, 1966

"The Dodgers put Jackie Robinson back in the infield and it must have given him ideas. All of a sudden he thinks he's a frisky kid again. . . . Jackie stole home for the first time in two years. He also stole second and third. . . . Jackie also chipped in with three hits including the double that beat the Pirates in the 13th, 6–5."

—Bill Roeder, *New York World-Telegram and Sun*, April 24, 1954

"Except for Jackie Robinson, all the Negro players with the Dodgers have decided to continue living at the colored hotel while in St. Louis rather than accept the long-delayed hospitality of the Hotel Chase, where the white players stay. . . . Last year the Giants got rooms at the Chase for their Negro players, and the Brooklyn management has been expecting to follow suit. 'Not for me,' said Roy Campanella. 'If they didn't want us for several years, I'd just as soon make it forever.' So Campanella, Don Newcombe, Joe Black, Junior Gilliam, and Sandy Amoros will live at the Adams."

—*New York World-Telegram and Sun*, about Robinson's lone decision to take the first step to integrate the Hotel Chase despite not being able to eat in the dining room, April 26, 1954

ROBBY AND CAMPY: A TROUBLED FRIENDSHIP

"Jackie was so pleased when Roy joined the team in 1948. Our son, Jackie Jr., was the same age as David, their first son. And Ruth and I were friends, so we were together a lot in the early years. Then both families moved to St. Albans. We were as close as two families [can be] for years. The rift between Jack and Campy came when questions of civil rights began to emerge, and Jack would take a very strong position, and he felt that Campy wasn't taking a strong position. This rift was years later, and we regretted it, Jack and I. The media was driving it. Dick Young enjoyed having anything controversial come up. I don't think he liked Jackie, so he publicized the things they were reported to have said, and that made it worse. That continued to the time of Campy's automobile accident prior to the Dodgers moving to Los Angeles."

—**Rachel Robinson to Danny Peary, 2012**

"My father was unfairly characterized by some sportswriters as being less committed to civil rights than Jackie Robinson. But the fundamental difference between them was style and not substance. In the early fifties, we lived in the same neighborhood, St. Albans, Queens, and they would drive to work together. There were no great debates. They both detested racism and wanted to see the full benefits of democracy extended to all Americans of African descent."

—**Roy Campanella II,** *Cult Baseball Players,* **edited by Danny Peary, 1990**

"Our friendship was one thing that many white writers didn't want to see."

—**J. R.,** *I Never Had It Made,* **as told to Alfred Duckett, 1972**

"THE SPORTSWRITERS USE ME TO ATTACK JACKIE—THAT'S WHY YOU CAN'T BELIEVE ANYTHING YOU READ."
—ROY CAMPANELLA TO ROY CAMPANELLA II, QUOTED BY CAMPANELLA II, *CULT BASEBALL PLAYERS*, EDITED BY DANNY PEARY, 1990

"Robinson's antagonistic attitude toward the umpires, his outspokenness on civil rights, and his growing difficulties with Walter O'Malley did not escape the scrutiny of the sportswriters, who became increasingly critical of him. They were accustomed to dealing with accommodating black athletes like Joe Louis . . . and Jesse Owens. . . . Predictably they flocked to Campanella, who was considered 'one of the boys,' according to Jack Lang, who covered the Dodgers in the 1950s for the *Long Island Press*. 'Campy was a fun-loving guy,' said Lang."

—**William C. Kashatus,** *Jackie and Campy,* **2014**

"Jack and Campy had distinctly different temperaments and approaches to dealing with white people. . . . Jack was reserved and direct at the same time, impatient for signs of progress, and unwilling to accept affronts to his dignity or challenges to the rights of others. Some sportswriters described his forcefulness as 'black rage' and said he had 'a chip on his shoulder.' Such labels made it easier for these journalists to belittle his point of view. . . . Campy's style and attitude made him more accepted. He was gentler and more accommodating, less apt to challenge. He was described by some as 'likable.'"

—**Rachel Robinson,** *Jackie Robinson: An Intimate Portrait,* **1996**

"Campy endeared himself to sportswriters by providing insightful analyses of games and humorous quotes. He also knew which writers to cultivate, like Dick Young of the *New York Daily News*, the most scrutinizing of all the city's scribes. . . . Because they favored him, the press protected him. . . . On the other hand, the writers viewed Robinson as 'oversensitive,' 'hot-tempered,' and 'irrational.' With the exception of Roger Kahn of the *Herald Tribune*, who believed that Jackie's 'bellicosity' was a more accurate reflection of 'what black attitudes should be,' Robinson had no close friends among the beat writers. They could not relate to his constant effort to make baseball a platform for civil rights or his tendency to interpret any difference of opinion as racially charged."

—**William C. Kashatus,** *Jackie and Campy,* **2014**

"Jackie, whenever I talk to Campy, I almost never think of him as a Negro. But any time I talk to you, I'm acutely aware of the fact that you're a Negro."

—**Dick Young, Dodgers beat reporter for the** *New York Daily News,* **stating a criticism that Robinson took as a compliment**

"I'm telling you as a friend, that a lot of newspapermen like Campanella because he doesn't talk about civil rights. But you wear your race on your sleeve and that makes enemies."

—**Dick Young, Dodgers beat reporter for the** *New York Daily News*

"Campy believes Jackie owes baseball everything. Jackie knows that baseball was ready to put the skids under him without his knowledge after having lived handsomely on him for years. . . . I like both players and I'm sorry this kind of thing must come up."

—A. S. "Doc" Young, author, contributing editor for *Jet* and *Ebony* magazines, the *Los Angeles Sentinel* and *Chicago Defender*, and the first black publicist in Hollywood

"Instead of being grateful to baseball, he's criticizing it. Everything he has he owes to baseball. That beautiful home of his, and this new job of his, too. Does he think those people would have had anything to do with him if he never played baseball?"

—Roy Campanella, angry that Robinson called him "washed up," *Sporting News*, February 6, 1957

"Both [my father, Roy Campanella, and Jackie Robinson] were inspiring role models to American youth and authentic heroes to African Americans. So it is a disservice for sportswriters such as [Jules] Tygiel and Lowell Reidenbaugh to stereotype Robinson as a 'militant' and my father a 'conservative.' Such labels are easily revealed as false when the actions of both men are examined in relation to the political persecution of Paul Robeson by the House Un-American Activities Committee."

—Roy Campanella II, pointing out that it was Robinson and not Campanella who agreed to testify, *Cult Baseball Players*, edited by Danny Peary, 1990

"In the early days we couldn't stay in the same hotels with the rest of the club, and when we did we couldn't eat in the dining rooms. Jackie was always annoyed by that. I didn't care that much. Jackie changed a little in his later years. He got a little more outspoken, and that was something that may have caused him trouble. He went after things his way, and I went after them my way. That's just the way things were."

—Roy Campanella, Dodgers catcher and Hall of Famer who refused to stay at the Hotel Chase when Robinson did in 1954 partly because blacks weren't allowed in the dining room, to Maury Allen, *Jackie Robinson: A Life Remembered*, 1987

"Jackie had built up this internal defense system. He had been hurt so much for so long that he had grown immune to all of it. At least publicly. Campy never seemed to get any abuse. Everybody liked him. . . . Jackie was still getting vicious hate mail by the time I got there, and Campy was getting letters requesting his autograph."

—Joe Black, Dodgers reliever and 1952 NL Rookie of the Year, to Maury Allen, *Jackie Robinson: A Life Remembered*, 1987

"A lot of people try to take different sides with me or Jack. I didn't push hard enough. He pushed too hard. Well, Jack had his moods and I had my moods, but deep down I believe we were always friendly. You'd never see Jack or me together. You might see Newk and me at a movie. On a day off at Chicago, I'd be in Shedd Aquarium. I'm just crazy about tropical fish. That's not Jack's speed; [Jackie] and Pee Wee and Duke would go to the track or play golf. I never did that. . . . So people figured that because [we] didn't pal around together that we were always having words. It wasn't true. . . . Jackie comes over here now when the weather is good for cookouts. You know I admire him. . . . Jack knows I admire him, too. It wasn't easy for any of us."

—**Roy Campanella to Roger Kahn,** *The Boys of Summer,* **1972**

"I'm happy that Roy Campanella and I survived the attempts at the old business of 'divide and conquer' that some people tried to use to make us enemies. It didn't work. There's no use in my pretending that we didn't have serious difficulties of opinion, but I think we always had mutual respect for each other. A coolness did exist between us for a number of years while I was in baseball and after I left. However, as time went by, my respect for Campy deepened."

—**J. R.,** *I Never Had It Made,* **as told to Alfred Duckett, 1972**

"As long as you have Jackie and what he stood for on your side, you've got a lot going for you."

—**Roy Campanella, at the renaming of William Ettinger JHS at 10th Street and Madison Avenue in Manhattan to Jackie Robinson Junior High, quoted by Peter Coutros,** *New York Daily News,* **March 26, 1974**

"Peter Wolinsky, a scrap metal dealer, and his wife came forward to identify themselves as having been hit by Jackie Robinson's thrown bat here [in Milwaukee] last night. . . . Robinson, for his part, has apologized profusely. He called Mrs. Wolinsky, tried to reach her husband, and visited their lawyer [James Stern]. . . . The bat-tossing occurred when Robinson, being ejected from the game, threw the club as he was walking back to the dugout. It bounced off the dugout roof and sailed into the box seats. . . . The main rhubarb started when Robinson came to bat, still angered by the fact that the Braves' Johnny Logan had been given a walk on a third called ball instead of a fourth. Jackie let umpire Lee Ballanfant know how he felt . . . and the heave-ho followed."

—**Bill Roeder,** *New York World-Telegram and Sun,* **June 3, 1954**

"It was raining. The Braves had a four-run lead. I feigned anger. I was stalling. I wanted to get the game called. The bat was slippery. I held it too long. I wasn't trying to throw it into the stands, but some people make it out that way."

—J. R., quoted by Jimmy Cannon, *New York Post,* July 22, 1962

"National League President Warren Giles told Jackie Robinson of the Brooklyn Dodgers today that he was convinced beyond doubt that Robinson did not intend to throw his bat into the stands last Wednesday night in Milwaukee."

—Associated Press, about Giles' conclusion after a "thorough investigation," June 8, 1954

"New developments in the Jackie Robinson bat-throwing incident, which supposedly had been 'settled' upon a promised payment of one public apology, have revived the case, it was learned today. The possibility of a suit against the fiery Dodger veteran and the Brooklyn Dodger club hangs on 'proper settlement' according to a Milwaukee attorney. The complainants, Mr. and Mr. Peter Wolinsky, who were struck by a bat tossed unintentionally into the stands by Robinson in a game played here January 2, have retained new counsel to press the case."

—Dick Young, *New York Daily News,* July 15, 1954

"I have a pretty good lawyer myself—Mr. O'Malley."

—J. R., July 15, 1954

"Alston . . . believes Robby is about to break out of his slump—a belief fostered by Jackie's long double in yesterday's All-Star Game."

—Dick Young, *New York Daily News,* July 15, 1954

"We lived in St. Albans, a mixed neighborhood in Queens, but we wanted something more. . . . We answered ads for some places near Greenwich [Connecticut]. When the brokers saw us, the houses turned out to be sold or no longer on the market, phrases like that. The brokers said they themselves didn't object. It was always the other people. The *Bridgeport Herald* got wind of the trouble and wrote it up and then a committee was formed in Stamford. . . . They asked what we wanted. We said view, privacy, water. . . . Then we saw this site. . . . But we had to find a builder, and some banks . . . were dead set against us. . . . But we finally found a bank operated by two Jewish brothers, and they'd take the chance."

—Rachel Robinson to Roger Kahn, *The Boys of Summer,* 1972

"My father and mother knew that our home, wherever it was, had to be a safe haven against an often turbulent world. . . . Toward this end, Mom and Dad made a hard decision, and in the fall of 1954, my family . . . exchanged our New York address in what was reported by *Ebony* magazine as the most exclusive Negro residential community in America for an all-white exclusive section of Fairfield County. . . . Our new address became 103 Cascade Road, Stamford, Connecticut. In Sugar Hill—less than an hour from Manhattan—our neighbors had been celebrities like Roy Campanella, Count Basie . . . and Ella Fitzgerald. In Stamford, our neighbors were exclusively white, mostly corporate businessmen; their wives were homemakers."

—Sharon Robinson, *Stealing Home,* 1996

"When we moved to Stamford . . . there was a wave of panic selling. Two families in fact did move out of our neighborhood. There are still problems in the North, but it's veiled because there hasn't been legislation against segregation."

—Rachel Robinson

"When we moved to North Stamford, which was predominantly white at the time, we fervently hoped that other black families would follow us. We wanted our children in good schools, and we wanted the neighborhoods and schools to be integrated so they would have black companionship. This did not occur soon enough for our children. We now realize how much being 'the only black' can hurt. In talks with us as they grew up, our children made us realize what a heavy burden had been placed on them. Sharon, as well as David and Jackie, went through a loss of identity."

—J. R., *I Never Had It Made,* as told to Alfred Duckett, 1972

"For several years before Jackie reached adolescence, I had been painfully aware of the widening gap between us. . . . I couldn't get through to him and he couldn't get through to me. . . . [Jackie] did display an interest in little league baseball and went all the way through to finish the Babe Ruth League. He enjoyed playing and he was good at it but he was exposed to cruel experiences not so much by the youngsters as their parents, who made loudly vocal comparisons between the way Jackie played and the way I played. . . . During his years in junior and high school, Jackie . . . seemed lost."

—J. R., who believed from personal experience that participation in sports could keep a boy out of trouble, *I Never Had It Made,* as told to Alfred Duckett, 1972

"[Jack] was explosive on the field and reporters used to ask if he was explosive at home. Of course he wasn't. No matter what he'd been called, or how sarcastic or bigoted others had been to him, he never took it out on any of us. After we moved up here, there was one clue to when he was upset, when things were going particularly badly. He'd go out on the lawn with a bucket of golf balls and take his driver and one after another hit those golf balls into the [lake]."

—**Rachel Robinson to Roger Kahn,** *The Boys of Summer,* **1972**

"THE GOLF BALLS WERE WHITE."

—J. R.

"Off the field, [Jackie's] acts were less intense but no less singular. Once some friends put him up for membership in a golf club near Stamford. When Jack learned that some members objected, he told his friends to forget it. So we played the Stamford public course. Weekends, that could mean a two-hour wait at the first tee. Jack never regretted the inconvenience that principle had caused him. Nor did he expect favors. We waited with all the other golfers, watching the foursomes tee off."

—**Leonard Gross, friend and West Coast editor of** *Look* **magazine,** *Los Angeles Times,* **November 3, 1972**

"Milwaukee won the [three-game] series' rubber game against the Dodgers, 6–4, as Jim Wilson—after pitching a no-hitter in his last start—gave up 7 extra-base hits but . . . gained his third victory without a defeat. Wilson's run-less streak ended at 24 frames. . . . Robinson was particularly troublesome for Wilson with 2 homers and 2 doubles."

—**James Kreis, about Robinson's most productive offensive game of his major league career on June 17, 1954, when he had four extra-base hits and a stolen base,** *1954—A Baseball Season,* **2011**

"Joe Adcock hit four home runs and a double in one game against the Dodgers in Ebbets Field [on July 31, 1954]. . . . Sure enough, [the next day, Clem Labine] hit him on the head. I was starting the next day and Adcock . . . said, 'Get one of them for me, will you?' . . . The guy I picked out to floor was Jackie Robinson. I knocked him down a couple of times. Then he started dropping bunts along the first base line, but they went foul. . . . I picked up the paper the next day and saw Jackie quoted as saying he wished he could have got one fair so he could have stepped on me at first base. And all the while I thought I was getting a break because Jackie was trying to bunt instead of swinging away. . . . But Robinson played that way."

—Gene Conley, Braves pitcher, to Donald Honig, *Baseball Between the Lines*, 1976

"Jackie Robinson . . . bailed the Dodgers out last night [against St. Louis]. He said this one was 'particularly sweet.' . . . Someone brought up [Cards manager] Eddie Stanky. Could it be that Robinson gets a special kick out of beating Stanky? . . . 'You said that,' he shouted, grinning and wiggling a finger in mock reproof. . . . It was really quite a night for Robinson. He hit the homer with a man on in the ninth to bring the Dodgers the victory by 8–7, and he set up two earlier runs with a beautiful bit of footwork on the bases."

—Bill Roeder, *New York World-Telegraph and Sun*, August 5, 1954

"Jackie Robinson . . . is proud and dedicated, loyal and tempestuous but basically he is an angry man. There is a need for angry men to fight stupidity and bigotry and conformity. There is a need for Jackie Robinson. That's why it is so troubling to hear so often the man dismissed with a shrug. 'It's too bad,' people close to baseball and far from baseball have said, 'that Robinson has gone wrong.' 'The reason we have beanball fights with the Dodgers,' a pitcher for the Milwaukee Braves insists, 'is Robinson. His needling starts things and it's too bad. If he didn't needle so much he could be the most respected man in baseball.' From umpires there come complaints about his penchant for argument. From newspaper men come reports of tantrums Robinson has thrown because of something which was written, perhaps rightly, perhaps wrongly, but almost always honestly. Not even Robinson himself claims that all his actions have been correct or even defensible. But to judge Jack by the standard which measures Leo Durocher as a pop-off man or Ed Stanky as a hot head is to make a mistake. The ordinary standards don't apply to Robinson. He is larger than life size."

—Roger Kahn, a passionate defense of a properly angry man,
***New York Herald Tribune*, August 29, 1954**

"While the 35-year-old Robinson stole only seven bases in 1954, the only time in his career he failed to reach double figures in steals, he did continue to hit well. His .311 average that season marked the sixth consecutive time he had batted over .300. It was also his last."

—Lyle Spatz, baseball historian, excerpt from paper presented at the Jackie Robinson anniversary conference, Long Island University, Brooklyn Campus, April 1997

"IT ISN'T FUN ANYMORE. . . . IT USED TO BE FUN BUT NOW IT HURTS WHEN I RUN AND IT HURTS WHEN I MOVE. IF IT ISN'T MY HEEL, IT'S MY KNEE OR MY GROIN. IF IT DIDN'T HURT TO PLAY, IT WOULD STILL BE FUN. BUT IT HURTS."

—J. R. TO ROGER KAHN, *NEW YORK HERALD TRIBUNE*, AUGUST 29, 1954

"To guard against a precipitant drop in the standings until the new blood jells and the pattern of a new championship structure begins to unfold, a skillful blend of rookie and veteran talent is indicated [for next year]. Pee Wee Reese, for instance, is certain to return. Just as certain to go is Jackie Robinson. If my informant is correct, Robinson's loss in popularity in Flatbush has been as conspicuous as his loss of proficiency."

—Joe Williams, needing a more credible informant, *New York World-Telegram and Sun,* September 9, 1954

"Concerning Robinson, Walter Francis insists that he will not be traded unless some club offers a first class pitcher for him. . . . O'Malley has no hope of being offered a first-rate hurler in exchange for Robinson. But Walter cannot be blamed for throwing up straws in the wind."

—Dan Daniel, *New York World-Telegram and Sun,* November 15, 1954

"It was [every winter my dad's] official job to test the ice on the lake to determine its safety. . . . When Dad was properly dressed for the frigid weather, he led the way carrying his equipment—a shovel and a broomstick. . . . The lake, which ran the length of our property . . . was . . . in winter . . . reserved for figure skating and ice hockey. . . . He was as brave then as when he entered baseball. . . . He had to feel his way along an uncleared path like a blind man tapping for clues. That was Jackie Robinson. And that was my dad—big, heavy, out there alone on the lake, tapping his way along so the ice would be safe for us. And he couldn't swim."

—Sharon Robinson, about Robinson enjoying his home life every winter, although there were rumors he'd be traded, as in 1954, *Stealing Home,* 1996

"About the closest we ever got was in 1954 and 1955 when Jackie was working real hard to break down the barriers for blacks staying in the [segregated] spring training hotels. We would talk on the phone about that and got together a couple of times over the winter to discuss how we might best go about this. He was very cordial and very concerned. . . . When the hotels down in Florida and the hotels in the big leagues began accepting all players on equal terms, I think he looked at that as one of his more notable achievements."

—Monte Irvin, outfielder for the 1954 world champion Giants and future Hall of Famer, to Maury Allen, *Jackie Robinson: A Life Remembered,* **1987**

"In 1955 the Dodger payroll was the largest in the league, but still, it totaled less than one million dollars. Jackie Robinson, Duke Snider, Pee Wee Reese, and Roy Campanella—each a Hall of Famer—never made as much as $50,000 in any one year."

—Carl Erskine, Dodgers pitcher, *Carl Erskine's Tales from the Dodger Dugout,* **2000**

"I'm staking a claim. I hope there's somebody here who can run me off the job. If there is, we'll have a hell of a club."

—J. R., who knew he'd have to battle Alston-favorite Don Hoak for the third base job after Billy Cox was dealt to Baltimore, quoted by Bill Roeder, *New York World-Telegram and Sun,* **March 7, 1955**

"In spring training Robinson [grew] increasingly agitated with how much time he spent on the bench while Alston evaluated other players. He asked Dick Young whether he heard anything about playing time he would get that season."

—Tom Clavin and Danny Peary, *Gil Hodges,* **2012**

"Walter hit the ceiling. Alston and I got into a shouting match that seemed destined to end in a physical fight. Gil Hodges kept tapping me on the arm, advising me, 'Jack, don't say anything. Cool down, Jack.' I listened to Gil because I had a tremendous amount of respect for him."

—J. R., *I Never Had It Made,* **as told to Alfred Duckett, 1972**

"If he's not going to play me, let him get rid of me. When I'm fit I've got as much right to be playing as any man on this team and Alston knows it. Or maybe he doesn't know it."

—J. R., miffed that Alston hadn't yet named him the Opening Day third baseman, Associated Press, April 4, 1955

"[On Opening Day] Carl Erskine . . . got [Brooklyn] off to a proper start with a 6–1 victory over the Pirates at Ebbets Field. . . . Robinson . . . was at third base and batting sixth in the lineup in the opener. . . . Brooklyn broke it open with five runs in [the seventh inning]. Jim Gilliam opened with a homer. . . . Two outs later, Robinson batted with Pee Wee Reese at third and Snider . . . at first. Jack brought Reese home with a well-placed bunt single to the right side. His hit also served to keep the inning alive and allowed Furillo to apply the crushing blow: a three-run homer to the seats in left."

—Lyle Spatz, baseball historian, excerpt from paper presented at the Jackie Robinson anniversary conference, Long Island University, Brooklyn Campus, April 1997

"[Before the Dodgers' second game, in the Polo Grounds] I looked over at the Giants [as they raised the 1954 NL flag and their world championship banner] and thought of the kick they must be getting out of it. . . . I just tried to realize how they were feeling at that moment."

—J. R., whose Dodgers still hadn't won a World Championship

"After a spring training dominated by doubts about aging hitters and untested pitchers, an injured Roy Campanella, an aging Jackie Robinson, and a Don Newcombe still rusty from two years in the military, the Dodgers simply ran away with the pennant."

—Thomas Oliphant, on how the Dodgers would win twenty-two of their first twenty-four games, *Praying for Gil Hodges,* 2005

"The Giants came to Brooklyn and ended the [Dodgers' season-starting ten-game] winning streak [5–4, as Alston was ejected for disputing Don Zimmer being called out at home on a Robinson squeeze bunt in the eighth inning that would have tied the game]. . . . The Dodgers came back the next day to win 3–1, as Erskine outdueled Maglie. . . . In the bottom of the fourth inning . . . after Maglie [threw behind him], Robinson bunted, hoping Maglie would be covering first base for retribution. But Maglie stayed out of the play and Robinson instead plowed into second baseman Davey Williams covering first. The dugouts emptied and there was plenty of shoving and shouting before order was restored. Unfortunately, the well-liked Williams hurt his back and would play only eighty-two games in his sixth big-league season and retire at the age of twenty-seven."

—Tom Clavin and Danny Peary, on a play that caused Robinson to feel remorse for hurting Williams, *Gil Hodges,* 2012

"Later in the game, Alvin Dark, Giants' captain, tried to retaliate by capsizing Robinson at third on a hard slide. Jackie saw the play coming and tagged Dark in the mouth—only the ball bounced free, to Robinson's dismay."

—**David Falkner,** *Great Time Coming,* **1995**

"A $40,000 damage suit has been filed in federal court against Jackie Robinson and the Brooklyn Dodgers by a Milwaukee husband and wife, who claimed they were hit by a bat thrown by Robinson June 2, 1954. Mr. and Mrs. Peter Wolinski charged they were both struck on the head when Robinson tossed his bat over the top of the Brooklyn dugout into the box seats. The Wolinskis claimed they both suffered brain concussions. . . . Mrs. Wolinski said she was confined to bed several weeks and Wolinski was unable to work."

—**Associated Press, about the couple called Wolinsky in 1954 newspapers, May 11, 1955**

"They're making a lot of claims they didn't make at the time. I called the man the day after it happened and he was out of town on business. That's how bad he [was hurt]."

—**J. R., who would settle out of court with the Wolinskys for supposedly about $300 each in early 1957,** *New York World-Telegram and Sun,* **May 12, 1955**

"I made a mistake when I popped off about the way I was being used. It seemed to me I was on the bench against all the weak pitchers and played third base against all the strong pitchers. . . . I realized I was wrong. I did Alston an injustice. If I were a manager I would admire a man's intense desire to be in the lineup every day, but I would not admire a repetition of the kind of pop-off to which I plead guilty here."

—**J. R., in an article titled "Why Can't I Manage in the Majors?," as told to Milton Gross, 1956**

"I'm going as lousy as I've ever gone in my life. It was all right when we were winning, but when we lost a couple I figured it might do some good to get me out of there."

—**J.R, who had been upset when Alston didn't play him,** *New York World-Telegram and Sun,* **May 13, 1955**

ROBINSON'S BIGGEST FAN

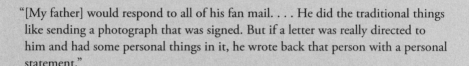

"[My father] would respond to all of his fan mail. . . . He did the traditional things like sending a photograph that was signed. But if a letter was really directed to him and had some personal things in it, he wrote back that person with a personal statement."

—Sharon Robinson, *Letters from Jackie* (MLB video), 2011

"One of his most enduring pen-pal relationships was with a young boy from [Sheboygan, Wisconsin] named Ronnie Rabinovitz. Jackie and Ronnie would . . . exchange letters for nearly a decade."

—*Letters from Jackie* (MLB video), about a friendship Robinson developed with
a seven-year-old Jewish boy whose lawyer father was
an advocate for civil rights, 2011

"WE WERE SO DIFFERENT. I WAS WHITE; HE WAS BLACK. I WAS A JEW; HE WAS A CHRISTIAN. I WAS FROM A SMALL MIDWEST TOWN; HE LIVED OUT EAST. I WAS A CHILD; HE WAS AN ADULT. BUT WE DEVELOPED THIS BOND THAT I CAN'T EVEN EXPLAIN."

—RON RABINOVITZ TO BOB NIGHTENGALE, *USA TODAY*, APRIL 13, 2007

"When the Dodgers came to Milwaukee in '55 for a game against the Braves, Ron [was taken to game by his father] and got to meet his hero. As a bonus, he took an unexpected trip to the Dodgers clubhouse."

—*Letters from Jackie* (MLB video), 2011

"[Jackie] got a brand new ball and took me from locker to locker to locker. Every one of these ballplayers signed [it]. Here was Duke Snider, Pee Wee Reese, Don Newcombe, Gil Hodges, Sandy Koufax was a rookie that year. I was numb. I was off the ground, floating for a week. It was so funny that he was so busy getting autographs for me that he forgot to sign the ball. Of course I got other autographs from him."

—Ron Rabinovitz, *Letters from Jackie* (MLB video), 2011

"On September [8], it was my birthday. We were at the game watching him play. He hit a home run [in the fifth inning off Ernie Johnson in a 10–2 Dodgers victory] and as he was rounding third, he waved to me. It was 'This one's for you.' . . . [Later] I have Jackie Robinson at my birthday. He was singing 'Happy Birthday' to me. It was like a dream come true. I couldn't believe it. He said to me, 'Keep in touch.'"

—Ron Rabinovitz, *Letters from Jackie* (MLB video), 2011

"It's really nice getting letters from you because you always seem to have a nice word when it's needed. I guess everyone in the public eye wants to have a friend like you and believe me, I am no exception. I can't tell you how much I appreciate you standing by me and I only hope I can always be worthy of your friendship."

—J. R. to Ronnie Rabinovitz, excerpt from letter, 1956

"Ronnie, one of the things that pleases me most is our friendship continues even though I am no longer connected with baseball. It is friends like you that make me feel everything that happened was worthwhile."

—J. R. to Ronnie Rabinovitz, excerpt from letter, 1958

"He [gave] me so much advice in the letters. In one letter, he said he learned a long time ago that 'a person has to be true to himself to succeed. He has to be willing to stand by his principles even at the loss of prestige.'"

—Ron Rabinovitz, Robinson's longtime friend who was featured prominently in the 2011 MLB documentary *Letters from Jackie,* to Bob Sansevere, *Pioneer Press,* April 16, 2012

"[After] about 1962, [Jackie and I] wrote less. As I got older, I would call him. He sent me a telegram when I graduated from high school. Then I got into the garment business and would get into New York a lot. We would get together for lunch, or if he was too busy, we would talk on the phone. We were in touch for almost 20 years. . . . Jackie had a great impact on me."

—Ron Rabinovitz to Bob Sansevere, *Pioneer Press,* April 16, 2012

"Everyone, including Robinson, realized that he was past his peak and his career was winding down. However, he wasn't pleased giving up so much playing time [at third and left field] to Don Hoak, [Sandy] Amoros, and his roommate, Junior Gilliam, who shifted to left field when [Don] Zimmer played second base and Hoak played third. Even Hodges made twenty-four appearances in left field, the first time in his career he didn't play in the infield. Unable to find his rhythm, Robinson would bat .256 with only 36 RBI."

—Tom Clavin and Danny Peary, *Gil Hodges,* 2012

"HE . . . PLAY[ED] IN ONLY 105 GAMES. MOST WERE AT THIRD BASE, WHERE HE SHARED DUTY WITH SECOND-YEAR MAN DON HOAK. DESPITE HIS OWN DECLINE, ROBINSON CONTRIBUTED TO AND SHARED THE JOY OF THAT GLORIOUS SEASON."

—LYLE SPATZ, BASEBALL HISTORIAN, APRIL 1997

"He was always ahead of you on the ballfield. I know when I was at second and he was playing third you had to be quick to keep up with him. He improvised his plays and you had to be alert."

—Jim Gilliam, Dodgers second baseman and future coach, quoted by Red Foley, *New York Daily Mirror,* October 28, 1972

"One day in the middle of the 1955 season, manager Walter Alston started a team that included Newcombe pitching, Campanella catching, Gilliam at second, Robinson at third, and Amoros in left—a majority [of black players]. This happened at a time when three of the sixteen teams (the Philadelphia Phillies, Detroit Tigers, and Boston Red Sox) were still segregated and the Yankees had only just succumbed by bringing up Elston Howard."

—Thomas Oliphant, *Praying for Gil Hodges,* 2005

"I think he was very happy when [the Yankees] finally got Elston Howard [their first black player in 1955]. Jack had known him from some barnstorming games, and he was a real fine man."

—Willa Mae Robinson Walker to Maury Allen, *Jackie Robinson: A Life Remembered,* 1987

"On Friday July 12 . . . my father called me excitedly to tell he had managed to get us tickets to the thirty-seventh-birthday celebration of Pee Wee Reese. . . . Just before the celebration was to begin, I caught Jackie Robinson's attention as he headed slowly to the dugout. I didn't care that Robinson's hair was now almost totally gray. The aging warrior remained my favorite player. I had traded for Robinson's autograph . . . but had never made direct contact with him myself, never looked him in the eye, and I wanted his name linked to me in a more intimate way. I leaned over the railing, and with my most beseeching smile waved my autograph book, opened to a page with an empty space surrounded by a wreath of florid messages: 'Let's never forget one another.' . . . 'Remember me until rubber tires and Niagara Falls.' . . . 'I will always cherish our relationship.' Before signing, Robinson scanned these silly, affectionate sentiments, and I could feel my face reddening. . . . 'Well,' he said. 'I can see I'm in good company.'"

—Doris Kearns Goodwin, a Dodgers fan who would become a famous historian,
***Wait Till Next Year,* 1997**

"Keep your smile a long, long while, Jackie Robinson."

**—J. R., writing an appropriately silly and affectionate sentiment in
Doris Kearns Goodwin's autograph book, July 12, 1955**

"Not only did the Man of the Hour double twice and score a run in the Dodgers' 8–4 victory, but the generous wit of Jackie Robinson had given me an unexpected moment I would treasure for the rest of my life. That night with my father, Reese, and Robinson remained fixed in my mind as the Dodgers continued their extraordinary season. On September 8, 1955, they clinched the National League pennant earlier than any team since 1904."

—Doris Kearns Goodwin, a Dodgers fan who would be come a famous historian,
***Wait Till Next Year,* 1997**

"After 63,000 Stadium spectators bowed their heads in silence for a minute to pray for the recovery of President Eisenhower from a heart attack, Whitey Ford and Don Newcombe opened the [1955 World Series] for their respective teams. Neither pitcher was sharp. . . . In the sixth inning [first baseman Joe] Collins . . . blasted a towering two-run shot . . . to give the Yankees a 6–3 lead and the game. The Dodgers scored two more runs on a sacrifice fly and a steal of home by the electric Jackie Robinson, but Bob Grim relieved in the ninth to protect Ford's win."

—Peter Golenbock, *Dynasty,* 1975

CLASSIC MOMENT: SEPTEMBER 28, 1955, YANKEE STADIUM, NEW YORK CITY

"Well, here we were in our seventh World Series in fifty years and there was hope that this would be the year, but our fans were also ready to shrug their shoulders and say 'Wait 'til next year' if we lost. The way we were playing the first game—down 6–4 in the eighth inning—it looked like we might have to wait. I was on third base and I knew I might not be playing next year. There were two men out, and I suddenly decided to shake things up. It was not the best baseball strategy to steal home with our team two runs behind, but I just took off and did it. I really didn't care whether I made it or not—I was just tired of waiting. I did make it and we came close to winning that first game."

—J. R., *I Never Had It Made,* **as told to Alfred Duckett, 1972**

"IT IS OUR MOST ENDURING IMAGE OF JACKIE ROBINSON. A DANCE OFF THIRD BASE, A BREAK FOR HOME, THE SLIDE FOR THE PLATE AND YOGI BERRA'S GLOVE AND—SAFE!—AND NOT EVEN ACKNOWLEDGING YOGI'S RHUBARB WITH THE UMPIRE AS HE PICKS HIMSELF UP AND CIRCLES AWAY. ROBINSON'S STEAL OF HOME IN GAME ONE OF THE 1955 WORLD SERIES MARKED HIM FOREVER AS THE DARING, ALMOST RECKLESS RUNNER WHO COULD AND WOULD STEAL ANY OPEN BASE AHEAD OF HIM."

—SHANE TOURTELLOTTE, *THE HARDBALL TIMES*, MARCH 2, 2012

"I knew he was going to try to steal home. . . . I almost dared him by taking a long windup as he danced off the bag. . . . I threw the ball to Yogi and got it there in plenty of time. The pitch was low, right where I wanted it, and Yogi just caught it and put his mitt down . . . in front of the plate and Robinson slid right into the tag. Robinson was out, there was no question about it. But the plate umpire, Bill Summers, was . . . too short to see over Yogi's head. Summers called Robinson safe and Yogi, who rarely argued with an umpire . . . started jumping up and down, yelling at Summers that he blew the call."

—**Whitey Ford, Yankees pitcher,** *Slick,* **1987**

"He was out!"

—Yogi Berra, Yankees catcher and future Hall of Famer, who would gripe about the safe call on Robinson's steal attempt until his death in 2015

"The batter for us when Jackie stole home was Frank Kellert, a reserve first baseman. Ordinarily in those situations, the batter is supposed to block out the catcher from getting a clear shot at tagging the runner coming home. But Kellert . . . stepped out of the way as Jackie slid right into Yogi. . . . After the game, some writers asked Kellert if he thought Jackie was out and he said 'yes.' The next day, Jackie lit into him like I'd never seen before, screaming at Kellert: 'What team are you playing for anyway?'"

—Don Zimmer, *Zim: A Baseball Life,* 2001

"From the first-base side of the field, it appeared that Yogi Berra had tagged him out; but I found a picture in the Hall of Fame library . . . from the third-base side showing Robinson's foot on the plate and Berra's tag a tad high on his leg. Home plate umpire Bill Summers called Robinson safe, Berra went delightfully berserk, and the rest is history."

—Thomas Oliphant, *Praying for Gil Hodges,* 2005

"My first husband, [agent and producer] Pat [DeCicco] and I had gone to New York for the . . . Series. We were guests of Dan Topping, then co-owner of the Yankees. . . . Dan was Pat's best man at our wedding [in 1953]. . . . With Pat and me were Topping; George Weiss, the Yankees' general manager; and Del Webb, the other Yankee co-owner; they were discussing Hank [Greenberg, my future husband, to whom I had earlier been introduced by Pat] with great respect, but . . . I remember them making joking references to Jews, and it was my first experience with anti-Semitism. . . . I sat there in Dan Topping's private box cheering madly for the Dodgers, and particularly Jackie Robinson. You can imagine how that went over. They weren't terribly crazy about Jews, so you know how they felt about Jackie. DeCicco wanted to kill me."

—Mary Jo Greenberg, widow of Hank Greenberg (who died in 1986), confirming Robinson's contention that the men who ran the Yankees were bigots, quoted by Hank Greenberg, *Hank Greenberg: The Story of My Life,* 1989

"As the Series moved across the East River [following New York's victory in Game 2], there was . . . talk about the fact that no team in fifty-two years of postseason play had come back to win after losing the first two games. . . . Alston suddenly went on a hunch and announced that instead of Erskine, he would pitch Johnny Podres [in Game 3]—on his twenty-third birthday. . . . Alston also . . . called a meeting of the team before the game, simply to tell them that he thought they were just as good as the Yankees and that he had faith in their ability. According to Jackie Robinson, whose occasional clashes with the manager had been much-publicized, it was an unusual gesture both noted and appreciated."

—Thomas Oliphant, *Praying for Gil Hodges,* 2005

"It looked bleak. . . . But when the Dodgers returned to Ebbets Field, they won all three games. Game Three was the turning point. . . . With the score 2–2 in the second, and with one out, Robinson singled. Amoros was hit by a Bob Turley fastball, Podres was safe on a bunt, and the bases were loaded. On third Robinson began his "will I, won't I" routine of making a series of mad dashes as though intent on stealing home . . . distracting Turley, who walked Gilliam . . . as Robinson, in his pigeon-toed walk, shuffled across the plate. In the seventh, Robinson . . . doubled, racing wide past the bag at second, and . . . when Robinson saw that [leftfielder Elston] Howard was throwing behind him, he continued to third and slid in safe as the relay came in high. The Yankees brought the infield in . . . and Amoros hit a dribbler through to the outfield for another run. Podres, baffling the Yankees with his change-up, won 8–3."

—Peter Golenbock, *Bums,* 1984

"I MUST ADMIT I HAD A PRETTY GOOD DAY FOR AN OLD, GRAY FAT MAN."
—J. R., SEPTEMBER 30, 1955

"The greatest competitor [I ever saw] in the clutch—Yogi Berra. When it meant something, Yogi always came through."

— J. R., about the three-time AL MVP whose eighth-inning homer pulled the Yankees to 4–3 in Game 5 with the Series even, quoted by Jimmy Cannon, *New York Post,* July 22, 1962

"The so-called insurance run that the Dodgers then proceeded to get was a thing of baseball beauty. . . . The mighty Gil Hodges . . . laid down a perfect sacrifice bunt . . . to move Furillo into scoring position at second. He scored when a Jackie Robinson ground ball just made it past a lunging Phil Rizzuto into left field for a single."

—**Thomas Oliphant, recalling being at the Dodgers' 5–3 Game 5 victory,**
Praying for Gil Hodges, **2005**

"Whether it was because of my stealing home or not, the team had new fire. We fought back . . . and the series came down to the wire in the seventh game."

—**J. R., who went 0-for-4 with an error at third base in the Dodgers' 5–1 Game 6 loss that would be his final Series game in 1955,** *I Never Had It Made,* **as told to Alfred Duckett, 1972**

"One break I got was Mickey Mantle didn't play that day [in Game 7]. But [neither did] Jackie Robinson [who had a strained Achilles tendon in his right heel]. Neither one started."

—**Johnny Podres, Dodgers pitcher and 1955 World Series hero, to Donald Honig,**
The October Heroes, **1979**

"Podres pitched a brilliant shutout, and in the sixth inning with men on first and second and only one out, Sandy Amoros saved the game with a spectacular running catch of Yogi Berra's fly ball down the left field line. It was one of the greatest thrills of my life to be finally on a World Series winner."

—**J. R.,** *I Never Had It Made,* **as told to Alfred Duckett, 1972**

"I can still see the Dodgers sprinting from their dugout, led by a courageous black man of legendary intensity named Jackie Robinson, to converge around the most improbable hero of all. . . . For two hours and forty-four minutes, Johnny Podres had simply defied defeat."

—**Thomas Oliphant, who celebrated the Dodgers' 2–0 victory,**
Praying for Gil Hodges, **2005**

"I went to every World Series [Jackie] was in except the 1955 World Series, and that's the one they finally won."

—**Willa Mae Robinson Walker to Maury Allen,**
Jackie Robinson: A Life Remembered, **1987**

"At the gala Dodgers victory party in Brooklyn's old Bossert Hotel, there was [Carl] Furillo ([who in 1947 said,] 'I ain't gonna play with no niggers') rushing to greet Jackie and Rachel Robinson as they came in. Carl and Jackie, friends, hugging ecstatically with cheeks pressed together, saying, 'We did it, we did it!'"

—Lester Rodney, sports editor of the *New York Daily Worker,* excerpt from paper presented at the Jackie Robinson anniversary conference, Long Island University, Brooklyn Campus, April 1997

"I was not just a baseball wife, I was a Brooklyn Dodgers fan. . . . It was that combination of being proud and very interested in what my husband could do, but also looking to see that the team is winning, so we would someday be known as champs—although it took us a long time to get there."

—Rachel Robinson to Danny Peary, 2012

"I was making about $6,000 . . . and we got World Series shares of $9,700. . . . Actually, who won the World Series didn't mean that much to me. Even the loser's share was more than my salary. Getting to the World Series was it. But it was very emotional for the older players who had lost in past years. Reese, Furillo, Hodges, Robinson, Snider, Newcombe, Erskine, Campanella—that's who got the most out of it."

—Ed Roebuck, Dodgers reliever, to Danny Peary, *We Played the Game,* 1994

"Jackie, Pee Wee, Gil, the guys who had been there so long, all needed a minute before we started pouring champagne or spoke to the press. Besides what it meant for us, there was this feeling that we had finally won one for our fans who had supported us so well all those years we didn't win. I honestly believe we were happier for the fans in Brooklyn than we were for ourselves."

—Carl Erskine to Danny Peary, *Gil Hodges,* Tom Clavin and Danny Peary, 2012

"I definitely want to play next year and naturally I'm going to fight any salary cut. I never held the club up when I could have gotten as much as anyone in the National League. They said they couldn't pay me any more because of the size of the park and I went along with them. . . . I didn't have as good as year as I did last season, but I never go on percentages. My value to the club is measured in other ways."

—J. R., quoted by the *New York World-Telegram and Sun,* October 12, 1955

"Brooklyn definitely needs a new park. This one is too small to play in. . . . A new park that is decent for the fans as [far as] parking and seating go will draw a lot more fans and will probably result in better baseball."

—J. R., not realizing that Walter O'Malley was considering building a new stadium not only a proposed site at Flatbush and Atlantic Avenues in Brooklyn but also on open land in Los Angeles, quoted by the *New York World-Telegram and Sun*, October 12, 1955

"ROBINSON MET BILL BLACK, A NEW YORK BUSINESSMAN WHO OWNED A CHAIN OF COUNTER RESTAURANTS CALLED CHOCK FULL O'NUTS. THE CHAIN HIRED MOSTLY BLACKS AT MINIMUM WAGE, AND TURNOVER WAS VERY HIGH. BLACK CONSIDERED ROBINSON FOR A JOB AS LIAISON BETWEEN MANAGEMENT AND BLACK EMPLOYEES. AFTER EIGHT YEARS IN THE MAJOR LEAGUES, ROBINSON BEGAN TALKING SERIOUSLY ABOUT RETIREMENT. AT 36, HE WAS LOOKING FOR A NEW ARENA."

—MATT MCHALE, *PASADENA STAR-NEWS*, APRIL 1987

"As an American citizen and as a human being concerned about the welfare of all people, I am writing to urge you not to sign extradition papers for Rev. Joseph A. DeLaine. I believe he is worthy of sanctuary and that of all states, the Empire State, New York, should provide a haven for a very courageous man whose only crime was being born a Negro and attempting to protect his person, his family and his home."

—J. R., pleading on the behalf of a prominent African American activist who fled South Carolina because he was charged with assault after returning gunfire fire on his home in October, to New York Governor Averell Harriman, who would not sign the extradition papers, excerpt from letter, December 6, 1955

"Brooklyn's having acquired third baseman Randy Jackson from the Cubs in exchange for Don Hoak and outfielder Walt Moryn today appeared to support the belief that Walter O'Malley was trying to sell Jackie Robinson, preferably to an American League club."

—**Dan Daniel,** *New York World-Telegram and Sun,* **December 7, 1955**

"I'm not sure whether I'll be playing next year or not so I am looking for other things. . . . Most [major] networks are not ready yet [for a black sports broadcaster] and I believe it's a shame because I am certain most people are. Our program at NBC has the highest local sports rating and it's creating considerable talk. . . . I am doing a spot with Marty Glickman and . . . Marty . . . usually throws a provocative question at me and, believe me, we say what we believe."

—**J. R., hoping he could host a national radio show after his baseball career ended, to friends David and Caroline Wallerstein, excerpt from letter, January 3, 1956**

"Dodger star Jackie Robinson says that anti-Negro statements are hurting the entire nation but helping his race 'achieve our goals just that much faster.' Robinson . . . attacked the 'few bigots' among Southern politicians yesterday before . . . the '100 Percent Wrong' Club, a Negro sports fan organization. Robinson, who was joined by Negro baseball players, Elston Howard of the Yankees and Brooks Lawrence and Tom Alston of the Cardinals, at the banquet, said the whole country suffers when Southern officials attempt to keep Negroes out of athletics or from having equal opportunities in other fields."

—**United Press, January 21, 1956**

"Two of the city's most distinguished ball players came to terms with their clubs today—Mickey Mantle with the Yankees and Jackie Robinson with the Dodgers. Mickey . . . signed . . . for an estimated $30,000. This is $8,000 over last season but less than the $35,000 he reportedly had sought. Jackie, according to Brooklyn veep Buzzie Bavasi, took a cut, but not the full 25 percent allowed under the rules. A good guess is that the veteran will get $33,000. Both players said they were quite 'satisfied.'"

—**Dan Daniel,** *New York World-Telegram and Sun,* **January 24, 1956**

"From the first moment I met Jackie Robinson [during spring training in 1956], I could see he was an awfully intense man. I could also see the frustrations he had to endure, and the battle scars. Wherever he went, Jackie had to put up with more insults, and he always had to walk that fine line. . . . I'll never forget a trip we took to New Orleans, where we played an exhibition game in Pelican Stadium. . . . The fans called him the worst possible names, and about the most polite thing I heard was 'Gator Bait.' It was brutal, and I was always braced for an incident of some sort. If there was a fight involving Jackie, I was damn well sure going to get in there and back him up."

—**Don Drysdale, Dodgers pitcher and future Hall of Famer,**
Once a Bum, Always a Dodger, **1990**

"A lot of the South wasn't integrated, so Jackie had to put up with problems right from the start of spring training. At Holman Stadium in Vero Beach, there were restrooms for whites and for 'colored.' . . . And the blacks also couldn't stay with us at our Miami headquarters, the MacAlister Hotel. But when we took a train through some town where blacks weren't permitted to stay at our hotel, Buzzie Bavasi made sure that we stayed together, anyway. The two or three sleeping cars . . . were just taken off the train and we slept overnight in the trainyard. It . . . kept the team together."

—**Don Drysdale, Dodgers Hall of Fame pitcher,**
Once a Bum, Always a Dodger, **1990**

"A MEANINGLESS SPRING-TRAINING GAME WAS NO EXCUSE FOR JACKIE TO GIVE LESS THAN HIS BEST. HE RAN THE BASES WITH A VENGEANCE. I SENSED THAT JACKIE HAD AN ALMOST PSYCHIC QUALITY. HE WOULD SIT IN THE DUGOUT . . . AND STARE AT THE MOUND. HE WOULD ANALYZE EVERY ASPECT OF THE PITCHER'S STANCE, HIS WINDUP, AND HIS DELIVERY. HE WAS A GREAT STUDENT OF THE GAME. I WOULD SIT NEXT TO HIM AND HE WOULD PREDICT EVERY SINGLE PITCH. TO A SEVEN-YEAR-OLD, THIS WAS LIKE SOME CIRCUS ACT. [HE] TAUGHT ME TO PREDICT PITCHES."

—STEVE GARVEY, DODGERS BATBOY DURING SPRING TRAINING IN 1956 AND THEIR FUTURE ALL-STAR FIRST BASEMAN, *MY BAT BOY DAYS,* 2008

"On the morning of the opener, the borough of Brooklyn held a victory parade down Flatbush Avenue to honor its world champions. . . . Eventually they got around to the game, the final one to open a National League season in Brooklyn. It matched the league's only twenty-game winners from a year ago: Don Newcombe and Robin Roberts. . . . Roberts held on to win 8–6. Robinson batted sixth in Alston's lineup and went 0-for-3, although he did drive in a run with a third-inning sacrifice fly."

—Lyle Spatz, baseball historian, excerpt from paper presented at the Jackie Robinson anniversary conference, Long Island University, Brooklyn Campus, April 1997

J. R. NOTE: Robinson had only two hitless Opening Days, in his first and last ones. He went 0-for-3 in both 1947 and 1956. Other than in those two years, he batted .438 on Opening Days. His overall batting average on Opening Days was a lofty .368.

"When I was traded [by the Cubs] to the . . . first-place Dodgers, I was delighted. . . . The players knew me and accepted me right away [and] no one resented that I was going to be playing Jackie Robinson's position. Robinson played third base in 1955, so theoretically I was supposed to replace him at third. . . . I knew that Jackie was on the decline. But he was a *great* player. He was the best all-around player I ever saw, including Willie Mays, Stan Musial, and Ernie Banks. He had the best instincts and would beat you doing something with the bat, his feet, or glove. . . . Jackie and I got along fine . . . though I never got to really know him on a personal basis. . . . Jackie was somewhat of a loner. I don't think he ran around much with the other guys."

—Randy Jackson, Dodgers third baseman, to Danny Peary,
We Played the Game, **1994**

"Jackie, hooted unmistakably [after making an error] by the 12,214 fans scattered in Roosevelt Stadium, let off steam in the dressing room, finally exploding, 'Whatever made 'em sign up for 24 games here!' That's the Dodger quota over a three-year span. . . . He added a few more comments about the fans in general and Jersey City in particular, and a couple of JC newspapermen tried to get him to repeat the more insulting quotes. . . . Ed Brennan of the *Jersey Journal* kept pressing him. Finally Robinson got sore and that got Brennan sore. 'Why don't you act like a gentleman?' he snapped. With that, Robinson blew up. He started toward Brennan but [Dodgers publicity director] Red Patterson stepped in."

—Bill Roeder, who was chastised by the *Post's* Milton Gross for not pointing out that Robinson was one of many Dodgers complaining about the facilities, *New York World-Telegram and Sun*, April 20, 1956

"I miss [Leo]. I miss that chatter over there [in the Giants dugout]. But this guy is the perfect image of him. Everything he does is Durocher all over."

—J. R., about the Giants' new manager Bill Rigney, quoted by Bill Roeder, *New York World-Telegram and Sun*, April 26, 1956

"[Jackie] had begun to gray, picked up a little weight, and had physically slowed down. However, his competitive drive had not diminished. . . . He saw [an] article quoting Tom Sheehan, chief New York Giant scout, [saying] 'The Dodgers are over the hill. Jackie's too old, Campy's too old and Erskine, he can't win with the garbage he's been throwing up there.' I also read that article Saturday morning, May 12, 1956, and it hurt, because I was having severe arm problems but was scheduled to pitch that afternoon at Ebbets Field against the Giants. . . . My spirits were low and I literally had nothing going for me but . . . I miraculously pitched a no-hit, no-run game—thanks to Jackie [robbing Mays of a hit]. Jackie rushed to the mound, shook my hand and then turned and raced toward the Giants dugout. . . . Jackie reached in the hip pocket of his Dodger uniform, pulling the clipping out, waved it at Sheehan and shouted, 'How do you like that *garbage*?'"

—Carl Erskine, Dodgers pitcher, *Carl Erskine's Tales from the Dodger Dugout*, 2000

"That there would be some anti-Semitism in baseball is hardly surprising. The national pastime was no bastion of enlightenment. . . . What Hank Greenberg did for Jackie Robinson, Robinson, Black, Campanella, and Newcombe did for Koufax, taking him under their sheltering wing."

—Jane Leavy, *Sandy Koufax*, 2002

"Jackie Robinson . . . clashed with Alston on many subjects, including [how little the manager pitched] Koufax."

—Jane Leavy, *Sandy Koufax,* 2002

"Jackie appreciated talent. If you were good, he was on your side. I think he saw that in Sandy. Added to that was the fact Jackie Robinson did not like Alston. Jackie always thought Alston was dumb. And the very fact that Sandy would every so often show this terrific flash of brilliance and pitch a terrific game and not pitch again for thirty days would add to Jackie saying how dumb this guy was."

—Tom Villante, Dodgers broadcast coordinator, quoted by Jane Leavy,
Sandy Koufax, 2002

J. R. NOTE: Jackie Robinson stole home for the final time in his career on April 25, 1956, against the Giants' battery of pitcher Jim Hearn and catcher Wes Westrum. It was the third time he stole home against the Giants but the first time since 1948. Although Robinson was considered the greatest stealer of home since Ty Cobb, he trailed Cobb significantly in career steals of home, as did everyone else in baseball history. However, he did sneak into the all-time top ten: (1) Ty Cobb, 54; (2) Max Carey, 33; (3) George Burns, 28; (4) Honus Wagner, 27; (5) Sherry Magee and Frank Schulte, 23; (7) Johnny Evers, 21; (8) George Sisler, 20; (9) Frankie Frisch and Jackie Robinson, 19. He also stole home against the Yankees in the 1955 World Series. Robinson was thrown out twelve times.

"Jackie Robinson was a helluva ballplayer even in 1956. . . . He still gave 110 percent all the time and would do anything to beat you, like bunting with 2 men out and a man on third, anything you wouldn't expect. He was a team player and we thought he was the leader of the Dodgers."

—Bob Buhl, Braves pitcher, who beat the Dodgers eight of nine times in 1956,
to Danny Peary, *We Played the Game,* 1994

"Jackie was always so mature. He instilled in you the idea that winning should be uppermost. But he also spoke of being a good sport when you lost. I know that sometimes when I used to let my head get too big with success, Jackie would bring me back to earth. He'd tell me, 'You can't be bigger than baseball. No one is bigger than baseball.'"

—Don Newcombe, Dodgers pitcher who went 27–7 and was voted the 1956 NL MVP and the majors' first Cy Young Award winner, quoted by Red Foley, *New York Daily Mirror*, October 28, 1972

"In 1956, Walter O'Malley had five black men on his payroll and was very eager to rid himself of one of them. Three times that season he told Bavasi to see what he could get for Robinson. . . . Bavasi did not underestimate the degree of O'Malley's dislike for Robinson. Nor did he doubt O'Malley's resentment of anyone on the team being more prominent than he was: 'Walter didn't like people taking any thunder away from him.' Still, Bavasi resisted. . . . 'Without him we lose,' he told O'Malley. 'With him we win.'"

—Michael Shapiro, *The Last Good Season*, 2003

"He called me a son of a ___ and several other things."

—Augie Donatelli, umpire, swearing Robinson used offensive language during a rhubarb at Ebbets Field, *New York World-Telegram and Sun*, June 29, 1956

"HE'S A LIAR. I DIDN'T CALL HIM ANYTHING THEN, BUT I DO NOW, THE NO-GOOD ___."

—J. R., WHO HAD DISAGREEMENTS WITH UMPIRES UNTIL THE END OF HIS CAREER, REFUTING DONATELLI'S CLAIM, TO REPORTERS, *NEW YORK WORLD-TELEGRAM AND SUN*, JUNE 29, 1956

"I grew up in Bedford-Stuyvesant and was a Brooklyn Dodgers fan, naturally, because of Jackie Robinson coming into the National League in 1947. . . . I was scouted by the Dodgers' Al Campanis, but the Yankees gave me more attention. . . . I guess he found out I was going to sign with the Yankees on a Tuesday afternoon and he had Jackie Robinson call me on Sunday night. That did it. All I needed to hear was Jackie's voice. . . . That Tuesday afternoon I signed with the Dodgers."

—Tommy Davis, who would become the LA Dodgers top RBI man in the early 1960s, *Tommy Davis' Tales from the Dodgers Dugout*, 2005

"A squabble between the Brooklyn Dodger star Jackie Robinson and a New Orleans sports writer has arisen over Louisiana's law banning sports contests between Negroes and whites. In a recent column, Bill Keefe, sports editor of the *Times Picayune*, said the new law received a push from the 'insolence of Robinson.'"

—**Associated Press, August 3, 1956**

"He has been the most harmful influence the Negro race has suffered in the attempt to give the Negro nationwide recognition in the sports field, and the surprising part of it is that he wasn't muzzled long ago."

—**Bill Keefe, sports editor of the *Times Picayune*, July 1956**

"You call me 'insolent.' I'll admit I have not been subservient, but would you use the same adjective to describe a white ballplayer—say Ted Williams, who is, more than I, involved in controversial matters? Am I insolent or am I merely insolent for a Negro who has courage enough to speak against injustices . . . ? I am deeply regretful that Lousiana has taken this step backward . . . because your sports fans . . . will be deprived of the right of free and equal competition—because of the damage it does to our country. I am happy for you, that you were born white. It would have been extremely difficult for you had it been otherwise."

—**J. R. to Bill Keefe, public letter, *Louisiana Weekly*, July 23, 1956**

"Jackie Robinson admitted today he issued a 'meet me outside' challenge to Lew Burdette, controversial Brave right-hander, during the hectic Milwaukee series, but the pitcher turned it down. . . . It all started Sunday afternoon when Burdette, who didn't pitch in the series, started 'jockeying' Robinson from the dugout [as he was warming up with Gil Hodges]. He said something about watermelon, which are fighting words to Robinson because of the racial inference."

—**Mike Gaven, *New York Journal-American*, August 28, 1956**

"When Gil assured me the remarks were meant for me, I fired the next ball over Hodges's head right at Burdette in the dugout. Lucky for him, I missed."

—**J. R., August 28, 1956**

"I saw his picture in a magazine and he looked hog fat. So I was kidding him about the watermelon on his stomach."

—**Lew Burdette, Braves pitcher who Roy Campanella had charged in a 1953 game because of two knockdown pitches followed by a racial slur, August 28, 1956**

"He didn't accept the challenge. He has no guts."

—J. R., about Burdette's unwillingness to face him alone, August 28, 1956

"It doesn't take guts to get yourself suspended, any moron can do that. We got a pennant to win. I am more interested in that than what Robinson has to say. . . . If he's going to get redneck like that I guess I'll just have to stop kidding him."

—Lew Burdette, who would apologize to Robinson during a September series, August 28, 1956

"In 1956, we had a very good ball club [in Milwaukee] and played very well, but we were young and inexperienced. As we headed into our last series with St. Louis, we heard that Jackie Robinson had said the Braves had a few playboys. He didn't name any names, so everybody started looking around and [thinking], 'Who could he be talking about? I wonder if he's talking about me. If my wife sees this in the paper, it's going to cause trouble.' . . . Robinson . . . was trying to put something into our minds so that we'd think about something other than baseball, and we were still thinking about it late in the game. And the Cardinals were out there doing business. They beat us two out of three. And meanwhile, Jackie's Dodgers took three straight and won the pennant [by one game over us]."

—Hank Aaron, Braves outfielder and Hall of Famer about a controversy that would dog Milwaukee in their 1957 world championship season, *The Tim McCarver Show*

"The finale was played on a sunny Sunday in Brooklyn. Alston chose Don Newcombe, with his 26–7 record and his strong right arm, and though the game ended Dodgers 8, Pirates 6, it wasn't nearly as close as the score might suggest. Duke Snider hit two towering home runs and made a spectacular catch to snuff a rally, and Jackie Robinson also hit a home run to give the Dodgers a 7–2 lead. . . . Once again the Dodgers of Brooklyn were champions of the National League, their sixth time in nine years."

—Peter Golenbock, *Bums,* 1984

"By the conclusion of the 1956 season . . . it was apparent that the illustrious career of Jackie Robinson was winding down. . . . However, his games played, batting average, home runs, and runs batted in were all improvements over his 1955 marks."

—Ron Briley, teacher and sports historian, excerpt from paper presented at the Jackie Robinson anniversary conference, Long Island University, Brooklyn Campus, April 1997

"The first two games of the 1956 [World Series] were played at Ebbets Field, and
. . . [in] the first game, before an aristocratic gathering including the Duke of
Windsor, President Eisenhower, J. Edgar Hoover, New York State Governor [Averell]
Harriman, and Mayor [Robert] Wagner of New York City, Sal 'the Barber' Maglie
defeated New York 6–3. Maglie, acquired by Brooklyn in May from the Cleveland
Indians [in a deal that shocked Dodgers fans], allowed Mantle a two-run homer and Billy
Martin a solo homer, but in Ebbets Field, a graveyard for lefties, Whitey Ford . . . lasted
only three innings. Jackie Robinson, in the last series of his illustrious career, hit a
long home run off Ford [in the second inning], and in the third inning Gil Hodges
hit a three-run home run for the lead and the game."

—Peter Golenbock, about Robinson's final home run, *Dynasty*, 1975

"[After throwing the first perfect game in World Series history in Game 5, Yankees
right-hander Don Larsen] was swarmed by writers, photographers, baseball officials.
Even Jackie Robinson and Walter O'Malley . . . came in to congratulate him."

—Yogi Berra, Yankees catcher and future Hall of Famer, *Ten Rings*, 2003

"We certainly won't see anything like [that] again. No matter who they pitch today
we ought to win."

**—J. R., before Game 6, quoted by the *New York World-Telegram and Sun*,
October 9, 1956**

"The sixth game [on October 9] was one of the finest pitching duels ever in a World
Series. Bob Turley and Clem Labine hooked up and it was 0–0 all the way to the
bottom of the tenth inning. The Dodgers got men on first and second with two
out and Jackie Robinson . . . hit one of those line drives that come out there like
it's shot out of a rifle. I went back as quick as I could and jumped against the wall,
but the ball hit up there and the winning run scored. Some of the newspapermen
wrote that I misjudged the ball, but that was wrong; it was hit just too quick for
me to get back on it."

**—Enos Slaughter, Yankees outfielder, about Robinson's final hit and RBI,
to Donald Honig, *Baseball Between the Lines*, 1976**

"I pitched the best game of my major league career but . . . ended up losing in the tenth
inning, 1–0. . . . I should have had a no-hit, no-run ball game myself but they got a
bad-bounce single to McDougald, and Enos Slaughter misplayed three balls in left
field: he lost Labine's hit in the shadows, Gilliam's hit in the sun, and on Robinson's
game-winning hit in the tenth, he lost the ball in the haze and white shirts and charged
in, only to have the ball shoot over his head. That was heartbreaking."

—Bob Turley, Yankees pitcher, to Danny Peary, *We Played the Game*, 1994

"Robinson went hitless [as Johnny Kucks pitched a three-hitter to win Game 7, 9–0]. In the first he grounded into a double play. In the fourth, he tried to bunt for a hit but . . . Kucks made a fine running catch at the third base line. In the seventh he walked. . . . Robinson came to bat . . . with two outs in the ninth inning. Kucks, summoning the last of his strength, struck him out. Yet Berra dropped the ball. . . . Another player in a similar situation, trailing by nine runs in the last game of the World Series, may have simply stood there and allowed the catcher to tag him. Jackie Robinson . . . dropped his bat and lit out for first, running hard down the line, just as he had when he entered the league, not running away from anything, but for something. Berra calmly tossed the ball to Moose Skowron, and Robinson was out. He ran hard until he passed the bag, then pulled up, turned and jogged back toward the Brooklyn dugout. The Yankees celebrated. Consequently, Brooklyn soon mourned."

—**Glenn Stout and Dick Johnson,** *Jackie Robinson: Between the Baselines,* **1997**

"No one knew it was Robinson's last major-league appearance."

—**Tom Clavin and Danny Peary,** *Gil Hodges,* **2012**

"I want to play one more year. I'm sure I can help them win another pennant. . . . Money is not the factor. I think my wife, Rachel, would like for me to manage and slow down some. But, to me, I'd be like a fire horse put out to pasture."

—**J. R., indicating he had no intention of retiring or managing, Associated Press, October 10, 1956**

"The last thing Alston told me [after the 1956 season] was to keep in shape. He needed me."

—**J. R., quoted by Jimmy Cannon,** *New York Post,* **July 22, 1962**

"There was never any question about Jackie Robinson's ability as a player, nor any question of his status as a man. And the effort he put forth those three years [I managed him] was everything he had despite bad legs. You could still see the greatness in him as a player. Sometimes something he would do would be phenomenal. He, like Campy, Gil, and Pee Wee, was best when you needed the best he had in him. You can't ask any more than that from anyone."

—**Walter Alston, Dodgers manager,** *A Year at a Time,* **1976**

"What I said [to you last year about being interested in managing the Montreal Royals] still stands. The door is open but I have heard nothing about [Montreal] and I don't believe what I read in the papers. . . . I haven't given too much thought about managing. . . . Managing would probably give me ulcers."

—J. R., to Bard Lindeman, Associated Press, October 15, 1956

"WE WILL HAVE A NEGRO MANAGER EVENTUALLY AND IT WILL BE THE FINEST THING THAT COULD HAPPEN TO BASEBALL WHEN IT COMES. . . . IT WOULD PROVE WE ARE MAKING STRIDES AND ARE SINCERE ABOUT EQUALITY."

—J. R., TOUCHING ON A TOPIC THAT HE'D BE TALKING ABOUT UNTIL HIS DEATH, TO BARD LINDEMAN, ASSOCIATED PRESS, OCTOBER 15, 1956

"Before one of the games at the old stadium, Jackie was warming up with somebody and he got pulled away for a minute. So I jumped in and got to play catch with him for five minutes, warming him up."

—Bob Corboy, batboy, recalling how he got a baseball autographed by Jackie Robinson at the age of fifteen when the Dodgers played an exhibition game in Honolulu before their post-season exhibition tour in Japan, to Jim Mendoza, *Hawaii News Now*, April 15, 2013

"An explosive outburst by Jackie Robinson, for which he was thrown out of the game, highlighted Brooklyn's 10–6 victory over all-Kansai Stars today [in Hiroshima]. Prior to the game, the Dodgers presented a plaque in memory of those who were killed by the A-bomb explosion here on August 6, 1945. Robinson's row with the umpire came in the third inning and he became the first player ejected from a game since the start of the Japanese tour."

—Leslie Nakashima, pointing out that Robinson couldn't turn off his competitiveness, even on a good will tour, United Press, November 1, 1956

"The players were told they were not allowed to have their wives ride with them in the same car of the train in Japan. Their wives rode in separate cars. But the top brass—O'Malley, the manager, and the coaches—had their wives with them in their car. So Jackie questioned that double standard in front of Reese, my dad, and the other players. Jackie protested and Pee Wee whispered to my dad, 'How much do you want to bet that Jackie won't be back next year?'"

—Roy Campanella II to Danny Peary, *Gil Hodges,* Tom Clavin and Danny Peary, 2012

"On December 8, 1956 . . . Robinson received the prestigious Spingarn Medal, awarded annually 'for the highest achievement of an American Negro.' Ed Sullivan, columnist and television celebrity, presented the gold medal at a New York dinner sponsored by the NAACP."

—Ron Briley, teacher and sports historian, excerpt from paper presented at the Jackie Robinson anniversary conference, Long Island University, Brooklyn Campus, April 1997

"THE NAACP'S PRESTIGIOUS SPINGARN MEDAL, WHICH THE ORGANIZATION AWARDED FOR DISTINGUISHED SERVICE TO BLACK AMERICA, WAS THE CIVIC HONOR HE PRIZED MOST. . . . IT CONFIRMED JACK'S BELIEF THAT HIS ACCOMPLISHMENTS ON THE FIELD HAD SIGNIFICANCE BEYOND SPORTS—AND THAT HE HIMSELF WAS NEEDED IN THE RANKS OF BLACK LEADERSHIP."

—RACHEL ROBINSON, *JACKIE ROBINSON: AN INTIMATE PORTRAIT*, 1997

"He played better in 1956 than he had in 1955, but not well enough to change the trajectory of his career. . . . He knew time was running out, but he didn't yet know what he would do with his life after baseball, nor how he would replace the lost income. He had a clothing store in Harlem, but business there was not good, and his new construction business had so far not constructed a thing."

—Jonathan Eig, *Opening Day: The Story of Jackie Robinson's First Season*, 2007

"On December 10, 1956, Robinson met with William Black, president of Chock full o'Nuts. . . . Black . . . offered Robinson a position as vice president in charge of personnel at annual salary of $50,000."

—Ron Briley, teacher and sports historian, April 1997

"Mr. Black happened to see a piece in the paper one day that I planned to retire from baseball. . . . He has many Negro employees and was having difficulty with a turnover in personnel. He thought I could handle the job because he felt the employees would have confidence in me."

—J. R. to Les Beberman, August 16, 1957

"I never saw him play."

—William Black

"Robinson attempted to reach the Dodgers' 'general manager,' 'Buzzy' Bavasi, to inform him of his intentions. However, Bavasi, who was negotiating [a trade of Robinson] with the Giants, was unavailable. The next day, Robinson signed a contract with Black."

—Ron Briley, teacher and sports historian, April 1997

THE UNIMAGINABLE TRADE

"On December 13, Buzzie Bavasi traded Jackie Robinson to the New York Giants for journeyman pitcher Dick Littlefield and $35,000. Robinson had aged and wasn't the player he once was, but he was still worth a lot more than what Bavasi got in return. Besides, Bavasi knew he was the symbol of the postwar Dodgers and had no business forcing him to don a Giants uniform. Earlier in the year, Robinson did Bavasi a favor by calling Tommy Davis and convincing him to sign with the Dodgers rather than the Yankees, so he had to believe he would be around when Davis arrived and that no trade was in the works. So what went wrong?"

—Tom Clavin and Danny Peary, *Gil Hodges*, 2012

"There are no hard feelings. The Brooklyn club had to protect its own best interest. [But] I thought I helped Brooklyn last year and didn't figure to be traded."

—J. R., making an official statement that didn't hint at his true feelings, December 13, 1956

"We all knew Jackie was coming to the end of the line. He was 38, had slowed down and couldn't get around on the inside fastball anymore, and Alston was playing him less and less. But we never expected the Dodgers to trade him, especially to the hated Giants."

—Don Zimmer, Dodgers infielder, *Zim: A Baseball Life*, 2001

"Many in baseball were shocked. . . . Dodger fans were outraged."

—Ron Briley, teacher and sports historian, April 1997

"THIS IS LIKE SELLING THE BROOKLYN-BATTERY TUNNEL. JACKIE ROBINSON IS A SYNONYM FOR THE DODGERS. THEY CAN'T DO THIS TO US."

—DODGERS FAN, *NEW YORK TIMES*, DECEMBER 14, 1956

"I got the feeling he had worn out his welcome with the Dodgers. Look what they traded him for: Dick Littlefield. The Dodgers were changing, and Jackie was getting older and more vociferous. . . . Jackie wasn't going to leave New York, and the Dodgers planned to move to Los Angeles. I think Walter O'Malley and Buzzie Bavasi had a meeting and decided to trade him."

—Don Newcombe, Dodgers pitcher, to Danny Peary, *We Played the Game*, 1994

"I am tickled that I will remain in the city. The Polo Grounds will make easier commuting. . . . I will play first, second, third, the outfield, anywhere I am placed. I will give the Giants the best I have."

—J. R., not revealing that he had other plans than to play for the Giants, to reporters, quoted by Dan Daniel, *New York World-Telegram and Sun*, December 13, 1956

"They traded him without discussing it with him, or preparing him for it, given his status, his importance to the team, and the years of service to the team. There was no ceremonial stuff planned to lead up to this. And to be traded to the hated Giants was of course another part of the disrespect kind of thing. It was not just because they wanted to trade him, but the way they went about it that was disturbing. Buzzie just picked up the phone and said, 'You're traded.'"

—Rachel Robinson, about the last Giants-Dodgers trade until 1968, to Danny Peary, *Gil Hodges*, Tom Clavin and Danny Peary, 2012

"I was hurt by it, yes. After you give everything you have for one team, it's hard to be traded."

—J. R. to Ron Rapoport, *Los Angeles Times*, June 5, 1972

"Jackie had taken a lot of abuse to become the first black ballplayer in the major leagues, and being traded from the Brooklyn Dodgers to our arch-rivals probably was the last straw, a slap in the face."

—Don Drysdale, Dodgers Hall of Fame pitcher, *Once a Bum, Always a Dodger*, 1990

"At the last moment, after all the things he'd done for the Dodgers, after everything he'd suffered, they found it necessary to trade a man of stature, a man who *was* the Dodgers. . . . It should have been understood that this man started with the Dodgers and that he would end up with the Dodgers. Certain people you never trade, and Jackie Robinson should never have been traded."

—**Hank Aaron, Braves outfielder and future Hall of Famer, introduction,** ***I Never Had It Made,*** **Jackie Robinson, as told to Alfred Duckett, 1972**

"My judgment is that Robbie is not through as a player at all. He'll have a great year with the Giants playing first base. If he gets his weight down, he'll have as good a year as he ever had. Jackie is a wonderful ball player, everyone knows that. And you get used to being with a guy after so many years. Jackie sure will look different in a Giant uniform. But we needed a left-handed relief pitcher. I think Dick Littlefield will make us a good one."

—**Roy Campanella, Dodgers catcher and future Hall of Famer, revealing mixed feelings toward Robinson, United Press, December 13, 1956**

"We had to do something to break the log jam of veterans that is keeping our younger stars out of action. We wanted to make the kind of deal that would be acceptable to Robinson. This we were able to do with the Giants. He'll help them. I just hope he doesn't hurt us."

—**Walter O'Malley, Dodgers owner, to Joe Williams,** ***New York World-Telegram and Sun,*** **December 14, 1956**

"To find similar cynicism [as O'Malley's], you had to go clear back to 1935 when the Yankees dumped Babe Ruth on the old Boston Braves. But then the star was being sent to another league. Robinson, the embodiment of the loud, brave, contentious Dodgers, was being assigned to his team's greatest adversary. Sports pages flapped with excitement."

—**Roger Kahn,** ***The Boys of Summer,*** **1972**

"After you've reached your peak, there's no sentiment in baseball. You start slipping and pretty soon, they're moving you around like a used car. You have no control over what happens to you."

—**J. R.**

"Robinson concluded that he would wait until January 10, 1957, to inform Giants owner Horace Stoneham whether he would retire or play for the Giants. . . . The reason for Robinson's apparent duplicity was an exclusive contract for $50,000 which he had signed with *Look* magazine. That contract stipulated that Robinson's retirement would first be announced in a magazine exclusive [in January]."

—Ron Briley, teacher and sports historian, excerpt from paper presented at the Jackie Robinson anniversary conference, Long Island University, Brooklyn Campus, April 1997

"I am glad Jackie has joined us. We sure got tired of seeing him against us. Jackie will help me. He knows all the answers, and there are a lot of them I want to learn. We are friends, and now that we are teammates, I am sure he will add to my education."

—Willie Mays, Giants outfielder and future Hall of Famer, quoted by Dan Daniel, *New York World-Telegram and Sun,* January 3, 1957

— TEN —

The Fight for Social Justice

"Dear Mr. Stoneham:

After due consideration I have decided to request to be placed on the voluntary retired list as I am going to devote my full time to business opportunities that have been presented.

My sincere thanks to you and to Mr. Feeney for your wonderful cooperation and understanding in this matter. I assure you that my retirement has nothing to do with my trade to your organization. From all I have heard from people who have worked with you it would have been a pleasure to have been in your organization. Again my thanks and continued success for you and the New York Giants.

Sincerely, Jackie Robinson"

— **J. R., letter to New York Giants owner Horace Stoneham, January 14, 1957**

"WHY I'M QUITTING BASEBALL"

—TITLE OF ARTICLE, WRITTEN BY ROBINSON AFTER HE WAS COMMISSIONED BY *LOOK* MAGAZINE PRIOR TO HIS BEING TRADED BY THE DODGERS TO THE GIANTS, JANUARY 5, 1957

"By selling the news of his retirement from baseball to *Look Magazine* and holding the announcement for that publication's deadline, he has embarrassed the Dodgers, dislocated the plans of the Giants and deceived the working newspaper men whose friendship he had and who thought they had his confidence."

— **Red Smith, one of several major reporters who preferred to attack Robinson's integrity rather than the Dodgers' for trying to dump their loyal longtime star, *New York Herald Tribune*, January 7, 1957**

"I run *Look*. Any statement Jack made that may have been misleading was out of respect for us. I've never met anyone more honest."

— **Dan Mich, at a press conference regarding Robinson's retirement, January 1957**

"I had given my best to Brooklyn for eleven years and my debt to baseball has been paid."

—J. R., about why he felt no obligation to the Dodgers' front office that had traded him, to reporters, January 1957

"And this is the way he repays the newspapermen for what they've done for him. He tells you one thing and then writes another for money. You fellows will find out that you've been blowing the horn for the wrong guy."

—Buzzie Bavasi, Dodgers general manager, showing his outrage that Robinson retired and his deal with the Giants had been nullified, January 1957

"I was as close to Buzzie as a ball player can get to a general manager. Basically he's a fine man but he hurt me very badly [by what he said]. I had made up my mind to quit and take [the] job. . . . But the people here told me it would be all right with them if I played with the Giants. They said the public relations would be worth a lot. I wanted to play. Then Buzzie said something about my integrity."

—J. R., who was tempted by the Giants' $60,000 salary offer, quoted by Jimmy Cannon, *New York Post*, July 22, 1962

"After what Bavasi said, I wouldn't play ball again for a million dollars."

—J. R., quoted by the *New York Times*, January 7, 1957

"I don't think that I ever said I'd play this year for the Giants. I naturally had to evade some questions about . . . what was going to happen next year. I did that simply because . . . I had a moral obligation not to reveal the exclusive story [*Look*] had paid for some three years ago."

—J. R. to audience member, *I've Got a Secret* television show, January 9, 1957

"It had absolutely nothing to do with my decision."

—J. R., about quitting because the team he was traded to was the Giants, to audience member, *I've Got a Secret* television show, January 9, 1957

"I love the game of baseball and I love what baseball has done for me . . . but at 38 I have to start thinking about my future."

—J. R. to audience member, *I've Got a Secret* television show, January 9, 1957

> ## "THE WAY I FIGURED IT, I WAS EVEN WITH BASEBALL AND BASEBALL WITH ME. THE GAME HAD DONE MUCH FOR ME, AND I HAD DONE MUCH FOR IT."
> ### —J. R., *I NEVER HAD IT MADE*, AS TOLD TO ALFRED DUCKETT, 1972

"President Warren Giles of the National League today received Jackie Robinson's official request to be placed on the voluntarily retired list."

—United Press, January 16, 1957

"News of Jackie Robinson's retirement in January 1957 left me feeling empty. His career had been my childhood."

—Doris Kearns Goodwin, Dodgers fan who became a famous historian, *Wait Till Next Year,* 1997

"I know I'll miss the excitement of baseball, but I'm looking forward to new kinds of satisfaction. I'll be able to spend more time with my family. My kids and I will get to know each other better. They won't have to look for me on TV. . . . Jackie still feels badly about my quitting the game. It's tough for a 10-year-old to have his dad suddenly turn from a ballplayer into a commuter."

—J. R., *Look* magazine, January 5, 1957

"For Major League Baseball my father's retirement signaled the end of an era; for me, it signaled the beginning of our family life."

—Sharon Robinson, *Stealing Home,* 1996

> ## "HE ENGENDERED MORE EMOTION, MORE HATRED, MORE PASSION THAN ANYBODY WHO EVER PLAYED THE GAME."
> ### —MAURY ALLEN, *JACKIE ROBINSON: A LIFE REMEMBERED*, 1987

"He established himself as a superb hitter, infielder, and base runner, but those skills are not his legacy. No man in the history of professional sports ever endured more abuse, performed under closer scrutiny, withstood heavier pressures. But always there was a sense of dignity. Jackie never let anyone, not his teammates or his opponents, forget that he was a man. All he really asked was to be treated as one."

—Mickey Herskowitz, *Houston Post,* April 14, 1987

"When Jackie Robinson played Major League Baseball, he turned an upside-down nation right side up."

—Roger Rosenblatt, Peabody and Emmy Award–winning author and playwright, keynote address, Jackie Robinson anniversary conference, Long Island University, Brooklyn Campus, April 1997

"[Jackie Robinson] helped inspire the image that this nation was capable of racial amity instead of racial anguish, and that was the best thing that ever happened to baseball."

—Howard Cosell, broadcaster and writer, *Cosell*, 1973

"Shortly after his retirement, Robinson agreed to postpone assuming his duties with Chock full o'Nuts. . . . Robinson could hardly refuse when NAACP Executive Secretary Roy Wilkins asked Robinson to chair the organizations' 1957 Freedom Fund drive. . . . Under the tutelage of veteran NAACP organizer Franklin Williams, Robinson became a successful orator and fund raiser, proudly pointing out that the 1957 tour was able to garner $1 million for the NAACP coffers."

—Ron Briley, teacher and sports historian, excerpt from paper presented at the Jackie Robinson anniversary conference, Long Island University, Brooklyn Campus, April 1997

"We have waited one hundred years for these rights. In my view, now is the time for Negroes to ask for all of the rights which are theirs."

—J. R. to Chicago audience during 1957 Freedom Fund drive tour, 1957

"Detroit is a great sports town. But you can't help but wonder about the absence of Negro players in both football and baseball."

—J. R. to Detroit audience during 1957 Freedom Fund drive tour, 1957

"Impressed with [Vice President Richard] Nixon's anticommunism as well as his occasional pro-civil rights statements, Robinson began to quote Nixon in his NAACP speeches, and the two began to write a series of letters."

—Michael G. Long, about Robinson and Nixon becoming strange bedfellows, *First Class Citizenship*, 2007

"I had found that there was a great deal of suspicion in the black community about Nixon, primarily because so many black people were disenchanted with the Eisenhower administration. . . . It sounded as if the vice president wanted me to disassociate him from Eisenhower since he knew that blacks, in the main, didn't like Ike."

—J. R., *I Never Had It Made,* as told to Alfred Duckett, 1972

"It is a privilege to be working along with someone like yourself to achieve the important objective of guaranteeing equal opportunity for all Americans, and your expression of approval will be a constant source of strength and encouragement to me."

—Vice President Richard Nixon, who Robinson, in retrospect, years later believed was conning him, to Robinson, excerpt from letter, March 22, 1957

"When the Dodgers assembled at Vero Beach in the spring of 1957, the absence of Jackie Robinson was conspicuous. Without his fiery presence on the field and in the clubhouse, the players felt the team's foundation was cracked. It cracked a little more when Walter O'Malley announced that the Dodgers had acquired . . . territorial rights in Los Angeles . . . a necessary hurdle for a move to take place."

—Tom Clavin and Danny Peary, *Gil Hodges,* 2012

"Robinson, you know, had a special talent for getting the club fired up emotionally, particularly for a big series, and that was important."

—Walter Alston, Dodgers manager, anticipating why Robinson would be missed in 1957, the Dodgers' final season in Brooklyn before moving to Los Angeles, quoted by Joe Williams, *New York World-Telegraph and Sun,* March 26, 1957

"My knee hurt so badly Opening Day, I couldn't get out of bed."

—J. R., about the exact moment he no longer had regrets about retiring, to Roger Kahn

"The Brooklyn Dodgers without Jackie Robinson were an engine without one of its biggest spark plugs. Our flaming competitor was gone, and the team that had won four pennants in the previous five years finished the 1957 season in third, 11 games behind the Milwaukee Braves."

—Duke Snider, *The Duke of Flatbush,* 1988

"In 1957, Jack, who had always been the epitome of health, strength, and physical indestructibility, suddenly began to lose weight. . . . Then when he also began to experience excessive thirst, we immediately went to the doctor, Charles Solomon, who told us Jack had diabetes. I don't know how Jack felt, for he was completely stoic. . . . I was stunned and sick at heart. I knew immediately that the condition was taking Jack further beyond my protective shield and would significantly restrict what he could and couldn't do."

—**Rachel Robinson,** *Jackie Robinson: An Intimate Portrait,* **1996**

"Jack set the pace. He told us that he would inject his own insulin, run his own tests, and give up sweets—from a man who could eat a pint of ice cream at a sitting. It was as close to a declaration of personal independence as I have heard. By radically changing his diet and managing his therapy, he could continue to travel alone if necessary. . . . As he grew older he kept painful thoughts to himself, and so did I."

—**Rachel Robinson,** *Jackie Robinson: An Intimate Portrait,* **1996**

"Recently retired Jackie Robinson . . . made several appearances in Detroit to help [Kansas City Monarchs' and Detroit Stars' popular African-American owner Ted] Rasberry promote his teams."

—**Larry Lester and Sammy J. Miller,** *Black Baseball in Kansas City,* **2000**

"Decked out in his new business suit in 1957, Jack plunged into his new role as Chock full o'Nuts vice president in charge of personnel with great enthusiasm. He commuted to New York City by car each day. . . . He studied traffic patterns, timed his trips, mapped out several different ways to get to work, and devised ways to set records for himself in the process. . . . He studied wage scales, benefits, training, and mobility patterns, and visited stores to talk to employees in person, solicit information, and identify problems. . . . He campaigned for more extensive training, promotions to managerial levels, and better pay for counterpeople."

—**Rachel Robinson,** *Jackie Robinson: An Intimate Portrait,* **1997**

"When I first joined Chock . . . my picture was used on the financial pages of the *New York Times,* and a very knowledgeable newsman told me that it was the first time a black man's picture had been featured in that section."

—**J. R.,** *I Never Had It Made,* **as told to Alfred Duckett, 1972**

"It was good seeing you in Washington on Friday. I considered it a great honor receiving an honorary degree with you. You have done a great work for the race and the nation and all the people of good will are indebted to you for your contribution. Mrs. King joins me in sending best regards. Please give our warm regards to your charming wife."

—**Martin Luther King Jr., who, along with Robinson on June 7, 1957, received an honorary degree of Doctor of Laws from Howard University, conclusion to letter, June 12, 1957**

"I READ YOUR STATEMENT IN THE PAPERS ADVISING PATIENCE. . . . IT IS EASY FOR THOSE WHO HAVEN'T FELT THE EVILS OF A PREJUDICED SOCIETY TO URGE IT, BUT FOR US WHO AS AMERICANS HAVE PATIENTLY WAITED ALL THESE YEARS FOR THE RIGHTS SUPPOSEDLY GUARANTEED US UNDER THE CONSTITUTION, IT IS NOT AN EASY TASK. NEVERTHELESS WE HAVE DONE IT. IT APPEARS TO ME NOW, MR. PRESIDENT, THAT UNDER THE CIRCUMSTANCES THE PRESTIGE OF YOUR OFFICE MUST BE EXERTED. A MERE STATEMENT THAT YOU DON'T LIKE VIOLENCE IS NOT ENOUGH. . . . I AM AWARE, MR. PRESIDENT, THIS LETTER EXPRESSES A MOOD OF FRUSTRATION. IT IS A MOOD GENERALLY FOUND AMONG NEGRO AMERICANS TODAY AND SHOULD BE A MATTER OF CONCERN TO YOU AS IT IS TO US."

—J. R., WHOSE LETTERS TO PEOPLE IN POWER WERE POLITE BUT POINTED IN CRITICISM BECAUSE HE HAD NO PATIENCE FOR CHANGE, TO PRESIDENT EISENHOWER, SEPTEMBER 13, 1957

"Dad's mission, which began with integrating Major League Baseball, continued in other arenas when he retired. He made a point of sharing with us his experiences in the civil rights movement. . . . He described battles in Georgia, Alabama, and Mississippi as children were put on the line because of the . . . *Brown v. Board of Education* decision [in 1954]. I was most fascinated by the story of the nine teenagers who were selected to integrate the Little Rock [Arkansas] school system. In the fall of 1957, news of their struggle was all over television. As the situation heated up, the families of the children contacted my father. I still remember the day he heard from the children directly."

—**Sharon Robinson, *Stealing Home*, 1996**

"Please accept my congratulations on the positive position you have taken in the Little Rock situation. I should have known you would do the right thing at the crucial time."

—J. R., pleased that the army was deployed to Little Rock to stop mob violence due to the integration of schools, to President Eisenhower, excerpt from letter, September 25, 1957

"*The Jackie Robinson Show* . . . aired on WRCA radio after he retired from baseball. . . . His idea of a stunt was asking President Dwight Eisenhower to read the Gettysburg Address. Eisenhower declined and Robinson did it himself, reciting words we are still struggling to live by."

—Michael Daly, *New York Daily News*, April 15, 2007

"Integration is coming here whether you like it or not and such progress will bring trouble along the way. . . . Some of my friends in New York were afraid I would be physically harmed if I came here. Isn't that a reputation for a state to have?"

—J. R., at a news conference prior to addressing a rally organized by the NAACP in Jackson, Mississippi, United Press, February 7, 1958

"That's preposterous. O'Malley had nothing to do with [introducing Negroes into the major leagues]. It was all Mr. Rickey's idea and I don't believe O'Malley knew anything about it. In fact, he wasn't too keen about it in the first place."

—J. R., expressing anger that Walter O'Malley was receiving an award from the Urban League for his contribution to the integration of baseball, quoted by the *New York Journal-American*, May 9, 1958

"Jackie must be miffed at something to pop off again."

—Walter O'Malley, Los Angeles Dodgers owner, quoted by the *New York Journal-American*, May 9, 1958

"Jackie is right in that O'Malley had nothing to do with introducing Negroes into the major leagues, but Walter wouldn't claim he did. He might have accepted the award to avoid embarrassment."

—Branch Rickey, Dodgers controlling partner in 1947, quoted by the *New York Journal-American*, May 9, 1958

"The award was presented to O'Malley for the entire Dodger organization and not to O'Malley individually for a single accomplishment. . . . I've written Jackie and explained the situation."

—**Wesley Brazier, Urban League director,**
quoted by the *New York Journal-American*, May 9, 1958

"Bayard Rustin, arguably the most important tactician of the civil rights movement, enlisted Robinson, Coretta Scott King, and Harry Belafonte to lead the 1958 Youth March for Integrated Schools in Washington, DC. [On October 25] Robinson thank[ed] James Hagerty, the White House press secretary, for showing interest in the march and [lobbied] for Eisenhower to welcome the young marchers. But Robinson was unsuccessful. A racially integrated group of students presented their petition at the White House gate, and a guard denied the group's request to meet with Eisenhower or any other White House official."

—**Michael G. Long, *First Class Citizenship*, 2007**

"The National Labor Relations Board refused today to set aside an employee election on the basis of union charges against Jackie Robinson, vice president of Chock full o'Nuts. The former baseball star . . . had been accused of injecting the racial issue and of threatening reprisal in the pre-election campaign last July at the company's plant in Harrison, NJ. The employees voted against Local 262 of The Retail, Wholesales Department Store Union. . . . Mr. Robinson expressed satisfaction with the NLRB ruling. He called it 'absolutely just' and said the charges against him were unfounded."

—***New York Times*, about a ruling that, despite exonerating Robinson, wouldn't**
sway his critics from believing one of his main roles at Chock full o'Nuts was to
prevent unionizing, June 6, 1968

"The June 1, 1946, issue of *People's Voice*, contained an article and photograph of Jackie Robinson reflecting. . . . He had accepted the chairmanship of the New York State organizing committee for the United Negro and Allied Veterans of America (UNAVA). . . . The *People's Voice* has been cited by the California Committee on Un-American Activities, report, 1948, 'to be a Communist initiated and controlled, or so strongly influenced as to be in the Stalin solar system.' . . . The November, 1946, issue of *Fraternal Outlook* contains an article and photography of Jackie Robinson in connection with the opening of the Solidarity Center of the International Workers Order (IWO) in Harlem, New York. The name of Jackie Robinson, ballplayer, is listed as one of the persons on the advisory board. . . . The IWO has been designated by the Attorney General of the United States pursuant to Executive Order 10450."

—**FBI mailing to an individual or agency requesting a name check,**
excerpt from FBI file on Jackie Robinson, September 2, 1958

"Jackie Robinson . . . has joined thousands of other persons in appealing for mercy for a Negro sentenced to die for a robbery that netted $1.95. [Alabama] Gov. James E. Folsom . . . is expected to commute the sentence to life in prison. Mr. Robinson wired Gov. Folsom asking to meet him 'at your convenience to discuss the possible exercise of clemency by you.' . . . Jimmy Wilson, 55, an illiterate Negro handyman, was sentenced to die for robbing Mrs. Estelle Baker, 82 [some sources say the Marion widow was 74], of $1.95 in 1957 at her home in Marion, Ala. At the trial [before an all-white jury], she testified Wilson attempted to rape her."

—*New York World-Telegram and Sun,* **about Robinson supporting Wilson, who spent sixteen years in prison after his death sentence was commuted because his case became a cause célèbre internationally, September 29, 1958**

"With the assistance of the ghostwriter and playwright William Branch, Robinson became a syndicated columnist for the *New York Post,* a leading liberal newspaper, in April 1959. The column appeared three times a week and addressed any subject of his choosing, usually politics and sports."

—**Michael G. Long,** *First Class Citizenship,* **2007**

"James A. Wechsler, editor of the *Post,* said Robinson's column is being offered to leading daily newspapers throughout the country. 'I believe this is the first time that a real national syndication has been attempted for a columnist who happens to be a Negro.' Robinson, in addition to his other activities, conducts the *Jackie Robinson Show* over WRCA radio at 6:30 p.m. on Sundays."

—*New York Post,* **April 24, 1959**

"Shaping public opinion on important issues was always an essential part of Robinson's own understanding of his vocation. . . . Robinson wrote to prod and provoke, inflame and infuriate, and sway and persuade, as he sought to build his readership. Indeed, as Robinson played to win, he also strove to win the arguments of his day."

—**Michael G. Long,** *Beyond Home Plate,* **2013**

"Robinson never attended a Yankee game for fun during the years away from the game [with the Dodgers and Giants in LA, and San Francisco respectively, beginning in 1958]. He returned to the Stadium only once, at a 1959 Old-Timers Day, and enjoyed cavorting with old teammates, including the recently retired Pee Wee Reese and Eddie Stanky. He popped up in that old-timers' game but still had that fluid swing."

—**Maury Allen,** *Jackie Robinson: A Life Remembered,* **1987**

"The historic moment [for the Boston Red Sox and Major League Baseball] came on July 21, 1959, in the eighth inning of a completely meaningless game. He stepped on the field . . . as a pinch runner for Vic Wertz. . . . Pumpsie Green had joined the major leagues and in the process the Red Sox joined the present. Baseball, some fourteen years after Jackie Robinson's infamous tryout at Fenway Park and twelve years after his Brooklyn debut, was now [fully] integrated. . . . Robinson called to remind Green of his historical place, that the two were, in a way, bookends to the long story of baseball's integration. . . . For Jackie Robinson to call . . . was a defining moment for Pumpsie Green."

—**Howard Bryant,** *Shut Out: The Story of Race and Baseball in Boston,* **2002**

"Jackie Robinson . . . was honored . . . by the Pasadena branch of the National Assn. for the Advancement of Color People yesterday afternoon at . . . Pasadena City College. . . . The guest of honor was introduced by a former school teammate, Ray W. Bartlett, who described his boyhood friend as 'one of the greatest Americans in the fight for freedom.' . . . In his talk Robinson paid tribute to his favorite teacher, Miss Beryl Haney, whom he described as having provided him with *tremendous* inspiration. Others in the audience of 400 who were acknowledged by Robinson included his mother, Mrs. Mallie Robinson; his brother Mack, also a great former athlete; and Kenny Washington and Harry Thompson, both former football stars at UCLA and later with the Rams."

—*Los Angeles Times,* **December 14, 1959**

> ## "IF IT SHOULD COME TO A CHOICE BETWEEN THE WEAK AND INDECISIVE DEMOCRATIC NOMINEE [FOR U.S. PRESIDENT] AND VICE PRESIDENT NIXON, I, FOR ONE, WOULD ENTHUSIASTICALLY SUPPORT NIXON."
>
> ### —J. R., WHOSE SUPPORT IN HIS COLUMN FOR THE [REPUBLICAN] NIXON WOULD LESSEN HIS CREDIBILITY WITH BLACKS AND WHITE LIBERALS AND DISMAY HIS BOSSES AT THE PAPER, *NEW YORK POST,* DECEMBER 30, 1959

"Some 5,000 Negroes will march to the Greenville, Airport on New Year's Day to protest a racial incident involving Jackie Robinson, the former baseball star. The plan was announced by the Rev. J. S. Hall, spokesman for . . . the Committee on Racial Equality and the Greenville Ministerial Alliance. Mr. Hall said that when Robinson visited Greenville last Oct. 25, he was asked to move to the air terminal's waiting room for Negroes. Mr. Robinson was here to address a meeting of the South Carolina chapter of the [NAACP]. Mr. Robinson reportedly refused to leave the white waiting room."

—*New York Times,* **December 24, 1959**

"Golf is the one major sport in America in which rank and open racial prejudice is allowed to reign supreme. Though often called the sport of gentlemen, all too often golf courses, clubs and tournaments apply the ungentlemanly and un-American yardstick of race and color in determining who may or may not compete. Even the president of the United States, Dwight D. Eisenhower, holds membership in a golf club which limits membership to 'Caucasians'—the Augusta National Golf Club. . . . And another famous and highly honored American, Bing Crosby, who annually sponsors a golf tournament bearing his name at Pebble Beach, California, has consistently refused to invite Negro professionals to compete."

—J. R., an avid golfer agitating to get Charlie Sifford, Ted Rhodes, and other qualified black golfers admitted to the PGA, *New York Post,* **February 24, 1960**

"Former President [Harry] Truman's outburst at the NAACP is a sad commentary on the man who, in 1948, gained the whole world's respect for thrashing the Dixiecrats. That he should now choose to attack those who are so valiantly fighting bigotry, rather than the bigots themselves is regrettable. . . . If Truman really means that he would 'throw out' any of the quiet, orderly peaceful students for merely asking to be served at a public lunch counter, I suggest he open an establishment and prepare to [do that] at once."

—J. R., responding to Truman's contention that students at sit-ins in the South should be physically removed because they weren't behaving like good citizens, *New York Post,* **March 25, 1960**

"Support the Southern Negro Students All the Way Buy Elsewhere"

—Words on the placard Robinson carried when he joined picketers at a demonstration organized by the NAACP outside a Cleveland branch of W. T. Grant, a store that refused to serve Negroes at its lunch counter in the South, April 1960

"[Jackie Robinson is] a pilgrim that walked in the lonesome byways toward the high road of Freedom. He was a sit-inner before sit-ins, a freedom rider before freedom rides."

—Martin Luther King Jr., arguing with those who contended Robinson, an ex-athlete, had no right to speak about civil rights

"[After his baseball career ended] Robinson toured the South to speak for civil rights and became the most requested speaker on the circuit: more requested than even Dr. King."

—David Brown, *Big League Stew,* **Yahoo! Sports, January 21, 2013**

"If I had to choose tomorrow between the Baseball Hall of Fame and full citizenship for my people I would choose full citizenship time and again."

—**J. R., stating words he used to end every speech**

"Soviet Premier Nikita S. Khrushchev rode up to Harlem this afternoon and held his first face-to-face meeting with Cuba's Fidel Castro. Thousands of Harlem residents gathered, some booing and others cheering. . . . Jackie Robinson . . . told reporters he strongly objected to the visits of both Khrushchev and Castro to Harlem. 'They have come up here to try to get the sympathy of the Negro. They should know that Negroes are Americans.'"

—**Thomas MacCabe,** *New York World-Telegram and Sun,* **September 20, 1960**

BACKING THE WRONG CANDIDATE

"A registered Independent, Jack had supported Hubert Humphrey's campaign for the Democratic nomination [for U.S. President]—he wholeheartedly admired his position on civil rights and other issues when he was mayor of Minneapolis and a US Senator. When Humphrey lost to [Massachusetts Senator John Kennedy], Jack studied Kennedy's and [Republican nominee Vice President Richard] Nixon's records and also met privately with the two men."

—**Rachel Robinson,** *Jackie Robinson: An Intimate Portrait,* **1997**

"It was good to see you . . . the other evening. I have long admired your contribution to the world of baseball and good American sportsmanship. Hearing your great personal concern about the denial of civil rights to American citizens by reason of their race or color and your dedication to the achievement of first-class citizenship for all Americans, I believe I understand and appreciate your role in the continuing struggle to fulfill the American promise of equal opportunity for all. I trust that you now understand better my own concern about this problem and dedication to these same ideals."

—**Massachusetts Senator John Kennedy, Democratic presidential nominee, futilely trying to persuade Robinson to back him by assuring him he was a civil rights advocate, excerpt from letter, July 1, 1960**

"The Kennedy camp assumed that my father would maintain his Democratic affiliation and automatically support JFK. The two sat down in a private meeting. My father came away still distrustful of Kennedy because the candidate didn't look him directly in the eyes. My father ultimately supported Richard Nixon, believing that it was important to have blacks affiliated with both parties so that their vote would not be taken for granted. As a registered Independent, my father was able to work on either side."

—**Sharon Robinson, *Stealing Home*, 1996**

"At the time [Robinson's] reasoning was that [Kennedy] simply knew little, and cared to know less about the black condition. To Robinson, such a quantifiable lack of desire to understand the black dilemma disqualified Kennedy as a viable political option."

—**Howard Bryant, *Shut Out: The Story of Race and Baseball in Boston*, 2002**

"I followed the logic of his thinking, but as a third-generation Democrat it pained me to see him cross over into alien and conservative territory."

—**Rachel Robinson, *Jackie Robinson: An Intimate Portrait*, 1997**

"The AFL-CIO . . . refused a request for $50,000 from [Robinson and] the NAACP for a crusade to register a million black voters."

—**Arnold Rampersad, *Jackie Robinson: A Biography*, 1997**

"Mr. Robinson is on leave as vice president of Chock full o'Nuts Corp., to stump for Nixon. The AFL-CIO, wholeheartedly in the Democratic camp, based its opposition not on Mr. Robinson's politics [and support for Nixon], but on the allegation that he has taken an 'anti-labor' position as personnel director for the food chain."

—**Joel Seldin, *New York Herald Tribune*, October 6, 1960**

"I am not now, nor could I ever become, anti-union."

—**J. R., differing from his boss William Black**

"Jackie . . . went for Nixon because [New York Republican Governor] Nelson Rockefeller, a master politician who had stroked him, had convinced him that Nixon was a man who would do great things for the Negro."

—**Irving Rudd, powerful press agent who had become Robinson's confidant when he was the publicist for the Brooklyn Dodgers, to Harvey Frommer, *Rickey and Robinson*, 1982**

"Following the Republican National Convention, Robinson praised Nixon for committing himself to a pro-civil rights platform and to a racially progressive running mate, UN ambassador Henry Cabot Lodge Jr. [who indicated that if Nixon was elected a black would be appointed to the cabinet]. . . . [However] while stumping for Nixon, Robinson frequently felt that the campaign ignored or dismissed opportunities to reach out to African American voters. He criticized the team, for instance, when it avoided Harlem during a campaign swing through New York."

—Michael G. Long, *First Class Citizenship*, 2007

"While campaigning for . . . Nixon, Dad became disenchanted and several times considered dropping out. . . . Ultimately it was the response of the two candidates to the [October 19] jailing of Martin Luther King Jr. [in Georgia] that swayed the black community in favor of Kennedy. The Kennedy group stepped in and worked on behalf of his release. Nixon refused, in spite of the urging of his black supporters, my father included, to use his influence to get King out of jail. King was released and the black community credited JFK."

—Sharon Robinson, *Stealing Home*, 1996

"I was in the behind-the-scene struggle to persuade Dick Nixon to express his concern for Dr. King [who had been sentenced to four months in a public works camp on a trumped-up antitrespassing law for not having a valid Georgia driving license], but apparently his most trusted advisers were counseling him not to rock the racial vote."

—J. R., *I Never Had It Made*, as told to Alfred Duckett, 1972

"He thinks calling Martin would be 'grandstanding.' Nixon doesn't deserve to win."

—J. R. to Nixon speechwriter William Safire, 1960

"At this point, Jack was ready to abandon the campaign. . . . At the last minute Robinson decided to stick with Nixon to the end. A telephone conversation with Branch Rickey, he said, made the difference."

—Arnold Rampersad, about Rickey telling him to keep campaigning for Nixon, *Jackie Robinson: A Biography*, 1997

"Mr. Rickey assured me that Mr. Nixon was still personally the fine man I thought he was. And that I didn't want this one emotional thing to completely color my overall expectations."

—J. R., who, despite pressure from Democrats, decided to make his four final personal appearances on Nixon's behalf, to a reporter, November 1960

"On November 4, 1960—Election Day—*Post* editor James Wechsler informed Robinson that he and owner Dorothy Schiff had decided not to resume his column. (Robinson had taken a leave of absence to serve on Richard Nixon's campaign team in September 1960.) Wechsler, a Kennedy supporter, apparently felt that Robinson's pro-Nixon sentiments had led to unfair reporting."

—Michael G. Long, about Robinson being fired the day Kennedy defeated Nixon to become president, *Home Plate,* 2013

"Jackie Robinson, a ballplayer known for his fight, charged yesterday that Richard M. Nixon had given up on the Negro vote in the 1960 presidential election. . . . He told the New York Republican Club . . . that President Kennedy was 'doing a really good job in almost everything including the field where I thought he might not—civil rights.'"

—*New York Times*, March 10, 1961

"After [Bill] Black nominated him, in 1961 Jack was elected to the board of directors [of Chock full o'Nuts]. . . . Jack kept thinking of ways to improve the quality of the employees' lives. He decided that they and their families needed a recreational place to go in the summer, free of charge. Thus, 'Camp Utopia' in Warwick, New York, was born. Unfortunately the camp, to which we sent our children for two summers, failed after several years of operation. . . . Despite the problems, Jack . . . learned to be an executive, he gained financial reward . . . and clearly had an impact on the organization."

—Rachel Robinson, about a summer camp that survived a few years before management let it fail, *Jackie Robinson: An Intimate Portrait,* 1997

"[One] aspect of our childhood was regular family vacations. Since Dad's vacation requirements were quite simple—an eighteen-hole golf course and decent tennis facilities—any resort could satisfy the whole family. Sometimes, Mom and Dad would take us to a Caribbean island for a week of sun and beach play, but one of our favorite spots was Grossinger's, a resort nestled in the Catskill Mountains . . . famous for its green hills, shimmering lakes, kosher food, and nonstop entertainment."

—**Sharon Robinson,** *Stealing Home,* **1996**

"Dad was a basic kind of guy. Meat and potatoes for dinner, grits and scrambled eggs every morning, a warm comfortable home, privacy, his family, golf, and television. . . . His only vice was an attraction to horse races. . . . When Dad wasn't traveling, we could count on him being home by six. We all ate together in the dining room and . . . over the years the dinner table conversation revolved around politics . . . along with homework, getting us kids to the dentist, dance classes, sports, and bed. In short, we were our own sort of normal."

—**Sharon Robinson,** *Stealing Home,* **1996**

"In 1961, when I was with the Cincinnati Reds in the World Series in New York . . . I met him at some Series event. We got to talking about the old days and how it was for him. He told me a few stories of segregation and the racism, and then he looked at me and said, 'Rachel had to rub my legs because the trainers wouldn't touch my black skin.' This was years later, but I could still see how much that hurt."

—**Vada Pinson, Reds star outfielder from 1958 to 1968 and a Tigers coach in 1987, quoted by Maury Allen,** *Jackie Robinson: A Life Remembered,* **1987**

"No one will ever convince me that the *Post* acted in an honest manner [when they discontinued my column in 1960]. I believe the simple truth is that they became somewhat alarmed when they realized that I really meant to write what I believed."

—**J. R., writing about his previous column in his first column for a new publication,** *New York Amsterdam News,* **January 6, 1962**

"A few days ago, from Louisville, Kentucky, it was announced that Pee Wee Reese . . . had quit under fire for membership on the Citizens Human Rights Commission. According to newspaper reports, Reese was criticized by a mixed group of citizens because he operates—or had connection with—a bowling alley which bars Negroes. As firmly as this writer is opposed to any and all forms of segregation, this news disturbs me deeply. For, in my book, Pee Wee Reese is and has been a decent, courageous guy who knew how to stand up and speak out on the race issue where and when it counted. . . . I am not defending Pee Wee Reese if he is guilty of discrimination against Negroes who want to use his bowling alley. I am saying simply that I hope a tragic mistake has been made and an injustice done against a guy whom I found to be 100 percent in the past."

—J. R., staying loyal to his friend who explained that a black bowling team had been turned away only because that night all the lanes were reserved by a league, *New York Amsterdam News,* **July 7, 1962**

CLASSIC MOMENTS: JANUARY 23 AND JULY 23, 1962, COOPERSTOWN, NEW YORK

"In 1962 there was a great deal of conjecture about whether I'd be elected to the baseball Hall of Fame. Hall of Fame winners are determined by the Baseball Writers of America . . . and since I was a controversial personality in the eyes of the press, I steeled myself for rejection."

—J. R., *I Never Had It Made,* **as told to Alfred Duckett, 1972**

"Jackie Robinson and I have a bet . . . I bet he would be elected to the Hall of Fame at Cooperstown as soon as he was eligible and Jackie bet he wouldn't. . . . He made few friends among the newsmen. [But] there is a distinct difference between not making friends and making enemies. An enemy feels strongly and plots revenge. A non-friend feels indifference. I am confident Jackie's non-friends will sweep him into the Hall of Fame. . . . Jackie Robinson made baseball history and that's what the Hall of Fame is, baseball history."

—Dick Young, suggesting he was a "non-friend" rather than an enemy of Robinson's after all, *New York Daily News,* **January 1962**

"Jackie rates the Hall of Fame on merit and merit should be color-blind. If that appraisal of his abilities be correct, he rates it still more because he was the trail-blazer for his race. Negroes in baseball are taken so much for granted these days that it isn't easy to remember the Jim Crow era and the enormous difficulties which faced the young man who broke the color line, unflinching and unafraid."

—Arthur Daley, *New York Times,* January 7, 1962

"[On January 23, 1962] Robinson and Bob Feller were the first elected to the Hall of Fame in their first year of eligibility since Lou Gehrig in 1939."

—*The Ballplayers,* edited by Mike Shatzkin, 1969

"In terms of his profession, being elected to the Baseball Hall of Fame in the first year of his eligibility was a high point for him. He had not expected to win this honor because he had challenged the baseball writers often, and had antagonized some. And they were the ones who had to vote for him for this honor. So, this was a great thrill."

—Rachel Robinson, about Jackie Robinson, the first black to be elected to the Hall of Fame, squeaking in with only four votes to spare, receiving 77½ percent of the vote when 75 percent was needed for induction, interview, *Scholastic* magazine, February 11, 1998

"Mr. Speaker, I take this time to inform the House that Jackie Robinson and 'Rapid Robert' Feller were chosen yesterday by the Baseball Writers' Association of America to become the newest members of the Baseball Hall of Fame at Cooperstown, N.Y. As the representative from the district which includes Cooperstown, where baseball was first played and where the Hall of Fame now stands, I extend my heartiest congratulations."

—New York Congressman Samuel S. Stratton, introducing the selection of Robinson and Feller into the Congressional Record, January 24, 1962

"JACKIE DESERVED IT AND HE MADE IT ON HIS MERITS WITHOUT REGARD FOR COLOR OR THE FACT HE IS A NEGRO. HE IS A GREAT BALLPLAYER. I CONGRATULATE THE SPORTSWRITERS. I DON'T THINK THEY LEANED OVER BACKWARDS TO PUT HIM IN."

—BRANCH RICKEY, 1972

"He was a superior ballplayer who made a mighty contribution to baseball and America and human rights. This above all is the reason he belongs in the Hall of Fame and the reason he is there."

—**Red Smith,** *New York Herald Tribune,* **January 25, 1962**

"Early in February, Essie [Robeson] confided that Paul had become 'very depressed.' . . . A second series of ECT treatments did again produce momentary relief. Within ten days the improvement was so pronounced that Paul was asking for the newspapers . . . He told his [wife] Essie he was glad to read in the paper that Jackie Robinson had been elected to the Baseball Hall of Fame."

—**Martin Duberman,** *Paul Robeson,* **1989**

"I have come here tonight to say that the Southern Christian Leadership Conference is deeply proud to have the opportunity to pay tribute to Jackie Robinson. Virtually, on the eve of his induction into the Baseball Hall of Fame, we are honored by the privilege of pausing one moment in time to speak with fervent gratitude of a man who has become a legend and a symbol of his own time; to a man who committed a rich legacy of pride held in escrow by destiny for unborn generations of black American babies who will be born into a new dawn of freedom because Jackie Robinson challenged the dark skies of intolerance and frustration."

—**Martin Luther King Jr., at Robinson's Hall of Fame dinner, excerpt from a toast ghostwritten by Alfred Duckett, July 16, 1962**

"Jack was thrilled to have Branch Rickey and his mother share the day with us. He paid tribute to each of us, and we basked in the reflected glory of his achievements."

—**Rachel Robinson,** *Jackie Robinson: An Intimate Portrait,* **1997**

"We have been up in cloud nine since the election. I don't ever think I'll come down."

—**J. R., as part of his speech when he was inducted into Cooperstown along with Bob Feller, Edd Roush, and Bill McKechnie, July 23, 1962**

"I only hope I'll be able to live up to this tremendously fine honor. It's something that I think those of us who are fortunate . . . must use in order to help others."

—**J. R., toward the end of his induction speech, July 23, 1962**

"JACK ROOSEVELT ROBINSON

Brooklyn N.L. 1947 to 1956

Leading N.L. batter in 1949. Holds

fielding mark for second baseman

playing in 150 or more games with

.992. Led N.L. in stolen bases in

1947 and 1949. Most Valuable

Player in 1949. Lifetime batting

average .311. Joint record holder for

most double plays by second

baseman, 137 in 1951. Led second

basemen in double plays

1949–50–51–52"

—Words on Jackie Robinson's Hall of Fame plaque

"In one of the great ironies of baseball, there is not one word on the Hall of Fame plaque for Jackie Robinson that attests to the real pressures he faced as the man who broke baseball's color barrier."

—Maury Allen, *Baseball's 100*, 1981

"When Jackie Robinson was on the Hall of Fame ballot in 1962, he requested that the voters among the Baseball Writers Association of America judge him only as a player."

—Dave Anderson, *New York Times*, June 26, 2008

"Cap Anson . . . would turn handsprings in his grave if he knew that I share a niche with him in baseball's Hall of Fame."

—J. R., *Baseball Has Done It*, 1964

"I tell you how bad it is. The Dodger organization keeps no news of Jackie Robinson in its files. The Hall of Fame people told me not to blame them but they asked the Dodgers for some pictures of me to distribute and were told by the Dodgers they have none."

—J. R., feeling snubbed by the Dodgers since his retirement, quoted by
Jimmy Cannon, *New York Post*, July 22, 1962

J. R. NOTE: Jackie Robinson was thrilled to be enshrined at Cooperstown, but in May he had received another honor that gave him much gratification. On May 10, the *Los Angeles Times* stated: "Jackie Robinson, the first Negro in Major League Baseball and the first in its Hall of Fame, has been named UCLA's Alumnus of the Year. . . . Robinson will receive the Dickson Achievement Award . . . presented annually to the alumnus who has 'rendered a special service to UCLA or who, by personal achievement, has brought honor and distinction to the university.' . . . Dickson was a regent of the university for 42 years and a Los Angeles editor and publisher."

"Pennsylvania Democrat Representative Francis E. Walter . . . has announced that his House Un-American Activities Committee is considering launching 'a very intensive investigation of a Negro group known as the Black Muslims.' . . . I cannot repeat too often that I consider black supremacy as dangerous as white supremacy [but] in spite of my personal differences with the Black Muslims, I believe they have as much right to hate the white man—if it is true that they do—as any white man has the right, legally, to hate the black man. . . . Certainly, no one has ever proven that the Black Muslims have perpetrated anything like the terrible deeds openly and boldly committed by the Klan or by Gestapo Southern police officers who beat pregnant women and bloody the heads of Negro attorneys."

—J. R., *New York Amsterdam News*, August 25, 1962

"There are some who were never touched about the situation here in the South until their moral conscience was alarmed by the destruction of our churches. . . . All I want for my children—and I think all you want for yours—is a fair and equal chance and respect for their dignity as human beings. Give us that and we'll do the rest."

—J. R., excerpt from his speech at the Southern Christian Leadership Council's
annual Freedom Dinner in Birmingham, Alabama, September 1962

"People used to tell me a lot of things about Dr. King, that he was trying to take over the world, that he was making money on the civil rights issues. I didn't believe them, of course. I knew this was a dedicated man and that he has made tremendous personal financial sacrifices in the cause. I sort of wondered why people would stoop to talk about him. Then I realized that the world has always talked against great men. The best way to keep from getting talked about is to do nothing."

—J. R., excerpt from a speech at the Southern Christian Leadership Council's annual Freedom Dinner in Birmingham, Alabama, September 1962

"Life is not a spectator sport. . . . If you're going to spend your whole life in the grandstand just watching what goes on, in my opinion you're wasting your life."

—J. R.

"HE HAD A FIRE IN HIM. HIS WHOLE LIFE, HE BELIEVED THINGS WERE WRONG, HE WANTED TO CHANGE THEM. HE . . . WAS NOT GOING TO TOLERATE INJUSTICES TO PEOPLE. JACKIE ROBINSON COULDN'T STAND BEING ON THE SIDELINES AND BEING LEFT OUT OF THE ACTION."

**—SHARON ROBINSON TO PAT WILLIAMS,
HOW TO BE LIKE JACKIE ROBINSON, 2005**

"My father . . . taught a lot, but he did not preach. He didn't just say you have to serve others. He just went out and served."

**—Sharon Robinson, quoted by Kevin Baxter,
Los Angeles Times, November 17, 1996**

"Day after day, an angry crowd marched outside Harlem's legendary Apollo Theater protesting against its Jewish owner, Frank Schiffman, and his plan to open a low-cost restaurant with prices that potentially would threaten the business of a more expensive black-owned eatery. The demonstrators carried anti-Semitic posters and hurled racial epithets, reportedly denouncing Schiffman as a Shylock who wanted to extract a pound of flesh from the black community. Schiffman turned to several black leaders for help but . . . all remained silent—except for [Jackie] Robinson. . . . Robinson used his syndicated newspaper column to condemn the protesters' blatant . . . use of anti-Semitism . . . Robinson was always quick to criticize anti-Semitism in the black community."

—Ami Eden, *St. Louis Jewish Light*, April 15, 2013

"It is the duty and responsibility of each and every one of us to refuse to accept the faintest sign or token of prejudice. It does not matter whether it is directed against us or against others. Racial prejudice is not only a vicious disease, it is also contagious."

—J. R., *New York Amsterdam News,* **January 28, 1967**

"[In January, Cardinals outfielder] Curt Flood, born in Houston but raised in Oakland, took a deep breath and joined Martin Luther King and Jackie Robinson at the tenth annual meeting of the NAACP in Jackson, Mississippi."

—**Allen Barra,** *Mickey and Willie,* **2013**

"In May 1963, Jackie Robinson and former heavyweight champion Floyd Patterson traveled to Birmingham, Alabama, to support the Rev. Martin Luther King Jr.'s nonviolent protest. Willie Mays, who was in a better position to know Birmingham's history of segregation than any other black athlete, was nowhere to be seen."

—**Allen Barra, about Mays, who, along with Dodgers star Maury Wills, were the two current black stars Robinson most criticized for not being vocal about civil rights,** *Mickey and Willie,* **2013**

"IS THERE A MEDAL ANYWHERE WHICH IS WORTH A MAN'S DIGNITY?"

—J. R., WHO DIDN'T UNDERSTAND HOW SUCCESSFUL BLACK ATHLETES WHO DIDN'T SPEAK OUT ABOUT CIVIL RIGHTS COULD LOOK THEIR CHILDREN IN THE EYE

"[Robinson and Patterson] had registered at the Gaston Motel, Birmingham's principal Negro hotel, but it had been firebombed before they got there."

—**Charles Einstein,** *Willie's Time,* **1979**

"The motel was a scene of destruction. State and local police were massed outside, facing Negroes who were prepared to defend victims of fresh violence. Rumors were current that Klansman were rallying in the city's outskirts. . . . The following morning Floyd and I paid our respects to the brother of Martin Luther King, the Reverend A. D. King, whose home had twice been bombed. . . . Among those we found in Rev. King's shattered house was a young man who said he had been stopped by police while returning from work the previous evening. . . . As he hesitated [following their orders] knuckles crashed into his face, bloodying his nose, knocking loose a tooth. . . . 'I saw five cops standing on a poor woman,' another young man told me."

—**J. R.,** *Baseball Has Done It,* **1964**

"Jackie Robinson and Floyd Patterson spoke to Negroes at a mass meeting last night and said Negroes here [in Birmingham] are fighting to end segregation everywhere."

—**Associated Press, May 14, 1963**

"[At Dr. King's request] my father spearheaded a New York fund-raising drive for the Southern Christian Leadership Conference. Several churches in the South had been bombed in protest of SCLC's work [including the Mount Olive Baptist Church]. There was a big affair at the Apollo Theater in Harlem and Dad had convinced Mr. Black of Chock full o'Nuts to give money. Governor [Nelson] Rockefeller personally gave ten thousand dollars."

—**Sharon Robinson,** *Stealing Home,* **1996**

"I felt that if Martin King could make the kind of sacrifices he was making, I had to do what little I could to support him. He was and is my idol [although] we don't always agree."

—**J. R.,** *I Never Had It Made,* **as told to Alfred Duckett, 1972**

"Satisfied with the success of the first fund-raiser, Dad planned a second: [their first annual Afternoon of Jazz] concert on the lawn of our Stamford home with the proceeds earmarked to provide a bail fund for jailed civil rights' activists. My brothers and I swelled with excitement when we learned that Dr. Martin Luther King Jr. would be coming to our home! . . . Standing in his presence was as close to God as I figured I would ever get. . . . People came, the music flowed throughout the afternoon, and Dad said we made lots of money. . . . Dad and Dr. King thanked the people for coming and he made a quiet exit. We had been listening to our parents for years, learning about our history second-hand. This day was special because it made us active participants."

—**Sharon Robinson,** *Stealing Home,* **1996**

"In the early 1960s, Jack grew increasingly determined to find specific ways to help improve the lives of black people, and decided he would concentrate on stimulating economic development and political power. . . . He considered a variety of proposals, but nothing got his full attention until Dunbar McLaurin, a Harlem businessman, approached him in 1963 with the idea of establishing a minority-owned-and-operated commercial bank in Harlem. . . . After some discussion, Jack signed on."

—Rachel Robinson, *Jackie Robinson: An Intimate Portrait,* 1997

"A group of Negroes and whites has applied to the federal government for a charter for a new national bank in Harlem in the vicinity of 125th and Lenox Avenue. The bank would be the first in New York State with Negro leadership. . . . Among the organizers of the proposed Freedom National Bank are Jackie Robinson, the former baseball player; Samuel B. Pierce Jr., a Republican and former judge of General Sessions; and Herbert B. Evans, a Democrat and former City Councilman who is now a commissioner of the City Housing and Redevelopment Board."

—Edward Cowan, *New York Times,* June 30, 1963

"Jackie Robinson, the onetime Pasadena resident who broke baseball's color barrier, stood alongside the Rev. Dr. Martin Luther King Jr. at the steps of the Lincoln Memorial and greeted the men and women who came to Washington in a peaceful demand for civil rights. Robinson brought his three children. He would be photographed on the mall talking to a reporter as he hugged his young son David."

—Frank C. Girardot, about Robinson's appearance at the March on Washington on August 29, 1963, *Pasadena Star-News,* August 24, 2013

"I know all of us are going to go away feeling we cannot turn back."

—J. R., addressing the enormous crowd at the March on Washington, August 29, 1963

"I HAVE NEVER BEEN SO PROUD TO BE A NEGRO. I HAVE NEVER BEEN SO PROUD TO BE AN AMERICAN. FOR THE MARVELOUS MULTITUDE WHICH POURED INTO WASHINGTON WAS AS AMERICAN AS A HAM SANDWICH. IT WAS SALT AND PEPPER."

—J. R., WHO WAS INSPIRED BY MARTIN LUTHER KING JR.'S "I HAVE A DREAM" SPEECH AND BY BLACK AND WHITE MARCHERS TOGETHER, "HAND IN HAND SINGING SONGS FOR FREEDOM," *NEW YORK AMSTERDAM NEWS,* SEPTEMBER 7, 1963

"A week later, on the morning of September 16, joy turned to horror and sorrow when a bomb thrown into the Sixteenth Street Baptist Church in Birmingham, Alabama, killed four girls at Sunday school and wounded twenty other persons. Behind the bombing Jack saw the evil hands of Bull Connor and Governor George Wallace. 'God bless Dr. Martin Luther King,' [Robinson] mused bitterly in his column. But if his child had been one of those killed, 'I'm afraid he would have lost me as a potential disciple of his credo of non-violence.'"

—**Arnold Rampersad**, *Jackie Robinson: A Biography,* 1997

"AS MUCH AS I LOVED HIM, I NEVER WOULD HAVE MADE A GOOD SOLDIER IN MARTIN'S ARMY. MY REFLEXES AREN'T CONDITIONED TO ACCEPT NONVIOLENCE IN THE FACE OF VIOLENCE-PROVOKING ATTACKS. MY IMMEDIATE INSTINCT UNDER THE THREAT OF PHYSICAL ATTACK TO ME OR THOSE I LOVE IS INSTANT DEFENSE AND TOTAL RETALIATION."

—J. R., *I NEVER HAD IT MADE,* AS TOLD TO ALFRED DUCKETT, 1972

"Jackie Robinson . . . was elected president today of United Church Men, a department of the National Council of Churches serving Protestant and Orthodox laymen. His three-year term begins next Jan. 1. . . . The church's General Synod cited him for 'Christian commitment of time, energy, and skill in the struggle for social justice.'"

—*New York Times,* **November 8, 1963**

"When the tragic news first hit, like millions of Americans, I gasped with disbelief that here in America in 1963, a president could be murdered simply because he was a man of courageous conviction. What a tragic year this has been, with two great Americans—John Kennedy and Medgar Evers—paying the supreme sacrifice because they had given the last full measure of devotion. A noble man is gone. This was a man whom I often criticized. But . . . in my opinion, the president had emerged as the chief executive who has done more for the civil rights cause than any other president. . . . In these last few months, I have felt a deep admiration for the courage of Mr. Kennedy, so much so that one his top aides said to me recently, 'Jackie, you are certainly in his corner now, aren't you?'"

—**J. R., still reeling from the assassination of President Kennedy in Dallas on November 22,** *New York Amsterdam News,* **December 7, 1963**

"The assassination of the president was a great shock. I did not idolize Kennedy as many did, but his death was a great loss. [He and his brother, Attorney General Robert Kennedy] did much for the cause of black rights. . . . I was deeply concerned because of grave doubts about the future of blacks under Lyndon Johnson."

—J. R., *I Never Had It Made,* as told to Alfred Duckett, 1972

"In 1963, Malcolm X had insulted Dr. Ralph Bunche, the then undersecretary of the United Nations, by saying he made statements to please white people. . . . Dad wrote a column in [Dr. Bunche's] defense. Malcolm X responded in writing with a scathing attack on my father. Dad wrote back thanking Malcolm X for putting him in such distinguished company as Dr. Bunche, Roy Wilkins, Dr. King and Mr. [A. Philip] Randolph."

—Sharon Robinson, *Stealing Home,* 1996

"I am proud of my associations with the men whom you choose to call my 'white bosses'—Branch Rickey, my boss at Chock full o'Nuts, Mr. William Black, and Governor Nelson Rockefeller. I am also proud that so many others whom you would undoubtedly label as 'white bosses,' marched with us to Washington and have been and are now working with our leaders to help achieve equality in America. . . . Personally, I reject your racist views. I reject your dream of a separate state. I believe that many Americans, black and white, are committed to fighting for those freedoms for which Medgar Evers, William Moore, the Birmingham children and President Kennedy died."

—J. R. to Malcolm X, excerpt from public letter, *New York Amsterdam News,* December 14, 1963

"I DISAGREED WITH MALCOLM VIGOROUSLY IN MANY AREAS DURING HIS EARLIER DAYS, BUT I CERTAINLY AGREED WITH HIM WHEN HE SAID, 'DON'T TELL ME ABOUT PROGRESS THE BLACK MAN HAS MADE. YOU DON'T STICK A KNIFE TEN INCHES IN MY BACK, PULL IT OUT THREE OR FOUR, THEN TELL ME I'M MAKING PROGRESS.'"

—J. R., *I NEVER HAD IT MADE,* AS TOLD TO ALFRED DUCKETT, 1972

ELEVEN

Man in the Middle

"Jackie Robinson was destined to be as much a loner in his political affairs as he had been during his playing days. Caught between young black militants who dubbed him an 'Uncle Tom' because he persisted in trying to work through the system and an older generation that wasn't activist enough to suit him, arguing publicly with figures as politically opposed as Malcolm X and Roy Wilkins, he would act independently and courageously, stubbornly forging his own path through these turbulent years. Each of his actions seemed to alienate someone. . . . Jackie was uninterested in adhering to any inflexible political perspective; his sole commitment was to integration and improved social conditions for black Americans."

—Patrick Henry, professor and author, excerpt from paper presented at the Jackie Robinson anniversary conference, Long Island University, Brooklyn Campus, April 1997

"Columbus Police Department . . . advised that Jackie Robinson was among the speakers at the Columbus Civil Rights Rally held at the Veterans Memorial Auditorium, Columbus, Ohio."

—Item added to Jackie Robinson's FBI file, January 19, 1964

"The *Tampa Times*, Tampa, Fla. Newspaper . . . advised that State Secretary Robert W. Saunders, NAACP, announced a 'massive freedom rally' would be held in the St. Paul AME Church, Tampa, on 2/23/64. Jackie Robinson would be among those participating in this rally. Robinson would also be a special speaker at another rally to be held at St. Mathews Baptist Church, Clearwater, Florida, on 2/14/64."

—Item added to Jackie Robinson's FBI file, February 7, 1964

"Many people have asked me if I am disturbed because, ideologically, Cassius has taken on a new trainer—Malcolm X. Why should I be disturbed? Clay has as much right to ally himself with the Muslim religion as anyone else has to be a Protestant or Catholic."

—J. R., a boxing fan, about Cassius Clay, who converted to Islam and changed his name to Muhammad Ali on February 26, 1964, the day he knocked out Sonny Liston to become heavyweight champion, *New York Amsterdam News,* March 14, 1964

"I KNEW THAT 1964 HAD BEEN A DIFFICULT YEAR FOR MY FATHER. HIS HEALTH WAS FAILING HIM. HE HAD BEEN TAKING INSULIN FOR EIGHT YEARS TO CONTROL HIS ADULT-ONSET DIABETES BUT IT HAD BEEN INCREASINGLY UNSTABLE. DAD'S POOR HEALTH WASN'T HIS ONLY PROBLEM. SINCE HIS CAMPAIGN FOR NIXON, DAD'S REPUTATION IN THE BLACK COMMUNITY HAD TAKEN A HARD HIT. HE WAS CONSIDERED A CONSERVATIVE BY MANY."

—SHARON ROBINSON, *STEALING HOME,* 1996

"Governor Rockefeller asked me to become one of six deputy national directors of his campaign [for the Republican nomination in the 1964 presidential election]. I had spent seven years at Chock full o'Nuts. I decided to resign from my job rather than ask for a leave. . . . I wanted to involve myself in politics as a means of helping black people and I wanted my own business enterprises. . . . I was not on the Republican party as I was on the governor."

—J. R., *I Never Had It Made,* as told to Alfred Duckett, 1972

"Robinson's Republicanism, although widely questioned and criticized, had firm roots. Robinson, despite his militancy on civil rights issues, had conservative instincts. He believed that the solution to the nation's racial problems lay in the economic realm and that without expansion of black business enterprise lasting gains for African Americans would be limited."

—Jules Tygiel, *The Jackie Robinson Reader,* March 1997

"In Nelson Rockefeller he saw a great dark hope. He might have been appointed to the cabinet if Rockefeller had been elected president."

—Roger Kahn, *The Boys of Summer,* 1972

"August 1964, in typical Robinson fashion, after the discovery of the bodies of [three] slain . . . civil rights activists [who had disappeared June 21], Jackie co-chaired the campaign to raise $25,000 to build a memorial center in Meridian, Mississippi, in their honor."

—Patrick Henry, professor and author, about Robinson's response to the murders of James Chaney, Andrew Goodman, and Michael Schwerner in Mississippi, April 1997

"You say that you are interested in breaking bread with me and discussing your views on civil rights. . . . If at this late date, I have to ask you your views on civil rights, Senator, I doubt if I would understand. I seek no private, privileged information which you are unwilling to give to the electorate."

—J. R., turning down an invitation from Rockefeller's adversary Barry Goldwater to meet because Robinson had been calling him publicly "a bigot," "menace to our country," and "advocate of white supremacy," to Barry Goldwater, excerpt from letter, August 1964

"When the [Republican] party went on to nominate Barry Goldwater, it signaled a shift to the right within the party and . . . Dad informed Rockefeller that he was so frustrated . . . that he planned to defect and campaign for [Democratic Vice President] Lyndon Johnson [who] within weeks of the Republican Convention . . . signed the Civil Rights Act of 1964."

—Sharon Robinson, *Stealing Home*, 1996

"I see that Barry Goldwater is now, in your opinion, a man of courage and integrity. . . . It seems to me that to support him is to reject the ideals and principles for which the Rockefeller name has always stood. Your doing so is one of the most disappointing things which has ever happened to me."

—J. R., displeased that Rockefeller endorsed Republican nominee Goldwater for president, to New York Governor Nelson Rockefeller, excerpt from letter, October 7, 1964

"The smashing defeat of Goldwater indicates that the vast majority of our citizens are interested in growth and development."

—J. R., expressing gratification that Lyndon Johnson defeated Barry Goldwater in the presidential election, to Connecticut Governor John Dempsey, November 4, 1964

"Your address at our annual SCLC banquet made it one of the highlights of our convention. I don't know what we would have done through these past years without your ardent support and interest. We certainly count you among our most valuable friends and it pleases me to say that you have continued to give the kind of leadership throughout your career that we are proud to be identified with."

—Martin Luther King Jr. to Jackie Robinson, excerpt from letter, October 7, 1964

"[Blackened out name of a person in the] Stamford Police Department, Stamford, Conn., advised that . . . there was to be a meeting of Civil Rights Leaders in Samford on 8/22/64. The . . . only individual he could consider in the Stamford area to hold such a meeting would be Jackie Robinson, 103 Cascade Road, Stamford, as Robinson was active in the Civil Rights movement on a national basis and has, in the past, held concerts at his residence for the purpose of fund raising. Present at at least one of these concerts were Civil Rights Leaders Reverend Martin Luther King and Roy Wilkins."

—Item added to Jackie Robinson's FBI file, August 1964

"The violent and vicious attack on Martin Luther King which came from the lips of J. Edgar Hoover gives one pause for reflection. Mr. Hoover's absurd accusation that Dr. King is a 'notorious liar' is evidence that the boss of the FBI is a much disturbed man. . . . Evidently the truth hurts. And Dr. King did tell the truth—as other civil rights leaders have done—about the seeming inability of the FBI to takes steps to protect American citizens of color in the South and to solve the many bombings of homes and churches."

—J. R., *New York Amsterdam News,* December 5, 1964

"I ALWAYS THOUGHT J. EDGAR HOOVER SHOULD BE DOWN ON HIS HANDS AND KNEES BLESSING MARTIN LUTHER KING, FOR IT IF HAD NOT BEEN FOR KING, THERE WOULD HAVE BEEN BLOODY RACE RIOTS. KING IN A WAY WAS DOING THE FBI'S JOB."

—J. R., PHONE INTERVIEW, JANUARY 3, 1965

"Toss a challenge at Jackie Robinson and you get immediate action. . . . Jackie is just as aggressive today as he was 15 years ago, when he was at the peak of his baseball powers. . . . If you haven't heard much from Robinson lately, you will shortly. He'll be doing color commentary on ABC's Saturday TV games. ABC viewers are assured of plenty of snap, crackle, and pop. No one ever accused Jackie of muffling his opinions on anything."

—C. C. Johnson Spink, editor and publisher, *Sporting News*, January 3, 1965

"Freedom National Bank was chartered in 1964 [and opened January 5, 1965, on 125th Street in Harlem] and through 1990 was the only African-American–owned and operated commercial bank in New York State. [Jack] became the first chairman of the board. . . . The bank's mission was to spur economic development and provide a full range of banking services in the Harlem community. . . . Participating in the leadership of Freedom was one of Jack's most significant post-baseball achievements. It certainly gave him the most joy and the deepest pain."

—Rachel Robinson, *Jackie Robinson: An Intimate Portrait,* 1997

"My dear Mr. President: Words cannot express the gratitude my wife and I felt for one of the most enjoyable evenings of our lives. The warmth and friendliness of your guests was inspiring. My wife is still floating on cloud nine because she had the honor of dancing with the president of the United States, and having a dream come true. Your inspired leadership more than justifies the confidence we all have in you."

—J. R., about seeing the president at a dinner honoring Vice President Hubert Humphrey and others on February 2, to President Lyndon Johnson, beginning of letter, February 4, 1965

"THE [FEBRUARY 21, 1965] ASSASSINATION OF MALCOLM [X] WAS A TRAGEDY OF THE FIRST ORDER. A LOT OF THE BLUE WENT OUT OF THE SKY AND SOME WARMTH FROM THE SUN WHEN THE SINISTER NEWS CAME."

—J. R., *I NEVER HAD IT MADE,* AS TOLD TO ALFRED DUCKETT, 1972

"Even when I sharply disagreed with what I thought was his philosophy of hatred and his taunting of other leaders who disagreed with him, I consistently gave [Malcolm X] credit as a man who said what he believed. When we clashed Malcolm stuck to his guns and I to mine. Many of the statements he made about the problems faced by our people and the immorality of the white power structure were [the] naked truth. It was our approach to solutions that we differed radically. . . . It was ironic that, just as he seemed [to be] rising to the crest of a new and inspired leadership, Malcolm was struck down, ostensibly by the hands of blacks. His murderers quieted his voice but clothed him in martyrdom and deepened his influence. In death Malcolm became larger than he had been in life."

—J. R., *I Never Had It Made,* as told to Alfred Duckett, 1972

"IMPORTANT YOU TAKE IMMEDIATE ACTION IN ALABAMA. ONE MORE DAY OF SAVAGE TREATMENT BY LEGALIZED HATCHET MEN COULD LEAD TO OPEN WARFARE BY AROUSED NEGROES. AMERICA CANNOT AFFORD THIS IN 1965."

—J. R., URGING THE PRESIDENT TO TAKE ACTION AFTER "BLOODY SUNDAY," THE MARCH 7 CLUBBING AND GASSING OF NONVIOLENT MARCHERS PROTESTING FOR VOTING RIGHTS BY STATE TROOPERS POSITIONED BEYOND THE EDMUND PETTUS BRIDGE ON THE OUTSKIRTS OF SELMA, ALABAMA, TO PRESIDENT JOHNSON, LETTER, MARCH 9, 1965

"On March 10, 1965, Mr. Charles Evers, [NAACP] Field Secretary . . . advised that Jackie Robinson, ex-Major League Baseball player, would make several appearances in Mississippi from March 12 through March 14, 1965 . . . at Meridian . . . at the Holbrook Benevolent Association Hall [and] Cade Chapel Church . . . and in Clarksdale . . . at the First Baptist Church."

—FBI mailing to unknown agency, March 12, 1965

"The president's recent actions must surely have convinced you of this government's total commitment to the cause of civil rights and opportunities for all citizens. In providing federal protection for marchers in Alabama, and in recommending to the Congress comprehensive voting legislation, the president has acted with unprecedented vigor and determination to guarantee these fundamental rights."

—Vice President Hubert Humphrey, after President Johnson sent federal troops into Alabama to protect the protesters on their march from Selma to Montgomery and also went before Congress to propose voting legislation, to Jackie Robinson, excerpt from letter, March 29, 1965

"Mayor [Robert F. Wagner] remained silently clapping when [archconservative William] Buckley called Dr. King 'defiant' and praised the Selma, Alabama, police for their 'restraint' in dealing with Dr. King. Are we to interpret this silence as approval of Buckley's views? . . . The mayor's failure to respond to the attack on the civil rights movement constitutes a tremendous injustice to what is going on. . . . He didn't say a word. That's the worst part of it."

—J. R., demanding that New York Mayor Wagner repudiate remarks made by Buckley that received an ovation from an overflow audience of policemen at the New York Hilton Hotel, April 5, 1965

"The name of Jackie Robinson keeps coming up in Republicans' conversation about a candidate to run against [New York City] Mayor Wagner in November. . . . It was learned that he scored 'incredibly well' in a poll conducted by the Young Republican Club of New York."

—Claude Lewis and Marshall Pack, about the political junkie who would never run for political office, *New York Herald Tribune*, April 11, 1965

"[Robinson] had a high, stabbing voice, great presence, and sharp mind. All he lacked was time."

—Chuck Howard, ABC Sports producer, praising Robinson, who, beginning on April 17, 1965, was the first black network broadcaster for Major League Baseball, partnering with Merle Harmon, Chris Schenkel, or Keith Jackson during ABC's single year of telecasting Saturday afternoon games nationwide

"Thank you for your recent letter urging me to sign the $1.50 minimum wage bill, which I was sorry to have to veto. . . . As I pointed out, any substantial increase must be made concurrent with an increase in the federal minimum wage if New York is to avoid a serious loss of employment and economic opportunity."

—New York Governor Nelson Rockefeller to Jackie Robinson, excerpt from letter, May 3, 1965

"Dear Mr. O'Malley: Thanks for helping make the 'Jackie Robinson Day' a big success, at least for my family. . . . Rachel sends her best and thanks as well. Regards to Mrs. O'Malley and the family."

—J. R., showing that fences between him and Walter O'Malley had been at least partly mended after the Dodgers honored him at Dodger Stadium on June 16, to Dodgers owner Walter O'Malley, excerpt from letter, July 2, 1965

"While it is true that Jackie Robinson supported the president with his right hand [in the 1964 election], he was doing everything with his left hand to defeat a variety of democratic senatorial and congressional candidates across the country."

—Clifford Alexander Jr., White House special deputy, expressing a distrust of the Republican-leaning Robinson, excerpt from White House memorandum, November 22, 1965

"I am terribly sorry to hear that your son was wounded in Vietnam; thank heaven it was no worse, particularly in view of the tragic death of his two companions. Please give Rachel my best wishes."

—New York Governor Nelson Rockefeller, about Jackie Jr. escaping with his life in Vietnam, to Jackie Robinson, excerpt from letter, December 2, 1965

"On November 13, 1965 . . . an ambulance sped [Branch] Rickey to Boone County Hospital [after he suffered a heart attack while making a speech following his induction into the Missouri State Hall of Fame in Columbia, Missouri]. Placed in the intensive care unit . . . his wife keeping a constant vigil at his bedside . . . Branch Rickey died at 10:00 p.m. on December 9. It was just eleven days before his eighty-fourth birthday. . . . Jackie Robinson was ashamed and angered at the skimpy black representation at the funeral. 'Not even flowers and telegrams, and they're earning all that money,' he raged."

—Harvey Frommer, *Rickey and Robinson,* 1982

"It's hard to describe how I feel. It's hard to say what is in my heart."

—J. R., when receiving a phone call that informed him of Rickey's death, to New York sportswriter Phil Pepe, *New York World-Telegram and Sun,* December 10, 1965

"Side by side [Jackie and I] mourned our great loss in the same pew at Mr. Rickey's funeral. The respect and admiration that we shared for our mutual 'father' served to cement our friendship."

—Bobby Bragan, Braves manager, to Donald Honig, *The Man in the Dugout,* 1977

"THE PASSING OF MR. RICKEY IS LIKE LOSING A FATHER. MY WIFE AND I FEEL WE'VE LOST SOMEONE VERY DEAR TO US. MR. RICKEY'S DEATH IS A GREAT LOSS NOT ONLY TO BASEBALL BUT TO AMERICA."

—J. R., WHO WOULD ALWAYS GIVE RICKEY FULL CREDIT FOR THE INTEGRATION OF BASEBALL

"While I sincerely believe there is not a more dedicated politician on the scene, your record toward the Negro regarding political appointments cannot be accepted by any self-respecting Negro. In New York, it seems to me inexcusable that on the state level, excluding a few appointments, you do not have anyone of color on your staff."

—J. R. to New York Governor Nelson Rockefeller, excerpt from letter, January 12, 1966

"Governor [Nelson] Rockefeller [who is seeking re-election this year] announced today the appointment of Jackie Robinson, the former baseball star, as a Special Assistant to the Governor for Community Affairs. The 46-year-old Robinson . . . will be on the governor's personal staff and not on the state payroll. . . . Mr. Robinson said it was 'important for the future of the two-party system that progressive Republicans such as Nelson Rockefeller be re-elected to public office.' Mr. Robinson said he would advise the governor 'concerning any problem areas where I feel I can be helpful. I also hope to bring the remarkable Rockefeller record to the attention of minority groups throughout the state.'"

—*New York Times*, about Robinson becoming the second black to be appointed to Rockefeller's staff in a week, following new assistant press secretary Warren E. Gardner Jr., February 7, 1966

"I am delighted to have Jackie Robinson on my team. New Yorkers and other Americans know of his reputation for unqualified integrity. Because of this and because he is the kind of person who constantly seeks advice and guidance on all levels of his wide acquaintance, I know that he will seek out the truth from people and report that truth to me."

—New York Governor Nelson Rockefeller, quoted by the *New York Times*, February 7, 1966

"Negro personalities are extolling the suburbs as 'a better way of life for yourself and your children' in an attempt to integrate housing in Nassau, Suffolk, and Queens counties. Jackie Robinson, the former baseball player, and Arthur Prysock, a singer, have taped short, soft-sell radio messages aimed at nonwhite listeners who desire information in housing opportunities in predominantly white suburban neighborhoods. . . . The commercials, which were made without charge by the prominent Negroes and broadcast without cost by radio station WINS in Manhattan and WWRL in Woodside, Queens, have been used since last summer."

—Roy R. Silver, *New York Times,* **February 6, 1966**

"My high school friend Linda . . . and I were rebellious and . . . the activism and revolutionary philosophy of the Black Panthers appealed to our sense of disenfranchisement. . . . Linda and I went into Harlem to our favorite bookstore and purchased an eleven-by-fourteen poster of Huey Newton. . . . My father knocked on my door. . . . I barely got [a] greeting out before I noticed my father's eyes rest on our new poster. 'Get that poster off the wall!' Dad shouted. I was shocked. In my lifetime, my father had denied me only one other thing: a cat. This was the first time he had ever yelled at me. . . . I was highly incensed, but smart enough to know I'd better do as told. . . . He did not embrace ideologies of violence, or black nationalism, or black separatism."

—Sharon Robinson, *Stealing Home,* **1996**

"I guess we, as Negro people, are really pretty naïve about this so-called Great Society in which we live. We have witnessed some pretty raw brutalities—from the murders of Emmett Till and Medgar Evars—through the burning of churches and the execution of two white young men and a Negro in Philadelphia, Mississippi. Somehow . . . we never did believe we would be reading newspaper accounts about a mob of sick sadists beating twelve- and thirteen-year-old school children [with ax handles, pipes, and chains on September 12, in response to the desegregation of public schools in Grenada, Mississippi]. . . . The situation in Mississippi is discouraging enough. But when I think of that terrific and traitorous fight against the civil rights bill led by aged Senator Everett Dirksen of Illinois, I really wonder where we are headed. . . . Some of the apologists for the legislators . . . have [pointed] to the progress the Negro has been making. This is the stalest argument ever and I, personally, am sick of hearing it used as a cover-up. The Negro cannot be partially free any more than a woman can be partially pregnant."

—J. R., *New York Amsterdam News,* **October 1, 1966**

"I didn't realize then that my father was also at a critical turning point in his life. After years of being an activist in the civil rights movement, he was now finding himself at odds with every organization from the Black Panthers to the NAACP. . . . Dad basically felt the militancy of the Black Panthers would never work in the black community, but felt equally certain that the other black organizations of the times were not meeting the needs of the people."

—**Sharon Robinson,** *Stealing Home,* **1996**

"He . . . resigned [from the NAACP] because he felt . . . the leadership 'had become a reactionary and undemocratic political group,' stifling the efforts of the younger, more progressive members. It was a decision he later regretted, feeling that he should have stayed on to fight from within."

—**Rachel Robinson,** *Jackie Robinson: An Intimate Portrait,* **1997**

"[Dr. King and Dad] had a public disagreement as well."

—**Sharon Robinson,** *Stealing Home,* **1996**

ROBINSON A HAWK, KING A DOVE

"Dr. King's antiwar position had created controversy and debate within the black community. . . . Even SCLC, Dr. King's own organization, issued a disclaimer."

—**Sharon Robinson, about her father having a negative reaction to King's "Beyond Vietnam" speech at Riverside Church in New York, when King criticized the United States for sending young blacks across the world to fight and die in a so-called "war of liberation"—which he believed instead to be an imperialistic war—when they didn't feel liberated at home,** *Stealing Home,* **1996**

"Dear Mr. President: First, let me thank you for pursuing a course toward civil rights that no president in our history has pursued. . . . While I am certain your faith has been shaken by demonstrations against the Vietnam war, I hope the actions of any one individual does not make you feel as Vice President Humphrey does . . . that Dr. King's stand will hurt the civil rights movement. It would not be fair to the thousands of Negro fighting men who are giving their lives because they believe, in most instances, that our Vietnam stand is just. There are hundreds of thousands of us at home who are uncertain why we are in the war. We feel, however, that you and your staff know what is best and we are willing to support your efforts for an honorable solution to the war. . . . I hope God gives you the wisdom and strength to come through this crisis at home, and that an end to the war in Viet Nam is achieved soon."

—J. R., urging the president to continue to fight for civil rights while winding down the war, to President Johnson, excerpt from letter, April 18, 1967

"You suggest that we stop the bombing [in North Vietnam]. . . . [But] why should we take [this] vital step . . . without knowing whether the enemy will use that pause to prepare for greater destruction of our men in Vietnam? . . . Why is it, Martin, that you seem to ignore the blood which is on their hands and to speak only of the 'guilt' of the United States? Why is it that you don't suggest that the Viet Cong cease, stop, withdraw also? . . . I am confused because I respect you so deeply."

—J. R. to Martin Luther King Jr. to get him to clarify why he was against the war in Vietnam, excerpt from open letter *New York Amsterdam News*, May 13, 1967

"King did personally phone Robinson [to respond] because he was an old friend and explain his opposition to the war. Robinson acknowledged the depth, forcefulness, and sincerity of King's argument. Perhaps the break between them was healed."

—David Falkner, about Robinson being touched by King's "humanity" for calling him despite having been hurt by Robinson's criticism, *Great Time Coming*, 1995

"I would not want bigots and those who secretly hate Dr. King to find comfort in my disagreeing with him. Let there be no doubt in any man's mind where I stand on the subject of Dr. Martin Luther King Jr. If ever a man was placed on this earth by divine force to help solve the doubts and east the hurts and dispel the fears of mortal man, I believe that man is Dr. King."

—J. R., *New York Amsterdam News*, July 1, 1967

"To the Editor: Your fine editorial 'Black Racism' was ruined in my view by the complete lack of understanding of the desires and ambitions of Negro Americans."

—J. R., showing annoyance at an editorial that he felt told African Americans they should be content with their lives now that they had become more economically prosperous than any group of nonwhites in the world, to the editor of the *New York Times*, July 30, 1967

"Because of Tom Yawkey I'd like to see [Boston] lose. Because he is probably one of the most bigoted guys in organized baseball."

—J. R., who hadn't forgotten his sham tryout in Boston in 1945, about his rooting interests in the 1967 World Series in which the Cardinals would defeat Yawkey's Red Sox in seven games, to the Buffalo Chamber of Commerce, September 21, 1967

"If the GOP should nominate Nixon or [conservative governor of California Ronald] Reagan [in the 1968 presidential election], it would be telling the black man it cares nothing about him or his concerns."

—J. R., expressing in his column his worry that the Republicans wouldn't pick a liberal presidential candidate such as Nelson Rockefeller, *New York Amsterdam News*, September 22, 1967

"For Robinson, 1968 opened on a promising note. A new business venture offered an opportunity to succeed where other schemes had stagnated or failed. On January 4, Sea Host Incorporated . . . hired him to launch its main project: the sale of franchises for 'fast food' restaurants specializing in . . . seafood. . . . For Jack, this job represented a hope not only for himself but also for cash-starved blacks eager for a chance to break into business on their own."

—Arnold Rampersad, *Jackie Robinson: A Biography*, 1997

"Our aim is to help people help themselves. With the company's training program and support, almost anyone prepared to work for his income can become a successful Sea Host franchise."

—J. R., 1968

"Of all the Dodgers, none seemed as able as Jackie Robinson to trample down the thorns of life. . . . But here, on the night of March 6, 1968 . . . Robinson stood among television reporters, a bent, gray man, answering questions in a whisper, and drawing shallow breaths, because a longer breath might feed a sob. Jackie Robinson Jr., no more the large-eyed imp, had been arrested in a one-night-cheap hotel. The police of Stamford, Connecticut, charged him with possessing a tobacco pouch filled with marijuana, a .22 caliber revolver, and several packets of heroin, which he may have wished to sell."

—**Roger Kahn,** *The Boys of Summer,* **1972**

"HE QUIT HIGH SCHOOL. HE JOINED THE ARMY. HE FOUGHT IN VIETNAM AND HE WAS WOUNDED. WE LOST HIM SOMEWHERE. I'VE HAD MORE EFFECT ON OTHER PEOPLE'S KIDS THAN ON MY OWN."

—J. R., WHILE BAILING OUT JACKIE JR., TO REPORTERS AT THE SCENE, MARCH 6, 1968

"[Robinson's son] was given a choice of jail time or entering a drug-rehabilitation program. He entered a program selected by his mother [that] some colleagues . . . had suggested."

—**Susan Muaddi Darraj,** *Jackie Robinson,* **2008**

"Rockefeller sent his personal concerns and an offer of assistance when he heard of the arrest—a move that most likely deepened Robinson's faith in the governor's character and integrity."

—**Michael G. Long,** *First Class Citizenship,* **2007**

"Your surprise announcement [about not being a candidate for president] has left me disappointed, hurt, and utterly confused. I am disappointed because I have pictured a Republican victory with Negroes giving overwhelming support to your candidacy and the dream of the two-party system becoming a reality. . . . I strongly feel . . . that Negroes cannot support Richard Nixon. . . . I am also confused about President Johnson. While, in my opinion, he has been the greatest influence in our domestic racial policies, he leaves so much to be desired on the foreign policy level. I cannot help but feel that Robert Kennedy is a vindictive opportunist. . . . Nevertheless I would have to support him over Richard Nixon."

—**J. R., upset that Rockefeller had decided not to run for president and to support Richard Nixon in the November election, to New York Governor Nelson Rockefeller, excerpt from letter, March 27, 1968**

"Like so many others Robinson was crushed by the news of King's [assassination on April 4]. He flew to funeral services in Rockefeller's private plane and devoted several columns to the man."

—Michael G. Long, about Robinson's response to King, the most prominent figure of the civil rights movement, being killed by a sniper when in Memphis, Tennessee, to support a strike by sanitation workers, *First Class Citizenship*, 2007

"AT THE FUNERAL SERVICES, I WAS PLUNGED INTO DEEP CONTEMPLATION AS I THOUGHT OF THE SADNESS OF SAYING FAREWELL TO A MAN WHO DIED STILL CLINGING TO A DREAM OF INTEGRATION AND PEACE AND NONVIOLENCE."

—J. R., *NEW YORK AMSTERDAM NEWS*, APRIL 1968

"Because I am an eternal optimist, I have passed the first plateau of grief over the passing of the Rev. Dr. Martin Luther King Jr. I do not pretend that I have begun to reach the mountaintop which God showed the man who, in my view, was the greatest leader of the twentieth century. But I have come to regard his death as perhaps one of those great mysteries with which the Almighty moves—his wonders to perform."

—J. R., *New York Amsterdam News*, April 13, 1968

"As I write this letter our country is in trouble. The terrible tragedy of the assassination of Dr. Martin Luther King Jr. has cast a shadow over this land. . . . Words will no longer suffice. Deeds are required. . . . I do hope that if I should decide to be a candidate [for president] that I would be privileged to have your support. . . . I know how much you helped me [in 1960]. I really believe that this time we could succeed."

—Vice President Hubert Humphrey, courting Robinson a day after Martin Luther King's assassination in Memphis, excerpt from letter, April 5, 1968

"Jackie [Jr.'s] arrest and hospitalization inaugurated a period in which a series of tragedies touched us personally and made 1968 one of the worst years of our lives. Martin Luther King was assassinated, his death provoking riots in more than one hundred cities. We went from Jackie's hospital to [King's] funeral in Atlanta. Robert Kennedy would be assassinated in June, reinforcing the national sense of danger and sadness. And within our own family, our dear Mallie Robinson died quietly in her garden in Pasadena on May 21. Jack went home to bury this wonderful woman, the wellspring of his being. Adding to our sudden sense of being star-crossed, Sharon made an unfortunate marriage, which soon failed."

—Rachel Robinson, *Jackie Robinson: An Intimate Portrait,* 1997

"MANY TIMES I FELT MY MOTHER WAS BEING FOOLISH, LETTING PEOPLE TAKE ADVANTAGE OF HER. I WAS WRONG. SHE DID KINDNESS FOR PEOPLE WHOM I CONSIDERED PARASITES BECAUSE SHE WANTED TO HELP THEM. IT WAS HER WAY OF THINKING, HER WAY OF LIFE. SHE HAD NOT BEEN A FOOL FOR OTHERS. SHE HAD GIVEN WITH HER EYES AS OPEN AS HER HEART. IN DEATH, SHE WAS STILL TEACHING ME HOW TO LIVE."

—J. R.

"Jackie Robinson came to the 'defense' of the Black Panthers . . . last week. . . . Robinson said it was disgraceful that 300 off-duty city cops jumped and beat up [ten] Black Panthers [and two sympathizers]. . . . The goals of the Black Panther Party are no different than those of major civil rights groups, said Robinson. 'The Black Panthers seek self-determination, protection of the black community, decent housing and employment, and express opposition to police abuse,' he said. . . . The former Brooklyn Dodgers great, who came to New York to meet with the militant black group, which has been stirring up a headline-storm, criticized police who are 'trigger-happy' and 'white people in general' who have 'their head sticking way down in the sand. . . . There are not enough people around who give a damn about what is going on as far as the black man is concerned.'"

—*Pan African Press,* quoting Robinson, who was at his most militant in recalling an incident the previous September in the Brooklyn Criminal Courts Building, July 17, 1968

"Even after the *Amsterdam News* dropped his column in 1968, [Robinson] continued to write letters to the editor, make speeches around the country, and offer interviews to newspapers and magazine and radio and television shows. Robinson *had* to speak his mind. . . . But it is also very clear that the public *wanted* to hear from Jackie Robinson."

—**Michael G. Long,** *Beyond Home Plate,* **2013**

"Although doctors have not yet okayed a resumption of normal activities, Hall-of-Famer Jackie Robinson is reported recovering at his home from a mild heart attack. The 49-year-old Robinson . . . suffered the attack while playing golf. He underwent an examination June 24 and was confined to bed for two weeks. Robinson . . . said he was now feeling fine."

—*Sporting News,* **July 27, 1968**

"The year continued to be a troubling one for Robinson. Jackie Jr.'s rehabilitation program was not succeeding—he was discharged, but he went back almost immediately to using drugs."

—**Susan Muaddi Darraj,** *Jackie Robinson,* **2008**

"Two arrests [of Jackie Jr.], one in March and one in August. The second time the court ruled that he was a narcotics-dependent person."

—**J. R. to Roger Kahn in 1968,** *The Boys of Summer,* **1972**

"The first reaction my wife and I had when we found out that our son was a drug addict was to sweep it under the rug—hide it from our neighbors. The second reaction was, 'The hell what people think—he's our son and we love him and we're going to stick with him.'"

—**J. R., about his and Rachel's decision to find professional help for Jackie Jr., quoted by Gene Spagnoli,** *New York Daily News,* **August 3, 1970**

"It could have been jail, but the sentence was suspended with the understanding that he'd go into treatment to cure himself of addiction. There's a place called Daytop, in Seymour, Connecticut, where rehabilitation is done by former addicts. That's where he decided to go."

—**J. R. to Roger Kahn in 1968,** *The Boys of Summer,* **1972**

"Robinson wrote later that the Daytop program helped restore his son's respect for and love of life. 'The Daytop philosophy states firmly that no one owes the addict a living. He owes a lot to life. And the task of recovering is his alone.'"

—Susan Muaddi Darraj, *Jackie Robinson*, 2008

"Jackie Robinson Splits with GOP Over Nixon Choice"

—First-page article title, about Robinson resigning from Rockefeller's staff to support Democrat Hubert Humphrey for president against Richard Nixon, *New York Times*, August 12, 1968

"Because I couldn't support Mr. Nixon and Mr. Rockefeller could. Since I couldn't support the Republican Party, I did not think it proper for me to continue to work for the governor."

—J. R., replying to being asked why he parted ways with Nelson Rockefeller, *This Week* magazine, October 12, 1969

"Jack campaigned for [Democrat] Hubert Humphrey in the 1968 presidential election [against Richard Nixon]. He spent many days on the road in private discussion refining his ideas and preparing speeches. He was deeply disappointed by Humphrey's defeat."

—Rachel Robinson, *Jackie Robinson: An Intimate Portrait*, 1997

"THE SECRET SERVICE KEEPS A COMPUTERIZED FILE OF PEOPLE WHO MIGHT POSE A POTENTIAL THREAT TO THE PRESIDENT. JACKIE ROBINSON WAS INCLUDED ON JANUARY 25, 1969—FIVE DAYS AFTER PRESIDENT NIXON TOOK OFFICE. ROBINSON JOINED A GROUP OF BLACKS WHO VISITED THE NORTHWEST GATE OF THE WHITE HOUSE UNANNOUNCED . . . AND STATED THEY WANTED TO SEE THE PRESIDENT. . . . THE REASON . . . WAS THAT THEY WANTED MORE JOBS FOR THE BLACK PEOPLE AND ALSO WANTED THE PRESIDENT TO DEFINE BLACK CAPITALISM."

—JACK ANDERSON, LIBERAL POLITICAL COLUMNIST, MOCKING THE PARANOID NIXON FOR PUTTING ROBINSON ON A POTENTIAL-THREAT LIST SIMPLY BECAUSE HE CAME TO THE WHITE HOUSE ASKING FOR MORE JOB OPPORTUNITIES FOR BLACKS, UNITED FEATURES SYNDICATE, 1972

"In April 1969, appearing on a radio interview, I took exception to the statement reportedly made [by Yankees GM Lee MacPhail] that black players can make it as players but not in the front office. . . . All managers are white and have been hired by white owners: no white owner has yet hired a black man as a manager. The inescapable conclusion was frankly stated by Frank Robinson: 'There's only one reason a Negro has never been a manager—his color,' he said. 'The reason there hasn't been a Negro manager is that no one has ever given a Negro a chance to be one.'"

—J. R., criticizing the Yankees GM for making a statement similar to the one that would get Dodgers GM Al Campanis fired in 1987 and quoting the two-time Triple Crown winner Frank Robinson, who would become the majors' first black manager in 1975, *I Never Had It Made,* **as told to Alfred Duckett, 1972**

"I wouldn't fly the flag on the Fourth of July or any other day. When I see a car with a flag pasted on it I figure the guy behind the wheel isn't my friend."

—J. R., revealing his increasing pessimism by condemning all the flag-waving Americans who think they are patriots yet don't believe in the principles of democracy, *New York Times,* **July 4, 1969**

"At very least, [counsel to the president John D.] Ehrlichman's request [of Robinson's FBI file in July 1969] suggests that the Nixon administration was strategizing about Robinson's public criticism of Nixon."

—Michael G. Long, *First Class Citizenship,* **2007**

"On July 22, 1969, organized baseball officially celebrated its centennial with the All-Star Game in Washington, DC, and a White House reception hosted by President Nixon. . . . Prior to the White House reception, Hall of Fame players Bob Feller and Jackie Robinson squared off at a press conference at the Sheraton Park Hotel. . . . Feller lashed out at Robinson for his criticism of baseball hiring practices."

—Ron Briley, teacher and sports historian, excerpt from paper presented at the Jackie Robinson anniversary conference, Long Island University, Brooklyn Campus, April 1997

"Robinson has always been bush. He's always been a professional agitator more than anything else. He's just ticked off because baseball never rolled out the red carpet when he quit playing and offered him a soft front office job. . . . Ability alone is what should count in the front office, too. I think there will be a Negro with that ability."

—Bob Feller, press conference at Sheraton Park Hotel in Washington, July 22, 1969

"An angry Robinson retorted that Feller had grown little since 1947, Robinson's rookie season, continuing to bury 'his head in the sand.'"

—**Ron Briley, teacher and sports historian, excerpt from paper presented at the Jackie Robinson anniversary conference, Long Island University, Brooklyn Campus, April 1997**

"MY BIG THING IS I DON'T BELIEVE THAT THE BLACK PLAYERS ARE GETTING AN EQUAL OPPORTUNITY WITH THE WHITES AFTER THEIR PLAYING DAYS ARE THROUGH."

—J. R., JULY 22, 1969

"There can be no question that on the playing field they are only looking for talent. But the problem [for] black ballplayers is what do they do after their careers are over at 31, 32, or 33? Baseball has not done what is right for black ball players in terms of providing them with opportunities for earning a living in the area they know best."

—**J. R., replying to being asked about the progress of black ball players since 1947, *This Week* magazine, October 12, 1969**

"I would have to point to Willie Mays and Hank Aaron, and then you have to consider Roy Campanella and Bob Gibson. They are comparable to any white ball players of the past decades."

—**J. R., replying to being asked who the best black baseball players had been in the past two decades, *This Week* magazine, October 12, 1969**

"Willie Mays has been chosen the greatest New York Giant and Jackie Robinson the greatest Brooklyn Dodger in a poll of fans conducted by the New York Mets. The voting was held in conjunction with the celebration of baseball's centennial season."

—**Associated Press, November 6, 1969**

"I think the way things are going, we are closer to having a George Wallace elected President of the United States than we are of having a black president."

—**J. R., replying to be asked when he thought a black would be elected president, *This Week* magazine, October 12, 1969**

"I leaped into the air with a big wide grin on my face. What went through my mind was that this was the culmination of a dream I had when I was a little boy [in Florida] and idolized Jackie Robinson and wanted to play Major League Baseball and be in the World Series like he did. Jackie Robinson opened the door and I got the opportunity in New York with that team and that manager and his coaches. I was very fortunate."

—Ed Charles, New York Mets third baseman, about his reaction when the Mets, managed by Robinson's friend and former teammate Gil Hodges, clinched the 1969 world championship over Baltimore on October 16, 1969, to Danny Peary, *Gil Hodges,* Tom Clavin and Danny Peary, 2012

"Concerned once again with the business side of civil rights, and with making money [himself], Robinson and several others founded Jackie Robinson Associates [in November 1969]—a group of business leaders committed to providing business loans and affordable housing for minorities."

—Michael G. Long, about one of Robinson's shaky business ventures that he hoped Nelson Rockefeller would support, *First Class Citizenship,* 2007

"Jackie Robinson praised the franchise business today as a potential solution to the problems of black capitalism, but he severely criticized President Nixon's efforts in the field. Mr. Robinson, a business executive . . . said that America's next real trouble would be in economics and politics as Negroes push for 'a piece of the pie,' they have long been denied. . . . He said that a black man would have a better chance of succeeding with a franchise than . . . starting out in business in any other way. But . . . 'the very poor relations between black America and the present administration are causing a serious rift in this country.'"

—Paul Delaney, about Robinson's appearance, ten months before Sea Host filed for bankruptcy, before the Senate's Small Business Committee's Subcomittee on Urban and Rural Development, *New York Times,* January 21, 1970

"In our meeting we discussed the possibility of forming a group to develop housing in minority areas within the state. I have had some discussion with our associates about this and we are of the opinion that Jackie Robinson Associates could handle the program well. . . . I believe we can play a role once again in your campaign. . . . However . . . we will need considerable work in Black areas and the sooner we can demonstrate your real concern, the easier the task."

—J. R. to New York Governor Nelson Rockefeller, excerpt from letter, November 14, 1969

"IF YOU ARE SINCERE IN WANTING TO WIN THE RESPECT OF BLACK AMERICA, YOU MUST BE WILLING TO LOOK AT YOUR OWN ADMINISTRATION'S ATTITUDE. THERE SEEM TO BE NO KEY OFFICIALS IN YOUR ADMINISTRATION WHO HAVE AN UNDERSTANDING OF WHAT MOTIVATES BLACK PEOPLE. I FIND IT DIFFICULT TO BELIEVE THERE WILL BE ANY, WHEN IT APPEARS YOUR MOST TRUSTED ADVISERS ARE VICE PRESIDENT AGNEW, ATTORNY GENERAL MITCHELL AND STROM THURMOND. HOW CAN YOU EXPECT TRUST FROM US WHEN WE FEEL THAT THESE MEN YOU HAVE SELECTED FOR HIGH OFFICE ARE ENEMIES? YOU WOULD NOT SUPPORT KNOWN ANTI-SEMITICS TO PLACATE JEWISH FEELINGS. WHY APPOINT KNOWN SEGREGATIONISTS TO DEAL WITH BLACK PROBLEMS?"

—J. R., WHOSE DAYS OF THINKING RICHARD NIXON CARED ABOUT CIVIL RIGHTS HAD LONG PASSED, TO PRESIDENT NIXON, EXCERPT FROM LETTER, FEBRUARY 9, 1970

"Jackie Robinson urged Congress Tuesday to spurn pleas to legalize marijuana. He said . . . Jackie Jr., 23, smoked marijuana, then 'took the next step' to heroin. 'Just as we lost much time as parents, we are losing much time as a nation,' Robinson told the Senate District of Columbia Committee."

—**United Press, February 15, 1970**

"Jack finally found the business opportunity he had been searching for since leaving baseball a decade earlier. Backed by a small group of investors organized by his lawyer and loyal friend, Marty Edelman, Jack established the Jackie Robinson Construction [Corporation] to build housing for families with low and moderate incomes. . . . With a contract from the New York State Urban Development Corporation and a joint-venture agreement with Halpern Building Corporation, the new company in 1970 broke ground for Whitney Young Manor, a 197-unit development in Yonkers, New York. Jack set up an office in Fort Lee, New Jersey."

—**Rachel Robinson, *Jackie Robinson: An Intimate Portrait,* 1997**

SUPPORTING CURT FLOOD

"Early in January 1970, Curt Flood filed a $1 million law suit against Commissioner Bowie Kuhn and Major League Baseball. The previous October, Flood had been traded by the St. Louis Cardinals to the Philadelphia Phillies, a team Flood did not wish to play for in a city he did not wish to play in. What he wanted was nothing less than the overthrow of the long-standing 'reserve clause,' a part of every player's contract that bound him to his team. . . . Despite the urging of players' union head Marvin Miller, no active major leaguer came out for Flood. . . . Jackie Robinson, who had been retired for more than a decade, showed up [in court] to support Flood."

—**Allen Barra**, *Mickey and Willie*, 2013

"A few former players like Jackie Robinson and Hank Greenberg [and Jim Brosnan] came to testify in Flood's behalf."

—**Lee Lowenfish**, *The Imperfect Diamond*, 1980

"IN MY OPINION, ANYTHING THAT IS ONE-SIDED IN THIS COUNTRY IS WRONG. THE RESERVE CLAUSE SHOULD AT LEAST BE MODIFIED TO GIVE THE PLAYER SOME CONTROL OVER HIS OWN DESTINY."

—J. R., TESTIFYING AT THE TRIAL OF CURT FLOOD, WHO WOULD LOSE HIS CHALLENGE BUT PAVE THE WAY FOR THE END OF THE RESERVE CLAUSE IN BASEBALL IN 1975, MAY 1970

"[On May 27] Bill Braucher, a sportswriter and columnist for the *Miami Herald*, criticized Robinson's appearance [prompting] Robinson's response [to his paper]."

—**Michael G. Long**, *First Class Citizenship*, 2007

"Why should Bill Braucher be so upset because Curt Flood's attorney asked that I testify at the hearing against the reserve clause? . . . He seems to feel I don't have the right to express my opinion. . . . None of us should be so bigoted that he would deny that person his or her right to freedom of speech. . . . Braucher's biggest concern seems to be that I end up 'into the civil rights league.' Well, Mr. Editor, this is one area where I do consider myself an expert. Being black in these United States, having to contend with the Bill Brauchers for over 50 years, I know a little about bigots and bigotry. Bill says, regarding the reserve clause, 'maybe Robinson has a solution. If he does, however, I'm not sure I want to hear from him again.' I have never spoken for his ears. One does not waste time on men as little as Bill Braucher. All one has to do is read his column carefully to know it was a narrow bigoted one that tells you of the level of his competence, not only as a writer but also as a man."

—J. R. to editor, *Miami Herald,* **excerpt from public letter, June 8, 1970**

"I paid more than my dues for the right to call it like I see it. And I could care less if people like me, so long as they respect me. The only way I know how to deserve respect . . . is to be honest."

—**J. R. to literary and talent agent, Michal Hamilburg, excerpt from letter, October 10, 1970**

"The former baseball star Jackie Robinson will deliver the commencement address at [Northfield] Mount Herman School June 6. His son, David, will be among the graduates."

—**Associated Press, May 26, 1970**

"In July the ax fell at Sea Host. . . . Jack now had no regular source of income other than a small salary from his construction company. But . . . Rachel and Jack had been careful in their [financial] planning. . . . Still, with Jack's failing health, Rachel could see the dark closing in. In the fall of 1969, she had resigned her position with the mental health program in New Haven and taken a one-year, unpaid leave of absence from Yale. . . . 'I really did spend a fair amount of time in the library. But I was also more available for Jack and Jackie.'"

—**Arnold Rampersad,** *Jackie Robinson: A Biography,* **1997**

"HIS EYESIGHT WAS FAILING, AND HE SILENTLY ENDURED EXTREME PAIN IN HIS LEGS. THE NEW [CONSTRUCTION] BUSINESS ADVENTURE HELPED JACK'S MORALE IMMENSELY, BUT IT COULD NOT PREVENT PHYSICAL DETERIORATION. AND YET HE KEPT GOING AT HIS USUAL RELENTLESS PACE."

—RACHEL ROBINSON, *JACKIE ROBINSON: AN INTIMATE PORTRAIT*, 1997

"[Jack] would not talk about death. Denial was his greatest prop, and he denied he was dying. But after a while I knew I had to do something, so I went into therapy to learn how to cope with this terrible fact."

—Rachel Robinson, about seeing her husband's health fail in 1970, especially in August when he suffered two mild strokes that impaired his balance and ruptured blood vessels in his eyes, to Arnold Rampersad, *Jackie Robinson: A Biography*, 1997

"Joe Black has been feeling out Negro ballplayers about chipping in to honor Jackie Robinson with a banquet and scholarship in his name and he is appalled by the cool receptions he receives from most of them—those who came later and benefited without a struggle."

—Dick Young, *New York Daily News,* February 13, 1971

"I TRIED TO TELL [TODAY'S BLACK BALLPLAYERS] THAT WITHOUT JACKIE, IF SOMEBODY ELSE HAD BEEN CHOSEN TO BE FIRST AND BLEW IT, CHANCES ARE NONE OF US WOULD HAVE HAD ANYTHING OUT OF BASEBALL. THEY SAY TO ME, 'SO WHAT, HE GOT PAID, DIDN'T HE?'"

—JOE BLACK, FORMER BROOKLYN DODGERS PITCHER AND VP WITH GREYHOUND BUS LINE, QUOTED BY DICK YOUNG, *NEW YORK DAILY NEWS*, FEBRUARY 13, 1971

"Baseball great Jackie Robinson confirmed his appointment to the three-man New York State Athletic Commission. The 52-year-old . . . said of the post in New York City: 'I'm told that everything is settled. To me the Boxing Commission is a challenge. I'm hopeful of relating it to the community, particularly in the area of narcotics.'"

—*Jet* magazine, March 11, 1971

"Dad was busy with . . . problems associated with the Freedom National Bank. As chairman, Dad had to confront the president of the bank [who would be forced to move to a different position] about some questionable loans. He was nervous and tense about the suggestion of impropriety. After ten successful years in corporate America, Dad's latest ventures into entrepreneurship had been less satisfying."

—**Sharon Robinson, who was studying at Howard University while David was at Stanford and Jackie Jr. was working at Daytop,** *Stealing Home*, **1996**

FROM JOY TO HEARTBREAK: A FAMILY TRAGEDY

"In May 1970, my parents had a picnic for the Daytop staff and residents. About fifty people came. . . . I was struck by how loving Jackie was toward the other members, the staff, and us. As the day came to a close each person came up to my mother and father to thank them. Jackie was last. He reached out and grabbed Mom, hugging her lovingly. Then he got to Dad. My father, remembering how his earlier efforts to hug Jackie had been rejected, reached out to shake his son's hand. Jackie brushed Dad's hand aside, pulled his father to him, and hugged him tightly."

—**Sharon Robinson,** *Stealing Home*, **1996**

"That single moment paid for every bit of sacrifice, every bit of anguish, I had ever undergone. I had my son back."

—**J. R.,** *I Never Had It Made*, **as told to Alfred Duckett, 1972**

"I was haunted by the image of being the son of a father who was a great man. So when I found I couldn't deal with him as a man and found that my father couldn't identify with me as his son, I stopped trying to find a man who wasn't there. I tried to eliminate the desire that I thought would never be fulfilled. Daytop helped me through discipline to find the father I had lost. In the process I lied, cheated, robbed, and dealt with prostitutes. After I tried marijuana I reached out for bigger and better thrills, egged on by my friends who called me square for being afraid. At Daytop I found not only myself but love. My family closed ranks to help me in every way possible. My father was always in my corner."

—**Jackie Robinson Jr., speaking before the U.S. Senate Subcommittee to Investigate Juvenile Delinquency, October 30, 1970**

"As the struggle at the bank grew more intense and his health suffered, Jack was heartened . . . mainly by his son Jackie's continuing progress. Steadily, Jackie was emerging as a respected, quietly eloquent leader in the Daytop community; he had become assistant regional director of Daytop. In March [1971], Jack and Jackie appeared together on a [radio] program . . . with Jackie speaking of the personal trauma of drug abuse, and Jack telling of the importance of family support based on love and discipline."

—**Arnold Rampersad,** *Jackie Robinson: A Biography,* **1997**

"[Jack and I] decided to make a sizable contribution to Daytop by dedicating the 1971 Afternoon of Jazz concert to them and donating all proceeds to the program. Jackie was delighted and joined our volunteer committee. He took the lead in contacting artists, starting with his favorite, Roberta Flack. The concert was scheduled for the last Sunday in June."

—**Rachel Robinson,** *Jackie Robinson: An Intimate Portrait,* **1997**

"Jackie Robinson Jr., son of former Pasadena baseball great, died early today in a one-car accident, state police said. The son of the first black man to break baseball's color barrier was on his way home from work at a drug rehabilitation center when his small sports car slammed into a bridge abutment on the Merritt Parkway, friends said."

—*Pasadena Star-News,* **about the death of the Robinsons' first child, June 17, 1971**

"YOU DON'T KNOW WHAT IT'S LIKE TO LOSE A SON, FIND HIM AND LOSE HIM AGAIN."

—J. R.

"We lost my brother Jackie when he was twenty-four. . . . At the funeral, my brother David read a poem that he'd written for Jackie called 'The Baptism.' The poem ended with the words 'and, he was free.' Cries erupted from every pew in the church. . . . I watched my parents over the next few months, needing to understand how we all would go on. They walked slower, rarely smiled broadly, but still they got up each morning and went to work."

—**Sharon Robinson,** *Jackie's Nine,* **2001**

"The loss of Jackie was the most traumatic and tragic moment in my parents' life. . . . Over the summer, I made frequent trips home. . . . On one visit . . . Dad was sitting alone in the darkness crying. . . . Dad was an emotional rock. I couldn't ever remember seeing him cry. . . . 'First Mr. Rickey and my mother, now your brother.' Dad's voice trembled as he spoke."

—**Sharon Robinson,** *Stealing Home,* **1996**

"As Jack waited for his construction company to gain momentum, he kept himself busy with other, smaller entrepreneurial ventures that brought in little money. . . . Once he sank money into a Chicken Shack fast-food franchise in St. Martin. . . . He invested in a cosmetics-distribution scheme. . . . At one point Jack . . . joined two associates in bidding for a license to operate a radio station in Stamford. . . . On May 27, following confirmation by the state senate, Jack was sworn in to a two-year term on the New York State Athletic Commission, which oversaw boxing and wrestling. But the job carried no salary. Members received $100.33 for each working day."

—**Arnold Rampersad,** *Jackie Robinson: A Biography,* **1997**

"Robinson undertook . . . the writing of his last autobiography, *I Never Had It Made.*"

—**David Falkner,** *Great Time Coming,* **1995**

"I WENT BACK TO SCHOOL AFTER MANY YEARS AS A HOMEMAKER, GOT MY MASTER'S DEGREE IN PSYCHIATRIC NURSING AT NEW YORK UNIVERSITY, AND WENT TO WORK IN MENTAL INSTITUTIONS. MY HUSBAND WAS NOT VERY HAPPY WITH MY GOING TO WORK."

—RACHEL ROBINSON, WHO BECAME THE DIRECTOR OF NURSING FOR THE CONNECTICUT MENTAL HEALTH CENTER AND ASSISTANT CLINICAL PROFESSOR AT YALE UNIVERSITY SCHOOL OF NURSING, INTERVIEW, *SCHOLASTIC* MAGAZINE, FEBRUARY 11, 1997

"[Rachel] did not want to go through her life being known only as Mrs. Jackie Robinson. She has a strong, independent spirit, and she wanted to be accepted as an individual in her own right. If I had my way, Rachel would not have a job. But having my own way would constitute selfishness as well as insensitivity to her needs as a person."

—J. R., *I Never Had It Made,* as told to Alfred Duckett, 1972

"[Dad's growing] dependence [on my mother] masked his fears. There was no denying that his health had become a serious problem and he must have sensed that he would not live much longer. A couple of times that fall, he was hospitalized and I was called home."

—Sharon Robinson, *Stealing Home,* 1996

"One day in September 1971 . . . Jack played nine holes in a charity golf tournament in Westchester County, New York [and] then . . . we hopped in the car and drove five hours to Washington, DC, to be in attendance as Sharon received her nurse's cap at Howard University. We were both so proud. . . . Jack's love for her would not let him think of missing it. He was extremely tired, but he stayed after the ceremony to sign autographs for Sharon's classmates who surrounded him. This was the way Jack had always lived his life. We didn't talk about the shadow hovering over us."

—Rachel Robinson, about attending the graduation ceremony of their daughter, who became a nurse, midwife, educator, and author, *Jackie Robinson: An Intimate Portrait,* 1997

TWELVE

The Final Year

"Black players have saved baseball, kept baseball on top, but I think football and basketball have moved beyond baseball in race relations. In many instances, they hire a man to do a job regardless of skin color. Baseball is still wallowing around in the 19th century, saying a black can't manage, a black can't go to into the front office. . . . I think baseball is very vindictive. . . . If you're a [black] man and you stand on your own two feet, look out. I think that is basically the problem today with baseball."

—J. R., who had drifted away from baseball and MLB had allowed it, quoted by Dave Anderson, *New York Times*, December 5, 1971

"[A few weeks] before we left for vacation in Jamaica [for the Christmas holidays], *Sport* magazine announced that Jackie Robinson had been named 'The Man of the 25 Years in Sports.' A luncheon in his honor marked the beginning of ten months of celebrating the twenty-fifth anniversary of his entry into the major leagues . . . and culminated in the ceremony at the [1972] World Series. It was quite a wonderful, happy time, beginning with the morning of December 6 when a limousine drove us into Manhattan to Mamma Leone's. It was one of my father's favorite restaurants and he had brought us there many times. Dad stood tall among the other giants being honored that day. Willie Mays, Arnold Palmer, Gale Sayers, John Unitas, Rocky Marciano, [Bill Russell, Kareem Abdul-Jabbar] and Vince Lombardi were just a few of the names."

—Sharon Robinson, *Stealing Home*, 1996

"In January, my father invited me to go with him to the Apollo Theater on 125th Street to hear Jesse Jackson speak in honor of Dr. King's birthday. . . . By the early seventies . . . King had proven the wiser [than my Dad about the Vietnam War]."

—Sharon Robinson, *Stealing Home*, 1996

"I have not embraced nonviolence, but I have become more cynical about this country's role in Vietnam. I have become more skeptical about the old domino theory; that the fall of Vietnam would bring communist domination to Southeast Asia. I feel that the regime we are supporting in South Vietnam is corrupt and not representative of the people. I am particularly upset about the plight of the black soldier. I cannot accept the idea of a black supposedly fighting for the principals of freedom and democracy in Vietnam when so little has been accomplished in this country. There was a time when I deeply believed in America. I have become bitterly disillusioned."

—J. R., *I Never Had It Made,* **as told to Alfred Duckett, 1972**

"I am sorry the President does not understand my concern. . . . Black America has asked so little, but if you can't see the anger that comes from rejection, you are treading a dangerous course. We older blacks, unfortunately, were willing to wait. Today's young blacks are ready to explode! . . . I hope you will listen to the cries of the black youth, we cannot afford additional conflict."

—J. R. to Roland Elliot, special assistant to President Nixon, excerpt from letter, April 20, 1972

"Today militants find me hard to take. Their attitude is: burn everything. But I haven't changed much. The times have changed around me. Now we're coming to the black-black confrontation, extreme against moderate. After that the rough one, black and white. Blacks aren't scared anymore. If the Klan walked into a black neighborhood now, the people would rip the sheets right off them."

—J.R to Roger Kahn, *The Boys of Summer,* **1972**

"Now I hear people putting him down. Black people. To Stokely Carmichael and Rap Brown, he's a period piece. When I hear that, I feel sorry for *them*. Carmichael and Brown can never understand what Robinson did. How hard it was. What a great victory. But he can understand them. He was a young black man once, and mad and hurt. He knows *their* feeling, and their ignorance must hurt him more."

—Carl Erskine, former Brooklyn Dodgers pitcher, to Roger Kahn, *The Boys of Summer,* **1972**

"I THINK JACKIE WAS SUBJECT TO SOME UNFAIR CRITICISM . . . BY THE YOUNG BLACK MILITANTS. THEY DIDN'T UNDERSTAND HIS POSITION. HE WAS SUPPORTIVE OF THE MOVEMENT BUT WANTED TO DO IT THROUGH THE SYSTEM. SOME OF THE YOUNGER PEOPLE WERE IMPATIENT, AND THEY PAINTED HIM WITH SOME DEROGATORY BRUSHES. THERE'S NO QUESTION IN MY MIND THAT JACKIE ROBINSON HAD THE BROADEST IMPACT ON AMERICAN SOCIETY OF ANY BLACK ATHLETE. . . . HE MAY WELL BE THE MOST SIGNIFICANT FORMER ATHLETE IN AMERICAN HISTORY WHEN IT COMES TO HIS INFLUENCE AFTER HIS PLAYING DAYS."

—ARTHUR ASHE, THE FIRST AFRICAN AMERICAN MALE TENNIS PLAYER TO WIN THE US OPEN, AUSTRALIAN OPEN, AND WIMBLEDON, QUOTED BY MAURY ALLEN, *JACKIE ROBINSON: A LIFE REMEMBERED*, 1987

"I remember my own dangerous confrontation with a white policeman in the lobby of the Apollo Theater recently . . . after a couple of police officers had been killed in Harlem. . . . On my way into the lobby . . . a plainclothesman accosted me. He asked me roughly where I was going, and I asked what the hell business it was of his. He grabbed me and spectators passing by told me later that he had pulled out a gun. . . . By this time people had started crowding around, excitedly telling him my name, and he backed off. Thinking over that incident, it horrified me to realize what might have happened if I had been just another citizen of Harlem. It shouldn't be necessary to be named Jackie Robinson to keep from getting brutalized in [New York Mayor] John Lindsay's Fun City or [Chicago Mayor] Dick Daley's Chicago."

—J. R., about the issue of abusive white police across America denying black men—and protesters of all colors at the 1968 Democratic Convention in Chicago—their civil liberties and dignity, *I Never Had It Made,* as told to Alfred Duckett, 1972

"Jack was no longer even a small force in national politics. He would attempt no intervention in either the Republican or the Democratic primaries. . . . However, Jack's support of young Jesse Jackson continued. Through the winter he did what he could to assist Jackson's PUSH. On March 26, he and Rachel were prominent in a Tribute to Black Heroes organized as a fundraiser [for Operation Breadbasket] at the 369th Armory in Harlem. Later they were honored at PUSH headquarters in Chicago."

—Arnold Rampersad, about an event at a packed auditorium at which Jackson presented Robinson with a plaque and medallion, *Jackie Robinson: A Biography,* 1997

"I was proud to become first vice president when Jesse organized the fast-growing PUSH (People United to Save Humanity) at the beginning of 1972 after he resigned from the Southern Christian Leadership Conference. . . . I think he offers the most viable leadership for black and oppressed minorities in America and also for the salvation of our national decency."

—J. R., *I Never Had It Made,* as told to Alfred Duckett, 1972

ROBINSON'S CLARION CALL FOR EQUALITY

"I look at my children now, and know that I must still prepare them to meet obstacles and prejudices. But I can tell them, too, that they will never face some of these prejudices because other people have gone before them. And to myself I can say that, because progress is unalterable, many of today's dogmas will have vanished by the time they grow into adults. I can say to my children: There is a chance for you. No guarantee, but a chance."

—J. R., recorded essay, Edward R. Murrow's radio series *This I Believe,* 1952

"Mr. President: As a proud Black American who feels Blacks have contributed greatly to whatever successes have been achieved as a nation, I am greatly concerned with your leadership at a time when understanding and courage is needed to head off what could be the worst racial turmoil we have witnessed. . . . You must realize that the idea that blacks want busing for racial balance is erroneous. This notion springs from white America. . . . As a black I could not care less about integration except that it is the only way to build a strong country. We want busing so our children can compete! You know, as all Americans know, our kids will make it only on the quality of their education. Non-integrated schools, no matter what, are not equal in terms of educational opportunities."

—J. R. to President Nixon, excerpt from letter, 1972

"It is up to us in the North to provide aid and support to those who are actually bearing the brunt of the fight for equality down south. America has its iron curtain too."

—J. R.

"Negroes aren't seeking anything which is not good for the nation as well as ourselves. In order for America to be 100 percent strong—economically, defensively, and morally—we cannot afford the waste of having second- and third-class citizens."

—J. R.

"I DON'T THINK THAT I OR ANY OTHER NEGRO, AS AN AMERICAN CITIZEN, SHOULD HAVE TO ASK FOR ANYTHING THAT IS RIGHTFULLY HIS. WE ARE DEMANDING THAT WE JUST BE GIVEN THE THINGS THAT ARE RIGHTFULLY OURS AND THAT WE'RE NOT LOOKING FOR ANYTHING ELSE."

—J. R.

"Civil rights is not by any means the only issue that concerns me—nor, I think any other Negro. As Americans, we have as much at stake in this country as anyone else. But since effective participation in a democracy is based upon enjoyment of basic freedoms that everyone else takes for granted, we need make no apologies for being especially interested in catching up on civil rights."

—J. R.

"I won't 'have it made' until the most underprivileged Negro in Mississippi can live in equal dignity with anyone else in America."

—J. R.

"The right of every American to first-class citizenship is the most important issue of our time."

—J. R.

"One evening in early 1972, Jack arrived home visibly shaken. He had almost hit a car on the parkway: the near-miss forced him to finally admit that he had completely lost all peripheral vision. I immediately hired a chauffeur."

—Rachel Robinson, *Jackie Robinson: An Intimate Portrait*, 1997

"Jackie was very upset by Gil Hodges's death [on April 2, 1972]. It was a shock. Jackie was quoted as saying he thought he'd be the one to go first [of the Brooklyn Dodgers]. . . . At the time of Gil's funeral, he was feeling very fragile, because we lost our son in 1971. Both of us were still devastated by that."

—**Rachel Robinson to Danny Peary,** *Gil Hodges,*
Tom Clavin and Danny Peary, 2012

"[He] was the core of the Brooklyn Dodgers. It's a saddening experience, losing a great man like Gil."

—**J. R., April 2, 1972**

"After my father's service, Howard Cosell grabbed me and he brought me to a car and put me in the backseat. Jackie was sitting there, crying hysterically. He held me and said, 'Next to my son's death, this is the worst day of my life.'"

—**Gil Hodges Jr. to Tom Clavin and Danny Peary,** *Gil Hodges,* **2012**

"Robinson had also become disillusioned with his favorite politician, [New York Governor] Nelson Rockefeller. . . . Robinson was angry at Rockefeller's decision [not to open a dialogue by coming in person and to instead] order an assault on Attica State Prison during the September 1971 riots (twenty-three of the thirty-nine inmates killed were African Americans). . . . Changes to welfare policies also continued to irritate Robinson, and it is highly likely that he was disturbed by Rockefeller's support for Nixon's one-year moratorium on busing as a tool for integrating schools."

—**Michael G. Long,** *First Class Citizenship,* **2007**

"It is with the greatest difficulty that I write this letter . . . because the one man in public life in whom I had complete faith and confidence does not now measure up to his previous highly laudable stand. . . . I believe you have lost the sensitivity and understanding I felt . . . when I worked with you. Somehow, it seems to me, getting ahead politically is more important to you than what is right."

—**J. R., as always being blunt, to New York Governor Nelson Rockefeller, excerpt from letter, May 2, 1972**

"He seemed to have trouble walking, and he absolutely couldn't see. It was so sad. . . . Jackie just seemed to get older faster than the rest of us. It had to be what he went through. I don't think Jack ever stopped carrying that burden. I'm no doctor but I'm sure it cut his life short. Jackie Robinson never could stop fighting."

—**Pee Wee Reese to Maury Allen,** *Jackie Robinson: A Life Remembered,* **1987**

"In 1971, Don Drysdale worked Expo television with me. The next year, he went to Texas, and Pee Wee Reese did a majority of our TV games. A couple of times . . . Jackie Robinson, filled in for him. . . . The first night that I worked with him in the booth, Jackie pointed to the monitor and said, 'Dave, I'll be able to discuss the game, but just point to the ball so I'll know where it is when I'm talking about replays.' Kind of hard to forget a moment like that."

—**Dave Van Horne, Montreal Expos broadcaster, to Curt Smith,**
The Storytellers, **1995**

ROBINSON RECONCILES WITH THE DODGERS (SORT OF)

"A Salute to Casey Stengel Day at Dodger Stadium brought out 43,818—plus one. And on the same evening, June 4, Walter O'Malley was honored at a $100-a-plate testimonial. . . . It was one of the happy days of Dodger history, not the least of which was the welcome return of Jackie Robinson, who had left the team in bitterness some 16 years ago. Don Newcombe, now in charge of community relations for the ball club, extended the invitation to the first modern black major leaguer."

—**Bob Hunter,** *Los Angeles Herald-Examiner,* **June 24, 1972**

"ROBINSON KNOWS HE'S BEEN BITTER ABOUT A LOT OF THINGS. . . . HE DOESN'T WANT PEOPLE TO REMEMBER HIM THAT WAY."

—DON NEWCOMBE, WHO, AT [DODGERS PRESIDENT] PETER O'MALLEY'S REQUEST, PERSUADED ROBINSON TO GET PAST HIS ESTRANGEMENT FROM BASEBALL AND THE DODGERS, TO BOB HUNTER, *LOS ANGELES HERALD-EXAMINER,* JUNE 24, 1972

"I called him on the phone."

—**Don Newcombe, quoted by Michael D'Antonio,** *Forever Blue,* **2009**

"Hell no, I'm not coming. F**k the Dodgers."

—**J. R. to Don Newcombe, quoted by Michael D'Antonio,** *Forever Blue,* **2009**

"Robbie, will you come for me?"

—Don Newcombe to Jackie Robinson, quoted by Michael D'Antonio,
Forever Blue, **2009**

"You're goddamned right I will."

—J. R. to Don Newcombe, quoted by Michael D'Antonio, *Forever Blue,* **2009**

"Despite poor health, Robinson attended the game on June 4, 1972, and spent a long time talking to Peter O'Malley."

—Michael D'Antonio, about Robinson speaking to Peter O'Malley, although he had recently been corresponding with O'Malley's father, Walter, *Forever Blue,* **2009**

"I told Peter I was disturbed at the way baseball treats its black players after their playing days are through. . . . I don't think we'll see a black manager in my lifetime."

—J. R. to Ron Rapoport, *Los Angeles Times,* **June 5, 1972**

"AS THE HIGHLIGHT . . . THE UNIFORM NUMBERS 39 OF ROY CAMPANELLA, 32 OF SANDY KOUFAX, AND 42 OF ROBINSON WERE RETIRED."
—BOB HUNTER, *LOS ANGELES HERALD-EXAMINER,* JUNE 24, 1972

"I could never believe that we'd come out together . . . in Los Angeles for an old-timers' game, that Jackie would hardly be able to see and that I would be in a wheelchair."

—Roy Campanella, who was confined to a wheelchair after a car accident on January 28, 1958, not long after Robinson was diagnosed with diabetes, to Harvey Frommer, *Rickey and Robinson,* **1982**

"They retired Jackie Robinson's uniform number Sunday, a significant and remarkable event that coincidentally commemorated the 25th anniversary of the breaking of the color barrier in America's national pastime."

—Ron Rapoport, *Los Angeles Times,* **June 5, 1972**

"[Roger] Kahn, who was aware of times when Robinson struggled financially and would have appreciated a job offer from [Walter] O'Malley, would recall most keenly the statements that showed 'he despised Walter.' But the totality of the evidence, including their [recent] letters, statements, and other gestures, show a more nuanced relationship. At the worst moments Robinson did express real hostility, but at other times he expressed regret and desire for a more positive relationship."

—**Michael D'Antonio,** *Forever Blue,* **2009**

"I HONESTLY BELIEVE THAT BASEBALL DID SET THE STAGE FOR MANY THINGS THAT ARE HAPPENING TODAY, AND I'M PROUD TO HAVE PLAYED A PART IN IT."

—J. R., WHO, AT DODGER STADIUM IN LA, CELEBRATED THE TWENTY-FIFTH ANNIVERSARY OF THE 1947 BROOKLYN DODGERS TEAM, TO RON RAPOPORT, *LOS ANGELES TIMES,* JUNE 5, 1972

"I like the sport, except if I could have picked a sport to break the color line in, it would have been basketball. That was my game. But it had to be baseball, and the men I played beside . . . I was fortunate to have experienced them. Remembering them clears away the bitterness."

—**J. R. to Roger Kahn, 1972**

"Jackie Robinson and Clyde Sukeforth, two men who made baseball history . . . no strike the word "baseball," were reunited yesterday after more than 15 years at Mamma Leone's Restaurant, where the US Virgin Islands government threw a testimonial to commemorate the 25th anniversary of the black man's entrance into Major League Baseball."

—**Phil Pepe,** *New York Daily News,* **July 20, 1972**

"While there has not been enough said of your significant contribution in the Rickey-Robinson experiment, I . . . have always considered you to be one of the true giants in this initial endeavor in baseball, for which I am truly appreciative. May you never find it convenient to underplay the role you played to make the Rickey-Robinson experiment a success."

—**J. R., letter to Clyde Sukeforth, July 21, 1972**

"In 1972, I collaborated with Robinson on a magazine story under his byline. I do not pretend that this assignment gave me any special insights or any claim on his friendship. He was wound tight and had an edge of anger in his voice and manner. He didn't go out of his way to charm you or exchange banter."

—**Mickey Herskowitz,** *Houston Post,* **April 14, 1987**

"The day of the black manager is coming."

—**J. R. to Mickey Herskowitz, 1972**

"Bob Feller is just a stupid ass, but Alvin [Dark] was talking out of ignorance. He had been brought up to believe that God made the white man superior, and put him on earth to take care of the black man."

—**J. R., about indelicate comments made by Feller and Dark, to Mickey Herskowitz, 1972**

"He told me that he made a lot of speeches, often to troubled young people. Many of them, he said, had only the faintest notion that he once played baseball for a living."

—**Mickey Herskowitz,** *Houston Post,* **April 14, 1987**

"When President Nixon named him as the best all-around athlete in Major League Baseball history, Jackie Robinson seemed surprised but very pleased with the 'real honor.'"

—**Associated Press, July 3, 1972**

"I can't read except very close and then the words kind of go together and it's difficult. I have been unable to read *The Boys of Summer,* but I've gotten tremendous thrills out of the few pages . . . Rachel has been able to read to me."

—**J. R., whose failing eyesight due to diabetes prevented him from reading Roger Kahn's new best seller in which Robinson and his Brooklyn Dodgers teammates looked back on their playing days, quoted by Milton Richman, United Press, July 20, 1972**

"He seemed to have made a stirring peace with life. He sat within his great stone mansion in Connecticut, blindness filming his eyes, and spoke slowly, gravely about the serious issues of his existence."

—**Roger Kahn,** *New York Times,* **June 2, 1974**

"I've lost the sight of one eye, but they think they can save the other. I've got nothing to complain about."

—J. R. to Roger Kahn, quoted by Red Smith, *New York Times* News Service, October 26, 1972

CLASSIC MOMENT: OCTOBER 15, 1972, RIVERFRONT STADIUM, CINCINNATI, OHIO

"In 1972, the twenty-fifth anniversary of his major league debut, Robinson was invited [by baseball commissioner Bowie Kuhn] to throw out the first pitch in the second game of the World Series [between the Oakland A's and Reds] in Cincinnati."

—David Conrads, baseball historian, Pasadena City College's website, 2013

"They were planning this whole big celebration. We're all, 'Great, wonderful!' And my father says, 'And Nixon's coming.' And we're, 'Oh, we're not going to get caught up looking at we're supporting Nixon for a second time.'" . . . And my father sits us all down . . . at the dining room table and says, 'I just need for you to trust me and come to this event. And one by one we made it happen . . . We all came from different directions and met up and it turns out it was the last time we were together as a family. And Nixon did not come so we didn't have the political tug-of-war we thought we were going to have. And it was a wonderful tribute."

—Sharon Robinson, interview, Michael G. Long's *Jackie Robinson—Last Words, First Class Citizenship* video, circa 2007

"Partaking in ceremonies [honoring Jackie's work in combating drugs] were Red Barber, Pee Wee Reese, and Joe Black . . . and Larry Doby. . . . Black, citing Robby's work with Daytop, presented that organization with a station wagon from Chrysler and a double-decked bus from Greyhound. . . . Gifts were made in the name of Jackie Jr."

—Dick Young, *New York Daily News,* October 16, 1972

"Many were shocked at [Robinson's] appearance. Crippled and nearly blind from a variety of physical ailments, his hair snow white, he was an old man at fifty-three."

—David Conrads, baseball historian, Pasadena City College's website, 2013

"Robinson decides he was not going to [throw out the ceremonial pitch] . . . because he's so disturbed by Major League Baseball's refusal to have any black managers. And he states this to Bowie Kuhn. . . . And Kuhn says, 'If I tell you that we're working on it, will that help?' And Robinson gives in and says, 'Yes, that will help.'"

—Michael G. Long, about Robinson agreeing to throw out the ceremonial first pitch to enthusiastic Reds catcher Johnny Bench following the awards ceremony, *Jackie Robinson—Last Words, First Class Citizenship* video, circa 2007

"Jackie Robinson is something special."

—Bowie Kuhn, introducing Jackie Robinson at the awards ceremony

"He accepted a plaque commemorating his achievements, then used the occasion to criticize baseball for not having a black manager."

—David Conrads, baseball historian, Pasadena City College's website, 2013

"He gets a dig in."

—Michael G. Long, *Jackie Robinson—Last Words, First Class Citizenship* video, circa 2007

"I AM EXTREMELY PROUD AND PLEASED TO BE HERE THIS AFTERNOON BUT MUST ADMIT I'M GOING TO BE TREMENDOUSLY MORE PLEASED AND MORE PROUD WHEN I LOOK AT THAT THIRD BASE COACHING LINE ONE DAY AND SEE A BLACK FACE MANAGING IN BASEBALL."

—J. R., STILL FIGHTING FOR THE END OF DISCRIMINATION IN BASEBALL

"He went out with a rhetorical flourish, typical Jackie."

—Michael G. Long, *Jackie Robinson—Last Words, First Class Citizenship* video, circa 2007

"He said baseball will always have its head buried in the sand until it can find the strength and the vision to have a black man coaching at third base. . . . It was the last time I heard him speak."

—Hank Aaron, Braves future Hall of Famer, saying he'd never forget Robinson's final words in a ballpark, introduction, *I Never Had It Made*, Jackie Robinson, as told to Alfred Duckett, 1972

"It was just a grand moment."

—Sharon Robinson, interview, Michael G. Long's *Jackie Robinson—Last Words, First Class Citizenship* video, circa 2007

"Sadly, Robinson's presence in the Reds' dugout that afternoon caused hardly a stir. Only one player, a black pitcher, reacted with enthusiasm to meeting the most historically significant player in the history of the game."

—David Conrads, baseball historian, Pasadena City College's website, 2013

"I was surprised by their indifference, especially the blacks. There seems to be a feeling among the current black players that they owe Jackie nothing."

—Dick Young, sportswriter for *New York Daily News*

"In the face of being written off by Mr. Nixon's party and being taken for granted by the Democrats, we must develop an effective strategy and learn how to become enlightenedly selfish to protect black people when white people seem consolidated to destroy us."

—J. R., *I Never Had It Made*, as told to Alfred Duckett, 1972

"I cannot stand and sing the anthem. I cannot salute the flag; I know that I am a black man in a white world. In 1972, in 1947, at my birth in 1919, I know I never had it made."

—J. R., the solemn last words of his preface to his soon-to-be published autobiography, *I Never Had It Made*, as told to Alfred Duckett, 1972

"At 6:26 in the morning, Tuesday, October 24, 1972, the phone rang at the office of the police dispatcher in Stamford, Connecticut, some ten minutes from the home of Jackie Robinson. 'Send an ambulance, quickly, please,' the dispatcher heard a distraught female voice ask. The fire department ambulance arrived at the Robinson home in less than twelve minutes. He was carried into the ambulance. He was unconscious. An oxygen mask was placed over his face, and an ambulance service volunteer massaged his heart as the vehicle sped toward Stamford Hospital. . . . 'When he arrived at the hospital he was not breathing,' said his personal physician, Dr. John Borowy. 'Despite all our attempts to revive him he did not respond.'"

—**Maury Allen, about Robinson being pronounced dead at 7:10 a.m.,**
Jackie Robinson: A Life Remembered, **1987**

"I love you."

—**J. R., his final words to Rachel Robinson, October 24, 1972**

"Jackie Robinson, the grandson of a slave, a man who emerged from a small house on Pepper Street in Pasadena to become one of the nation's greatest athletes and a symbol of hope for black America, died Tuesday. The 53-year-old Robinson succumbed of a heart attack in the 25th year since his debut with the Brooklyn Dodgers shattered baseball's color barrier."

—**Ross Newhan,** *Los Angeles Times,* **October 25, 1972**

"His dominant characteristic, as an athlete and as a black man, was a competitive flame. Outspoken, controversial, combative, he created critics as well as loyalists. But he never deviated from his opinions."

—*New York Times,* **October 25, 1972**

"At a time when American society desperately needs every man who has brought better understanding to human beings, the passing of Mr. Jackie Robinson is coldly brain numbing. It calls all of America to take a good look at itself."

—**Allan Barron, publisher of** *Black Sports Magazine,* **quoted by the Associated Press, October 25, 1972**

"The most colorful ballplayer I've ever seen was Babe Ruth; the most dynamic, Jackie Robinson."

—**Milton Richman, United Press, October 25, 1972**

"The Word for Jackie Robinson Is 'Unconquerable'"

—**Title of article written by Red Smith,** *New York Times* **News Service,**
October 26, 1972

BROOKLYN DODGERS PAY TRIBUTE

"His death saddens me greatly. Jackie was quite a person. I grew to know and admire him a great deal, off the field as well as on. Of course, he was a very controversial guy and some of the things he said made some of the players on the old Dodger teams pretty mad. But for all that he was a great person and I had to admire him for having the guts to say what was on his mind."

      —**Pee Wee Reese, quoted by Shav Glick,** *Los Angeles Times,* **October 25, 1972**

"Baseball has just lost one of the greatest players that ever put on a pair of spikes."

      —**Eddie Stanky, quoted by Shav Glick,** *Los Angeles Times,* **October 25, 1972**

"I'm shocked. I did feel real bad about this. We were the best of friends."

      —**Duke Snider, quoted by Bob Anderson,** *New York Daily News,* **October 25, 1972**

"His death is a shock and a tragedy. He was one of the greatest and smartest ballplayers of all time."

      —**Jim Gilliam, quoted by Bob Anderson,** *New York Daily News,* **October 25, 1972**

"He was a helluva ballplayer, and he started it all for the black players, which was good. He was an inspiration to all of us."

      —**Billy Cox, quoted by Bob Anderson,** *New York Daily News,* **October 25, 1972**

"He had to be a great ballplayer on the field. To be black and the best player in the league was an extremely difficult assignment."

      —**Carl Erskine, quoted by Bob Anderson,** *New York Daily News,* **October 25, 1972**

"He was a real team leader."

—Johnny Podres, quoted by Bob Anderson, *New York Daily News,*
October 25, 1972

"SOCIOLOGICALLY, ALL AMERICA CHANGED, THE WHOLE WORLD CHANGED, BECAUSE OF JACKIE. DID JACKIE WIN? NO, HE TRIUMPHED."

—RALPH BRANCA, *THE TIM MCCARVER SHOW*

"I really hope that the world will mourn the passing of a man, not just an athlete. I don't want him to be a martyr but I want the people to know that they've lost a battler."

—Joe Black, quoted by Bob Anderson, *New York Daily News,* October 25, 1972

"He was a great man. He accomplished so much in his lifetime. On and off the field Jackie could do it all. . . . He had to do it all."

—Roy Campanella, December 1972

"No one surpassed his contribution in sports. His entire life was courage. Courage as the black pioneer of the game; courage as a player; courage in the way he fought for what he believed; courage in the way he faced his final illness."

—Bowie Kuhn, baseball commissioner, quoted by Shav Glick, *Los Angeles Times,*
October 25, 1972

"Our nation in general and black people in particular have lost a pioneer, a champion, and a heroic fighter for justice and freedom in the person of Jackie Robinson. He was an inspiration to countless numbers of young black people; he opened the door through which many have entered; and proved to young people they could go even to the Hall of Fame, regardless of the color of their skin."

—Ralph Abernathy, successor to Martin Luther King Jr. as the president of the
Southern Christian Leadership Conference, telegram to the Robinsons,
October 25, 1972

"The country has lost a great man, and I have lost a friend."

—**New York Governor Nelson Rockefeller, October 25, 1972**

"His courage, his sense of brotherhood and his brilliance on the playing field brought a new human dimension not only to the game of baseball but to every area of American life where black and white people work side by side. This nation to which he gave so much in his lifetime will miss Jackie Robinson, but his example will continue to inspire us for years to come."

—**President Richard Nixon, statement, October 25, 1972**

"The LA City Council and the Board of Supervisors both adjourned out of respect for Robinson's memory. Mayor Yorty ordered flags in municipal buildings to be flown at half-mast."

—**Shav Glick, sportswriter and Robinson's friend at Pasadena Junior College,** *Los Angeles Times,* **October 25, 1972**

"Pasadena—The community that nurtured Jackie Robinson's spirit and sent him out to cross the racial Rubicon in sport, paid him tribute Friday on the steps of City Hall. Nearly 300 persons, including more than a dozen childhood friends of Robinson, attended. John Muir High School, from which Robinson graduated and went on to Pasadena Junior College (now Pasadena City College) sent it's a capella choir, and a college bugle corps member sounded taps."

—**Bert Mann,** *Los Angeles Times,* **October 28, 1972**

"In silence we were driven [by a limousine] from our home in Stamford to 122nd Street and Riverside Drive in New York City . . . in front of Riverside Church. . . . The casket was opened briefly before the service began. . . . I looked around at the packed chapel. Thousands gathered outside and listened to the service on loudspeakers. . . . I remember seeing Joe Louis, Dick Gregory, Hank Aaron, Vida Blue, Elston Howard, and Willie Mays. A. Philip Randolph, the labor union executive, sat tall and imposing, while Roy Wilkins, executive director of the [NAACP], looked unusually somber. Bowie Kuhn, commissioner of baseball, rubbed his eyes."

—**Sharon Robinson, about Jackie Robinson's funeral on October 29, 1972,** *Stealing Home,* **1996**

"Jackie's death hit Elston hard. Elston had idolized him since that day in 1947 when he decided like Jackie, he . . . would play professional baseball for the Kansas City Monarchs. In spirit, Jackie Robinson was the big brother Elston never had. He was a big brother for all of us."

—Arlene Howard, wife of Elston Howard until his death in 1980,
Elston and Me, 2001

"MOST OF THE BLACK PLAYERS FROM JACKIE'S DAY WERE AT THE FUNERAL, BUT I WAS APPALLED BY HOW FEW OF THE YOUNGER PLAYERS SHOWED UP TO PAY HIM TRIBUTE. AT THE TIME I WAS 41 HOMERS SHORT OF BABE RUTH'S CAREER RECORD, AND WHEN JACKIE DIED, I REALLY FELT THAT IT WAS UP TO ME TO KEEP HIS DREAM ALIVE. I WAS INSPIRED TO DEDICATE MY HOME RUN RECORD TO THE SAME GREAT CAUSE TO WHICH JACKIE DEDICATED HIS LIFE."

—HANK AARON, BRAVES OUTFIELDER AND FUTURE HALL OF FAMER,
***TIME* MAGAZINE, JUNE 14, 1999**

"Today we must balance the tears of sorrow with the tears of joy. Mix the bitter with the sweet in death and life. Jackie as a figure in history was a rock in the water, creating concentric circles and ripples of new possibility. . . . Jackie, as a co-partner with God . . . didn't integrate baseball for himself. He infiltrated baseball for all of us, seeking and looking for more oxygen for black survival. . . . This mind, this mission, could not be held down by a grave. . . . No grave can hold this body down. It belongs to the ages, and all of us are better off because the temple of God, the man with convictions, the man with a mission passed this way."

—Jesse Jackson, at Riverside Church in New York, excerpt from eulogy,
October 29, 1972

"Active Pallbearers: Bill Russell, Larry Doby, Monte Irvin, Martin Edelman, Jim Gilliam, Don Newcombe, Arthur Logan, Ralph Branca, Pee Wee Reese, Ray Bartlett, Joe Black. Honorary Pallbearers: Willie Mays, Joe Louis, Nelson Rockefeller, Richard Cohen, Willie Stargell, Peter Long, Roy Campanella, A. Philip Randolph, Bayard Rustin, Martin Stone, Robert Boyd, Frank Schiffman, Roy Wilkins, Elston Howard, Kiah Sayles."

—Listed by Rachel Robinson, *Jackie Robinson: An Intimate Portrait,* 1997

"My son David and Reverend Jesse Jackson assist[ed] me as we [left] Riverside Church [after Jack's service]. I have no comforting perspective on the moment, except to understand that I had to descend into the depths of grief, unrestrained, before I could rise again and step back into living. The loss felt unbearable."

—**Rachel Robinson,** *Jackie Robinson: An Intimate Portrait,* **1997**

"The mile-long motorcade traveled a carefully planned route through Harlem and ended just a few blocks from the site of the old Ebbets Field at Cypress Hills Cemetery in Brooklyn. Thousands of mourners lined the streets as if providing a protective shield. People hung out their windows, others waved from rooftops. Children tried to touch the hearse. People cheered 'Good-bye Jackie, good-bye.' Adults openly mourned the passing of a friend and symbol of the community. . . . The limo pulled up next to the curve on a hill. It was a peaceful setting."

—**Sharon Robinson,** *Stealing Home,* **1996**

"I couldn't bear to see the burial and remained in the car. My last visual memory of Jack was one of the vibrant living person."

—**Rachel Robinson,** *Jackie Robinson: An Intimate Portrait,* **1997**

"I KNEW THAT MY FATHER WAS TO BE BURIED IN THE GRAVE ALONGSIDE MY BROTHER. I FELT STRANGELY HAPPY ABOUT THIS ARRANGEMENT. AT LEAST THEY WERE TOGETHER."

—SHARON ROBINSON, *STEALING HOME,* 1996

— THIRTEEN —

From Legend to Icon

"The top seven hitters in the National League in 1972 were black. Twenty-three years ago, in 1949, only one black player made the top 10 among NL batters. His name led all the rest: 'Robinson, Jack R., Brooklyn, .342.' Those seven who dominated National League hitters this year got there on ability, yet they owe something to Jackie Robinson, too."

—*Sporting News,* **which had criticized Robinson's signing in 1947,
November 11, 1972**

"Jackie Robinson will be remembered on the spot where he made history as the first black player in baseball's major leagues. The 1,321-unit Brooklyn apartment complex built in 1963 where Ebbets Field once stood will be named for Robinson, Gov. Nelson A. Rockefeller has announced."

—**Associated Press, about the modest housing facility that Robinson was glad
replaced the deserted ballpark, December 10, 1972**

"Rebirth became a theme for Mom, David, and me. We each had to find our way in our newly defined world. Mom had a choice when Dad died. She could remain at Yale University or enter the business world. Choosing the latter, she stepped forward as president of the Jackie Robinson Construction Company and founder and chairman of the newly formed Jackie Robinson Foundation. David and I are active board members of the Jackie Robinson Foundation, but it is Mom's baby."

—**Sharon Robinson,** *Stealing Home,* **1996**

"In 1973, after the business was underway, my brother Chuck Williams, Marty Edelman, and Franklin Williams met with me to consider how we could create a 'living memorial' to Jack. . . . We incorporated as the Jackie Robinson Foundation (JRF), a public, not-for-profit national organization which would provide education and leadership development opportunities principally for minority youth with strong capabilities and limited financial resources."

—**Rachel Robinson, about the birth of a foundation that would be growing
strongly forty-five years later,** *Jackie Robinson: An Intimate Portrait,* **1997**

"As described on its web page: 'The Jackie Robinson Center [on North Oaks Avenue in Pasadena] is a multi-purpose social service delivery center that provides assistance to a culturally, economically, and socially diverse population in the northwest area of Pasadena. The 1974 dedication of this 17,800 square feet facility is of significant importance because the center is named after one of this country's great African American leaders.'"

—Sid Galley, Pasadena Museum of History volunteer, March 2, 1974

"Jackie would always say, 'Be somebody, be somebody' and 'Do the tough things, don't pass them by.'"

—Rachel Robinson, at the renaming of William Ettinger JHS at 10th Street and Madison Avenue in Manhattan to Jackie Robinson Junior High, quoted by Peter Coutros, *New York Daily News*, March 26, 1974

"IF I HAD ONE WISH I WAS SURE WOULD BE GRANTED, IT WOULD BE THAT JACKIE ROBINSON COULD BE HERE, SEATED ALONGSIDE ME, TODAY."

—FRANK ROBINSON, AT THE PRESS CONFERENCE ANNOUNCING HE WAS HIRED BY THE CLEVELAND INDIANS TO BE THE MAJOR LEAGUE'S FIRST BLACK MANAGER AND REALIZE JACKIE ROBINSON'S DREAM, OCTOBER 3, 1974

"Everyone of color who's come through baseball or [was] connected with baseball should be very conscious of what Jackie Robinson did and what he had to endure and what he put up with, And without him doing it the way he did it and the respect he collected over those years, it would have been very difficult for others to follow."

—Frank Robinson, baseball's first black manager and a future Hall of Famer, NPR, April 13, 2007

"The Interior Department is designating the homes of baseball player Jackie Robinson, jazz musician Duke Ellington and Nobel Peace Prize winner Ralph Bunche as National Historic Landmarks as part of a 1970s campaign to honor the achievements of black Americans."

—Associated Press, about Robinson's New York home, March 20, 1977

"Jackie Robinson changed the face and soul of baseball and, indeed, of all sports in America. By a remarkable display of athletic skill and personal courage, he earned our enduring respect and affection. Every black athlete owes Jackie Robinson a debt of gratitude, as does every individual who believes in the principles of fair play. Jackie was a pioneer in the finest sense of the word and set an example that can be our constant guide. I am pleased to join in saluting his memory and honoring his inspiring legacy to our society."

—President Jimmy Carter, commemorating the thirtieth anniversary of Robinson's rookie season, statement, July 8, 1977

"The Los Angeles Dodgers will commemorate the 30th anniversary of the late Jackie Robinson's historic first season in the major leagues by staging Jackie Robinson Night on Thursday, July 21, at Dodger Stadium . . . prior to the Dodgers' . . . game with Montreal. . . . Those in attendance for the ceremonies will include Mrs. Jackie Robinson, Commissioner Bowie Kuhn and former teammates Don Newcombe, Jim Gilliam, Duke Snider, and Al Campanis."

—Steve Brener, Los Angeles Dodgers Publicity Director, press release, July 1977

"Mes Amis, I want to tell you un grand merci. It is a great thrill to come home to Montreal and to know that Jack is going to have a permanent place in your hearts, in your memory, and in your stadium."

—Rachel Robinson, unveiling a plaque of Jackie Robinson at Olympic Stadium in Montreal, the city where he first played organized baseball, July 30, 1977

"THIS IS THE CITY FOR ME. THIS IS PARADISE."

—J. R., WHOSE DESCRIPTION ABOUT MONTREAL IN 1946 WERE THE FIRST WORDS ENGRAVED ON HIS BRONZE PLAQUE, JULY 30, 1977

"The Dodger organization will be well represented when the dedication ceremonies of UCLA's Jackie Robinson Stadium are held on Saturday, Feb. 7. Representing the Dodgers will be President Peter O'Malley . . . Vice President Al Campanis, Ben Wade (scouting), Don Newcombe (community relations) and Roy Campanella (community relations) [and] Dodger manager Tommy Lasorda and Dodger pitching instructor Sandy Koufax."

—Steve Brener, Los Angeles Dodgers Publicity Director, press release, January 1981

"Pasadena citizens gathered Friday to honor the late Jackie Robinson as a great athlete and humanitarian. The occasion was Pasadena's tribute in a series of celebrations marking the creation of a Jackie Robinson Black Heritage Commemorative Stamp. Pasadena Postmaster Kathryn Wilson presented a replica of the stamp which will be issued Aug. 2 in Cooperstown, NY, home of the Baseball Hall of Fame. The framed poster will be displayed at the Jackie Robinson Center. . . . On hand to accept the accolades were the famed athlete's brother and sister, Mack Robinson and Willa Mae Walker. . . . Don Newcombe, director of community relations for the Los Angeles Dodgers, was the featured speaker. . . . Newcombe ranked Robinson with Martin Luther King in helping bring equal opportunity to black people in all areas of endeavor."

—Pasadena Star-News, **July 24, 1982**

"I MAKE SURE I TALK ABOUT JACKIE WHEREVER I GO. HE WAS MY IDOL, MY MENTOR, MY HERO. AS LONG AS I'M ALIVE, AS LONG AS I HAVE A BREATH TO BREATHE, I WON'T LET ANYBODY FORGET JACKIE ROBINSON."

—DON NEWCOMBE, DIRECTOR OF COMMUNITY RELATIONS FOR THE LOS ANGELES DODGERS AND FORMER BROOKLYN DODGERS PITCHER, *PASADENA STAR-NEWS,* JULY 24, 1982

"The late Jackie Robinson . . . was lauded here [in Cooperstown, New York] Monday in ceremonies marking the issuance of a commemorative US postage stamp bearing his likeness. . . . The Robinson stamp [is the] fifth in the Black Heritage USA series [following stamps of Harriet Tubman, Martin Luther King Jr., Benjamin Banneker, and Whitney Young Jr.]."

—Claude Rose, Cooperstown News Bureau, August 3, 1982

"Henry Aaron, Frank Robinson, Travis Jackson, and Happy Chandler were inducted into the Baseball Hall of Fame but this first day of August was dominated by Jackie Robinson. Robinson's spirit, pride and determination as he carried the torch for the acceptance of black players in Major League Baseball 35 years ago were close to the hearts and lips of those at the rostrum."

—Dick Kaegel, about the ceremony in which three inductees—Aaron, Frank Robinson, and Chandler—had ties to Jackie Robinson, *Sporting News,* **August 9, 1982**

"As an individual of courage and conviction, and as a skilled and dedicated athlete, Jackie Robinson stood tall among his peers. His courage opened the door of professional sports to all Americans when, in 1947, he became the first black baseball player in the major leagues. He bravely demonstrated to all that skill and sportsmanship, not race or ethnic background, are the qualities by which athletes should be judged. In doing so, he struck a mighty blow for equality, freedom, and the American way of life. Jackie Robinson was a good citizen, a great man, and a true American champion."

—President Ronald Reagan, who, with Rachel Robinson in attendance, presented Jackie Robinson with the nation's highest civilian award, the Medal of Freedom, March 26, 1984

"It hurt me to read that [Cardinals star] Vince Coleman says he 'don't know nothing about no Jackie Robinson.' Are black athletes so blinded by greed for dollars and ego trips that they fail to remember that someone had to 'open the doors?' . . . Vince, Jackie Robinson was more than an athlete. He was a man. . . . He accepted and overcame the slings, slams, and insults so that young black youths, such as you, could dream of playing Major League Baseball."

—Joe Black, former Dodger pitcher and teammate of Jackie Robinson and a prominent businessman, to Vince Coleman, excerpt from a letter, 1986

"I know his name, but I'm not sure what he did."

—Mookie Wilson, Mets outfielder who played a key role in his team's 1986 World Series victory over the Red Sox, quoted by Maury Allen, *Jackie Robinson: A Life Remembered*, 1987

"I'm not sure who he is. . . . Am I supposed to know him?"

—Dwight Gooden, Mets star pitcher, quoted by Maury Allen, *Jackie Robinson: A Life Remembered*, 1987

"JACKIE ROBINSON?"

—RICKEY HENDERSON, A'S STAR OUTFIELDER AND FUTURE CAREER STOLEN-BASE KING AND HALL OF FAMER, QUOTED BY MAURY ALLEN, *JACKIE ROBINSON: A LIFE REMEMBERED*, 1987

"No black ball player today should ever take the field without thinking of Jackie Robinson and how much he owes him. For me, even when I broke in to the big leagues in 1958, baseball *was* Jackie Robinson."

—**Frank Robinson, MLB's first black manager and Hall of Famer,**
quoted by Maury Allen, *Jackie Robinson: A Life Remembered,* **1987**

"Al Campanis was the man who signed me to my first professional contract, so I took it a little hard when he said the things he said on ABC's *Nightline* show. It was April of 1987 when he was on the show to mark the 40th anniversary of Jackie Robinson breaking the color barrier. . . . When Ted Koppel asked Al why there were no black managers or general managers in baseball at the time, his answers seemed to take on a racist tone. When Koppel asked if there was prejudice in baseball, Al answered, 'No, I don't believe it's prejudice. I truly believe that [blacks] may not have the necessities to be, let's say, a field manager, or perhaps a general manager.' . . . He was fired within two days. . . . That killed me. That was the worst thing he could have said."

—**Tommy Davis, former Los Angeles Dodgers third baseman/outfielder,**
Tommy Davis' Tales from the Dodgers Dugout, **2005**

"Campanis had played shortstop to Robinson's second base in Montreal, 1946, but apparently learned nothing. His comments desecrated Jack's legacy and laid bare what black sociologist Harry Edwards called 'the plantation system' perpetuated by such rich baseball club owners as Peter O'Malley [of the Dodgers]."

—**Roger Kahn,** *Los Angeles Times,* **September 22, 1996**

"The other day I learned something new about Jackie Robinson and his legacy. In 1987 [on July 14], the American and National League Rookie of the Year Awards were renamed the Jackie Robinson Awards to honor the 40th anniversary of Robinson breaking the color barrier [and winning the first NL rookie award]. A fact, it seems, that is almost universally overlooked."

—**Nick Scott, espn.com, February 13, 2011**

"On Jan. 30, 1988, the old baseball diamond Number 1 at . . . Brookside Park . . . was renamed The Jackie Robinson Memorial Field. . . . Everyone from Vice Mayor William Thompson and Mack Robinson, Jackie's brother, to [his childhood friend and former mayor Warren] Dorn and [pitcher] Ken Howell of the Los Angeles Dodgers, spoke of Robinson. . . . The ceremony . . . was part of the celebration of February as Black History Month."

—**Bryon Okada,** *Pasadena Star-News,* **January 31, 1988**

"When I was a kid, I wanted more than anything else to play baseball at Ebbets Field with Jackie Robinson."

— Terrance Mann, James Earl Jones's black activist writer in the popular fictional baseball movie *Field of Dreams,* 1989

"A LIFE IS NOT IMPORTANT EXCEPT IN THE IMPACT IT HAS ON OTHER LIVES."
—J. R., HIS FAMOUS WORDS THAT WERE ENGRAVED ON HIS NEW HEADSTONE AT CYPRESS HILLS CEMETERY IN BROOKLYN, JUNE 30, 1990

"Wherever he was, he fought injustices."

—Bill White, the first African American National League President and one-time outspoken Cardinals first baseman, at the unveiling of Robinson's new headstone, June 30, 1990

"I don't think that today, Jackie Robinson belongs to one family."

—David Robinson, Jackie's surviving son who, along with Rachel, Sharon, granddaughter Ayo, and grandson Jesse, were present at the unveiling, June 30, 1990

"I was never a baseball fan [so] I wasn't attracted to the role because of his athleticism. . . . What I saw was a strong man, gifted and articulate, who fought for what is most precious—his manhood. He refused to believe or accept what other people thought of him, that he was inferior. Society in the '40s conspired to destroy this man, and others like him, but he refused to permit it. He fought and survived."

—Andre Braugher, actor who played Jackie Robinson in TNT's 1990 film *The Court-Martial of Jackie Robinson,* quoted by Shav Glick, *Los Angeles Times,* October 14, 1990

"Pasadena has never appreciated the accomplishments my brother attained. It seems like it would a good starting point to use what he attained as a role model for kids. The celebration is based on doing something to help the kids recognize who Jack is and what he accomplished coming from the poverty side of the tracks."

—Mack Robinson, about a celebration to honor Jackie and give awards to excellent students at the Cleveland Elementary School in Pasadena that both brothers attended, to Jane Estes, *Pasadena Star-News,* January 31, 1991

"Spike Lee has sealed the deal for the screen rights to the Jackie Robinson story. Lee will write and direct the film. And, he tells the show-biz paper *Variety*, he's working on getting Denzel Washington to star."

—*New York Post,* **about the genesis of the famous African American director and passionate sports fan's doomed attempt to bring his dream project to the screen, October 5, 1994**

"The widow of Jackie Robinson . . . urged students yesterday at a school named for her husband to make the most of their chances in life. Rachel Robinson attended the dedication of the Jackie Robinson Academy, a 550-student, state-of-the-art school that officials called the first of its kind in the Long Beach [California] school district."

—**City News Service, printed in the** *Pasadena Star-News,* **October 21, 1994**

"ALTHOUGH JACKIE ROBINSON NEVER PLAYED ON THE CAIRO (GA.) HIGH BASEBALL FIELD, TODAY THE CITY WHERE THE FORMER BROOKLYN DODGERS INFIELDER WAS BORN IS DEDICATING IT IN HIS HONOR."

—USA TODAY, MARCH 11, 1996

"In 1997, we will celebrate the fiftieth anniversary of my father's entry into baseball. While my family will join the country in celebrating this stellar aspect of Dad's life, we will also celebrate the loving father and husband that he was, and the proud family tradition of service that resulted from his example."

—**Sharon Robinson, final passage of her autobiography,** *Stealing Home,* **1996**

"It was baseball's proudest moment. It still is baseball's proudest moment."

—**Bud Selig, MLB commissioner, who announced that the 1997 baseball season would be dedicated to Jackie Robinson and that all major and minor league players would wear "Breaking Barriers" arm patches all year, quoted by Lynn Zinser, Knight Ridder newspapers, March 5, 1997**

"No single person is bigger than the game. No single person other than Jackie Robinson. Number 42 belongs to Jackie Robinson for the ages. Uniform number 42 will never again be issued by a major-league club."

—**Bud Selig, MLB commissioner, retiring Jackie Robinson's uniform number, 42, for all of Major League Baseball at a ceremony during the fifth inning of a Mets-Dodgers game at Shea Stadium to celebrate Jackie's fiftieth-year anniversary in the major leagues, April 15, 1997**

"Maybe one day we will all wear 42. That way they won't be able to tell us apart."

—**Pee Wee Reese to Robinson years before**

J. R. NOTE: While Jackie Robinson is identified with Number 42 that he wore for his entire tenure with the Brooklyn Dodgers (1947–1956), he had previously worn Number 9 with the Montreal Royals (1946), and Number 5 with the Kansas City Monarchs (1945). Some people contended the Dodgers gave him a fairly high number as a rookie to protect him from aggressive reporters who assumed teams gave low numbers only to those players they expected to become stars; others insisted the high number indicated the team's lack of faith that the new black player would be successful.

"[Jackie Robinson] changed the face of baseball and the face of America forever."

—**President Bill Clinton, who joined Rachel Robinson on the field during a ceremony at a Mets-Dodgers game at Shea Stadium, April 15, 1997**

"On April 15, 1997, Sanford, Florida, issued a public apology regarding the events of 1946 and proclaimed it Jackie Robinson Day."

—**Joel Schipper, reporter for Bright House Sports Network, mynews13.com, February 7, 2014**

"In one of the most important honors . . . Congress and President Clinton authorized the minting of gold and silver coins in honor of Jackie Robinson. Jack is the first African American to be honored by the United States with a coin. The proceeds will assist the Jackie Robinson Foundation to provide students with strong academic capabilities and leadership potential with the financial resources to carry on Jack's legacy."

—**Rachel Robinson, writing an article to promote the foundation, *USA Today*, October 31, 1997**

"In 1997, Jackie became the first athlete to appear on three different Wheaties boxes at the same time, regular Wheaties, Honey Frosted Wheaties, and Crispy Wheaties 'n Raisins."

—**Larry Lester, baseball historian, larrylester42.com**

"Georgia Gov. Zell Miller will be on hand Wednesday to rename a stretch of southwest Georgia highway for Jackie Robinson, who was born near Cairo, Ga. The 10-mile section of Georgia 93 connects Cairo with Beachton, the birthplace of Major League Baseball's first African American player."

—*USA Today,* **August 26, 1997**

"It took awhile but Pasadena, Calif., has a memorial ready honoring hometown heroes Jackie Robinson and his Olympian brother Mack. It will be dedicated and unveiled Nov. 6 at Centennial Square across from City Hall."

—*USA Today Baseball Weekly,* **about an honor to the two brothers (whose sister, Willa Mae, passed away in 1997), November 1, 1997**

"On Monday, she was in Los Angeles for a golf tournament to benefit the Jackie Robinson Foundation. On Tuesday, she traveled more than nine hours to reach Louisville. And on Wednesday morning at Southeast Christian Church, Rachel Robinson was among those who attended the funeral service for [Harold "Pee Wee"] Reese. The Captain was 81 when he died Saturday, but he was still The Captain, the guy whose comments and actions delivered the word that Jackie Robinson was welcome in this no longer all-white world."

—**Rick Bozich,** *USA Today,* **August 19, 1999**

"To the city he called home for 17 years, Jackie Robinson is even bigger than his immense legend in baseball. So it is fitting, his friends and family say, that he get a larger than life tribute in Samford, Conn: a 7½-foot-tall, bronze statue in a full batting stance. The statue was unveiled yesterday in a ceremony filled with accolades for Robinson. . . . It took community activists three years to raise the $150,000 needed to pay for the statue."

—**Associated Press, October 16, 1999**

"After years of suffering in . . . bed, the victim of a debilitating stroke brought on in part by the diabetes that claimed the life of his more famous brother, Jackie, nearly 30 years earlier, Mack Robinson died quietly over the weekend at the age of 85."

—**Stephanie Cuadra,** *Pasadena Weekly,* **March 6, 2000**

"Jackie Robinson and Babe Ruth were picked as the most important figures in New York sports in the 20th century. The baseball greats were selected in a poll of veteran sports writers, broadcasters and executives announced Monday by Chase Manhattan Bank."

—**Associated Press, December 5, 2000**

"IT SEEMS TO ME LIKE HE'S ALWAYS BEEN WITH ME. HIS THOUGHTS, HIS INFLUENCE, HAVE COME DOWN TO ME. HIS PRESENCE IS VERY STRONG. THE THING I'VE LEARNED FROM HIM, THE THING THAT I HAVE TRIED TO MAKE A PART OF MY OWN LIFE, IS HIS BELIEF THAT A LIFE IS UNIMPORTANT EXCEPT FOR THE IMPACT IT HAS ON OTHER LIVES."

—JESSE SIMMS, SHARON'S SON AND JACKIE ROBINSON'S GRANDSON, WHO WORE A BROOKLYN DODGERS NUMBER 42 UNIFORM AND REPRESENTED HIS GRANDFATHER AT THE 2002 ALL-STAR GAME AT MILLER PARK IN MILWAUKEE, QUOTED BY CROCKER STEPHENSON, *MILWAUKEE JOURNAL-SENTINEL,* JULY 10, 2002

"Even symbolically to have Jack represented here in Brooklyn is of great importance to me. Our roots are here, and a lot of our history is here."

—Rachel Robinson, prior to a ceremony in which the New York Mets' affiliate Brooklyn Cyclones retired his number, Associated Press, August 4, 2003

"To honor the enduring impact of Jackie Robinson and his legacy, Major League Baseball has established April 15 as Jackie Robinson Day throughout the major leagues, it was announced today."

—Office of Commissioner Bud Selig, starting a tradition in which every player would wear Number 42 one day a year, publicity release, March 3, 2004

"I'm very saddened by that fact. Change can occur, but it has to be sustained, and I wish I could see that happen in my lifetime."

—Rachel Robinson, about there being a drop from 25 percent in 1974 to 9 percent in 2004 of African Americans on major league rosters, an unfortunate downward trend that would get worse, quoted by Bill Plaschke, latimes.com, April 14, 2005

"His story is one that shows what one person can do to hold America to account to its founding promise of freedom of equality."

—President George W. Bush, awarding Jackie Robinson the Congressional Gold Medal and presenting it to the Robinson family, at the Capitol Building in Washington, DC, March 2, 2005

"Those showing up at Dodger Stadium tonight will receive the first-ever action figure of Jackie Robinson, sliding into home plate, elbows up, spikes high. . . . Its head does not bobble."

—Bill Plaschke, on the fifty-eighth anniversary of Robinson breaking the color barrier, latimes.com, April 15, 2005

"I will not allow a bobblehead, ever. It's not keeping with his manner."

—Rachel Robinson, at the unveiling of Jackie Robinson's plaque in the Memorial Hall of Honor at Dodger Stadium, quoted by Bill Plaschke, latimes.com, April 14, 2005

"The coffee farmer from Africa used to build houses in Harlem. [David Robinson] used to study at Stanford and protest war and racism. He fought with his fists as a black kid under siege by first-grade classmates at a white private school in Connecticut. . . . He is here for the Smithsonian Folklife Festival, where his Tanzanian Arabica coffee is being featured. . . . 'I was blessed to have gone to Tanzania when I was 15, in the company of my mother; went back at 19; settled there in 1984,' says Robinson. 'I went to be involved in international economics. Coffee is the largest foreign exchange earner for Tanzania.' . . . His father [Jackie], after baseball, was an executive for Chock full o'Nuts coffee empire in New York. But Robinson doesn't think that influenced his choice of vocation. His workplace is deep in the African bush, a place his father would have never gone."

—Lynne Duke, *Washington Post,* July 4, 2005

"On November 1, New York City Mayor Michael Bloomberg unveiled the Jackie Robinson and Pee Wee Reese Monument. . . . The monument depicts the late Brooklyn Dodgers shortstop Harold Henry 'Pee Wee' Reese draping his arm around follow Dodger Jack Roosevelt 'Jackie' Robinson. . . . It stands before KeySpanPark, home of the Brooklyn Cyclones."

—Michael Jay Friedman, *Washington File (DC),* November 2, 2005

"The Yankees paid tribute to Jackie Robinson last night, dedicating a memorial in Monument Park to the Brooklyn Dodgers Hall of Famer. [Manager] Joe Torre, [captain and shortstop] Derek Jeter, [relief pitcher] Mariano Rivera and [second baseman] Robinson Cano helped unveil the plaque during a ceremony before the Yankees [played] the Indians."

—Michael Morrissey, *New York Post,* April 18, 2007

DEREK JETER'S DEBT TO JACKIE ROBINSON

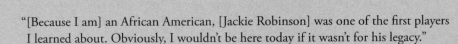

"[Because I am] an African American, [Jackie Robinson] was one of the first players I learned about. Obviously, I wouldn't be here today if it wasn't for his legacy."

—**Derek Jeter, Yankees shortstop, mlb.com, 2008**

"I would choose Jackie Robinson, Lou Gehrig, and Martin Luther King. I think that would be a good group—some interesting stories."

—**Derek Jeter, Yankees shortstop, on the three people he'd choose for a golf foursome, to Jeff Rude, golfweek.com, February 6, 2012**

"Jackie Robinson was the one person I would have loved to have had the opportunity to sit down and talk to."

—**Derek Jeter, Yankees shortstop**

"Unfortunately I never got the opportunity to meet him, but [I got] to meet his wife [Rachel]—she had just as much a role as he did, maybe even bigger. There were times when he felt he couldn't deal with it, and she was the one who made him feel like he could again."

—**Derek Jeter, Yankees shortstop and supporter of the Jackie Robinson Foundation, *Inside Sports* magazine, August 1997**

"Being the first, I'm sure he went through things that people couldn't even imagine. . . . I don't know how I could have handled it. . . . You'd like to think you'd deal with it in the same way he did, but you don't know. Who knows if anyone is strong enough to do that. . . . You're talking about adversity while you're playing, and then you're dealing with things away from the field that no one else has to deal with. I think how strong he was mentally is probably the one thing that sticks out most."

—**Derek Jeter, Yankees shortstop, mlb.com, 2008**

"Anything that draws attention to what Jackie was able to do is a positive thing. Anytime you can draw attention to what he stood for, what he did and what he went through in a positive light—I think it should be celebrated every year."

—**Derek Jeter, Yankees shortstop, approving of Major League Baseball's celebrating Jackie Robinson Day every year, mlb.com, 2008**

"I've always been proud and pleased that Mariano [Rivera] was the one chosen to wear that number [42] because I think he brought something special to it. . . . Jack appreciated dignity in anyone he met, especially someone in the public eye who influenced young people through his behavior like Mariano does."

—Rachel Robinson, on the last major leaguer permitted to wear Jackie Robinson's retired number, to Ian O'Connor, ESPN, June 14, 2013

"God's plan. . . . It is a privilege and honor to wear Number 42. Especially because of what Jackie represents to us."

—Mariano Rivera, Yankees' Hall of Fame-bound Panamanian reliever who was the last player to wear Jackie Robinson's retired number before retiring at the end of the 2013 season, on the fifty-fourth anniversary of Robinson's first major league game, quoted by Alden Gonzalez, mlb.com, April 15, 2011

"The Dodgers solemnly lined up along the third-base line, each and every one wearing Number 42 [as] the sport celebrated the 60th anniversary of [Jackie Robinson's] debut throughout the country Sunday, when more than 200 players, managers and coaches wore his number. . . . Hank Aaron and Frank Robinson threw out ceremonial first pitches, and fellow Hall of Famers Joe Morgan and Dave Winfield were on hand. . . . Broadcaster Vin Scully paid tribute to Rachel Robinson [as] Don Newcombe . . . looked on. [Bud] Selig presented Mrs. Robinson with the Commissioner's Historic Achievement Award for her work with the Jackie Robinson Foundation."

—Associated Press, April 16, 2007

"One special day each year, April 15, we have the privilege of wearing Number 42 as we pay tribute to this baseball icon."

—Curtis Granderson, Yankees outfielder, *Lettters from Jackie,* MLB video, 2011

"Ray Bartlett . . . has died. He was 88. . . . Bartlett had a long close friendship with baseball pioneer Jackie Robinson. They lettered in football, baseball, basketball and track at Pasadena Junior College 1937–39 and at UCLA where they were two of four black players on the 1939 Bruins team."

—Janette Williams, *Pasadena Post-News,* June 25, 2008

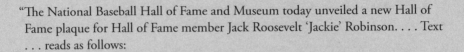

"The National Baseball Hall of Fame and Museum today unveiled a new Hall of Fame plaque for Hall of Fame member Jack Roosevelt 'Jackie' Robinson. . . . Text . . . reads as follows:

JACK ROOSEVELT ROBINSON

"JACKIE"

BROOKLYN, NL, 1947–1956

A PLAYER OF EXTRAORDINARY ABILITY RENOWNED FOR HIS ELECTIFYING STYLE OF PLAY. OVER 10 SEASONS HIT .311, SCORED MORE THAN 100 RUNS SIX TIMES, NAMED TO SIX ALL-STAR TEAMS AND LED BROOKLYN TO SIX PENNANTS AND ITS ONLY WORLD SERIES TITLE, IN 1955. THE 1947 ROOKIE OF THE YEAR, AND THE 1949 NL MVP WHEN HE HIT A LEAGUE-BEST .342 WITH 37 STEALS. LED SECOND BASEMEN IN DOUBLE PLAYS FOUR TIMES AND STOLE HOME 19 TIMES. DISPLAYED TREMENDOUS COURAGE AND POISE IN 1947 WHEN HE INTEGRATED THE MODERN MAJOR LEAGUES IN THE FACE OF INTENSE ADVERSITY.

The text of the original plaque for Jackie Robinson [was written] in 1962."

—Baseball Hall of Fame, about how the original plaque differed from the new one in that it failed to mention Robinson broke the color barrier in the majors, press release, June 25, 2008

"At his induction in 1962, his plaque reflected his wishes—it only recounted his magnificent playing career. But as we all know, there's no person more central and more important to the history of baseball, for his pioneering ways, than Jackie Robinson. Today, his impact is not fully defined without mention of his extreme courage in crossing baseball's color line."

—Jane Forbes Clark, Hall of Fame Board chairman, press release, June 25, 2008

> "A VERY IMPORTANT PART OF JACK'S LIFE HAS BEEN ACKNOWLEDGED TODAY IN A MORE TOTAL WAY. . . . AS YOUNG PEOPLE VIEW JACK'S NEW HALL OF FAME PLAQUE, THEY WILL LOOK BEYOND STATISTICS AND EMBRACE ALL THAT JACK HAS MEANT AND ALL THAT THEY CAN BE. WE WANT IT TO BE AN INSPIRATION, NOT SOMETHING TO TAKE PICTURES OF. WE WANTED TO GIVE THEM A SENSE OF DIRECTION."
>
> —RACHEL ROBINSON, QUOTED BY JOHN KEKIS, ASSOCIATED PRESS, JUNE 25, 2008

"Jackie Robinson was inducted into the College Baseball Foundation's Hall of Fame yesterday in Lubbock, Texas."

—*New York Post,* July 4, 2008

"Jackie Robinson once said, 'A life is not important except in the impact it has on other lives.' And when his widow, Rachel, walked under a 70-foot brick archway yesterday and into the majestic Jackie Robinson Rotunda that bore the inscription of that famous quote, she was nearly moved to tears. Yesterday—62 years to the day after Robinson broke Major League Baseball's color barrier, and made the sport, for the first time, America's pastime—the Mets honored the iconic trailblazer by dedicating the rotunda as the gateway to their gleaming new Citi Field home."

—Brian Lewis, *New York Post,* April 16, 2009

"The story of Jackie Robinson, the first black Major League Baseball player of modern times, is headed to the big screen with the help of his widow, producers Legendary Pictures said on Wednesday. . . . Oscar-winning filmmaker Brian Helgeland, the writer of *L.A. Confidential,* will write the script and direct the film. Rachel Robinson will serve as a consultant. Robinson, 88, told Reuters she has wanted to bring her husband's story to the big screen 'for years—back when Sidney Pointier (now 84) could have played Jack.' . . . She said the movie will 'tell the story of how it all occurred' and focus on 'Jack breaking into baseball, our lives at home and in the ball park, the players . . . Branch Rickey.' Warner Bros . . . will release the project."

—Zorianna Kit, *Reuters,* June 1, 2011

"If you think about him being an icon and a hero anyway, that actually is the pitfall in playing the role. It's the biggest pitfall you can fall into because he didn't know that he was going to be an icon. He didn't know that he was going to be a hero. In fact, [Jackie] has to deal with that heroism throughout the movie when he finds out that [being in Major League Baseball] is a bigger deal to everyone than he thought it would be. You can't completely block out that feeling of responsibility, but you can focus the same way he did—one thing at a time, moment to moment. Eventually all the pieces will be there."

—Chadwick Boseman, about playing Robinson in *42*, to Julie Miller, *Vanity Fair* magazine, April 12, 2013

"They got it right. Don't you think they got it right?"

—Rachel Robinson, very happy about the new major movie, *42*, featuring exceptional performances by Chadwick Boseman as Jackie Robinson, Nicole Beharie as Rachel, and Harrison Ford as Branch Rickey, at the All-Star Game at Citi Field in Queens, New York, July 16, 2013

"Last week, vandals defaced the statue of Jackie Robinson and Pee Wee Reese, located outside MCU Park [formerly KeySpan Park] in Coney Island, with hateful [anti-black and anti-Semitic] words and symbols which have since been removed. . . . In light of these recent events, the Cyclones and Alliance for Coney Island will join together with community leaders to host Diversity Day in Coney Island . . . on Monday, August 19th, in conjunction with the Coney Island Flicks on the Beach screening of *42* later in the evening. Prior to the Brooklyn Cyclones taking on the Staten Island Yankees in a doubleheader, the Cyclones, along with the Jackie Robinson Foundation, the Jackie Robinson Little League, Major League Baseball and other local community leaders will host a rededication ceremony for the Jackie Robinson and Pee Wee Reese statue, which stands as a monument to these men of 'courage and conviction' as engraved on the base of the statue which was originally erected in November 2005."

—*Brooklyn Daily Eagle*, August 2013

"THIS ATTACK [ON THE STATUE] HITS CLOSE TO HOME. THIS IS ABOUT SO MANY THINGS, ABOUT NEW YORK, AND ABOUT BASEBALL, ABOUT REAL HEROES MOST OF ALL. AND IS A CRIME AGAINST ALL OF US."

—MIKE LUPICA, *NEW YORK DAILY NEWS*, AUGUST 7, 2013

"The city will host Robinson Family Weekend Friday and Sunday to commemorate the lives and contributions of historical icons and Pasadena residents Matthew 'Mack' . . . and Jackie Robinson. The events will kick off with two celebrations Friday for the centennial birthday of Mack Robinson. . . . On Sunday, the weekend celebration will conclude with an induction ceremony for Rachel Robinson, wife of baseball star and civil rights activist Jackie Robinson, into the Baseball Reliquary's Shrine of Eternals."

—**Lauren Gold,** *Pasadena Star-News,* **July 14, 2014**

"UCLA is honoring Jackie Robinson by retiring the former four-star athlete's iconic Number 42 for all its athletic teams. The Bruins announced the honor Saturday night during the Bruins' football game against USC. . . . UCLA is honoring the 75th anniversary of Robinson's arrival on campus. On Friday, the school collectively named 22 sports facilities the Jackie Robinson Athletics and Recreation Complex."

—**Associated Press, November 22, 2014**

"JACKIE ROBINSON'S UNIFORM NUMBER WAS ON THE BACK OF EVERY PLAYER AT DODGER STADIUM ON WEDNESDAY NIGHT AND NUMBER 42 WAS ETCHED IN THE INFIELD DIRT. . . . AS PART OF CIVIL RIGHTS GAME FESTIVITIES THAT PRECEDED A 5–2 VICTORY OVER THE SEATTLE MARINERS, THE DODGERS ANNOUNCED PLANS TO ERECT A STATUE OF ROBINSON ON THEIR STADIUM GROUNDS. THE STATUE WOULD BE THE FIRST OF ITS KIND AT DODGER STADIUM. 'I'VE BEEN WAITING 20 YEARS,' SAID ROBINSON'S WIDOW, RACHEL ROBINSON. 'IT'S THE FULFILLMENT OF A DREAM.'"

—DYLAN HERNANDEZ, *LOS ANGELES TIMES*, APRIL 15, 2015

"Rachel Robinson is hopeful that a museum honoring her late husband's legacy will [soon] open for business. . . . The 92-year-old [widow of Jackie Robinson] told WFAN's *Boomer & Carton* show . . . 'We're not only celebrating Jack's life and learning about his experiences and his legacy, but we're also celebrating African American heroes of the past. So it's a combination of who and what people have been involved in social change in America. . . . It's going to be a destination for families and children. We want to educate, inspire and challenge people.'"

—**cbsnewyork.com, January 15, 2015**

"We had a wonderful marriage. A lot has been said about how much I helped Jack and how much he needed me. I needed him just as much."

—Rachel Robinson to Pat Williams, *How to Be Like Jackie Robinson*, 2005

"Jackie's courage helped me hurdle the racism and bigotry I encountered, particularly in the early years of my career."

—Orlando Cepeda, Hall of Famer who was NL Rookie of the Year with the San Francisco Giants in 1958 and NL MVP with the Cardinals in 1967, *Baby Bull*, 1998

"I was glad Jackie came along. He was a great ballplayer. He made a big difference with our way of life in our society, and he opened a lot of doors. And I am sure Robinson took more abuse than we really, really know about."

—Stan Musial

"That man had tons and tons of guts."

—Ted Williams to documentarian Ken Burns

"If I were in Jackie Robinson's shoes, I probably never would have made it."

—Bob Gibson, Cardinals pitcher and Hall of Famer

"When I look at my house . . . I say, 'Thank God for Jackie Robinson.'"

—Joe Black, former Dodgers pitcher, quoted by Phil Pepe, *New York Daily News*, July 20, 1972

"I think he brought a country together with his play on the field. He showed the people that blacks should be treated equal, and can be just as good if not better than the white players."

—Frank Robinson, Hall of Famer and the majors' first black manager, NPR, April 13, 2007

"I think what Jackie Robinson did off the field was even more significant."

—Frank Robinson, Hall of Famer and the majors' first black manager, NPR, April 13, 2007

"They say certain people are bigger than life, but Jackie Robinson is the only one I've known who truly was."

—Hank Aaron, Braves Hall of Famer, *Time* magazine, June 14, 1999

"Jackie was the only person without prejudice I ever met."

—Buck O'Neil, Monarchs teammate, to Pat Williams, *How to Be Like Jackie Robinson,* 2005

"He opened minds. He opened hearts. . . . He caused America to reconnect itself to honor."

—Carl Erskine, Brooklyn Dodgers pitcher

"There should be a national holiday for Jackie Roosevelt Robinson."

—Don Newcombe

"Thank you, Jackie Robinson."

—Robinson Cano, star second baseman for the Yankees and then the Mariners who was named after his hero, *Letters from Jackie Robinson,* MLB video, 2011

"Without a doubt, the most important person in the history of baseball is Jackie Robinson."

—Ken Burns, director and producer of the 2016 PBS documentary *Jackie Robinson*, at a Television Critics Association gathering on Martin Luther King Jr. Day, January 18, 2016

"THE FUNDAMENTAL QUESTIONS THAT FACED JACK IN 1947 ARE ABOUNDING TODAY. WE'VE GOT TO GO BEYOND CELEBRATING THE PAST AND USE OUR EMOTIONS, SENTIMENTS, IDEAS, AND ANALYSIS TO MOVE FORWARD. THIS WOULD BE THE GREATEST TRIBUTE TO JACKIE ROBINSON."

—RACHEL ROBINSON

J. R. NOTE: Jackie Robinson insisted that his value as a player could not be summed up by statistics alone. Nevertheless, they were quite impressive.

CAREER BATTING

YEAR	TEAM	GP	AB	R	H	2B	3B	HR	RBI	BB	SO	SB	CS	AVG	OBP	SLG	OPS
1947	BKN	151	590	125	175	31	5	12	48	74	36	29	0	.297	.383	.427	.810
1948	BKN	147	574	108	170	38	8	12	85	57	37	22	0	.296	.367	.453	.820
1949	BKN	156	593	122	203	38	12	16	124	86	27	37	0	.342	.432	.528	.960
1950	BKN	144	518	99	170	39	4	14	81	80	24	12	0	.328	.423	.500	.923
1951	BKN	153	548	106	185	33	7	19	88	79	27	25	8	.338	.429	.527	.956
1952	BKN	149	510	104	157	17	3	19	75	106	40	24	7	.308	.440	.465	.905
1953	BKN	136	484	109	159	34	7	12	95	74	30	17	4	.329	.425	.502	.927
1954	BKN	124	386	62	120	22	4	15	59	63	20	7	3	.311	.413	.505	.918
1955	BKN	105	317	51	81	6	2	8	36	61	18	12	3	.256	.378	.363	.741
1956	BKN	117	357	61	98	15	2	10	43	60	32	12	5	.275	.382	.412	.794
Total	Total	1382	4877	947	1518	273	54	137	734	740	291	197	30	.311	.409	.474	.883

Bibliography

Aaron, Hank. *If I Had a Hammer: The Hank Aaron Story*. With Lonnie Wheeler. New York: HarperCollins, 1991.

Alexander, Charles C. *Our Game: An American Baseball History*. New York: Henry Holt, 1991.

Allen, Maury. *Baseball's 100: A Personal Ranking of the Best Players in Baseball History*. New York: A&W Publishers, 1981.

————. *Brooklyn Remembered: The 1955 Days of the Dodgers*. Champaign, IL: Sports Publishing, 2005.

————. *Jackie Robinson: A Life Remembered*. New York: Franklin Watts, 1987.

Alston, Walter. *A Year at a Time*. With Jack Tobin. Waco, TX: Word Books, 1976.

Barber, Red, and Robert Creamer. *Rhubarb in the Catbird Seat*. Garden City, NY: Doubleday, 1968.

————. *1947: When All Hell Broke Loose in Baseball*. Garden City, NY: Doubleday, 1982.

Banks, Ernie. *Mr. Cub*. With Jim Enright. Chicago: Follet, 1971.

Barra, Allen. *Mickey and Willie: Mantle and Mays, the Parallel Lives of Baseball's Golden Age*. New York: Crown Archetype, 2013.

————. *Yogi Berra: Eternal Yankee*. New York: W. W. Norton, 2009.

Barthel, Thomas. *Baseball Barnstorming and Exhibition Games, 1901–1962: A History of Off-Season Major League Play*. Jefferson, NC: McFarland, 2007.

Berkow, Ira. *Red: A Biography of Red Smith*. New York: Times Books, 1986.

Berra, Yogi. *Ten Rings: My Championship Seasons*. With Dave Kaplan. New York: HarperCollins, 2003.

Berra, Yogi, and Ed Fitzgerald. *Yogi*. Garden City, NY: Doubleday, 1961.

Black, Martha Jo, and Chuck Schoffner. *Joe Black: More Than a Dodger*. Chicago: Academy Chicago Publishers, 2015.

Bragan, Bobby. *You Can't Hit the Ball With the Bat on Your Shoulder: The Baseball Life and Times of Bobby Bragan*. With Jeff Guin. Fort Worth, TX: Summit Group, 1992.

Brashler, William. *The Story of Negro League Baseball*. New York: Houghton Mifflin, 1994.

Broeg, Bob. *Memories of a Hall of Fame Sportswriter*. Champaign, IL: Sagamore, 1995.

Bruce, Janet. *The Kansas City Monarchs: Champions of Black Baseball*. Lawrence, KS: University of Kansas Press, 1985.

Bryant, Howard. *Shut Out: A Story of Race and Baseball in Boston*. New York: Routledge, 2002.

Cannon, Jack, and Tom Cannon, eds. *Nobody Asked Me, But . . . : The World of Jimmy Cannon*. New York: Holt, Rinehart and Winston, 1978.

Charlton, James, ed. *The Baseball Chronology: The Complete History of the Most Important Events of the Game of Baseball*. New York: Macmillan, 1991.

Clavin, Tom, and Danny Peary. *Gil Hodges: The Brooklyn Bums, the Miracle Mets, and the Extraordinary Life of a Baseball Legend*. New York: New American Library, 2012.

Campanella, Roy. *It's Good to Be Alive*. Boston: Little, Brown, 1959.

Cohen, Marvin A. *The Dodgers-Giants Rivalry, 1900–1957: A Year by Year Retrospective*. Vestal, NY: M C Productions, 2000.

Conlan, Jocko, and Robert Creamer. *Jocko*. Philadelphia: J. B. Lippincott, 1967.

Cosell, Howard. *Cosell*. Chicago: Playboy Press, 1973.

Creamer, Robert W. *Stengel: His Life and Times*. New York: Simon & Schuster, 1984.

D'Antonio, Michael. *Forever Blue: The True Story of Walter O'Malley, Baseball's Most Controversial Owner, and the Dodgers of Brooklyn and Los Angeles*. New York: Riverhead Books, 2009.

Davis, Tommy. *Tommy Davis' Tales from the Dodgers Dugout*. With Paul Gutierrez. Champaign, IL: Sports Publishing, 2005.

Dorinson, Joseph, and Joram Warmund, eds. *Jackie Robinson: Race, Sports, and the American Dream*. Armonk, NY: M. E. Sharpe, 1998.

Drysdale, Don. *Once a Bum Always a Dodger: My Life in Baseball from Brooklyn to Los Angeles*. With Bob Verdi. New York: St. Martin's Press, 1990.

Duberman, Martin. *Paul Robeson: A Biography*. New York: Alfred A. Knopf, 1988.

Durocher, Leo. *Nice Guys Finish Last*. With Ed Linn. New York: Simon & Schuster, 1975.

Eig, Jonathan. *Opening Day: The Story of Jackie Robinson's First Season*. New York: Simon & Schuster, 2007.

Einstein, Charles. *Willie's Time: A Memoir*. New York: J. B. Lippincott, 1979.

Erskine, Carl. *Carl Erskine's Tales from the Dodger Dugout*. Champaign, IL: Sports Publishing, 2000.

Falkner, David. *Great Time Coming: The Life of Jackie Robinson from Baseball to Birmingham*. New York: Simon & Schuster, 1995.

———. *Nine Sides of the Diamond: Baseball's Great Glove Men on the Art of Defense*. New York: Crown, 1990.

Farrar, Hayward. *The Baltimore Afro-American, 1892–1950*, Westport, CT: Praeger, 1998

Foner, Philip S., ed. *Paul Robeson Speaks: Writings, Speeches, Interviews, 1918–1974*. New York: Bruner/ Mazel, 1978.

Ford, Whitey. *Slick: My Life in and Around Baseball*. With Phil Pepe. New York: William Morrow, 1987.

Frommer, Harvey. *Rickey and Robinson: The Men Who Broke Baseball's Color Barrier*. New York: MacMillan, 1982.

Garvey, Steve. *My Bat Boy Days: Lessons I Learned from the Boys of Summer*. With Ken Gurnick and Candace Garvey. New York: Scribner, 2008.

Golenbock, Peter. *Bums: An Oral History of the Brooklyn Dodgers*. New York: G. P. Putnam's Sons, 1984.

———. *Dynasty: The New York Yankees, 1949–1964*. Englewood Cliffs, NJ: Prentice Hall, 1975.

Greenberg, Hank. *Hank Greenberg: The Story of My Life*. Edited by Ira Berkow. Norwalk, CT: Easton Press, 1989.

Halberstam, David. *Summer of '49*. New York: William Morrow, 1989.

Hirsch, James S. *Willie Mays: The Life, the Legend.* New York: Scribner, 2010.

Honig, Donald, ed. *Baseball Between the Lines: Baseball in the Forties and Fifties, As Told by the Men Who Played It.* New York: Coward, McCann & Geoghegan, 1976.

——, ed. *Baseball When the Grass Was Real: Baseball from the '20s to the '40s, Told by the Men Who Played It.* New York: Coward, McCann & Geoghegan, 1975.

——, ed. *The Man in the Dugout: Fifteen Big League Managers Speak Their Minds.* Chicago: Follet, 1977.

——, ed. *The October Heroes: Great World Series Games Remembered by the Men Who Played Them.* New York: Simon & Schuster, 1979.

Howard, Arlene. *Elston and Me: The Story of the First Black Yankee.* With Ralph Wimbish. Columbia, MO: University of Missouri Press, 2001.

Jones, K. C. *Rebound: The Autobiography of K. C. Jones and an Inside Look at the Champion Boston Celtics.* With Jack Warner. New York: Warner Books, 1986.

Kahn, Roger. *The Boys of Summer.* New York: Harper & Row, 1972.

——. *The Era: 1947–1957 When the Yankees, the Giants, and the Dodgers Ruled the World.* New York: Ticknor & Fields, 1993.

——. *Rickey & Robinson: The True, Untold Story of the Integration of Baseball.* New York: Rodale, 2014.

Kashatus, William C. *Jackie and Campy: The Untold Story of Their Rocky Relationship and the Breaking of Baseball's Color Line.* Lincoln, NE: The University of Nebraska Press, 2014.

Kearns Goodwin, Doris. *Wait Till Next Year: A Memoir.* New York: Simon & Schuster, 1997.

Kreis, James. *1954—A Baseball Season.* Bloomington, IN: AuthorHouse, 2011.

Kiner, Ralph. *Baseball Forever: Reflections on 60 Years in the Game.* With Danny Peary. Chicago: Triumph Books, 2004.

Koufax, Sandy. *Koufax.* With Ed Linn. New York: Viking, 1999.

Lacy, Sam. *Fighting For Fairness: The Life Story of Hall of Fame Sportswriter Sam Lacy.* With Moses J. Newson. Centreville, MD: Tidewater, 1998.

Lamb, Chris. *Blackout: The Untold Story of Jackie Robinson's First Spring Training.* Lincoln, NE: University of Nebraska Press, 2004.

——. *Conspiracy of Silence: Sportswriters and the Long Campaign to Desegregate Baseball.* Lincoln, NE: University of Nebraska Press, 2012.

Lanctot, Neil. *Negro League Baseball: The Rise and Ruin of a Black Institution.* Philadelphia: University of Pennsylvania Press, 2004.

Leavy, Jane. *Sandy Koufax: A Lefty's Legacy.* New York: HarperCollins, 2002.

Lester, Larry, and Sammy J. Miller. *Black Baseball in Kansas City.* Chicago: Arcadia, 2000.

Linge, Mary Kay. *Jackie Robinson: A Biography.* Westport, CT: Greenwood, 2007.

Long, Michael G., ed. *Beyond Home Plate: Jackie Robinson on Life After Baseball.* Syracuse, NY: Syracuse University Press, 2013.

——, ed. *First Class Citizenship: The Civil Rights Letters of Jackie Robinson.* New York: Henry Holt, 2007.

Lowenfish, Lee. *Branch Rickey: Baseball's Ferocious Gentleman*. Lincoln, NE: University of Nebraska Press, 2007.

———. *The Imperfect Diamond: The Story of Baseball's Reserve System and the Men Who Fought to Change It*. New York: Stein & Day, 1980.

Mann, Arthur. *The Jackie Robinson Story*. New York: Grosset & Dunlap, 1950.

Mantle, Mickey. *All My Octobers: My Memories of 12 World Series When the Yankees Ruled Baseball*. With Mickey Herskowitz. New York: HarperCollins, 1994.

Muaddi Darraj, Susan. *Jackie Robinson*. New York: Chelsea House, 2008.

Okrent, Daniel, and Harris Lewine, eds. *The Ultimate Baseball Book*. New York: Houghton Mifflin, 1979.

Oliphant, Thomas. *Praying for Gil Hodges: A Memoir of the 1955 World Series and One Family's Love of the Brooklyn Dodgers*. New York: Thomas Dunne Books, 2005.

O'Neil, Buck. *I Was Right on Time: My Journey from the Negro Leagues to the Majors*. With Steve Wulf and David Conrads. New York: Simon & Schuster, 1996.

Paper, Lew. *Perfect: Don Larsen's Miraculous World Series Game and the Men Who Made It Happen*. New York: New American Library, 2009.

Parr, Royce and Bob Burke. *Allie Reynolds: Super Chief*. Oklahoma City: Oklahoma Heritage Association, 2002.

Parrott, Harold. *The Lords of Baseball*. Atlanta: Long Street, 1976.

Peary, Danny, ed. *Baseball Immortal: Derek Jeter: A Career in Quotes*. Salem, MA: Page Street, 2015.

———, ed. *Cult Baseball Players: The Greats, the Flakes, the Weird, and the Wonderful*. New York: Fireside, 1990.

———, ed. *We Played the Game: 65 Players Remember Baseball's Greatest Era, 1947–1964*. New York: Hyperion, 1994.

Peterson, Robert W. *Only the Ball Was White: A History of Legendary Black Players and All-Black Professional Teams*. Englewood Cliffs, NJ: Prentice Hall, 1970.

Prince, Carl E. *Brooklyn's Dodgers: The Bums, the Borough and the Best of Baseball*. New York: Oxford University Press, 1996.

Prager, Joshua. *The Echoing Green: The Untold Story of Bobby Thomson, Ralph Branca, and the Shot Heard Round the World*. New York: Pantheon Books, 2006.

Rampersad, Arnold. *Jackie Robinson: A Biography*. New York: Alfred A. Knopf, 1997.

Reisler, Jim, ed. *Black Writers/Black Baseball: An Anthology of Articles from Black Sportswriters Who Covered the Negro Leagues*. Jefferson, NC: McFarland, 1994.

Robinson, Jackie, *Baseball Has Done It*. Philadelphia: J. B. Lippincott, 1964.

———. *I Never Had It Made: An Autobiography*. As told to Alfred Duckett. New York: Putnam, 1972.

———. *Jackie Robinson: My Own Story*. As told to Wendell Smith. New York: Greenberg, 1948.

Robinson, Rachel. *Jackie Robinson: An Intimate Portrait*. With Less Daniels. New York: Harry N. Abrams, 1996.

Robinson, Sharon. *Jackie's Nine: Jackie Robinson's Values to Live By*. New York: Scholastic, 2001.

———. *Promises to Keep: How Jackie Robinson Changed America*. New York: Scholastic, 2004.

———. *Stealing Home: An Intimate Family Portrait by the Daughter of Jackie Robinson*. New York: HarperCollins, 1996.

Rowan, Carl T. *Wait Till Next Year: The Story of Jackie Robinson*. With Jackie Robinson. New York: Random House, 1960.

Shapiro, Michael. *The Last Good Season: Brooklyn, the Dodgers, and Their Final Pennant Race Together*. New York: Doubleday, 2003.

Simon, Scott. *Jackie Robinson and the Integration of Baseball*. Hoboken, NJ: John Wiley & Sons, 2002.

Smith, Red. *Red Smith on Baseball: The Game's Greatest Writer on the Game's Greatest Years*. Chicago: Ivan R. Dee, 2000.

Snider, Duke. *The Duke of Flatbush*. With Bill Gilbert. New York: Zebra Books, 1988.

Stout, Glenn, and Dick Johnson. *Jackie Robinson: Between the Baselines*. San Francisco: Woodford, 1997.

Strode, Woody, and Sam Young. *Goal Dust: The Warm and Candid Memoirs of a Pioneer Black Athlete and Actor*. Lanham, MD: Madison Books, 1990.

Trouppe, Quincy. *20 Years Too Soon: Prelude to Major-League Integrated Baseball*. Los Angeles: S & S Enterprises, 1977.

Turner, Frederick. *When the Boys Came Back: Baseball and 1946*. New York: Henry Holt, 1996.

Tygiel, Jules. *Baseball's Great Experiment: Jackie Robinson and His Legacy*. New York: Oxford University Press, 1983.

———, ed. *The Jackie Robinson Reader: Perspectives on an American Hero*. New York: Dutton, 1997.

Vincent, Fay. *We Would Have Played for Nothing: Baseball Stars of the 1950s and 1960s Talk About the Game They Loved*. New York: Simon & Schuster, 2008.

Whitaker, Matthew C., ed. *Icons of Black America: Breaking Barriers and Crossing Boundaries*. Vol. 1. Santa Barbara, CA: Greenwood, 2011.

Williams, Pat. *How to Be Like Jackie Robinson: Life Lessons from Baseball's Greatest Hero*. With Mike Sielski. Deerfield Beach, FL: HCI, 2005.

Wills, Maury, and Mike Celizic. *On the Run: The Never Dull and Often Shocking Life of Maury Wills*. New York: Carroll & Graf, 1991.

Young, Andrew S. "Doc." *Great Negro Baseball Stars and How They Made the Major Leagues*. New York: A. S. Barnes, 1953.

Young, Dick. *Roy Campanella*. New York: A. S. Barnes, 1952.

Zeiler, Thomas W., ed. *Jackie Robinson and Race in America: A Brief History with Documents*. Boston: Bedford/St. Martin's, 2014.

Zimmer, Don. *Zim: A Baseball Life*. With Bill Madden. Kingston, NY: Total Sports, 2001.

Acknowledgments

It was my great fortune to work with many of the same people that helped me with the first of the Baseball Immortal books, *Baseball Immortal Derek Jeter: A Career in Quotes.* As before, I first must express gratitude to my esteemed agent, Al Zuckerman, and my publisher, Will Kiester. Without them there would be no book. And without my super sharp and reliable editor, Sarah Monroe, the quality of this book would be diminished. I thank each of you.

I am delighted to acknowledge the great work done by everyone else at Page Street Publishing—Meg Palmer, Harriet Low, Marissa Giambelluca, Laura Gallant, Meg Baskis, as well as my publicist Kim Yorio and my copyeditor, Nichole Kraft. Likewise, I once again thank Mickey Novak and others behind the scenes at Writers House.

Again I availed myself of the services of Matt Rothenberg in Cooperstown, New York. Thank you, Matt, and Bill Francis at the HOF, as well as Tim Wiles and Marty Appel. I have tremendous appreciation for my California researcher, Carol Summers, who found more obscure material than I thought possible. She acknowledges the help she received from Manya Hakopyan, the archivist at Shatford Library at Pasadena City College. I am indebted to Julia Hsiyi-Yi Wang, the adult services librarian at the Pasadena Public Library and her crack team: Tiffany Duenas, Greene Lopez, and Asmik Gevokyan.

I respectfully salute all the people I have quoted in this book—excluding the bigots, sorry politicians, and others who gave Jackie Robinson trouble—particularly sports figures and journalists, whether I met them or not. Special thanks to Carl Erskine and Roy Campanella II. I must also express gratitude to the remarkable Rachel Robinson.

I thank Jeanie Dooha, Cory Gann, Anne Kostick, Gene Ohler, Gerald Peary, and Amy Gellar. Finally, I thank my wife, Suzanne, daughter Zoë, and granddaughter Julianna, an unbeatable team.

About the Author

Danny Peary is a sports and film historian who has published 25 books, including *Baseball Immortal Derek Jeter: A Career in Quotes* with Page Street Publishing. He collaborated on the biographies of Roger Maris and Gil Hodges, the autobiographies of Ralph Kiner and Shannon Miller, and three books with Tim McCarver. He also edited the anthology *Cult Baseball Players*, the oral histories *Super Bowl: The Game of Our Lives* and *We Played the Game: Memories of Baseball's Greatest Era*. He is the writer-researcher of *The Tim McCarver Show*. Danny divides his time between New York City and Sag Harbor, New York.

Index